영어독해를 위한

영어특수구문

영·특·구

English Special Constructions

Preface

머리말

이 책을 독자 여러분들과 공유하게 된 것을 진심으로 기쁘게 생각합니다. 한 권의 책을 써서 세상에 내놓는다는 것이 저자에게는 결코 쉬운 일이 아니었습니다. 무엇보다도 저자의 지식이 부족하다는 점과 그 위에서 만들어진 책이 독자 여러분들께 잘못된 지식을 전달하지나 않을까 하는 두려움 때문이었습니다. 그럼에도 불구하고 저자는 감히 이 책을 세상에 내놓기로 결심을 했습니다. 여기에는 크게 세가지 이유가 있습니다.

첫째는 개인적인 지적욕구에서 끊임없는 관심을 갖고 자료를 하나 둘 모으면서 1992년부터 약 9년 동안 모은 자료가 지금은 방대한 분량이 되어 혼자만 가지고 있기 보다는 공유하는 것이 좋겠다는 생각을 하였기때문입니다.

둘째는 강의 중에 학생들로부터 받은 질문이 저자의 학창시절의 궁금증과 너무 흡사하다는 생각에 그런 질문들을 체계적으로 정리해서 책으로 내놓으면 그런 궁금증이 있는 다른 독자들에게도 다소 도움이 될 수 있을 것이라고 판단하였기때문입니다.

마지막으로 이런 주제로 책을 쓰시는 분들께 다소나마 도움이 되어 뒤이어 보다 좋은 책이 나오길 기대하는 마음에서 비롯된 것입니다.

이 책이 보다 정확한 지식을 전달하여 독자 여러분들께 도움이 될 수 있도록, 발견되는 문제점들은 바로 수정할 것이며 질문 사항에 대해서는 성의껏 답변에 응하겠습니다. 이 책은 전문가들이 아닌 영어 실력을 쌓으려는 분들을 위하여 쓰고 있기 때문에 전문적인 용어 및 접근법에서 약간 차이가 있을 수 있습니다. 그리고 가능한 깊은 설명이나 어색한 용어의 사용을 최대한 자제하고 실용성을 높이는데 주안점을 두고 있습니다. 독자 여러분들의 적극적인 참여를 환영하며 여러분들을 isjeong@gmail.com으로 초대합니다.

이 책에서 사용된 용어로서 규범적 구문, 일반 구문, 혹은 보통 어순이라 함은 어니언스(Onions)가 제시한 5개의 기본 문형(제1문형; 제2문형; 제3문형; 제4문형; 제5문형)을 말하는 것입니다. 그리고 이런 일반적인 어순의 문장 요소가 원래 위치로부터 문두(文頭)나 문미(文尾)로 이동되어 자리 바꿈이 있는 구문을 특수구문(Special Construction)이라 부르고 있습니다. 이런 구문은 단순히 자리 이동만 일어난 것이 아니고 이동에 따른 기능의 변화가 있어서 그런 표현들이 언제 그리고 왜 쓰이는지에 초점을 맞추고 있습니다. 이런 부류의 구문은 아니지만 별도로 설명이 필요하다고 생각되어 이 책에 "WITH 주술구문"이 첨가되어 있습니다.

사람들은 같은 뜻의 문장을 아주 다양한 표현으로 나타낼 수 있습니다. 그러나 뜻이 같다고 해서 아무 상황에서나 다른 표현의 문장을 임의로 바꿔 쓸 수 있는 것은 아닙니다. 같은 의미의 문장이라도 구조나 어순이 다른 문장은 상황에 따라 다른 중요한 역할을 하기 때문입니다. 한 예로서 우리는 중학교 시절 능동태와 수동태에 대해서 배웠습니다. 그때 이래로 능동태와 수동태는 의미가 같다는 것을 잘 알고 있습니다. 어쩌면 지금까지도 뜻이 같아서 아무 때나 바꿔 쓸 수 있는 것으로 생각하고 있는지도 모르겠습니다.

Preface

(1) a. Columbus discovered America in 1492.
    b. America was discovered in 1492 by Columbus.

물론 위의 두 문장 (1a)와 (1b)의 의미는 같습니다. 위의 능동태에서는 "Columbus"가 주어인 반면 수동태에서는 "America"가 주어입니다. 그러나 중요한 것은 의미가 같다고 그래서 어느 때나 바꿔 쓸 수 있는 것은 아니라는 점입니다. 다음 질문 (2a)에 가장 적절한 답을 하나 선택해보세요.

(2) a. What did the police do yesterday?
    b. ___________________

ⓐ They blocked the bridge.
ⓑ The bridge was blocked by them.
ⓒ It was them that blocked the bridge.
ⓓ The bridge they blocked.

위의 네 문장 (a), (b), (c), 그리고 (d)는 모두 의미가 같습니다. 그렇다면 모두가 질문 (2a)에 대한 대답으로 쓰일 수 있을까요? 많은 사람들은 능동태 (a)와 수동태 (b)는 뜻이 같기 때문에 하나만 고른다면 둘 모두가 답은 될 수 없기 때문에 아마 (c)번 아니면 (d)번을 선택할 수도 있을 것입니다. 그러나 가장 자연스럽고 적절한 답은 (a)번 입니다. 왜냐하면 영어에서도 한국어와 마찬가지로 주제(Topic)가 되는 말이 앞에 놓이기 때문입니다. 위의 질문에서는 "경찰"에 대해서 묻고 있습니다. 따라서 이런 경우에 답변을 할 때에는 역시 "경찰"에 대해서 이야기를 하게 됩니다. 그래서 이런 경우에는 "경찰"이 주어로 오는 것이 가장 자연스러운 답이 되는 것입니다. 이런 흥미로운 사실들을 독자 여러분들이 한 단원씩 공부해가면서 체험하길 바랍니다.

이 책을 펴내면서 감사의 말씀을 드리고 싶은 분들이 있습니다. 우선 이곳 어스틴에서 생활하는 동안 물심양면으로 많이 도와주신 신상렬 박사님 내외분께 깊은 감사를 드립니다. 아울러 여러 가지 질문에 대해 좋은 답변을 주신 이곳 University of Texas at Austin에 계시는 Knud Lambrecht교수님과 Lisa Green교수님께도 감사를 드립니다. 이분들은 필자가 이곳 대학에서 Visiting Scholar로 있는 동안 많은 학문적인 교류와 도움을 아끼지 않은 분들로서 이 책을 펴내는데 많은 도움을 주셨습니다. 원고의 수정 및 보완과 관련해서 이곳 대학에 다니는 Joe Shin과 Ben Shin 형제 그리고 Louis Divino와 Jane Jantha 그리고 언어학과 박사과정의 최인철(현. 경북대학교 교수), 오치성(현. 상명대학교 교수), 이은정 선생님 그리고 외국어 교육과 박사과정의 박명수 선생님(현. 상명대학교 교수)께 감사를 드립니다. 자료 수집 및 정리를 위해 많은 시간을 할애해준 김은현양과 이원복군 그리고 정영진군과 최선정양에게도 감사를 표하고자 합니다. 그리고 무엇보다도 이 책의 구성의 근간은 지금은 고인이 되신 저자의 은사님이신 양인석 교수님의 책에 있음을 밝히며 부족하지만 그분 영전에 이 책을 바칩니다.

끝으로 이 책을 흔쾌히 출판해주신 도서출판 새암 이재철 사장님께 감사를 드리며 독자 여러분들에게 이 책이 좋은 벗이 되길 바랍니다.

어스틴에서

정인식

English Special Constructions

Table of Contents 목 차

English Special Constructions

English Special Constructions

Chapter 01

전 치 / Preposing

Chapter 01

전 치 (前置) Preposing

전치란 무엇인가?

영어에서 전치구문이란 보통 문장의 어순과는 달리 동사 뒤에 있는 일부 구성 요소 즉 목적어, 보어, 혹은 부사적 요소가 문장의 왼쪽, 즉 문두(文頭: 주어 앞)에 나타나는 구문을 말한다. 전치 구문은 대개 보통의 문장어순으로 바꾸어 사용하는 것은 적절하지만, 반대로 아무 상황에서나 임의로 전치구문을 사용하는 것은 적절치 못하다. 전치 가능한 요소들은 명사구, 형용사구, 전치사구, 동사구 등이 있다.

01 a. I know this song.

b. **This song** I know. (명사구)

02 a. He isn't humble.

b. **Humble** he isn't. (형용사구)

03 a. There grows a willow tree out of the hedge.

b. **Out of the hedge** there grows a willow tree. (전치사구)

04 a. And he got a hundred.

b. And **get a hundred** he did. (동사구)

이렇게 전치된 요소는 문장과 문장을 자연스럽게 연결해줌으로써 글 전체의 응집력 (coherence)을 높여 주고 그 문장에서 대개 주제 역할을 하게 된다. 전치와 관련해서 주제화(Topicalization), 좌향전이(Left-dislocation), 그리고 동사구 전치(VP-Preposing)구문이 다루어진다.

전치는 언제 쓰이는가?

어떤 요소가 전치된 위치에 나타나기 위해서는 앞의 문맥에서 이미 명시적으로 언급되었거나, 또는 추론 가능한 선행요소를 통해 적절한 관계를 이루어야 한다. 선행하는 요소를 A라 하고 전치 될 요소를 B라 할 때에 앞에서 이미 언급되었다 함은 A와 B가 똑같은 것을 가리키고, 선행요소를 통해 추론 가능하다 함은 A가 B보다 크거나 혹은 작은 관계에 있다. 흔히 B와, 청자(Hearer)가 이미 알고 있다고 판단되는 요소를 구정보(Old Information)라하고, 어떤 요소가 그 문맥에서 처음 쓰이거나, 혹은 청자가 이미 알지 못하고 처음 접하게 되는 요소를 신정보(New Information)라 한다. 예를 들어보자.

05 A: You know this album?
(너 이 앨범 알고 있지?)

B: **This song** I know.
((그 앨범에 들어있는) 이 노래는 내가 알아.)

06 A: What do you think of John?
(너는 존에 대해서 어떻게 생각하니?)

B: He's a very successful, but **humble** guy.
(그는 아주 성공했지만 겸손한 사람이지.)

A: Successful, yes. But **humble** he's not.
(그래 성공은 했지. 하지만 겸손하지는 않아.)

07 Cabbage and potatoes are the only plants cultivated in **the gardens**, but out of **the hedge** there grows a willow tree.
(양배추와 감자가 이 정원에서 재배되는 유일한 식물이다. 그러나 울타리 밖으로는 버드나무 한 그루가 자라고 있다.)

08 Andy claims that he **got a hundred** on his exam. And **get a hundred** he did.
(Andy는 그가 시험에서 100점을 받았다고 주장한다. 그런데 그는 사실 100점은 받았다.)

위 예문이 보여주는 바와 같이 (5)와 (7)에서는 전치된 요소 "This song"과 "the hedge"는 선행하는 명사 "this album"과 "the gardens"을 구성하고 있는 요소들이다. (6)과 (7)에서는 전치된 요소 "humble"과 "get a hundred"가 이미 앞에서 언급되어 있음을 알 수 있다. 이와 같이 전치된 요소는 반드시 선행하는 요소와 긴밀한 관계가 있을 때에만 문두에 나타나는 것이 가능하다. 그렇지 않은 다음과 같은 경우에는 옳지 못한 표현이다.

09 a. Someone broke into the garage last night. #**My father** I need to talk to.

b. Someone broke into the garage last night. I need to talk to my father.
(지난 밤에 누군가 차고에 침입해 들어왔다. 그래서 나는 아버지께 말씀을 드려야 하겠다.)

참고 이 책에서 사용되는 기호로써 #은 문법적으로는 맞지만 문맥상 적절하지 못하다는 것을 나타내고, ?는 일부는 문법적으로 옳지 못하다고 또 일부는 문법적으로 옳다고 주장하여 문법성에 이견이 있는 경우를 나타내고, 그리고 *은 문법적으로 옳지 못하다는 것을 나타낸다.

10 a. Tchaikovsky was one of the most tormented men in musical history. But he did produce music.

b. Tchaikovsky was one of the most tormented men in musical history. But #**produce music** he did.

c. Tchaikovsky was one of the most tormented men in musical history. In fact, one wonders how he managed to produce music at all. But **produce music** he did.
(Tchaikovsky는 음악 역사상 가장 많은 고문을 받은 사람 중에 한 사람이다. 사실 사람들은 도대체 그가 어떻게 음악 창작을 했는지 궁금해 하고 있다. 그렇지만 음악 창작은 해냈다.)

이상에서 본 바와 같이 의미는 같다 하더라도 문장의 어순이 변할 때에 그 문장의 적절성은 문맥에서 결정된다.

Unit 1 주제화 (主題化: Topicalization)

어떤 문장이 있을 때에 "그 문장이 무엇에 대하여 이야기하고 있는가?"라는 질문을 받았을 때에 그에 대한 답을 주제(Topic)라 한다. 주제를 명시적으로 나타내줌으로써 담화의 의도 또는 방향을 분명하게 전달하는 동시에, 주제에 관한 정보를 받아들일 준비를 하도록 하기 위한 것이다. 그리고 일반적으로 영어에서의 주제의 위치는 문두가 된다. 다음 예문을 보자.

01 The children went to school.

위 문장은 주어"The children"에 대해서 이야기를 하고 있다. 따라서 주어가 주제로 쓰이고 있는 것이다. 이와 같이 문장의 주제는 흔히 문장의 주어와 일치한다. 그러나 항상 그런 것은 아니다. 다음 예문을 보자.

02 These steps he used to sweep with a broom.
(이 계단은 그가 비로 쓸곤 했었다.)

위 문장은 주어 앞에 있는 "These steps"에 대해서 이야기를 하고 있다. "These steps"는 문장의 주어가 아니고 엄밀히 말하면 동사 "sweep"의 목적어로 쓰이고 있는데 이 문장에서는 주제 역할을 하기 위하여 전치되어 있는 것이다.
이처럼 주제화라는 것은 문장의 주어가 아닌 요소를 주제로 만들기 위하여 문두에 놓는 것을 말한다. 그리고 문장의 주제가 되는 요소를 전치시켜 놓음으로써 문장과 문장을 자연스럽게 연결해주며 글의 응집력(Coherence)을 높여준다. 한국어로 옮길 때에도 가능하면 주제화된 요소를 먼저 해석하며 조사 "은"이나 "는"을 붙여주는 것이 문맥을 자연스럽게 해준다.

1 주제화 되는 요소

1.1. 명사구 / 절

03 a. I could have endured the private pain.

b. **The private pain** I could have endured. (타동사의 목적어)
(그런 개인적인 고통은 참을 수 있었을 것이다.)

04 a. We elected the boy's employer president.

b. **The boy's employer** we elected president. (불완전 타동사의 목적어)
(그 소년의 고용주는 우리가 회장으로 선출했다.)

05 a. We are proud of our ancestors.

b. **Our ancestors** we are proud of. (전치사의 목적어)
(우리의 조상은 우리가 자랑스럽게 여긴다.)

06 a. They are not the average American family of four.

b. **The average American family of four** they are not. (보어)
(평균 미국의 4인 가족은 그들이 아니다.)

07 a. No one ever expected Bill to find out that you were coming.

b. **That you were coming** no one ever expected Bill to find out.
(네가 오리라는 것을 Bill이 알고 있을 거라고 기대한 사람은 아무도 없었다.)

1.2. 형용사구

08 a. Our hearts are heavy that prayer has become a controversial and divisive issue. It is controversial.

b. Our hearts are heavy that prayer has become a controversial and divisive issue. **Controversial** it is.
(우리의 마음은 기도가 논쟁과 불화를 가져오는 문제가 되고 있어서 울적하다. 그것이 논쟁거리가 되고 있는 것은 사실이다.)

09 A: This is not another vulgar disgusting sexploitation film.
(이것은 또 하나의 저속하고 구역질 나는 섹스플로이테이션 영화가 아니다.)

B: **Vulgar** it's not. **Dumb** it is.
(저속한 것은 아니지만, 있어야 할 것이 빠져있다.)

참고 예문 (9B)에서 "Vulgar"는 선행 문장에서 언급되어 있지만 "Dumb"은 그렇지 않다. 그럼에도 불구하고 후자 형용사의 전치가 가능한 것은 전자 형용사와 대립되고 있기 때문에 가능하다.

1.3. 전치사구

10 a. We asked him to put the bananas into the basket.

b. **Into the basket** we asked him to put the bananas.
(우리는 그에게 바구니 안에다 바나나를 담으라고 했다.)

11 a. It pierced its way through the snow to the root, and there was a stirring within the root.

b. It pierced its way through the snow to the root, and **within the root** there was a stirring.
(그것은 눈을 헤치고 뿌리까지 깊숙이 뚫고 들어갔습니다. 그리고 그 뿌리 안에서는 흔들림이 있었습니다.)

1.4. 동사구

12 a. They expect that John will pass the exam, and he will pass the exam.

b. They expect that John will pass the exam, and **pass the exam he** will.
(그들은 존이 시험에 합격할 것으로 기대하고 있는데 그는 정말 그 시험은 합격할 것이다.)

참고 동사구 전치에 대한 설명은 뒤의 "동사구 전치" 단원에서 자세히 다루어짐.

2 보충 설명

13 a. The principal caught a guy in our school smoking in the john.

b. *A guy in our school the principal caught smoking in the john.
(우리학교의 어떤 학생이 화장실에서 담배 피우는 것을 교장 선생님이 발견하셨다.)

주제화 구문에서 주제화 되는 요소는 이미 앞에서 언급된 정보이거나 혹은 청자가 이미 알고 있다고 가정되는 구정보(Old Information)이어야 한다. 그러나 위 예문 (b)는 주제화 된 요소가 신정보(New Information)임으로 적절치 못한 문장이다.

14 a. Eat these apples up.
(이 사과를 남기지말고 다 먹어치워라)

b. *These apples eat up.

명령문에서 사용되는 명사구 목적어는 주제화시킬 수 없다. 따라서 예문(b)에서처럼 목적어를 전치시키는 구문은 비문이다.

15 a. John bought three of the apples.
(John이 그 사과중에서 셋을 샀다.)

b. *The apples John bought three of.

"수량사 + 전치사 + 목적어"가 동사의 목적어로 쓰일 때에는 전치사의 목적어는 주제화 시킬 수 없다.

16 a. I believe that Mary is genuinely ill.

b. *Mary, I believe that is genuinely ill.

c. Mary, I believe is genuinely ill.
(Mary가 나는 정말 아프다는 생각이 든다.)

목적어절의 주어를 주제화 시켜 문두에 놓을 때는 접속사 "that"을 생략해야 한다. 따라서 위 예문(b)는 적절치 못한 문장이다.

17 a. I suppose that you'll want to wear this dress.

b. This dress, I suppose you'll want to wear.

c. This dress, I suppose that you'll want to wear.
(이 옷은 네가 입고 싶어할 것으로 생각이 든다.)

목적어절의 목적어를 주제화 시켜 문두에 놓을 때는 접속사 "that"을 위 예문(b)에서처럼 생략해도 되고, 위 예문(c)에서처럼 생략하지 않아도 된다.

18 a. I saw your brother last night.

b. Your brother I saw last night.
(너의 형은 내가 지난 밤에 보았다.)

c. As for your brother, I saw him last night.

주제화 구문은 주제가 되는 요소를 반드시 이동시키지 않더라도 그 자리에 대명사를 남겨두고 문두에 "as for" 나 "about"을 사용해 같은 기능을 하게 할 수 있다. 이것은 뒤에서 다루는 좌향 전이(Left Dislocation)와 비슷한 형태이다.

Practice Examples

Reading 01

As a proud son of the world's greatest city, I am deeply pained to have to address the issue I am about to address. But I must. So many bizarre and irresponsible rumors-and, yes, outright lies-have been circulated lately about our redoubtable mayor, the canards at last must be countered to save our civic reputation. The rest of America and the world must know the truth. He is a strong and dedicated man, Rudolph Giuliani of New York, and unafraid. He is also an innovator, bursting with new ideas. Of course such a man has enemies. Of course he inspires vitriolic opposition from reactionaries and nihilists in the media, the opposition party and the city's entrenched interests. But the stories! **The outrageous fabrications you read and hear**. Let me list just a few of the ludicrous mendacities flying about-immediately exploded by the facts. /Time

Word Bank

- redoubtable: 존경할만한.
- circulate: 퍼뜨리다. 유포하다.
- canard: 허위보도, 유언비어.
- vitriolic: 신랄한, 통렬한.
- reactionary: 반동주의자, 보수주의자.
- nihilist: 허무주의자.
- inspire: 고무시키다. 불러 일으키다.
- interest: 이해 관계자.
- entrench: 확립하다.(= to establish solidly).
- fabrication: 꾸며낸 일. 거짓말.
- let me R = I will(wish to) R.
- ludicrous: 우스운, 바보 같은.
- mendacity: 거짓.
- explode: 뒤엎다, 타파하다.

구문 설명

"He is a strong and dedicated man, Rudolph Giuliani of New York."에서 "He"는 뒤에 있는 "Rudolph Giuliani"이다. 이런 표현은 우향전이(Right Dislocation)라고 하는데 뒤에서 자세히 다루고 있다.

Reading 02

Once upon a time there lived an unhappy young girl. **Unhappy she was**, for her mother was dead, her father had married another woman, a widow with two daughters, and her stepmother didn't like her one little bit. All the nice things, kind thoughts and loving touches were for her own daughters. And not just the kind thoughts and love, but also dresses, shoes, shawls, delicious food, comfy beds, as well as every home comfort.

/Cinderella

Word Bank

- widow: 과부.
- thought: 생각, 사고, 배려.
- touch: 접촉, 만지기.
- comfy: 편안한 (=comfortable).
- stepmother: 계모.
- loving: 애정어린, 사랑이 깃든.
- shawl: 어깨걸이, 숄.

구문 설명

And not just the kind thoughts and love, but also dresses, shoes, shawls, delicious food, comfy beds, as well as every home comfort."다음에 "were for her own daughters"가 생략된 표현임.

Reading 03

Cabbage and potatoes are the only plants cultivated in the gardens, but **out of the hedge there grows a willow tree, and under this willow tree sat a little girl**, and she sat with her eyes fixed upon the old oak tree between the huts.

/H. C. Andersen. What the Moon Saw

Word Bank

- cabbage: 양배추.
- hedge: 울타리.
- oak: 참나무.
- cultivate: 경작하다, 재배하다.
- willow: 버드나무.
- hut: 오두막.

Reading 04

My parents were always devising ways to help me overcome my fears and learn to trust in God. For example, they had a little exercise for me to conquer my uncontrollable fear of the dark. At the end of the long hallway was my room. **On the floor they placed my stuffed tiger.** The hallway was dark; my parents and I were standing in the living room. "Now go down the hall and get your tiger," they told me, "and stop this foolishness." I needed tiger, but I was afraid of the dark hallway and what might be waiting in my dark room. They refused to turn on the light or walk with me, because, as they told me, they were trying to teach me something for my own good. Finally, after a long-period of tears and pleading, I steeled myself to walk down the hallway, because I couldn't stand to think of tiger alone in the dark. /Elizabeth Kim. Ten Thousand Sorrows

Word *Bank*

- devise: 궁리하다, 고안하다.
- overcome: 극복하다, 압도하다.
- controllable: 관리할 수 있는, 통제할 수 있는.
- hallway: 통로, 복도.
- stuffed: 속을 채워넣은.
- living room: 거실, 응접실.
- good: 이익, 복리.
- pleading: 변명, 변론.
- steel: 마음을 굳게 하다.
- stand: 〈보통 부정문〉 …을 참다, 견디다 (to do / doing).

Reading 05

Until recently, the ability to make tools was considered one of the characteristics that distinguished humans and their ancestors from all other animals. In 1964, Dr. Jane M. Goodall shattered this belief when she observed that chimpanzees in the African forest frequently make simple tools for catching termites. The ape first looks for the right materials. It carefully selects a twig of the correct size and shape and then strips off the leaves. **This the ape inserts into a hole in the termite nest.** When the twig is pulled out, it is covered with delectable insects. /TOEFL.

Word Bank

- shatter: 깨다, 꺾다.
- strip: 벗기다, 없애다.
- correct: 정확한, 적절한, 알맞은.
- twig: 작은 가지.
- termite: 흰개미(=white ant)
- delectable: 즐거운, 맛있는.

Reading 06

In the spring of 1963, graduation ceremonies were held at Carnegie Hall. As I walked across the stage to accept my medical degree, **tears I saw in my mother's eyes and in Aunt Lottie's, and the pride I saw in my father's smile**. I hugged them all. With their support I had made it. But why I'd had to work so hard was still a mystery to me.

/Reader's Digest.

Word Bank

- ceremony: 의식, 제전.
- make it: 어떤 일을 이룩하다. 성공하다.
- degree: 학위

Reading 07

The way women score points is not just a preference but a true need. Women need many expressions of love in a relationship to feel loved. One or two expressions of love, no matter how important, will not, and cannot, fulfill her. **This can be extremely hard for a man to understand**. One way to look at it is to imagine that women have a love tank similar to the gas tank on a car. It needs to be filled over and over again. Doing many little things (and scoring many points) is the secret for filling a woman's love tank. A woman feels loved when her love tank is full. She is able to respond with greater love, trust, acceptance, appreciation, admiration, approval, and encouragement. Lots of little things are needed to top off her tank.

/John Gray. Men are from Mars. Women are from Venus

Word Bank

- score: 채점하다, 받다.
- fulfill: 이행하다, 만족시키다.
- appreciation: 감사, 감상.
- top off: 가득 채우다.
- preference: 더 좋아함, 편애.
- over and over again: 몇 번이고
- admiration: 감탄, 찬미.

구문설명

One way to look at it is to imagine ~ = One way to understand it is to imagine ~

Reading 08

The emotion is just as prevalent among adults as among children. Take, for example, maid-servants: I remember when one of our maids, who was a married woman, became pregnant, and we said that she was not to be expected to lift heavy weights, the instant result was that none of the others would lift heavy weights, **and any work of that sort that needed doing we had to do ourselves.**

/Bertrand Russell. The conquest of Happiness

Word Bank

- prevalent: 널리 퍼진, 일반적인(among, in).
- pregnant: 임신한.
- weight: 무거운 짐.

구문설명

and any work of that sort that needed doing we had to do ourselves. = and any work of that sort that needed to be done we had to do ourselves. 동사 "need" 다음에서 능동형 동명사는 수동의 의미를 갖는다. 이런 표현을 쓰는 단어로는 want, need, require, bear, stand, deserve, merit, worth, past 등이 있는데 이들 다음에서 동명사형이 쓰일 때에 수동의 의미를 갖는다. 일부(want, need, require, deserve, merit, worthy)는 동명사 대신에 "to be + 과거분사"를 쓰기도 한다.

Reading 09

The exact moment I can remember that fog lifted. It was on a trek up a small mountain. Climbing it had not been my idea. I am afraid of heights, and so was Matthew--until he saw the view from the top. "But Mom, it's so beautiful," he gasped. "Why didn't you tell me?"

/Reader's Digest.

Word Bank

- lift: 올라가다, 걷히다.
- trek: 여행.
- gasp: 헐떡이며 말하다. 헐떡거리다.

구문 설명

(1) The exact moment I can remember that fog lifted. = (2) The exact moment that fog lifted I can remember. = (3) I can remember the exact moment that fog lifted. 문장 (1)은 (2)에서 보여주는 바와 같이 "The exact moment"가 관계대명사절의 수식을 받는데 너무 길어지는 것을 피하기 위해 그 절을 뒤로 옮겨놓은 구문이다. 이런 구문을 "탈명사구 외치 구문"이라 하는데 뒤에서 자세히 설명되고 있다.

Reading 10

The pictures on television and in the press had wrenching impact. **The cameras sick and dying seals with dark liquid eyes were staring reproachfully into**. They were among the estimated 7,000 victims of a mysterious epidemic first detected off the Danish coast last April; it then spread into West German waters and now threatens Britain's 20,000 harbor seals. The images haunted West Europeans. In Britain, where issues like air pollution have not stirred much passion, the response to the seals plight was described as staggering.

/New York Times.

Word Bank

- wrench: 비통한 느낌을 가지게 하다(= to cause to suffer mental anguish).
- seal: 바다표범.
- harbor seal: 점박이 바다표범.
- reproachfully: 비난에 찬, 책망하는 듯한.
- epidemic: 유행병.
- detect: 찾아내다, 발견하다.
- off: ~의 앞바다에서.
- waters: 해역, 영역.
- haunt: 끊임없이 떠오르다.
- staggering: 깜짝 놀라게 하는, 엄청난.

Reading 11

Man is the only creature that consumes without producing. He does not give milk, he does not lay eggs, he is too weak to pull the plough, he cannot run fast enough to catch rabbits. Yet he is the lord of all the animals. He sets them to work, he gives back to them the minimum that will prevent them from starving, and **the rest he keeps for himself**. Our labor tills the soil, our dung fertilizes it, and yet there is not one of us that owns more than his bare skin.

/George Orwell. Animal Farm

Word Bank

- creature: 피조물, 동물.
- give: 산출하다(=produce).
- plough: 쟁기(=plow).
- lord: 주인, 지배자, 우두머리.
- till: 경작하다, 갈다.
- dung: (동물의) 똥, 거름.
- fertilize: 기름지게 하다, 비옥하게 하다.
- bare: 벌거벗은, 겨우 ~인 뿐인.

구문 설명

"he gives back to them the minimum that will prevent them from starving"에서 "the minimum ~ starving"은 동사 "give"의 목적어인데 너무 길어 후치시켜 놓은 구문이다. 이런 구문은 "복합 명사구 이동"편에서 다루어 지고 있다.

Reading 12

S'right. It's a shell. I seen one like that before. On someone's back wall. **A conch, he called it**. He used to blow it and then his mum would come. It's ever so valuable.

/William Golding. Lord of the Flies

Word Bank

- conch: 소라.
- mum: 엄마 (= mummy, mom)
- blow: 불다.

구문 설명

1. S'right = It's right.
2. A conch, he called it. = He called it a conch.
3. I seen one like that before. = I have seen one like that before.

Reading 13

If daughter was as concerned as mother about living on Easy Street, my guess is that she would have dumped Arnie long ago. I vehemently disagree with your advice to the mother to have a talk with her daughter. Abby, it's the MOM who needs a talking-to. **Well-meaning she may be**, but I wish she'd wake up to the idea that love and wealth do not go hand-in-hand.

/Universal Press Syndicate, Dear Abby 1999. 2

Word Bank

- concerned: 염려하는, 걱정스러운.
- Easy Street: 유복한 신분(= a situation with no worries).
- dump: 을 버리다, 을 쓰레기로 버리다.
- talking-to: 잔소리, 꾸중.
- hand in hand: 손을 마주잡고, 협력하여.
- vehemently: 열렬히, 격렬하게.
- well-meaning: 선의의, 사람이 좋은.
- wake up to: 알아채다, 깨닫다.

Reading 14

As a matter of fact, the event which they were hypocritically lamenting had not taken place, though a few examples of eccentric behavior had given rise to the rumor. **Of all characteristics of ordinary human nature envy is the most unfortunate;** not only does the envious person wish to inflict misfortune and do so whenever he can with impunity, but he is also himself rendered unhappy by envy. Instead of deriving pleasure from what he has, he derives pain from what others have.

/Bertrand Russell. The Conquest of Happiness

Word Bank

- as a matter of fact: 사실은, 실은.
- lament: 한탄하다, 슬퍼하다.
- give rise to: 낳다, 일으키다.
- nature: 천성, 본성.
- misfortune: 불행, 불운.
- render: 로 하다(=make).
- hypocritically: 위선적으로.
- eccentric: 괴상한, 이상한.
- characteristic: 특징, 특질.
- inflict: 을 가하다, 주다.
- impunity: 처벌을 받지 않음.
- derive: 얻다, 끌어내다.

구문 설명

"not only does the envious person wish to inflict ~"에서는 부정요소 "not only"가 문두에 놓여 주어 조동사가 도치된 구문이다. 자세한 설명은 "주어 조동사 도치" 구문 참조.

Reading 15

And even the miserable lives we lead are not allowed to reach their natural span. For myself I do not grumble, for I am one of the lucky ones. I am twelve years old and have had over four hundred children. Such is the natural life of a pig. But no animal escapes the cruel knife in the end. You young porkers who are sitting in front of me, every one of you will scream your lives out at the block within a year. **To that horror we all must come** - cows, pigs, hens, sheep, everyone. Even the horses and the dogs have no better fate. You, Boxer, the very day that those great muscles of yours lose their power, Jones will sell you to the knacker, who will cut your throat and boil you down for the fox-hounds. As for the dogs, when they grow old and toothless, Jones ties a brick round their necks and drowns them in the nearest pond.

/George Orwell. Animal Farm

Word Bank

- natural span: 천수(= natural span of life).
- porker: 식용돼지.
- Out: 없어질 때까지, 소멸하여.
- knacker: 도살업자.
- block: 푸줏간의 도마.
- come: 이르다.
- fox-hound: 여우사냥개.

Reading 16

We know that the law is spiritual; but I am unspiritual, sold as a slave to sin. I do not understand what I do. **For what I want to do I do not do**, but what I hate I do. And if I do what I do not want to, I agree that the law is good. As it is, it is no longer I myself who do it, but it is sin living in me. I know that nothing good lives in me, that is, in my sinful nature.

/Holy Bible-New International Version. Romans 7:14-18

Word Bank

- law: 법, 율법.
- as it is: 그러나 실상은, 실제로.
- spiritual: 영적인, 신성한.

구문 설명

1. if I do what I do not want to ~ = if I do what I do not want to do ~.
2. but it is sin living in me. = but it is sin living in me.

Reading 17

The Dutch have just appointed their physicians doctors of death. The Senate in the Netherlands voted to pass a law last week allowing physicians to end patients′ lives if they have terminal "unbearable suffering." In so doing, the Netherlands has become the first country to legalize assisted suicide and to turn medicine from the purpose of healing to one of killing. For Europe, all this has haunting implications. From the religious community to politicians to the press, there was an outcry in Germany against a government-approved euthanasia practice. While the Nazis secretly eliminated 100,000 men, women and children who were physically or mentally handicapped between 1939 and 1941, the Dutch are now openly embracing the killing of children, the aged, and the psychologically challenged. **Among the victims of the Nazi regime** were the Dutch themselves. Dutch parliamentarians have shown they have decided not to remember those lessons. With this new law, life in the Netherlands has been cheapened.

/Washington Times. 2001. 4

Word Bank

- Dutch: 네덜란드인.
- Senate: 상원. (cf. Senator: 상원 의원).
- vote: 을 투표로 결정하다, 가결하다.
- pass: 통과시키다.
- terminal: 말기의. 종말의.
- medicine: 의학, 의약품.
- haunting: 잊혀지지 않은, 자주 마음에 떠오르는.
- outcry: 절규, 격렬한 항의.
- eliminate: 제거하다, 죽이다.
- psychologically: 심리적으로, 정신적으로(= mentally).
- challenge: 도전하다. 자극하다.
- embrace: 포옹하다, 포용하다. regime: 정부, 체제.

Reading 18

Harry made a grab for the letter but Uncle Vernon knocked his hand out of the way. The woman stared. "I'll take them," said Uncle Vernon, standing up quickly and following her from the dining room.
"Wouldn't it be better just to go home, dear?" Aunt Petunia suggested timidly, hours later, but Uncle didn't seem to hear her. **Exactly what he was looking for, none of them knew**. He drove them into the middle of a forest, got out, looked around, shook his head, got back in the car, and off they went again. The same thing happened in the middle of a plowed field, halfway across a suspension bridge, and at the top of a multilevel parking garage.

/J. K. Rowling. Harry Potter and the Sorcerer's Stone

Word Bank

- grab: 잡아채기, 움켜쥐기.
- knock: 치다. 때리다.
- out of the way; 방해가 되지 않을 곳에, 손이 미치지 않을 곳에.
- timid: 소심한, 겁 많은.
- get out: 내리다.
- go off: 떠나다, 도망치다.
- plow: 쟁기질하다. 일구다.

구문 설명

"~and off they went again."에서 방향부사 "off"는 "went"뒤에 주로 나타나는데 전치되어 있다. 이런 경우에는 다음 예문에서와 같이 동사와 주어도 서로 위치가 바뀌는데 주어가 대명사일 때에는 그렇게 되지 않는다. Down the street rolled a baby carriage. (= A baby carriage rolled down the street.). 자세한 설명은 "주어 동사의 도치"편 참조.

Reading 19

When I opened the newspaper today, **in the front section was a photograph of Lucille Ball**. Her blue eyes, red hair and lovely smile reminded me of my mother. My mother was only 49 when she passed away last month. Mom had a hard life. She was weak from the beginning. She weighed 1 pound at birth and had only one lung. Her whole life, she hated going to doctors. I try to comfort my stepfather because he blamed himself for not forcing Mother to consult a doctor when she first started feeling sick.

/Universal Press Syndicate, Dear Abby. 2001. 2

Word Bank

- lovely: 아름다운.
- lung: 폐.
- consult: 상담하다, 의견을 구하다.
- pass away: 죽다. 사망하다.
- comfort: 위로하다, 달래다.

Reading 20

It seems that we should look in vain for evidence in her work of many of the main historical and political events which occurred during her lifetime. She saw -or lived through- the French Revolution, the rise (and fall) of Napoleon Bonaparte; the American War of Independence (and the war with England of 1812). She died (1817) midway between Waterloo (1815) and Peterloo (1819) and she lived through much of the turmoil which accompanied what E. P. Thompson has described as 'The Making of the English Working Class.' She must also have been aware of the Jacobin and anti-Jacobin struggle which went on in England as a result of the French Revolution, a struggle most easily (though not adequately) described as the opposition of the views expressed in Edmund Burke's Reflection on the French Revolution (1790) and in Thomas Paine's Rights of Man (1791). These tumultuous revolutions, changes and arguments seem to have left very little mark on her fiction, and yet of course she knew what was going on. **What effect, if any, all these events had in her writing we shall have to consider in due course.**

/Tony Tanner. Jane Austen

Word Bank

- in vain: 헛되이(문장부사: "주어 조동사 도치" 연습문제 15번 해설 참조).
- go on: 일어나다(= happen).
- midway: 중간에(= halfway).
- accompany: 동시에 일어나다. 수반하다.
- tumultuous: 소란스러운, 소동을 일으키는.
- in due course: 순서를 따라, 결국.
- turmoil: 혼란, 소요, 소란.

Reading 21

Americans now have 60 percent of their savings and investment in the stock market-double the ratio in 1982-and crumbling stock prices represent a loss of real wealth. What happened to the New Economy? Can we get it back? **At the center of the new economy were advances in telecommunications, microelectronics, software, and management practices**. These created new products and unleashed innovations in the workplace and corporate supply chain that raised potential productivity growth to levels not seen since the 1960s. Better products and productivity resurrected American competitiveness. From 1989 to 1998, exports accounted for 25 percent of U.S. growth.

/Washington Times. 2001. 4

Word Bank

- savings: 저축.
- stock: 주식, 재고.
- crumble: 멸망하다, 붕괴하다.
- telecommunication: 장거리 통신.
- unleash: 풀어 놓다, 폭발 시키다.
- workplace: 일터, 작업장.
- corporate: 법인의, 기업의.
- account for: 설명하다, 해당하다.
- investment: 투자.
- ratio: 비율.

Reading 22

Accept the fact that your mother-in-law is trying to show her love and concern for you, so smile, nod and tune her out. Once the twins arrive, assure her that they are under the care of an excellent pediatrician-and you'll mention her suggestions to the doctor to be sure they don't conflict with the medical advice you are already receiving. **As for your sister-in-law, tell her sweetly that you would LOVE to see her** - perhaps during the holidays-after you have regained your strength and you and the babies have a firmly established schedule. To do so is not "alienating her"-it's asserting your right to recover from the delivery.

/Universal Press Syndicate. Dear Abby.

Word Bank

- -in-law: 법률상의.
- nod: (동의, 인사, 명령등에 대하여 수긍하는 뜻으로) 머리를 끄덕이다(= make a quick downward motion of the head as in expressing assent, salutation, or command).
- tune out: 상관치 않다.
- suggestion: 암시, 제안.
- conflict: 모순되다, 상충되다.
- alienate: 소원하게 하다.
- delivery: 출산, 분만.
- assert: 단언하다, 주장하다.
- delivery: 분만, 출산.

Reading 23

Enter an unlikely alliance of the U.S. government, environmental groups and security agencies. In 1977 a moratorium was placed on nuclear recycling in the hopes that foreign countries would not recycle their waste; the idea was to prevent nuclear proliferation among non-nuclear nations. **For their part, anti-nuclear activists believe there is no safe way to handle waste**, so they prefer to close down plants rather than recycle, even today, when the real choice is between more coal-generated electricity, or more nuclear plants being built. Environmental and anti-nuke groups, led by Ralph Nader's Public Citizen, are fighting even the suggestion of recycling a small amount of nuclear waste. /Washington Times.

Word Bank

- enter: 등장하다(명령형으로).
- unlikely: 있을 법하지도 않은, 가망이 없는.
- moratorium: 지불유예, 일시적 정지.
- recycle: (폐기물을) 재처리하다, 재생 이용하다.
- proliferation: 확산, 증식.
- close down: 폐쇄하다.
- nuke: 핵무기(의), 원자력 발전소(의)

Reading 24

I think you came up short in your reply to "Dreading September," the woman expecting twins. She is concerned about having to deal with both her controlling mother-in-law and a potential visit from her sister-in-law's family immediately after the children are born. You advised her to accept her mother-in-law's love, reassure her, and tune her out. **As for her sister-in-law, you said she should have them put off the visit until she has a firmly established schedule.** Good advice - but it's directed at the wrong person. /Universal Press Syndicate. Dear Abby.

Word Bank

- short: 부족한, 불충분한.
- reassure: 안심 시키다.
- tune out: 에 귀를 기울이지 않다, 무시하다.
- put off: 연기하다(= postpone).
- established: 확립된.
- direct: 향하게 하다.

구문 설명

"she should have them put off the visit until ~"에서 "have"는 사역 동사이고 "them"은 "her sister-in-law's family"를 가리킨다.

Unit 2 좌향 전이 (左向 轉移: Left-Dislocation)

좌향 전이는 앞에서 다루었던 주제화 구문과 아주 비슷하다. 보통 문장 어순에서 명사구를 문두 위치에 놓으며 전치되어 있는 요소는 주제화 구문과 마찬가지로 주제역할을 한다. 그러나 다른 점은 전치된 요소가 원래 있던 자리에 그것의 성(gender)과 수(number)가 일치되는 대명사를 남겨둔다. 게다가 주제화 구문에서는 구정보에 해당되는 요소만 전치되지만, 좌향전이에서는 구정보뿐만 아니라 신정보도 전치될 수 있다.

1 좌향 전이 되는 요소

1.1. 주 어

01 a. The report really depressed him.

b. **The report,** it really depressed him.
(그 보도에 그는 정말 낙담했다.)

02 a. John's sister won't do anything rash.

b. **John's sister, she** won't do anything rash.
(John의 누이는 경솔한 짓은 하지 않을 것이다.)

1.2. 목 적 어

03 a. I bought these books at the university bookstore.

b. **These books,** I bought **them** at the university store.
(이 책들을 나는 대학서점에서 샀다.)

04 a. I told you you wouldn't like this movie much.

b. **This movie,** I told you you wouldn't like it much.
(이 영화를 네가 그리 좋아하지 않을 거라는 것을 너에게 말했었다.)

1.3. 소 유 격

05 a. I will marry Harry's pretty sister, when she becomes 25.

b. **Harry,** I will marry **his** pretty sister, when she becomes 25.
(나는 Harry의 예쁜 누이와 그녀가 스물 다섯이 되면 결혼할 것이다.)

06 a. Steve's mother likes Mary.

b. **Steve, his** mother likes Mary.
(Steve의 어머니는 Mary를 좋아한다.)

1.4. 전 치 사 구

07 a. Lisa put the beans in this cupboard.

b. **In this cupboard,** Lisa put the beans **there**.
(이 찬장 안에다 Lisa가 콩을 넣어두었다.)

2 보충 설명

08 a. I have met the boy who was wearing a big straw hat.
(나는 큰 밀짚 모자를 쓰고 있는 소년을 만난 적이 있다.)

b. *The boy, I have met him who was wearing a big straw hat.

c. The boy who was wearing a big straw hat, I have met him.

09 a. I agree to the common belief that women like to talk more than men.
(나는 여자들이 남자들보다 이야기하는 것을 더 좋아한다는 통념에 공감한다.)

b.*The common belief, I agree to it that women like to talk more than men.

c. The common belief that women like to talk more than men, I agree to it.

명사가 관계절, 부정사구, 혹은 동격절의 수식을 받을 때에 그것을 복합명사구라고 하는데, 수식하는 요소를 제외하고 명사만 전치시킬 수는 없다. 따라서 위의 예문 (8b)와 (9b)는 비문이다.

10 a. They let him have a holiday yesterday.
(그들은 그를 어제 하루 쉬도록 해주었다.)

b. *He, they let him have a holiday yesterday.

c. *Him, they let him have a holiday yesterday.

위 예문 (10b)와 (10c)가 보여주는 바와 같이 대명사는 좌향전이가 될 수 없다.

11 a. Sally made the hamburgers.

b. The hamburgers Sally made.(주제화)

c. The hamburgers, Sally made them.
(그 햄버거는 Sally가 만들었습니다.)

d. *The hamburgers, Sally made it.

위 예문 (11d)가 좌향 전이 구문이라면 "The hamburgers"와 "it"은 같은 것을 지시하여야 한다. 그러나 하나는 복수이고 다른 하나는 단수이므로 수의 일치가 이루어지지 않고 있다. 그래서 예문 (11d)는 적절치 못하다.

12 a. A teacher of the discipline was about to join a public protest against the crackdown.

b. **A teacher of the discipline, he** was about to join a public protest against the crackdown.
(그 훈련 사범인 그는 당국의 탄압에 항의하기 위한 대중집회에 참여하려 하고 있었다.)

여기에서 주어 "A teacher of the discipline"은 실제 문맥에서 볼 때에 그리고 청자에게도 신정보이다. 이런 신정보가 주어 위치에 놓이는 것은 좋지않으므로 그것을 전치 시키고 주어 위치에 그에 상응하는 대명사를 놓는다.

13 a. A real prodigal son is what you are.

b. **A real prodigal son, that's** what you are.
(진짜 탕아는 바로 현재의 당신입니다.)

좌향전이 구문에서 전치된 명사의 원래 위치에 성과 수가 일치하는 대명사가 아닌 "that"이 가끔 쓰이기도 한다.

Practice Examples

Reading 01

The son of poor parents, he planned to become a teacher. As a student in the normal school, he become interested in germs and prepared to follow his studies throughout his lifetime. As a teacher of science, he continued his research, discovering germs and studying the evil effects of dread diseases, thereby improving conditions in his country, curing anthrax and other diseases.

/Richard A. Flinn. Choosing Your Work

Word Bank

- normal school: 사범학교, 2년제의 교원 양성학교.
- germs: 세균, 병균.
- follow: 에 종사하다.
- anthrax: 탄저병.

구문 설명

As a student in the normal school, = As (When) he was a student in the normal school,.

Reading 02

The girls had reached the meat counter and were asking McMahon something. He pointed, they pointed, and they shuffled out of sight behind a pyramid of Diet Delight peaches. All that was left for us to see was old McMahon patting his mouth and looking after them sizing up their joints. **Poor kids, I began to feel sorry for them, they couldn't help it.** Now here comes the sad part of the story, at least my family says it's sad but I don't think it's sad myself. The store's pretty empty, it being Thursday afternoon, so there was nothing much to do except lean on the register and wait for the girls to show up again.

/John Updike. A & P

Word Bank

- shuffle: 발을 질질 끌며 걷다.
- look after: 을 지켜보다. 을 돌보다.
- size up: 을 평가하다. 의 치수를 재다.
- pat: 가볍게 두드리다.
- joint: 고기 덩어리.

구문 설명

All that was left for us to see was old McMahon patting his mouth... = All that was left for us to see was that old McMahon was patting his mouth··· 여기에서 "old McMahon"은 동명사 "patting ~"과 "looking ~"의 의미상의 주어.

Reading 03

Across the plain, puffs of dust mark the occasional approach of a long-distance truck. Volcano Sajama waits continually on the horizon. En route, you pass the remarkable Ciudad de Piedra. Large stone towers and free standing boulders, some as huge as buses, cover the landscape. The effect is eerie, almost lunar. You might see a 'Puya raimondi'. **This magnificent cactus, 25 to 32 feet tall, with the largest blossoms in the world, it flowers only once a century.**

/David Sanger. The Jewel of the Andes

Word Bank

- plain: 평야, 평원.
- puff: 한 번 불기, 한 번 부는 양.
- en route: 도중에
- free-standing: 지주 없이 서있는.
- boulder: 둥근 돌, 호박 돌.
- eerie: 무시무시한
- long-distance: 멀리 떨어진.

구문설명

~, puffs of dust mark the occasional approach of a long-distance truck. = ~, puffs of dust occasionally mark the approach of a long-distance truck. 때때로 형용사를 부사로, 혹은 반대로 부사를 형용사로 전환해서 생각하는 것이 문장을 이해하는데 좋은 경우가 많다. They spend an occasional night in a fancy hotel. = They occasionally spend a night in a fancy hotel. He is a real idiot. = He is really an idiot.

Reading 04

Into this important commercial region the timid Carrie went. She walked east along Van Buren Street through a region of lessening importance, until it deteriorated into a mass of shanties and coal-yards, and finally verged upon the river. She walked bravely forward, led by an honest desire to find employment and delayed at every step by the interest of the unfolding scene, and a sense of helplessness amid so much evidence of power and force which she did not understand. **These vast buildings, what were they? These strange energies and huge interests, for what purposes were they there?** She could have understood the meaning of a little stone-cutter's yard at Columbia City, carving little pieces of marble for individual use, but when the yards of some huge stone corporation came into view, filled with spur tracks and flat cars, transpierced by docks from the river and traversed overhead by immense trundling cranes of wood and steel, it lost all significance in her little world.

/Theodore Dreiser. Sister Carrie

Word Bank

- important: 현저한, 커다란.
- until: 그리고 마침내(= and at last).
- shanty: 판자촌, 변두리 빈민가.
- verge: 인접하다.
- helplessness: 무력, 무능.
- yard: 작업장, 뜰.
- lessen: 적어지다, 감소하다.
- deteriorate: 악화되다, 나빠지다.
- coal-yard: 저탄장, 석탄 적하장.
- evidence: 징표, 명백함.
- stone-cutter: 석공, 돌 자르는 기계.
- carve: 새기다, 조각하다.

- spur track: (철도) 단거리의 지선.
- flat car: 화차(railroad car without a roof or sides, for carrying freight).
- transpierce: 을 꿰뚫다, 관통하다.
- Traverse: 가로 지르다.
- overhead: 머리 위에, 하늘 높이.
- trundle: 돌리다, 운반하다.

구문 설명

", but when the yards of some huge stone corporation ~ by immense trundling cranes of wood and steel, it lost all significance in her little world." 에서 주절의 "it"은 밑줄 친 부분을 대신하고 있다.

Reading 05

Television, it has great positive potential for learning and development. It gives children different mental skills from those developed by reading and writing. Television is a better medium than the printed word for conveying certain types of information, and it makes learning available to groups of children who do not well in traditional school situations, and even to people who cannot read.

/Culture Watch .The Electronic Media

Word Bank

- potential: 가능성, 잠재력.

Reading 06

David Breashears and Ed Viesturs were in radio contact with Hall as he made his decision. **Filmmakers and climbers who had known the famous guide for years, they were 2,400m below him, in the relative safety of a mountainside campsite.** Hall, on the other hand, was 120m shy of Everest's 8,848m summit-the highest peak in the world-stuck on an outcrop where he had spent the night after a sudden blizzard pounded the mountain. The situation was probably not survivable, and yet the other climbers were determined to help Hall live through it.

/TIME.

Word Bank

- radio: 무선통신의, 라디오의.
- mountainside: 산허리, 산중턱.
- campsite: 캠프장, 야영지.
- shy: 이 부족한(of).
- stick: 을 꼼짝 못하게 하다.
- outcrop: 노출부, 노두(that part of a rock which can be seen above the surface of the ground).
- blizzard: 눈보라, 폭풍설.
- pound: 세게 치다, 맹렬히 포격하다.
- skinny: 말라 빠진, 피골이 상접한.
- snowsuit: 방한복.

구문 설명

The situation was probably not survivable. = He could probably not survive the situation. 무생물주어 + be + ~ible/able 형용사 = 무생물 주어 + can be + 과거분사. Not a sound was audible. = Not a sound could be heard.

Reading 07

A girl carries her baby brother on one of the back streets in Lhasa. Despite the presence of Chinese troops, people try to go about their daily lives undisturbed. **"The younger generation, they enjoy their life too much.** They are always playing, drinking beer, not working hard."

/USA Today.

Word Bank

- back street: 뒷거리, 뒷골목.
- go about: 열심히 하다.

Reading 08

Take again such a matter as travel: some men will travel through many countries, going always to the best hotels, eating exactly the same food as they would eat at home, meeting the same idle rich whom they would meet at home, conversing on the same topics upon which they converse at their own dinner-table. When they return, their only feeling is one of relief at having done with the boredom of expensive locomotion. **Other men, wherever they go, they see what is characteristic, make the acquaintance of people who typify the locality, observe whatever is of interest either historically or socially, eat the food of the country, learn its manners and its language, and come home with a new stock of pleasant thoughts for winter evenings.**

/Bertrand Russell. The conquest of Happiness

Word Bank

- onverse: 대화를 나누다.
- relief: 안도, 안심.
- locomotive: 운동, 이동, 여행.
- characteristic: 독특한, 특유의.
- locality: 장소, 지방성, 지방색.
- typify: 대표하다, 상징하다. 의 전형이 되다.
- manners: 예의 범절, 풍습.
- stock: 저장, 축적, 재고품.
- have done with: 을 마치다, 와 이제 관계가 없다.

구문 설명

wherever they go ~ = no matter where they go ~. whatever is of interest ~ = anything which is of interest ~.

Reading 09

It's sometimes best to hide in a public place. Liu Zhanguo slipped into a Beijing Starbucks last Tuesday for a quiet rendezvous. A Communist Party member from northern Fushun city, Liu wanted to tell Newsweek why he was willing to risk his life in a show of support for Falun Gong. The state had arrested thousands of his fellow believers in an effort to smash what authorities call an "evil cult". Liu, 50, credits its mystical blend of Buddhism, Taoism and deep-breathing exercises with curing his hypertension and his wife's psychological problems. **A teacher of the discipline, he was about to join a public protest against the crackdown.** "It doesn't matter if I live or die," said Liu. Gesturing around the upscale coffeehouse, he added; " The next time we talk it may not be here. Maybe I'll be in jail. After we finish talking I plan to go to the square to be arrested."

/Newsweek.

Word Bank

- slip: 살짝 들어가다(나오다), 미끄러지다.
- rendezvous: 만나기, 회합 약속.
- state: 국가. (여기에서는 중국).
- smash: 분쇄하다, 박살 내다.
- Buddhism: 불교.
- Taoism: 도교.
- credit: 에게 ~이 있다고 간주하다(with).
- hypertension: 고혈압(≠hypotension).
- discipline: 훈련, 규율.
- protest: 항의, 저항.
- crackdown:엄중한 단속.
- gesture: 몸짓으로 나타내다.
- upscale: 수준 높은, 부유층의.
- jail: 감옥.

Reading 10

Alfonso Orefice, who owns Alfonso's Pizzeria in Tampa, raised his price for extra cheese to $3, nearly double the $1.60 for other toppings. Orefice says he'll likely raise pizza prices, too, if the cheese stays pricey. "It's getting tough," he said. **"The cows, they are driving us crazy."**

/Chicago Tribune.

Word Bank

- topping: 요리에 얹거나 치는 것.
- pricey: 비싼(=expensive).
- drive: 하게 하다.

Reading 11

Tom and me found the money that the robbers hid in the cave, and it made us rich. We got six thousand dollars apiece-all gold. It was an awful sight of money when it was piled up. **Well, Judge Thatcher he took it and put it out at interest,** and it fetched us a dollar a day apiece all the year round. The Widow Douglas she took me for her son, and allowed she would civilize me; but it was rough living in the house all the time, considering how dismal regular and decent the widow was in all her ways; and so when I couldn't stand it no longer I lit out. I got into my old rags and my sugar-hogshead again, and was free and satisfied. **But Tom Sawyer he hunted me up and said he was going to start a band of robbers, and I might join if I would go back to the widow and be respectable.** So I went back.

/Mark Twain. The Adventures of Huckleberry Finn

Word Bank

- interest: 이자.
- rags: 누더기 옷
- put out: (이자 목적으로) 대부하다.
- take A for B: A를 B라고 생각했다.
- allow: 생각하다, ~할 작정이다.
- civilize: 교화하다.
- regular: 정연한, 질서 있는.
- light out: 도망치다, 갑자기 떠나다.
- get into: 착용하다(= put on), 몸에 배다.
- hogshead: 큰 통.
- hunt: 뒤쫓다, 찾아내다.
- band: 무리, 떼.
- respectable: 훌륭한, 점잖은.

구문설명

"Tom and me found the money that the robbers hid in the cave,"에서 "Tom and me"는 "Tom and I"가 표준어법 이다.

Reading 12

The writings of Captain John Smith (1580~1631) probably satisfied readers of both kinds. **A real adventurer, he had fought the Turks in Hungary, where he was wounded and taken prisoner.** He was sold as a slave and escaped by killing his master. In 1607, he helped found Jamestown, the first English colony in America. Although the details are not always correct, his True Relation of Virginia (1608) and Description of New England (1616) are fascinating "advertisements" which try to persuade the reader to settle in the New World. The Puritans, for instance, studied his Description of New England carefully and then decided to settle there in 1620. Smith was often boastful about his own adventures in his books.

/Peter B. High. An Outline of American Literature

Word Bank

- Turk: 터키 사람. 터키 족.
- boastful: 자랑하는, 허풍 떠는(of)
- Jamestown: 미국 버지니아주 동부의 마을(북미 최초의 영국 식민지).
- colony: 식민지.
- fascinating: 매혹적인, 황홀케 하는.
- study: 연구하다, 유심히 보다.
- settle: 정착하다.

Reading 13

A womanizing churchgoer and moralizer, he lived in conspicuous opulence and gluttony, holding business meetings amid damask and tapestries from the palaces of Europe, next to vaults containing Leonardo da Vinci notebooks and Shakespeare folios. Morgan looked down his monumental nose at Jews and other minorities, hated trade unions, sneered at new money, and fought ceaselessly with the other "robber barons" of his era.

/Alvin Toffler. Power Shift

Word Bank

- womanize: 여성화하다.
- churchgoer: 독실한 신자.
- moralizer: 도학자, 도덕론자.
- vault: 둥근 천장, 금고.
- opulence: 부, 풍요.
- gluttony: 대식, 폭식.
- damask: 단자(silk or linen material with designs shown up by reflection of light).
- tapestry: 태피스트리(cloth into which threads of colored wool are woven by hand to make designs and pictures, used for covering walls and furniture).
- conspicuous: 눈에 잘 띄는, 돋보이는.
- folio: 2절, 2절판의 책.
- monumental: 기념비의, 엄청나게 큰.
- look down one's nose at: 경멸하는 눈초리로 내려다보다, 경멸하다.
- trade union: 노동 조합(= labor union).
- sneer: 비웃다, 조소하다.
- baron: 남작(duke: 공작 marquis: 후작 earl: 백작 viscount: 자작)

Reading 14

In the last few weeks the killings have become even more brazen. **On Sunday, July 5, a band of armed men, it stormed a Richmaond tavern where patrons were playing darts and watching the World Cup.** Firing indiscriminately, the attackers killed eight people. The next weekend a woman and her 3-year-old daughter were gunned down in Magoda.

/Newsweek

Word Bank

- killing: 살인, 살해.
- brazen: 놋쇠로 만든, 파렴치한.
- storm: 습격하다, 에 밀어닥치다.
- patron: 손님, 후원자.
- indiscriminately: 무차별적으로
- gun: 을 총을로 쏘다. 사살하다.

Reading 15

She nagged me for more responsibilities, like standing a night watch by herself. That would have made my life a lot easier, but whenever she was on duty I only dozed. **The boat, I couldn't trust her to handle it alone, especially in this squally weather.**

/Guideposts

Word Bank

- nag: 괴롭히다, 귀찮게 볶아치다.
- on duty: 근무 시간 중에, 당번인(off duty).
- doze: 선잠을 자다.
- squally: 질풍의, 폭풍우가 휘몰아 칠 것 같은.
- night watch: 야경, 야경꾼.

Reading 16

In the three short decades between now and the twenty-first century, millions of ordinary, psychologically normal people will face an abrupt collision with the future. **Citizens of the world's richest and most technologically advanced nations, many of them will find it increasingly painful to keep with the incessant demand for change that characterizes our times.** For them, the future will have arrived too soon.

/Alvin Toffler. Future Shock

Word Bank

- abrupt: 갑작스러운, 뜻 밖의.
- keep with: 와 보조를 맞추다. 에 뒤지지 않다.

Reading 17

Bill was, by all accounts, a bit of a character. **A traveling salesman, he was also an avid golfer.** He twice won the Missouri Amateur Championship and even played in the US Open in 1955. But most people remember Bill Stewart for his loud sports coats.

/Reader's Digest.

Word Bank

- by all accounts: 모든 사람들의 이야기에 따르면, 누구에게(어디서) 들어도(= according to what everybody says).
- a bit of a : 좀, 다소.
  He is a bit of a scholar. (그는 좀 학자다운 데가 있다).
- avid: 열광적인.
- play: 경기에 나가다.
- sports: 운동용의, 스포츠의.

Reading 18

It was strange that only one man was wounded. A distinct impression existed that there should have been many more. And of course there were, in other outfits around them. The one man wounded in C-for-Charlie was Pfc Marl, a Nebraska cornball and dry-dirt farmer. Long and work-gnarled, **a draftee who had not wanted to leave his father's farm, he had never much liked the army anyway.**

/James Jones. The Thin Red Line

Word Bank

- distinct: 확실한, 분명한.
- impression: 느낌, 생각.
- outfit: 여행 용품, 부대.
- corn ball: 시골뜨기.
- work-gnarled: 일을 많이 해서 손에 마디가 많은.
- draftee: 징집병.

구문 설명

A distinct impression existed that there should have been many more. = A distinct impression that there should have been many more existed. (탈명사구 외치 참조)

Reading 19

"Honest. She'll be very happy. Ruth is a country girl and hasn't met many Filipinos. I mean Filipinos younger than I, cleaner looking. We're just poor farmer folk, you know, and we don't get to town very often. **Roger, that's my boy; he goes to school in town.** A bus takes him early in the morning and he's back in the afternoon. He's nice boy."

/Bienvenido N. Santos . Scent of Apples

Word *Bank*

- honest: 정말이야, 틀림없어.
- I bet: ~라고 생각하다.
- Filipino: 필리핀 사람.

Unit 3 동사구 전치 (Verb Phrase Preposing)

동사구(動詞句)라 함은 주어와 조동사를 제외한 동사와 그 뒤의 요소들을 말한다. 따라서 동사구 전치는 동사구들이 원래 있던 자리에서 주어 앞으로 이동된 것을 말한다. 동사구 전치가 일어나기 위해서는 선행문장에서 미리 언급되어야 하며 전치된 동사구는 해당 문장에서 주제 역할을 한다.

1 동사구 전치 조건

- 동사구 전치구문은 전치된 동사구와 같은 동사구가 앞에 있다.
- 동사구 전치가 이루어진 구문 바로 앞에는 접속사가 있다.
- 동사구 전치가 이루어진 구문에서는 주어 다음에 조동사가 있어야 한다.

2 동사구 전치 유형

2.1. 독립적 명제 확인 (Proposition Affirmation)

전치된 동사구가 들어있는 문장은 앞에서 그 사실성이 주장되지 않은 명제에 대해 사실인지 아닌지를 확인시켜주는 역할을 한다. 사실성이 주장되지 않은 명제의 사실성을 강조하기 때문에 주로 They say that p, It seems that p, I think/believe/expect/hope that p (p: proposition 명제)와 같은 문장이 이전 담화에 나타난다. 또 명제의 사실성을 보장하지 못하는 부정사, 동명사 등이 이전 담화에 나타나기도 한다. 그리고 이런 경우에는 전치된 동사구 앞에 접속사 "and"가 있다.

01 a. They expect that John will pass the exam, and he will pass the exam.

b. They expect that John will **pass the exam, and pass the exam** he **will**.
(그들은 John이 시험에 합격하리라 기대하고 있는데 사실 그는 그 시험에 합격할 것이다.)

02 a. Mary went to the bookstore to buy a book, and she bought one.

b. Mary went to the bookstore to **buy a book, and buy one** she **did**.
(Mary는 책을 사러 서점에 가서 책을 샀다.)

동사구 전치가 일어난 문장은 주어 뒤에 반드시 조동사가 있어야 한다. 일반 동사인 경우에는 뒤에 인칭과 시제에 맞게 "do", "does" 혹은 "did"가 쓰인다.

03 a. Running into a robber on the street is a bad luck, and I ran into a robber yesterday.

b. **Running into a robber on the street** is a bad luck, **and run into a robber I did** yesterday.
(거리에서 도둑을 만난다는 것은 불행한 일이다. 그런데 나는 어제 도둑을 만났다.)

2.2. 양보적 명제 확인 (Concessive Affirmation)

전치된 동사구가 들어있는 문장이 앞에서 이미 언급된 내용과 의미적 대립이나 대조가 일어나는 경우에 해당된다. 이런 경우에는 전치된 동사구 앞에 "but" 이나 "yet"과 같은 연결사가 쓰인다.

04 a. John hoped that Mary would find his hat, but she could not find it.

b. John hoped that Mary would **find his hat, but find it** she **could** not.
(John은 Mary가 그의 모자를 찾기를 바랐는데 그녀는 그것을 찾을 수가 없었다.)

05 a. John expected that Tom would find his book in the living room, but he found it in the toilet.

b. John expected that Tom would **find his book in the living room, but find it in the toilet he did.**
(John은 Tom이 거실에서 그의 책을 찾을 것으로 기대했었는데 사실은 그는 그것을 그의 화장실에서 찾았다.)

예문 (4b)에서는 긍정과 부정으로 의미적 대립이 일어나고 있지만 예문 (5b)에서는 "in the living room"과 "in the toilet"이 대립을 이루고 있다.

2.3. 명제 유보 (Proposition Suspension)

전치된 동사구가 들어있는 문장과 선행 문맥에서 언급된 명제의 사실성을 확인하는 것과는 반대로, 오히려 그 명제의 사실성과 관련하여 화자가 생각을 보류하는 경우에 해당된다. 이런 경우에는 전치된 동사구 앞에 "if"가 주로 쓰인다.

06 a. It is strange that John objected to the proposal, if he objected to it.

b. It is strange that John **objected to the proposal, if object to it** he **did**.
(John이 그 제안에 이의를 제기했다는 것은 이상한 일이다. 만약 정말로 그가 그것에 이의를 제기했다면은.)

07 a. It is shocking that she killed her baby, if she killed it.

b. It is shocking that she **killed her baby, if kill it** she **did**.
(그녀가 자신의 아이를 죽였다는 것은 충격적인 일이다. 만약 실제로 그녀가 그 애를 죽였다면은.)

3 보충 설명

08 a. Yesterday John **bought a book, and** #**buy a book** he **did**.

b. We urged him to go there, and **go** he did.
(우리는 그에게 그곳으로 가라고 했는데 그는 실제로 갔다.)

동사구 전치는 앞의 문장에서 사실성이 분명하지 않은 동사구의 경우에 대해 그것이 사실인지 아닌지 분명히 나타낼 때 사용된다. 예문 (7a)는 "and ~ did ." 앞에 있는 문장은 이미 사실임이 분명하다. 이런 경우에 뒤에서 다시 사실성을 덧붙일 필요가 없다. 그래서 동사구 전치구문을 쓸 수 없다. 반면에 예문 (7b)에서는 "and ~ ." 앞에 있는 문장에서 그에게 가라고 했지만 그가 거기에 갔는지 혹은 가지 않았는지가 분명하지 않다. 따라서 이 경우는 사실 여부가 분명하지 않으므로 동사구 전치를 통해서 사실성을 나타낼 수 있다. 그리고 예문 (2b), (3b), (5b), (6b) 그리고 (7b)에서 처럼 별도의 조동사가 없을 때는 동사구 전치가 이루어지며 조동사 "do"가 사용된다.

09 a. We thought someone would fail the exam, and plenty of people have failed it.

b. We thought someone would fail the exam, and fail it plenty of people have.

c. We thought someone would fail the exam, and *failed it plenty of people have.
(우리는 누군가 그 시험에 떨어질 것으로 생각했었는데 실제로 그 시험에 많은 사람들이 떨어졌다.)

10 a. They hoped that Koreans would unify the country, but they have not unified it yet.

b. They hoped that Koreans would unify the country, but unify it they have not yet.

c. They hoped that Koreans would unify the country, but *unified it they have not yet.
(그들은 한국인들이 통일을 이루고 살기를 희망하고 있습니다. 하지만 한국인들을 아직 통일을 이루지 못하고 있습니다.)

예문 (9)와 (10)에서 처럼 완료시제를 취하고 있는 구문에서 동사구를 전치하게 되면 전치되는 동사는 원형을 취해야 한다.

11 a. I told my boss I was going to quit today. And quit I did.
(나는 사장님께 오늘 그만두겠다고 이야기를 했다. 그리고 사실 그만 두었다.)

b. I told my boss I was going to quit today. #And resign I did.

12 a. Betty wasn't hungry today. But she ate.
(Betty는 오늘 배는 고프지 않았지만 음식을 먹었다.)

b. Betty wasn't hungry today. #But eat she did.

동사구 전치의 조건에서 언급된 바와 같이 전치된 동사구와 같은 동사구들이 앞에서 언급될 때에만 전치는 가능하다. 같은 동사구라는 말은 의미가 같다는 뜻이 아니라 형태가 같아야 한다는 뜻이다. 그래서 (11b)와 (12b)는 적절치 못한 표현이다.

13 a. Many people doubt that John will marry Lisa, but marry her he will.
(많은 사람들이 John이 Lisa와 결혼할 지 의심쩍게 보고 있지만 그는 그녀와 결혼할 것이다.)

b. Many people doubt that John will marry Lisa, #but married by him she will be.

예문 (13)에서처럼 능동 - 수동은 의미상으로 차이가 없지만 동사구 전치에서는 형태가 다른 것으로 간주된다. 따라서 예문 (13b)의 경우에서는 동사구 전치가 허용되지 않는다.

Practice Examples

Reading 01

Austin police have cited the 19-year-old Bush twin daughters in connection with using a fake ID to buy alcohol at Chuy's Tuesday night. Barbara Bush, Jenna Bush and a friend, Jesse Day-Wickham, were all issued misdemeanor citations for the incident. Jenna was cited for misrepresentation of age by a minor. Barbara and 20-year-old Jesse Day-Wickham were both cited for possession of alcohol by a minor. APD and the Texas Alcoholic Beverage Commission (TABC) have been investigating the incident for possible violations involving use of a fake ID at the bar. The story has made national headlines because it involves the president's daughters. **But the Bush family is trying to keep the matter private. They have yet to make any public statement about the incident and show no inclination they will.**

/News 8 Austin.

Word Bank

- cite: 인용하다, 소환하다.
- fake: 가짜의, 위조의.
- misdemeanor: 나쁜 행실, 경범죄.
- misrepresentation: 잘 못 전하기, 부당 표기.
- APD: 오스틴 경찰국(= Austin Police Department)
- TABC: 텍사스 주류 위원회(Texas Alcoholic Beverage Commission).
- investigate: 조사하다, 수사하다.
- violation: 위반, 침해.
- headline: 표제, 제목.
- have yet to: 아직 ~하지 않다.

Reading 02

It was almost ten years back that a friend rushed into my house, summoned me urgently and took me to this beach. Puzzled and bemused I asked what he had in mind. In response, he would just shyly gaze at the sea and the crashing waves. Then after an hour or so, he opened up and spoke slowly, looking at the sea. He said that he had fallen in love. However, he had not revealed his tender love to the girl. He wanted advice. I promptly asked him to express it to her. He followed my advice and did that; but the girl said 'No'. Later, he took me again to the same beach, told me about the refusal and declared again to the sea that he would wait. **And wait he did**. For seven long years. Again, I was off to the beach with him where he told me that his wish had come true--she had finally said yes. They got married almost immediately.

/The Indian Programmer.

Word Bank

- summon: 호출하다, 소환하다.
- urgent: 다급한, 긴급한.
- bemused: 넋을 잃은, 몽롱한.
- have ~ in mind: ~의 일을 생각(계획)하고 있다.
- shy: 부끄럼 타는, 수줍어하는.
- crash: 꽝 하고 박살 나다, 충돌하다.
- reveal: 드러내다, 밝히다.
- tender: 온화한, 다정한.
- promptly: 신속히, 즉각적으로.
- declare: 선언하다, 단언하다.
- be off: 출발하다, 떠나다.

Reading 03

The political arena runs contrary to the ethical interactions expected among persons of science. Politicians are elected by deceitfully putting together voting blocs of people with conflicting interests. They make promises impossible to keep just to be elected and to gain power. A businessperson or scientist would be discredited or even jailed for using similar "situation ethics." This is not to say that those in business and in science are always ethical--they are only human. But it is a chimera to expect ethical behavior from a politician. Pass the baton, John--you've worked hard and accomplished much. **But if pass it you must, give it to someone or some group worthy of its stewardship.**

/Simulation in the Service of Society.

Word *Bank*

- arena: 투기장(鬪技場), 활동무대.
- contrary: 거꾸로, 반하여.
- interaction: 상호작용, 상호영향.
- deceitfully: 속여서, 부정직하게.
- put together: 모으다, 조립하다.
- interest: 이해관계.
- discredit: 신용을 손상하다, 명예에 손상을 입히다.
- chimera: 키마이라, 환상.
- baton: 지팡이, 지휘봉.
- stewardship: 관리, 책임.

Reading 04

Before the party, the president huddled with his private lawyer, David Kendall. A day earlier, Lewinsky had agreed to cooperate with independent counsel Kenneth Starr, and to say that she and Clinton had had a sexual relationship. Faced with that, and a subpoena from Starr, Clinton made his own deal. He would "voluntarily" testify to a grand jury on Aug. 17 in a live link from the White House. **Kendall announced the bargain, and go to the East Room Clinton did.** Then, White House lawyers in the counsel's office were channel-surfing for news.

/Newsweek.

Word Bank

- huddle: 토론하기 위하여 모이다.
- testify: 증인이 되다, 증언하다.
- jury: 배심(grand jury: 대배심,
- bargain: 계약, 협정(agreement).
- independent counsel: 특별 검사.
- subpoena: 소환장.
- live: 생방송의, 실황의.
- petty jury: 소배심).
- counsel: 변호사, 법률 고문.
- surf: 파도타기를 하다.

구문 설명

Faced with that, and a subpoena from Starr, Clinton made ~ = When he was faced with that, and (he was faced with) a subpoena from Starr, Clinton made ~ .

Reading 05

The ambulance did not come until the next day, which was the day before we marched to San Juan. It arrived after nightfall, and as soon as Bell heard it coming, he crawled out of the hospital tent into the jungle, where he lay all night; and the ambulance went off without him. The men shielded him just as school-boys would shield a companion, carrying his gun, belt, and bedding. I found him the morning of the San Juan fight. **He told me that he wanted to die fighting, if die he must, and I hadn't the heart to send him back.** He did splendid service that day, and afterward in the trenches, and though the rupture opened twice again, and on each occasion he was within a hair's breadth of death, he escaped, and came back with us to the United States.

/Theodore Roosevelt. The Rough Rider

Word Bank

- nightfall: 황혼, 해질녘.
- go off: 가버리다, 떠나다.
- belt: 혁대, 탄띠.
- out of sight: 안 보이는 곳에.
- stagger: 비틀거리다.
- service: 근무, 복무.
- rupture: 파열, 불화.
- within hair's breadth: 근소하게, 아슬아슬하게.
- crawl: 기어가다, 살금살금 다가가다.
- shield: 보호하다, 막다.
- bedding: 침구류.
- column: 종대.
- splendid: 화려한, 훌륭한.
- trench: 참호.

Reading 06

No country is so wild and difficult but men will make it a theatre of war; concealed in the forest at the bottom of that military rat-trap, in which half a hundred men in possession of the exits might have starved an army to submission, lay, say, five regiments of federal infantry. They had marched all the previous day and night and were resting. At nightfall they would take to the road again, climb to the place where their unfaithful sentinel now slept and descending the other slope of the ridge fall upon a camp of the enemy at about midnight. Their hope was to surprise it, for the road led to the rear of it. In the case of failure, their position would be perilous in the extreme; **and fail they surely would should accident or vigilance apprise the enemy of the movement**.

/Ambrose Bierce. A Horseman in the Sky

Word Bank

- country: 지역, 땅.
- bottom: 기슭.
- rap-trap: 쥐 덫.
- army: 군(army (corps(군단) (division(사단) (brigade(여단) (regiment(연대) (battalion(대대) (company(중대) (platoon(소대) (squad(분대)).
- exit: 출구.
- submission: 항복, 굴복.
- starve: 굶겨 죽이다. 굶주려서 ~ 하게 하다.
- say: (보통 수사 앞에서) 이를테면, 대략.
- infantry: 보병.
- nightfall: 해질녘, 땅거미.

- take to: 로 가다.
- fall (up)on: 을 기습하다, 공격하다.
- rear: 후방.
- position: 진지.
- apprise: 알리다.
- ridge: 산등성이.
- surprise: 기습하다.
- vigilance: 경계, 불침번.

구문 설명

1. No country is so wild and difficult but men will make it a theatre of war. = No country is so wild and difficult that men will not make it a theatre of war. "not so/not such ~ but (that) . . ."에서 "but (that)"은 "that ~ not"과 같은 뜻으로 쓰인다: He is not so old but that he can work. (그는 일을 못 할 만큼 늙지는 않았다.) He is not such a fool but he knows it.(그가 그것을 모를 만큼 바보는 아니다.)
2. 결과 구문을 만드는 전치사 "to": They starved an enemy to submission. (그들은 적을 굶주려 항복 시켰다.) He was struck to death. (그는 맞아 죽었다.)
3. "fail they surely would should accident or vigilance apprise the enemy of the movement." = "they surely would fail if accident or vigilance should apprise the enemy of the movement." "if"가 생략되면 주어 조동사가 도치되었으며 동사구 "fail"이 전치된 구문이다.

Reading 07

Once upon a time lived a poor prince; his kingdom was very small, but **it was large enough to enable him to marry and marry he would.** It was rather bold of him that he went and asked the emperor's daughter: Will you marry me?" but he ventured to do so, for his name was known far and wide, and there were hundreds of princesses who would have gladly accepted him.

/Hans Christian Andersen. The Swineherd

Word Bank

- kingdom: 왕국.
- bold: 대담한, 용감한.
- emperor: 황제.
- venture: 과감히 ~하다, 감히 ~하다.
- far and wide: 도처에, 널리.

Reading 08

On July 4, they surrendered. Vicksburg and the Mississippi were lost. In time they would learn of Lee's great defeat at Gettysburg the same day. But for now, John Wright stepped forward with his fellow officers and signed his oath not to take up arms against the North again. They were released a few days later. **But go home they did not.** Much has been written and speculated about Southern will and morale during the war. Pemberton's men had every opportunity to spread to the four winds. Some surely did. For John it must have been a tough choice.
/John Edward Wright. The Civil War Record of Lt. John Edward Wright

Word Bank

- in time: 조만간, 결국.
- for now: 우선, 당분간.
- oath: 맹세, 서약.
- will: 의지, 소망.
- morale: 사기, 의기.
- Pemberton: 뉴저지 주에 있는 도시.
- wind: 바람, 방향(direction).

Reading 09

Antony Yip seems too young to order food in a smart restaurant, let alone set up an Internet company that just raised $6.5 million from an American venture capital firm. **But order he does--fish and chips, followed by ice cream--"two scoops of strawberry, one chocolate."** Nor is his age--he's a boyish 21 and dresses in baggy trousers and sneakers--the only anomaly. Yip runs a collection of 15 Chinese-language websites assembled under his umbrella site, Myrice.com--though he can neither write nor speak Chinese properly. "It's ridiculous, really," he says, smiling disarmingly.

/Time.

Word Bank

- smart: 멋진, 세련된.
- set up: 설립하다, 시작하다.
- firm: 회사, 기업.
- sneakers: 고무창의 즈크화.
- umbrella: 우산 같은, 포괄적인.
- let alone: 은 말할 것도 없이.
- raise: 모금하다, 조달하다.
- baggy: 축 늘어진, 헐렁한.
- anomaly: 변칙, 예외.
- disarming: 애교 있는, 천진난만한.

Reading 10

After the play opened, Joan and I took the girls to Florida. Suddenly the limp was back again. Joan held on to the railing when climbing steps, breathed a little harder, moved a little slowly. A few days later the pain got shaper, and she could no longer get around without the cane. **I knew she would die not much later, and die she has.**

/Reader's Digest.

Word Bank

- limp: 절름 거리기. 절뚝거림.
- hold on to: 을 꼭 잡고있다, 에 매달리다.
- railing: 난간, 울타리.
- get around: 돌아 다니다, 여기 저기 여행하다.

구문 설명

get + 보어: ~되다. "get"은 변화를 나타내는 동사로서 비슷한 동사로 "become, go, come, grow, make, fall, run, turn"등이 있다. 예를 들면, He became a doctor. (그는 의사가 되었다.) She went red with anger. (그녀는 화가 나서 얼굴이 빨개졌다.) Her dream came true. (그녀의 꿈은 실현되었습니다.) He has grown old and sick. (그는 나이가 들어 병이 들었습니다.) She will make a good wife. (그녀는 훌륭한 아내가 될 것입니다.) He suddenly fell grave. (그는 갑자기 심각해졌습니다.) The well has run dry. (그 우물은 메말랐습니다.) The leaves of trees turned red and yellow. (나뭇잎이 단풍이 들었습니다.)

Reading 11

In mature democracies around the world, exalted people 'resign' to save their good name from blemish. But, this noble word left our shores and our political lexicon a long time ago-yes, when was the last time we had one of our politicians resigning? **But, if resign you shall not, the least you can do for our people is to stand up and speak out, and speak out loud so that we can hear.** Tell us that you will lead and not be led by the ignorant minions around you.

http://www.lacnet.org/island/i990228/letters.htm

Word Bank

- mature: 성숙한, 완전히 발달한.
- save: 구하다, 지키다.
- noble: 고상한, 숭고한.
- lexicon: 사전, 용어집.
- speak out: 솔직하게 의견을 말하다.
- minion: 앞잡이, 부하.
- exalted: 지위가 높은, 고귀한.
- blemish: 흠, 오점.
- shore: 물가, 나라.

Reading 2

Puffins can fly, but they are clearly not the world's greatest "aviators." Indeed, their arrival on shore can resemble a crash landing! Furthermore, the puffin's takeoff is somewhat clumsy, and at times it seems that the bird's wings will not support its stout body. Some puffins even have trouble getting out of the water. But once those wings are beating?and they may beat as rapidly as 400 times a minute?the puffin can achieve a cruising speed of 50 miles per hour. Puffins are obviously more comfortable at sea than on land. **But come to land they must, for a puffin couple will have to prepare a burrow for their young.** Upon reaching land, a couple will clean the burrow, which may measure anywhere from 20 inches in length to about four times that size. They line the burrow with bedding consisting of grass, twigs, and feathers. Some puffins nest in cracks under boulders or in rocky crevices. Using its bill, the puffin picks its way through dirt and then shovels the dirt away with its webbed feet. /Awake.

Word Bank

- puffin: 바다 오리.
- aviator: 비행사, 항공기 조종사.
- crash-landing: 불시착.
- takeoff: 이륙, 도약.
- clumsy: 어색한, 서투른.
- stout: 뚱뚱한, 튼튼한.
- have trouble (in) ~ing: 을 하느라 애쓰다.
- beat: 날개 치다, 퍼덕거리다.
- cruise: 순항하다.
- burrow: 구멍, 은신처.
- young: (집합적) 새끼.
- measure: (길이 및 크기 따위가) 이 되다.
- line A with B: A를 따라 B를 놓다.
- crevice: 틈(= cleft).
- bedding: 침구류, 잠자리.
- crack: 빈 틈.
- nest: 둥지를 짓다.
- boulder: 둥근 돌, 호박 돌.
- pick one's way through: 을 쪼며 나아가다.(이와 같은 표현은 "TOUGH"이동 연습 문제 (6)에서 설명되고 있다).
- shovel: 을 (삽으로) 파내다.
- webbed: 물갈퀴가 달린.

구문 설명

about four times that size = about four times of that size. (up) on ~ing/동사 파생 명사: ~하자 마자(=as soon as + 절). Upon reaching land, a couple will ~ = As soon as it reaches land, a couple will ~.

Reading 13

It is a senseless thing to turn day into night, light into darkness, and to exchange good works for mere trifling follies. Moreover, those who frequent balls almost inevitably foster their Vanity, and vanity is very conducive to unholy desires and dangerous attachments. I am inclined to say about balls what doctors say of certain articles of food, such as mushrooms and the like--the best are not good for much; **but if eat them you must, at least mind that they are properly cooked.** So, if circumstances over which you have no control take you into such places, be watchful how you prepare to enter them. Let the dish be seasoned with moderation, dignity and good intentions. The doctors say (still referring to the mushrooms), eat sparingly of them, and that but seldom, for, however well dressed, an excess is harmful. So dance but little, and that rarely, lest you run the risk of growing over fond of the amusement.

/ St. Francis De Sales. Introduction To The Devout Life

Word Bank

- senseless: 지각 없는, 무의미한.
- trifling: 하찮은, 사소한.
- folly: 어리석음, 우매.
- frequent: 종종 가다, 자주 방문하다.
- ball: 무도회, 아주 즐거운 한때.
- foster: 불러일으키다, 품다.
- conducive: 도움이 되는, 촉구하는.
- unholy: 신성하지않은, 부정한.
- attachment: 부착, 애정.
- inclined: 할 생각이 있는, 하는 경향이 있는.
- mushroom: 버섯.
- and the like: 기타 등등.
- mind: 주의하다, 마음을 쓰다.
- watchful: 조심하는, 주의하는.
- sparingly: 절약하여, 드물게.
- dish: 접시, 요리.
- season: 맛을 들이다, 양념을 치다.
- moderation: 알맞음, 중용.
- dignity: 품위, 위엄.
- and that: 게다가, 그것도.
- dress: 요리를 소스 등으로 마무르다, 드레싱을 치다.
- amusement: 즐거움, 여흥.

Reading 14

If you looked at the political facts, it seemed impossible to imagine democracy would ever arrive. But if you looked at the changing culture, it seemed inevitable. It had come in 1987 with a huge display of people power, which led to a democratic presidential election. These developments had all the feel of a miracle. It was the people, rather than individual leaders, who had brought it about. The following year, Korea hosted the Olympics. I was really looking forward to seeing the miracle-makers host the Olympic Games. I didn't expect my Koreans to rain on my parade. **But rain they did.**

/Michael Breen. The Koreans

Word Bank

- inevitable: 불가피한, 필연적인.
- huge: 거대한, 막대한.
- display: 보여주기, 전시.
- development: 발전의 소산.
- bring about: 가져오다, 야기하다.
- host: 주최하다.
- look forward to: 학수고대하다.
- parade: 행렬, 퍼레이드.
- rain on: 에 불행을 가져오다. rain on my parade는 비유적 표현으로 "망쳐놓다"의 의미로 쓰이고 있다.

구문 설명

"~, it seemed inevitable."에서 "it"은 앞에서 언급된 "to imagine ~."을 가리킨다고 볼 수도 있지만 "inevitable"다음에 "to imagine ~ arrive."가 생략된 것으로 볼 수 있다.

Reading 15

Theirs was a rigid two-class society (bottom and top, but no middle), with a mercantilist and feudal landholding system, and a religious pattern of orthodoxy that reinforced the political absolutism of their government. In contrast, the North American colonies were for the most part settled by persons fleeing the feudal restraints of the older world so vividly personified by the conquistadors. The United States, settled and colonized in the 17th and 18th centuries, belonged from its beginning to the modern world. Two societies in one hemisphere, starting from different sources and remaining different. Mr. Wiarda describes in detail the various political doctrines, including Marxism, which influenced Latin American thought. Quite contrary to American thinking the individual alone had no rights but played a part in governance through his corporate identity. Although Mr. Wiarda describes the heart and soul of Latin America exceedingly well, in viewing the future of the area he fails to discuss the influence of the North American Free Trade Agreement (NAFTA) on Mexico, which many economists see as profound. **When NAFTA expands, and expand it will, it could well sweep away many of the oligarchic holdovers that still exist in the countries.**

/Washington Times.

Word Bank

- rigid: 단단한, 엄격한.
- feudal: 영지의, 봉건제도의.
- orthodoxy: 정통성.
- absolutism: 전제주의, 절대주의.
- settle: 정착시키다, 자리잡게 하다.
- restraint: 억제, 제지.
- conquistador: 정복자.
- source: 원천, 근원, 출처.
- governance: 지배, 통치.
- identity: 동일성, 정체성.
- profound: 심원한, 심오한.
- oligarchic: 과두 정치의, 소수독재 정치의.
- holdover: 남은 것, 잔존물, 유임자.
- mercantilist: 중상주의자(의).
- landholding: 토지소유(의).
- reinforce: 강화하다, 보강하다.
- colony: 식민지.
- flee: 도망치다. 피난하다.
- personify: 의인화하다, 구체화하다.
- hemisphere: 반구.
- doctrine: 교의, 학설, 주의, 정책.
- corporate: 법인의, 단체의.
- exceedingly: 대단히, 굉장히.
- sweep: 쓸어버리다, 소탕하다.

구문 설명

1. Theirs was a rigid two-class society (bottom and top, but no middle), with a mercantilist and feudal landholding system, and a religious pattern of orthodoxy that reinforced ~ = Theirs was a rigid two-class society (bottom and top, but no middle), which had a mercantilist and feudal landholding system, and a religious pattern of orthodoxy that reinforced ~.
2. Two societies in one hemisphere, starting from different sources and remaining different. = There are two societies in one hemisphere, starting from different sources and remaining different.

Reading 6

Then he returned through the kitchen, and gravely taking the awed and wondering little fellow by the hand, he led him silently into the study, and placing him before him, began an admonition on the importance of truthfulness, meaning to conclude with what he believed to be the moral of all punishment: "As you cannot remember this of yourself, I must give you a little pain to make you remember it. I am sorry it is necessary, and that you cannot recollect without my doing so." But before he had reached this very proper and desirable conclusion, and while he was yet working his way, his heart aching with the terrified look of the child at the solemnly sad face and words of upbraiding, Sally burst in?"And what may you be going to do with that fine switch I saw you gathering, Master Thurstan?" asked she, **her eyes gleaming with anger at the answer she knew must come, if answer she had at all.**

/Elizabeth Gaskell. Ruth

Word Bank

- gravely: 진지하게, 심각하게.
- truthfulness: 정직, 성실.
- ache: 아프다, 쑤시다.
- burst in: 말을 가로막다, 끼어 들다.
- admonition: 충고, 훈계.
- moral: 도덕, 전형(=type).
- upbraiding: 나무람, 꾸짖음.
- switch: 회초리, 스위치.

구문 설명

~ asked she, her eyes gleaming with anger at the answer~ = ~ asked she, with her eyes gleaming with anger at the answer ~

Reading 17

Before long I was back to my old pattern, trying to find out where he was and what he was up to. One day, when I called and heard people laughing and loud music playing in the background, my imagination went wild. I started firing questions. "You still haven't learned how to make small talk, Mom." He said, and hung up. I ran past the back door into the woods behind on a log out of breath, my heart pounding, angry thoughts chasing me like hounds after a rabbit. **I hated the way I was behaving, but help it I couldn't.**

/Guideposts.

Word Bank

- before long: 곧(= soon).
- up to: 에 종사하여, 을 하여.
- fire: 을 퍼붓다.
- small talk: 잡담, 일상적인 이야기.
- hang up: 전화를 끊다.
- out of breath: 숨을 헐떡이고.
- pound: 두근거리다.

Reading 18

It might take a madman to build a restaurant in the middle of the desert, but that is exactly what Mike Dabour did when he opened his restaurant in Baker, California. Several acquaintances told Mr. Dabour that he was out of his mind to build so far from civilization, but Mike had his own mind firmly in place. The restaurant was built and appropriately named "The Mad Greek Cafe". This was not the first. Michael had built several in sparsely populated places where others felt a Greek Restaurant could not succeed. **But succeed they did.** Maybe it was due to the tough determination that the young Greek possessed. Michael Dabour, together with his wife, Angela, immigrated to the U. S. in 1968 from Athens, Greece.

/http://www.mediaguilds.com/voices%20and%20faces.htm

Word Bank

- take: 가 들다, 필요로 하다.
- acquaintance: 아는 사람, 교우관계.
- mind: 생각, 건전한 정신상태.
- out of one's mind: 제정신이 아닌.
- in place: 있어야 할 곳에 있는, 그 자리에.
- Mike: Michael의 별칭.
- tough: 힘든, 불굴의.
- determination: 결의, 결단력.

Reading 19

Barnard ordered electrodes placed on each side of the heart and the current applied. The heart leaped at the shock and began a swift beat. Dr. Barnard's heart leaped too. Through his mask, he exclaimed: 'Christ, it's going to work!' **Work it did.**

/Time.

Word Bank

- electrode: 전극
- leap: 뛰다.
- current: 전류(= electric current).
- work: 움직이다, 작동하다.

Reading 20

Taiwan now wants to join the United Nations, and the mainland China would like to keep it out. It seems like a replay of the diplomatic tug of war between the two parties from 1949 to 1971, only with their roles reversed. Back then, it was the mainland China that wanted to join the UN, and Taiwan was doing all it could to keep China beyond the pale. **It took the mainland China 22 years to succeed, but succeed it did, at Taiwan's expense.** Taiwan's campaign now is apparently much more daunting than the mainland China's then, as the mainland China is now a much more formidable foe to Taiwan than Taiwan was then to the mainland. But Taiwan's appetite is also much smaller. China then wanted not only to join but also to join as a major power, recognized with a permanent seat at the Security Council. In addition, China also insisted that its entry be preceded with the removal of any and all of Taiwan's representation at the UN, no matter under what name. Taiwan now just wants to join, under any name, as an ordinary member so that it does not have to be excluded from the international community.

/Herb Ho. Chinese Community Forum 1995. Can Taiwan Join the United Nations?

Word Bank

- mainland: 본토, 대륙.
- tug of war: 줄다리기, 주도권 싸움.
- beyond the pale: 상궤를 벗어나, 범위 밖에.
- campaign: 전투, 운동.
- daunt: 위협하다, 위압하다.
- formidable: 무서운, 만만치 않은.
- appetite: 욕구, 욕망.
- seat: 의석, 회원.
- representation: 대표, 대표자.

Unit 4 Tough 이동 ("TOUGH" Movement)

"TOUGH" 이동이란 "It – (be) – 형용사/명사 – to 부정사 – 목적어" 형태의 구문에서 혹은 "주어 – 동사 – it – 형용사/명사 – to 부정사 – 목적어" 형태의 구문에서 "It"은 흔히 예비의 주어이거나 목적어 인데 그것을 없애고 그 자리에 부정사구 뒤에 있는 목적어를 옮기는 규칙을 말한다. 이렇게 전치된 요소는 이미 앞에서 언급된 구정보이며 전치된 요소를 주제화 시키기 위한 경우가 많다. 주제화(Topicalization)구문과 다른 점은 주제화 구문에서는 주어는 그대로 두고 주제화할 요소를 주어 앞에 놓는다. "TOUGH"이동은 주어나 목적어 역할을 하는 "It"을 없애고 그 자리에 부정사구내에 있는 목적어를 놓는다.
여기에서 "TOUGH"는 형용사 "힘들다"의 뜻으로서, 일반적으로 "힘들다"나 "쉽다"의 의미를 가지고 있는 형용사나 명사를 대신해서 사용된 말로 "TOUGH" 이동은 여기에서 비롯된 명칭이다. 이런 부류의 단어에는 "tough, hard, easy, difficult, painful, delightful, pleasant, convenient, dangerous, impossible, natural, necessary, important, satisfactory, joy, delight, pleasure, a bitch(불쾌한 일), a breeze(쉬운 일), a snap(쉬운 일), a cinch(쉬운 일)" 등이 있다.

1 "Tough" 이동되는 요소

1.1. 타동사의 목적어

01 a. Sometimes it is hard to distinguish the questions of a fool from those of a genius.

b. Sometimes **the questions of a fool** are hard to distinguish from those of a genius.
(때때로 바보들이 하는 질문과 천재들이 하는 질문을 구별하기는 어렵다.)

02 a. The English will find it hardest to bear the consequences.

b. The English will find **the consequences** hardest to bear.
(영국인들은 그런 결과를 참기가 가장 힘들 다는 것을 알게 될 것이다.)

1.2. 전치사의 목적어

03 a. It is easy to work with her.

b. **She** is easy to work with.
(그녀와 함께 일하기는 쉽다.)

04 a. Her advisers privately say she finds it difficult to work with him.

b. Her advisers privately say she finds **him** difficult to work with.
(그녀에게 조언을 해주는 사람의 개인적인 말에 의하면 그녀는 그와 함께 일하는 것이 힘들 다는 것을 알고 있다는 것이다.)

2 보충 설명

05 a. It is delightful to play Mozart on this violin.

b. **Mozart** is delightful to play on this violin.
(Mozart의 음악을 이 바이얼린으로 연주하는 것은 매우 기쁜 일이다.)

c. **This violin** is delightful to play Mozart on.
(이 바이얼린으로 Mozart음악을 연주하는 것은 매우 기쁜 일이다.)

일반적으로 "TOUGH"이동은 전치된 요소를 주제화 시키기 위한 것이기 때문에 부정사절 내에 타동사의 목적어와 전치사의 목적어 둘 모두가 있을 때는 주제가 되는 말을 앞으로 이동시킨다. 위 예문 (5a)에서는 문장의 억양에 따라 "Mozart"나 "this violin" 둘 중 하나가 주제가 될 수 있다. 반면에 예문 (5b)에서는 "Mozart"만이, 예문 (5c)에서는 "This violin"만이 주제가 될 수 있다.

06 a. It would be easy to kill someone with a gun like that.
(그와 같은 총으로 누군가 죽이기는 쉬울 것이다.)

b. #**Someone** would be easy to kill with a gun like that.

07 a. It was a delight to talk to someone interesting.

b. #**Someone** interesting was a delight to talk to.

"TOUGH"이동 구문은 주제화 구문에서처럼 일반적으로 앞으로 이동되는 요소는 구정보(Old Information) 이어야 한다. 따라서 위 예문 (6b)와 (7b)는 전치된 요소가 신정보(New Information)임으로 비문이다.

08 a. It is necessary for the children to learn English.

b. **English** is necessary for the children to learn.
(영어는 아이들이 배울 필요가 있다.)

c. *The children are necessary to learn English.

d. *English is necessary for the children to learn it. (English = it)

"TOUGH"이동 구문에서 술어로 쓰이는 형용사나 명사는 피상적으로 나타나는 주어를 서술하는 것이 아니라 일반적으로 부정사절 전체를 서술한다. 예문 (8c)의 술어 "is necessary"는 주어인 "The children"을 서술하는 것은 의미적으로 적절치 않다. 다만 예문 (8b)는 문장구조의 특수성에 의해 용인되는 문장일 뿐 역시 술어가 서술하고 있는 것은 주어인 "English"가 아니고 그것을 포함해 "for"이하 절이다. 예문 (8d)에서는 부정사절의 "learn"의 목적어는 의미상 "English"인데 이동된 후에 그 자리에 대명사를 다시 반복해서는 안 된다는 것을 보여주고 있다.

Practice Examples

Reading 01

It may seem like a dream come true -- being able to buy things without having the money. But racking up debt by using credit cards is no way to ensure a good financial future. **Credit cards are fairly easy to get, but you have to be disciplined and responsible to use them wisely.** "Credit cards are a good way to establish credit and show you're responsible enough" to manage payments, said Paul Lavoie, a credit counselor with American Consumer Credit Counseling. "But if young people don't get their education on how to use credit cards responsibly, bad things happen."
/CNN.

Word Bank

- credit: 신용.
- discipline: 훈련하다, 통제하다.
- rack up: 달성하다, 올리다.

Reading 02

There are times when it is important to remove or obliterate a large animal carcass (horse, mule, moose, etc.) from locations such as a recreation area, where a carcass might attract bears; a popular picnic area, the side of a road or trail. **Large animal carcasses can be particularly difficult to remove, especially if they are located below a steep slope or in a remote area.** /Harper's Magazine.

Word Bank

- obliterate: 말소하다, 제거하다.
- mule: 노새.
- trail: 흔적, 오솔길.
- slope: 비탈, 경사.
- carcass: 시체.
- moose: 큰 사슴.
- steep: 험준한, 가파른.

Reading 03

Think better of it, young man, while there is still time. To me two millions are a trifle, but you are losing three or four of the best years of your life. I say three or four, because you won't stay longer. **Don't forget either, you unhappy man, that voluntary confinement is a great deal harder to bear than compulsory.** The thought that you have the right to step out in liberty at any time will poison your whole existence in prison. I am sorry for you.

/Anton Chekhov. The Bet

Word Bank

- trifle: 시시한 일, 하찮은 일.
- bear: 참다, 견디어내다.
- poison: 오염시키다, 망치다.
- confinement: 감금, 제한.
- compulsory: 강제적인, 의무적인.

Reading 04

One of my co-workers is being married next month and has invited most of the office to her wedding. I had planned on buying her a gift, but probably won't attend. We are not close. **She has been very difficult to work with.** She's possibly the most two-faced person I have ever known. I have overheard this woman putting me down to co-workers, clients and vendors during the entire 4 1/2 years we have worked together. I am seriously considering leaving this company because of her. My supervisor has told me on several occasions that I am "on my own with her."

/Universal Press Syndicate. Dear Abby.

Word Bank

- office: 사무소, 전직원.
- two-faced: 양면의, 표리가 부동한.
- put down: 창피를 주다, 당황케 하다.
- vendor: 매각인, 상인.
- on one's own: 독력으로, 자신의 책임으로.
- close: 가까운, 친한.
- overhear: 우연히 듣다, 엿듣다.
- client: 고객, 단골.
- supervisor: 감독자, 관리자.

Reading 05

Mexico's experience, of course, reaffirmed the importance of sensible, and mutually compatible, economic policies. **Without those, financial upsets are hard to prevent.** But Mexico also rewrote the textbook on the best way to keep problems from turning into crisis. This now contains two main lessons.

/The Economist.

Word Bank

- reaffirm: 을 재확인하다.
- sensible: 양식 있는, 현명한.
- compatible: 양립할 수 있는, 모순이 없는.
- policy: 정책, 방침.
- financial: 재저의, 금융의.
- upset: 전복, 혼란.

Reading 06

Privacy is one of the necessities of human life, and to lose one's privacy makes life hard to bear. This is the reason why people who have had the misfortune to be born royal sometimes make frantic effort to break their way out into private life. To be born royal means being condemned in advance to live one's life in public, and this is an almost intolerable servitude.

/A. Toynbee. America and the World Revolution

Word Bank

- privacy: 사생활.
- bear: 참다, 견디다.
- royal: 국왕의, 왕실의.
- frantic: 광란한, 미친 듯한.
- break one's way: 헤치고 나아가다, 탈출하다.
- condemn: 을 비난하다, 을 운명짓다.
- intolerable: 참을 수 없는.

구문 설명

1. have the 추상명사 + to R = = have the + 추상명사 + of ~ing = 추상명사의 부사 + V = be + 추상명사의 형용사 + enough to R = be so + 추상명사의 형용사 + as to R. They had the misfortune to be born royal. = They unfortunately was born royal.
2. 동사 (feel, push, elbow, shoot…) one's way ~ ; 동사하며 나아가다. 여기에서 "way"는 전진(=advance)의 의미로 쓰인다. He made his way through the snowstorm. (그는 눈보라를 헤치며 나아갔다.) He pushed his way through the crowd. (그는 밀며 군중을 헤쳐 나아갔다.) He elbowed his way through the crowd. (그는 팔꿈치로 밀어 제치며 군중을 헤쳐 나아갔다.)

Reading 07

Now that a tunnel has been built through the mountain, the pass is less dangerous to cross, but each year, the dogs are still sent out into the snow whenever a traveler is in difficulty. Despite the new tunnel, there are still a few people who rashly attempt to cross the pass on foot.

/L.G. Alexander. Developing Skills

Word Bank

- pass: 고갯길, 산길.
- rashly: 경솔하게, 무모하게.

Reading 08

Whenever a single wave of change predominates in any given society, the pattern of future development is relatively easy to discern. Writers, artists, journalists, and others discover the "wave of the future." Thus in nineteenth-century Europe many thinkers, business leaders, politicians, and ordinary people held a clear, basically correct image of the future.

/Alvin Toffler. The Third Wave

Word Bank

- predominate: 우세하다, 세력을 떨치다.
- discern: 분간하다, 식별하다.

Reading 09

Aeh was a 22-year old secretary at a Bangkok news agency when she obtained her first credit card in 1993, the height of the country's economics boom. Her salary was only $360 a month, but soon she was buying expensive clothes, a St. Bernard puppy and lots of costly presents for her friends. When the bills mounted, she got three more credit cards and started charging cosmetics at department stores to sell to office-mates at a profit. (They were to repay her when they could afford it.) **The ending wasn't hard to foretell: the friends couldn't pay, neither could Aeh, her cards were cancelled and she disappeared more than a year ago.** Friends worry that she has ended up as a prostitute. /Time.

Word Bank

- secretary: 비서.
- puppy: 강아지.
- mount: 올라가다, 늘다.
- cosmetic: 화장품.
- repay: 돈을 갚다, 돌려주다.
- afford: (경제적, 시간적으로) 여유가 있다.
- foretell: 예고하다, 예언하다.
- end up: 결국 마지막에는 ~이 되다 (as ~).
- news agency: 통신사.
- bill: 계산서, 청구서.
- charge: 청구하다, 외상으로 사다.
- profit: 이익, 이윤.
- cancel: 취소하다.

구문 설명

1. "~ in 1993, the height of the country's economic boom."에서 "1993"과 그 이하는 동격.
2. the friend couldn't pay, neither could Aeh, her cards ~ = the friend couldn't pay, she could not also pay, her cards ~. 자세한 설명은 "주어 조동사 도치" 참조.

Reading 10

The materials, which span Kennedy's years in office from 1960 to 1963, should help give a clearer picture of the administration's foreign policy decisions, said David Coleman, an assistant professor at the University of Virginia's Miller Center of Public Affairs. But the historian, who been eagerly anticipating the release of the documents, cautioned against expecting any stunning revelations. Coleman is working on a project to transcribe tapes Kennedy secretly recorded in the White House. **CIA-related documents are especially valuable because they have been the most difficult to obtain, he said.** In addition to Cuba and Vietnam, the files also include documents concerning the United States' relations with the Dominican Republic, Germany, India, and the Soviet Union.

/CNN.

Word Bank

- span: 걸치다.
- caution: 경고하다, 충고하다.
- stunning: 놀랄만한, 기절 시키는.
- revelation: 폭로, 계시.
- transcribe: 을 베끼다, 녹음을 재생하다.

Reading 11

The United States has sent a delegation to Peru to investigate the April 20 shooting down of a missionary plane which killed Veronica Bowers and her daughter Charity. One would hope the delegation accurately and honestly assesses how vigorously a CIA plane in the area intervened to try to prevent a Peruvian air force jet from shooting at the plane, before having identified it. Indeed, there are many lessons that can be learned from the tragic deaths of the Bowers. The war on drugs pits good versus evil. **But the counter-narcotics struggle has also created a nebulous area that is very difficult to define or negotiate.** Nothing better exemplifies that dangerous gray area than the fatal shooting of a missionary plane in Peru.

/Washington Times.

Word Bank

- delegation: 대표단.
- assess: 평가하다.
- narcotic: 마취제, 마약.
- exemplify: 예증하다, 예시하다.
- missionary: 선교사, 전도사.
- pit: 싸우게 하다.
- nebulous: 안개 낀, 모호한.
- fatal: 치명적인, 중대한.

Reading 12

The essence of principled negotiation lies in remaining open to persuasion by objective facts and principles. By cautiously treating his view of the objective facts as possibly inaccurate and asking Mrs. Jones to correct it, Turnbull establishes a dialogue based on reason. He invites her to participate by either agreeing with the facts as presented or setting them right. This approach makes them two colleagues trying to establish the facts. The confrontation is defused. If Turnbull simply asserted the facts as facts, Mrs. Jones would feel threatened and defensive. She might deny the facts. The negotiation would not start off constructively.

If Turnbull is genuinely mistaken, asking for corrections beforehand will make them easier to accept. To tell Mrs. Jones that these are the facts, only to learn he is wrong, would make him lose face. Worse yet, she would then doubt all the more anything else he says, making it difficult to negotiate.

/Fisher, Roger & William Ury. Getting to Yes

Word Bank

- essence: 본질, 기본 요소.
- open: 받기 쉬운, 면할 수 없는.
- invite: 초청하다, 요청하다.
- confrontation: 대결, 대질.
- defensive: 방어적인, 수세에 있는.
- genuinely: 진실로.
- face: 체면, 면목.
- negotiation: 협상, 교섭.
- persuasion: 설득, 권유.
- colleague; 동료, 동업자.
- defuse: 제거하다, 완화시키다.
- mistaken: 잘못한, 오해한.

구문 설명

~, asking for corrections beforehand will make them easier to accept. = ~, asking for corrections beforehand will make it easier to accept them.

Reading 13

Relative to other reefs in the area, the marine biologists found the reefs of Raja Ampats to be in good condition. However, the scientists were particularly concerned by signs of damage from increased illegal fishing by local people and commercial fishing boats from Thailand and the Philippines. A growing number of fishers use dynamite and cyanide blasts to stun the fish. The **fish then float at the surface of the water, making them easy to catch and sell.** The dynamite and cyanide also kill the corals, which biologists liken to rain forests in the uniqueness and importance of their biodiversity. In some regions of Indonesia, fishing with explosives has reduced coral cover by as much as 80 percent, according to the World Fish Center, based in Penang, Malaysia

/National Geographic Today.

Word Bank

- relative: 관계 있는, 상대적인.
- marine: 바다의, 해양의.
- cyanide: 청산칼리, 청산염.
- stun: 기절 시키다, 멍하게 하다.
- liken: 비유하다.
- reef: 암초.
- biologist: 생물학자.
- blast: 폭발, 폭약.
- coral: 산호.
- biodiversity: 생물학적 다양성.

Reading 14

I am the youngest of five siblings. There is a large age gap between my older siblings and me, and quite frankly, despite the fact that I am now a 38-year-old physician, they seem not to take me seriously. My problem is that my family members insist upon calling me while I am at work. **I am a surgeon, and although you might find this hard to believe, these folks think that because they are "family" it's OK to contact me at any time during the day.** I have tried to explain that I need to focus on my patients during office hours, but they continue to call, write and send packages to me at the office.

/Universal Press Syndicate. Dear Abby.

Word Bank

- sibling: 형제, 자매.
- insist: 고집하다, 주장하다.
- contact: 연락하다, 접촉하다.
- physician: 의사.
- folk: 사람들, 가족.
- package: 꾸러미, 소포.

Reading 15

The legislative move to give people who live near Del. 1 and those who regularly commute among the three Delaware counties a break on tolls is a good idea. As welcome as the state's new north-south toll road is, it puts some financial burden on those who live in New Castle County and work in Kent or Sussex. **And it is particularly irritating to those who live near the new road and would find it convenient to use, but are reluctant to pay the high tolls.**

/The News Journal.

Word Bank

- legislative: 법률을 제정하는, 입법부의.
- move: 이사, 조치.
- commute: 통학하다, 통근하다.
- county: 군.
- break: 휴식, 우대.
- toll: 사용료, 통행료.
- financial: 재정상의, 금융상의.
- irritating: 화나는, 짜증나는.
- reluctant: 싫어하는, 마음 내키지 않는.

구문 설명

1. As welcome as the state's new north-south toll road is, it puts ~ = Though the state's new north-south toll road is welcome, it puts ~.
2. "those who live near the new road and would find it convenient to use, but ~" 에서 "it"은 앞에 나오는 "the new road"를 가리키며 "use"의 목적어 자리에서 "TOUGH"이동이 적용된 구문이다.

Reading 16

My late wife and I were married for more than 60 years. My reason for writing is to express how shocking it is to find many friends and relatives have given me the cold shoulder since my wife's funeral. I cannot understand why. **The isolation and sense of loss at a time of life when one needs support and encouragement have been hard to cope with.** The funeral expenses and the need to curb my activities because of the decrease in income are heavy enough changes to absorb, but the rejection by people I thought were friends hits even harder. Is there a specific reason for these cold shoulders and lack of phone calls - just when the opposite is needed? Several of these previous "friends" are strong church attendees. I served my country in World War II and was wounded twice. During my years of service, I never met any servicemen who turned their backs on me.

/Universal Press Syndicate. Dear Abby.

Word Bank

- relative: 일가, 친척.
- cold shoulder: 냉대, 경시.
- give (show, turn) the cold shoulder to: 냉대하다.
- funeral: 장례식, 장의.
- isolation: 고립, 고독.
- cope with: 대처하다.
- curb: 구속하다, 억제하다.
- attendee: 출석자.
- serve: 봉사하다, 복무하다.
- service: 복무, 봉사.
- serviceman: 군인.
- turn one's back on: 무시하다, 저버리다.

Reading 17

A few of the items are intimidating because they mean a serious commitment of some sort. I would like to publish a novel before I die, and I would like to get a Ph.D. in English literature. I also would like to learn to draw and play piano with a string quartet. **I know these things are difficult for me to accomplish.** If I'm going to accomplish these things, I need to start writing every day and polishing my piano skills.

/Reader's Digest.

Word Bank

- intimidating: 위협적인.
- draw: 그림을 그리다.
- quartet: 4중주.
- commitment: 헌신, 전념.
- string: 현, 현악기부.
- polish: 윤을 내다, 세련되게 하다.

Reading 18

He had originally hoped to send a probe this year to check mining prospects on a heavy metal asteroid. But finding investors for this specific journey has been a challenge, as has figuring a way to bring back the goods. "How do you chip a piece of a one-mile mountain of steel? I haven't solved that one in my mind," Bensen said. Yet the former Internet mogul is upbeat. "The natural resources in near-Earth space are unimaginable. **All these asteroids have untold wealth and they are easy to get to.**" A prospecting mission to an asteroid would access the economic value, establish an ownership claim and cost under $50 million, Bensen said. /CNN.

Word Bank

- probe: 시험, 우주탐측기.
- prospect: 전망, 채광 유망지.
- chip: 깎아내다, 잘라내다.
- upbeat: 낙관적인. 명랑한.
- wealth: 부, 풍부, 자원.
- mission 사절단, 임무.
- cost: 비용을 계산하다.
- mining: 채광, 지뢰 부설.
- asteroid: 소행성.
- mogul: 거물, 중요 인물.
- untold: 헤아릴 수 없는, 막대한.
- prospect: 답사하다, 조사하다.
- claim: 주장, 소유권의 자격.

구문 설명

1. "But finding investors for this specific journey has been a challenge, as has figuring a way to bring back the goods. = But finding investors for this specific journey has been a challenge, as figuring a way to bring back the goods has been a challenge." "as"이하는 도치 되어 있다. 자세한 설명은 "주어 조동사 도치"편 참조.
2. "the former Internet mogul"은 앞에서 언급된 "Bensen"을 말한다.

Reading 19

Recently I sat beside another woman whom I found difficult to visit. She had developed an enormous grotesque tumor on her head and neck. Her tongue was so distorted that she couldn't speak. Since I had known her when she was well, my first thought on walking into her bedroom was: How can I escape quickly without hurting her feelings?

/Guideposts.

Word Bank

- develop: 발병시키다, 에 걸리다.
- distorted: 비틀다, 왜곡하다.
- escape: 도망하다, 달아나다.
- grotesque: 괴상한, 우스꽝스러운.
- well: 건강한.

Reading 20

I schedule an appointment. Just a day prior to my doctor's appointment, I started to notice two new alarming side effects to my condition. One, I started developing these sores that begin small, and started literally eating my flesh, growing bigger as they do. They seemed contained to only my legs, so for that I was thankful. **The other effect was an arthritis effect that I was experiencing in my hands, making them painful to use.**
I first noticed this the day before my doctor's appointment. As the problem progressed, my hands became much more sore and much harder to use.

/Ultima Futuria Tones.

Word Bank

- schedule: 예정하다, 의 예정표를 만들다.
- notice: 알아차리다, 주목하다.
- effect: 효과, 작용.
- condition: 상황, 몸 상태
- sore: 아픈, 염증을 일으키는; 상처, 종기.
- contain: 담고 있다, 억제하다.
- shifting: 이동, 변화.
- alarming: 놀라운, 위급을 알리는.
- side effect: 부작용.
- arthritis: 관절염.

Reading 21

As a young girl growing up in California, I frequently dreamed of a career in law enforcement. I always had a great deal of respect for the law, and especially admired women in uniform, but girls weren't encouraged to be police officers. I didn't really think that was something I could do. After high school, I started out on my own, and began taking classes at the local community college. Needing to support myself, I took a job at Sears, Roebuck and Co., and worked my way up from a candy shop cashier to furniture sales. The minimum wage salary was tough to live on. I thought again about law enforcement as a career, but I didn't know anything about firearms. I'd never even learned to drive a car. I didn't think I could do it. So I kept working at my low-paying job, thinking about doing something better with my life.
/http://www.chp.ca.gov/recruiting/html/ditzenberger.html

Word Bank

- career: 직업, 출세.
- enforcement: 집행, 시행.
- on one's own: 독립하여, 혼자 힘으로.
- Community school: 지역 사회 학교(어린이의 사회 교육 외에 오락•성인 교육 등도 실시한다), 전문대학.
- Sears, Roebuck and Co.: 시어스로벅앤드컴퍼니(세계 최대의 소매기업).
- cashier: 출납원, 회계원.
- work one's way: 나아가다, 노력하여 ~얻다.
- firearm: 소화기(소총, 권총 등).

Reading 22

Iguanas are pretty cool animals. **They are among Americas favorite reptile pets. They can be a little tough to take care of, and they sometimes aren't the best beginning reptiles to keep.** I have had several iguanas. If you have any questions, suggestions, comments, feedback, or anything, you can e-mail me whenever you want.
/http://www.reptilerealm.com/iguana/

Word Bank

- iguana: 이구아나, 초식성 도마뱀.
- reptile: 파충류의 동물, 기어 다니는 동물.
- take care of: 돌보다, 관리하다.
- feedback: 피드백, 반응.

Reading 23

Watkins and Pearce took care of their business, but hadn't planned out other aspects of their new lives. The two arrived in San Antonio last June, armed with their entrepreneurial dream, but without Social Security numbers, insurance, transportation or even a residence. **All of those details were tough to take care of, Watkins says, when one doesn't have a history in the country.**
/San Antonio Business Journal.

Word Bank

- arm: 무장시키다, 갖추다.
- entrepreneurial: 기업의, 기업가의.
- insurance: 보험, 보험업.
- transportation: 운송, 수송 수단.

Reading 24

Immigration is a topic that affects all her students in one way or another. Kathleen asked students to interview their relatives about how their families came to America. They collected artifacts such as photographs and medals and created a web site that included the artifacts and stories. **Many of the students had never heard the stories before, because relatives found them painful to talk about.**
/http://pblmm.k12.ca.us/PBLGuide/Guide/Book/Real_World.pdf

Word Bank

- affect: 영향을 주다, 감동을 주다.
- artifact: 인공물, 공예품.
- relative: 친척, 일가.

Reading 5

It is of utmost importance that parents keep their eyes, ears, and minds open and objectively view their child's behavior and seek professional help immediately before the illness progresses. I tried desperately to convince other family members and professionals that my son, age 20 at the time, was suffering severely. He would sleep for 16-20 hours a day and was extremely sensitive to light and noise. He would roam at night for a few hours, restless. **He complained of severe headaches and his bizarre behavior made him impossible to live with.** He had hallucinations, delusions, heard voices including the voice of God, became socially withdrawn and isolated. He suffered from paranoia and could not concentrate. He was afraid to watch TV for fear that "things" would come out of it and "get him." He displayed obsessive-compulsive behavior by constantly washing his hands and face. He would stare at himself in the mirror while making weird facial expressions.

/http://www.mentalhealth.com/p.html

Word Bank

- objectively: 객관적으로.
- desperately: 자포자기가 되어, 필사적으로.
- severe: 엄한, 심한.
- restless: 침착하지 못한, 불안한.
- hallucination: 환영, 환상.
- withdrawn: 수줍은, 내성적인.
- paranoia: 망상증, 편집증.
- obsessive: 강박관념의, 귀신들린 듯한.
- compulsive: 강제적인, 강박관념에 사로 잡힌.
- professional: 직업의, 전문적인.
- bizarre: 기괴한, 별난.
- delusion: 망상, 착각.
- isolated: 고립된, 격리된.

Reading 26

And there was Bobby. He had lived in an institution all his life and had learned braille and could get around fine within his surroundings. He was 36 when I knew him and I was young enough to believe that as a rehab teacher I could give Bobby the training and confidence he needed so he could leave that institution and get a job and have more friends and, in short, live up to the huge potential I saw in him. After my first few visits, the administration of the institution begged me not to come back. **Bobby, who had been well-adjusted and comfortable, had suddenly started beating his head against the wall and acting out in ways that made him impossible to deal with.** He is old now but I guess he's still there. Is he happy?

/The Braille Forum Magazine. Vol. 37.

Word Bank

- institution: 기관, 원(院)
- braille: 점자(법).
- rehab: 갱생 시설, 사회 복귀 (= rehabilitation).
- live up to: 에 맞는 생활을 하다.
- administration: 통치, 집행부.
- comfortable: 마음이 편한.
- act out: 행동으로 나타내다.

English Special Constructions

Chapter 02

후 치 / Postposing

Chapter 02

후 치 (後置) Postposing

후치란 무엇인가?

영어에서 후치구문이란 보통 문장의 어순에서 일부 구성 요소가 문장의 오른쪽에, 즉 문미에 나타나는 구문을 말한다. 후치와 관련해서는 우향전이(Right-Dislocation), 외치(Extraposition), 탈명사구 외치(Extraposition from Noun Phrase), 그리고 복합 명사구 이동(Complex Noun Phrase Shift)구문이 있다.

01 a. They had all read about this jungle for months now in the papers.

b. They had all read about it for months in the papers, this jungle. (우향전이)
(그들 모두 신문에서 여러 달 동안 이 정글에 대한 글을 읽었다.)

02 a. For the neighbors to doubt that he was telling the truth was impossible.

b. It was impossible for the neighbors to doubt that he was telling the truth. (외치)
(이웃 사람들은 그가 진실을 이야기 하고 있다는 것을 의심하기란 불가능했다.)

03 a. A rumor that he will resign attracts students' attention.

b. A rumor attracts students' attention that he will resign. (탈명사구 외치)
(그가 사임할 거라는 소문이 학생들의 관심을 끌고 있다.)

04 a. Mary called the man who had stepped on her foot an elephant..

b. Mary called an elephant the man who had stepped on her foot. (복합명사구 이동)
(Mary는 그녀의 발을 밟았던 사람을 코끼리라고 불렀다.)

후치는 언제 쓰이는가?

후치는 전치와 달리 보다 다양한 특성을 가지고 있다. 예문 (1)에서 사용되는 우향 전이는 앞에서 이미 언급된 요소만 후치가 가능한데 이것은 후치된 요소를 주제화 시키거나 혹은 대명사만으로는 의사전달이 충분하지 못하다고 생각되어 보다 더 분명한 정보를 주고자 할 때에 사용된다. 예문 (2)와 같은 외치는 주어나 목적어 위치에 있는 요소가 너무 길 때에 사용된다. 그리고 예문 (3)과 (4) 역시 주어나 목적어가 너무 길 때에 일어나는 현상들인데 (3)과 같은 경우는 명사구에서 수식하는 요소만을 후치 시키는 것이며 (4)와 같은 경우는 명사구 전체를 문미로 이동시키는 구문이다.

Unit 1 우향 전이 (右向 轉移: Right-Dislocation)

우향전이는 앞에서 다루었던 좌향전이와 비교된다. 보통 문장 어순에서 명사구를 문두 위치에 놓았던 좌향전이와 달리 문미(文尾) 위치에 둔다. 좌향전이구문과 마찬가지로 후치된 요소는 원래 있던 자리에 성(gender)과 수(number)가 일치되는 대명사를 남겨둔다. 게다가 좌향전이 구문에서는 구정보뿐만 아니라 신정보도 전치가 가능하지만, 우향전이 구문에서는 구정보만 후치가 가능하다. 우향전이된 요소는 주제 역할을 하거나, 앞에서 언급된 대명사만으로는 의사전달이 충분하지 못하다고 생각되어 보다 더 분명한 정보를 주고자 할 때에 혹은 명사구가 너무 길어 뒤로 옮기고자 할 때에 사용된다.

1 우향 전이되는 요소

1.1. 주 어

01 a. The cops spoke to the janitor about that robbery yesterday.

b. **They** spoke to the janitor about the robbery yesterday, **the cops**.
(경찰들이 어제 도난사고와 관련해 관리인과 이야기를 나누고 있었다.)

02 a. Is that friend whom you like so much sick?

b. Is **he** sick, **that friend whom you like so much?**
(네가 정말 좋아하는 저 친구는 몸이 아프니?)

1.2. 목 적 어

03 a. Jane visits this park every week.

b. Jane visits **it** every week, **this park**.
(Jane은 매주 이 공원을 방문한다.)

04 a. We told the most stupid and dishonest man in the village to leave instantly.

b. We told **him** to leave instantly, **the most stupid and dishonest man in the village.**
(우리는 마을에서 가장 상식 없고 부정직한 사람에게 즉시 떠나라고 했다.)

05 a. I told you you wouldn't like this movie much.

b. I told you you wouldn't like **it** much, **this movie**.
(나는 네가 이 영화를 그리 좋아하지 않을 거라는 이야기를 네게 해주었다.)

1.3. 소 유 격

06 a. I met that guy's sister yesterday.

b. I met **his** sister yesterday, **that guy**.
(나는 어제 그 사람의 여동생을 만났다.)

2 보충 설명

07 a. I hear the Art Institute has a new exhibit on 19th Century Post-Impressionism. That Van Gogh was a genius.
(예술원에서 19세기 후기 인상주의의 새로운 전람회가 있다는 이야기를 들었다. 저기 고호는 참 천재 였지.)

b. I hear the Art Institute has a new exhibit on 19th Century Post-Impressionism. #**He** was a genius, **that Van Gogh**.

우향전이 구문에서는 주제화와 좌향전이 구문의 경우에서와 달리 후치되는 요소는 이미 앞에서 언급된 정보로서 구정보이어야 한다. 따라서 위 예문 (b)는 후치된 요소가 신정보임으로 비문이다.

08 a. They let him go yesterday.

b. *They let **him** go yesterday, **he**.

c. *They let **him** go yesterday, **him**.

좌향 전위 구문에서와 마찬가지로 우향 전위 구문에서도 대명사는 후치될 수 없다. 따라서 위 예문 (8b)와 (8c)는 적절치 못하다.

Practice Examples

Reading 01

He maneuvered his small craft toward the island, his eyes narrowed in the bright sun. The island wavered and danced before his gaze, seeming one moment to disappear amidst the swelling tide of the sea then to thrust up again like a proud fist. **It was the last rampart of land, this place;** beyond it, the Atlantic stretched into the distant horizon. As they neared the lonely island, the pounding hammer of the surf became louder. The swells crashed against the stone cliffs, sending spray higher, higher.

/Kristin Hannah. Waiting For the Moon

Word Bank

- maneuver: 이동시키다, 움직이다.
- craft: 배, 선박, 항공기.
- narrow: 좁게 하다, 가늘게 하다.
- waver: 흔들리다, 너울거리다.
- swell: 넘실거리다(명사: 넘실거림, 큰 파도).
- thrust: 뻗어나다.
- rampart: 성벽, 방벽.
- pound: 세게 치다, 연거푸 치다.
- surf: 밀려드는 파도.
- swell: 부풀기, 큰 물결 (= surf).
- crash: 부딪치다, 요란한 소리를 내다.
- spray: 물보라.

구문 설명

~ the island, his eyes narrowed in the bright sun. = ~ the island, with his eyes narrowed in the bright sun. 자세한 설명은 "WITH" 주술관계 참조

Reading 02

Outside an airport in Aspen, Colo., a group of seriously ill kids, some without hair, some on crutches, waited for vans to take them to a barbecue. It was 1992, and Andrea had invited them to a week-long camp sponsored by her nonprofit organization, Kids' Stuff Foundation. Here in Aspen, she hoped, they'd be able to recapture some of the joy they'd lost to illness. Andrea was anxious about every detail--especially about how well she'd relate to the children. Looking about, she noticed a dark-haired young woman putting her arm around one kid, teasing another, adjusting a baseball cap on another's head. She moved among the children with an ease that Andrea admired. **She was the oldest camper, 18-year-old Rhea Olsen.** As Andrea stood before the 15 kids to give them a pep talk about the day's activities, she noticed Rhea staring cynically, her hands on her hips. Andrea decided she'd better seek out this skeptical teen-ager.

/Reader's Digest.

Word Bank

- crutch: 목발.
- barbecue: 바베큐, 야외 파티.
- van: 소형 트럭.
- relate: 사이가 좋다, 친한 관계에 있다.
- look about(around): 주변을 둘러보다.
- tease: 놀리다.
- adjust: 단정히 하다,
- camper: 야영자, 캠프 생활을 하는 사람.
- admire: 놀라다, 감탄하다.
- pep talk: 격려의 말.
- skeptical: 의심 많은, 회의적인.
- had better: ~ 하는 편이 낳다, 해야 한다.

Reading 03

The book I was reading was this book I took out of the library by mistake. They gave me the wrong book and I didn't notice it till I got back to my room. They gave me Out of Africa, by Isak Dinesen. I thought it was going to stink, but it didn't. It was a very good book. I'm quite illiterate, but I read a lot. My favorite author is my brother D.B., and my next favorite is Ring Lardner. My brother gave me a book by Ring Lardner for my birthday, just before I went to Pencey. It had these very funny, crazy plays in it, and then it had this one story about a traffic cop that falls in love with this very cute girl that's always speeding. **Only, he's married, the cop, so he can't marry her or anything.** Then this girl gets killed, because she's always speeding. That story just about killed me. What I like best is a book that's at least funny once in a while. I read a lot of classical books, like The Return of the Native and all, and I like them, and I read a lot of war books and mysteries and all, but they don't knock me out too much.

/Salinger, J. D. The Catcher in the Rye

Word Bank

- stink: 몹시 나쁘다
- illiterate: 무식한, 문맹의.
- play: 극, 연극.
- crazy: 무모한, 이상한.
- speed: 질주하다, 제한 속도 이상으로 달리다.
- or anything: ~이라든가 뭐라든가.
- about: 거의(= almost).
- kill: 매료시키다, 즐겁게 해주다.
- once in a while: 가끔, 이따금.
- and all: ~등. mystery: 추리, 탐정.
- knock out: 에게 감명을 주다, 을 깜짝 놀라게 하다.

구문 설명

1. "They gave me the wrong book and I didn't notice it till I got back to my room."에서 "it"은 "and" 앞의 문장을 받는다.
2. 형용사를 부사로 혹은 반대로 부사를 형용사로 전환해서 생각하는 것이 문장 이해에 좋은 경우가 많다. I read a lot of classical books. = I read classical books a lot. They spend an occasional night in a fancy hotel. = They occasionally spend a night in a fancy hotel; Often, while Pierre worked at some chemical experiment, she prepared hasty meals which they ate as

they continued their task. = Often, while Pierre worked at some chemical experiment, she prepared in haste meals which they ate continued their task; He is a real idiot. = He is really an idiot.

Reading 04

It was always a great affair, the Misses Morkan's annual dance. Everybody who knew them came to it, members of the family, old friends of the family, the members of Julia's choir, any of Kate's pupils that were grown up enough, and even some of Mary Jane's pupils too. Never once had it fallen flat. For years and years it had gone off in splendid style, as long as anyone could remember: ever since Kate and Julia, after the death of their brother Pat, had left the house in Stoney Batter and taken Mary Jane, their only niece, to live with them in the dark, gaunt house on Usher's Island, the upper part of which they had rented from Mr Fulham, the corn-factor on the ground floor.

/James Joyce. Dubliners

Word Bank

- affair: 것, 일(=thing).
- choir: 합창단, 성가대.
- flat: 지루한, 재미없는.
- go off: 행해지다, 되어가다.
- splendid: 화려한, 호화로운.
- gaunt: 말라빠진, 으스스한.
- corn-factor: 곡물 도매상.
- rent: 임대하다(to), 임차하다(from).
- ground floor: 1층(미국에서는 first floor하고 한다).

구문설명

1. "Never once had it fallen flat." 은 부정어 "never"가 전치됨으로써 주어와 조동사가 도치된 구문임. 자세한 설명은 주어 조동사 도치 구문 참조.
2. "fall, become, go, come, grow, get, make, run, turn + 보어"은 "보어 하게 되다"의 뜻. He suddenly fell grave/asleep/sick.
3. "in (a/the) 형용사 + way"는 양태부사를 형성한다.
4. the corn-factor on the ground floor = with the corn-factor on the ground floor. 자세한 설명은 "WITH"주술관계 참조.

Reading 05

"It's her share in the family trait, the independence she speaks of." Her son's appreciation of the matter was more favorable. "Whatever the high spirit of those young ladies may be, her own is a match for it. She likes to do everything for herself and has no belief in any one's power to help her. She thinks me of no more use than a postage-stamp without gum, and she would never forgive me if I should presume to go to Liverpool to meet her." /Henry James. The Portrait of a Lady

Word Bank

- trait: 특성, 특색.
- appreciation: 평가, 이해.
- high: 숭고한, 고상한.
- gum: 접착제, 고무.
- presume to R: 감히 ~하다(= dare)
- independence: 독립, 자립.
- favorable: 호의적인, 유리한.
- match: 상대, 엇비슷한 사람/것.

구문 설명

1. no 비교급 than = as 반대어 원급 as : He is no wiser than his wife. = He is as foolish as his wife.
2. no less 원급 as = as 원급 as : She is no less beautiful than her mother. = She is just as beautiful as her mother.

Reading 06

The whole world heard the teacher that day, we all know you don't have a Daddy. **It lasted for a while, this kind of numbness.** I spent a lot of time feeling sorry for myself. And then one day I met this wino in a restaurant. I'd been out hustling all day, shining shoes, selling newspapers, and I had googols of money in my pocket. Bought me a bowl of chili for fifteen cents, and a cheeseburger for five cents, and a piece of chocolate cake for ten cents. That was a good meal. I was eating when this old wino came in. I love winos because they never hurt anyone but themselves.

/Dick Gregory. I never Learned Hate

Word Bank

- numbness: 감각을 잃음. 마비.
- wino: 포도주 중독자, 주정뱅이.
- hustle: 기운차게 일하다.
- googol: 10의 100제곱.

구문 설명

1. bought me a bowl of chili ~ = I had bought me a bowl of chili ~. 이 문장과 바로 앞 문장에서 과거 완료가 쓰이고 있는 것은 식당에서 만나기 이전 상황을 설명하기 때문이다.
2. "S1 + P1 when S2 + P2."의 문장은 자주 "When S1 + P1, S2 + P2." 또는 "S2 + P2 when S1 + P1."으로 바꾸어 쓸 수 있다. 따라서 위의 "I was eating when this old wino came in."은 "When I was eating, this old wino came in."으로 바꾸어 생각할 수도 있다.

Reading 07

Like the rest of my family, I have no idea how old I am; I can only guess. We lived by the seasons and the sun, planning our moves around our need for rain, planning our day around the span of daylight available. Our home was a tentlike domed hut woven from grass and built on a framework of sticks; it was about six feet in diameter. **When it came time to move, we dismantled the hut and tied it to the backs of our camels.** Then when we found a spot with water and foliage, we'd set up again. The hut provided shelter from the midday sun and storage space for fresh milk. At night we children slept outside under the stars, cuddled together on a mat. My father slept off to one side, our guardian.

/Reader's Digest.

Word Bank

- around: ~ 쯤에, ~에 입각하여.
- domed: 돔 모양의, 둥근 지붕의.
- weave: 을 짜다, 엮다.
- dismantle: 철거하다, 분해하다.
- foliage: 잎, 무성한 잎.
- set up: 세우다, 설립하다.
- storage: 저장, 창고.
- guardian: 보호자, 수호자.
- span: 한 뼘, 짧은 시간.
- hut: 임시 가옥, 오두막.
- framework: 구조물, 뼈대.
- shelter: 피난처, 은신처.
- cuddle: 껴안다,

Reading 08

They sat side by side, these men who had spent their professional lives pointing nuclear missiles at each other, inside the windowless room at Peterson Air Force Base in Colorado. Officers of the U.S. Space Command and their Russian counterparts had gathered, the day before New Year's Eve, to keep the world from ending: together they would monitor the early-warning system so that no Y2K-befuddled computer would mistakenly signal an ICBM launch, precipitate an all-too-real response and make this a really short millennium. Russian Lt. Col. Viktor Grigorenko kept glancing nervously from his desktop computer to the wall clock showing the time in Moscow. "Three minutes" to midnight, someone called out. "Two minutes..." And then, as the room fell silent, the officers stared at the TV screen showing the first fireworks arcing over Red Square in the final seconds of the old millennium. Three Russians in the room grabbed their hot lines to Moscow.

/Newsweek.

Word Bank

- side by side: 나란히.
- point: 겨누다.
- Space Command: 우주군(宇宙軍).
- counterpart: 상대물, 상대쪽.
- befuddle: 혼란하게 하다, 곤혹스럽게 하다.
- ICBM: 대륙간 탄도 미사일(intercontinental ballistic missile).

- launch: 진수, 발사.
- precipitate: 재촉하다, 촉진하다.
- all-too-real = very real. Lt. Col.: 중령(lieutenant colonel).
- nervously: 초조하게.
- firework: 발광, 불꽃.
- arc: 호광(전호)를 이루다.
- signal: 에 신호를 보내다.
- Red Square: (모스크바 크렘린궁 앞에 있는) 붉은 광장.

Reading 09

Each morning they made the journey together, and Mark would take a cab back to his office. Although this routine was even more costly and exhausting than the previous one, Mark knew it was only a matter of time before Susan would be able to ride the bus on her own. **He believed in her, in the Susan he used to know before she'd lost her sight,** who wasn't afraid of any challenge and who would never, ever quit.

/Jack Canfield, et al. Chicken Soup for the Couple's Soul

Word Bank

- journey: 여행, 여정. cab: 택시(= taxicab).
- routine: 일상적인 일, 일과.
- costly: 비용이 많이 드는, 값비싼.
- exhausting: 녹초가 되게 하는.
- a matter of: 대략, 의 문제.
- ride: 타다.
- on one's own: 자력으로, 독립해서.
- sight: 시력, 광경.
- quit: 포기하다. 단념하다.

구문 설명

"He believed in her, in the Susan he used to know before she'd lost her sight, ~"에서처럼 우향전이가 일어날 때에 전치사와 함께 후치되는 경우도 자주 나타난다.

Reading 10

President Nelson Mandela let South Africa's worst-kept secret out of the bag when he married her, the former Mozambican first lady, Graca Machel. Mr. Mandela and Mrs. Machel, 52, took their vows on Mr. Mandela's 80th birthday in a private, multi-denominational ceremony at his presidential home in the affluent Johanesburg suburb of Houghton.

/New York Times.

Word Bank

- tlet the cat out of the bag: (무심코) 비밀을 누설하다. 여기에서는 "the cat"을 "~secret"로 대체했음.
- vow: 맹세, 서약.
- multi - denominational: 많은 종파의.
- affluent: 부유한, 유복한.

Reading 11

When Theseus asked the reason, his father said, "As we were defeated in war, we must pay a terrible price to the king of Crete. Every year we must send seven of our best youths and seven of our most beautiful girls to the Island of Crete to be eaten by monster called the Minotaur. **The messenger to take them away on a black-sailed ship arrived this morning, the poor children.** So you have found everyone of us very sad."

/Myth of Greece. The Monster of Crete

Word Bank

- defeat: 이기다, 패배시키다.
- messenger: 사자, 전령.
- black-sailed: 검은 돛을 단.("형용사-명사ed"에서 접미사 "-ed"는 "~을 가진"의 뜻을 갖는다. kind-hearted: 마음씨가 착한. short - handled: 손잡이가 짧은).

구문 설명

능동태의 동사 표현이 수동태로 쓰이게 되면 우리말로 옮길 때 주의가 필요하다. 가끔 동사를 반대 의미로 해석하는 것이 더 좋은 경우가 많다. She defeated him at tennis. (그녀는 그와 테니스를 쳐 이겼다) ⇨ He was defeated at tennis by her.(그는 테니스에서 그녀한테 졌다.) She gave me a book.(그녀는 나에게 책을 한 권 주었다.) ⇨ I was given a book by her. (나는 그녀한테 책을 한 권 받았다.) He outpolled me in the survey of public opinion. (그가 이번 여론 조사에서 나보다 더 많은 표를 얻었다.) ⇨ I was outpolled by him in the survey of public opinion.(나는 이번 여론 조사에서 그보다 더 적은 표를 얻었다.)

Reading 12

Asian consumers feel comfortable with Japan's values and lifestyle, too. Hong Kong TV audiences love the Japanese drama "Under the Same Roof," partly because it stresses themes they can relate to: family ties and respect for elders. **It features three generations living together, a scenario not common in Western soap operas.** Indonesians, whose culture is steeped in mysticism, say they relate to Japanese cartoons' heroism and magic more than to the slapstick tales of American cartoons. On the most popular kids' channel, 95 percent of the children's lineup is from Japan. "The Japanese shows have a lot more different, strange characters," says Aditya Daniswara, 9, who lists Doraemon, a robot cat in a blue spacesuit, as one of his favorites. The cat uses magic to right wrongs. Asian tastes also veer toward the emotional. If Hollywood is big on special effects, Japanese productions scrutinize personal relationships and brim with feelings and schmaltz, which Asians lap up.

/TIME.

Word Bank

- relate: 관련이 있다, 친한 관계에있다.
- theme: 주제, 논제.
- feature: 의 특징을 그리다.
- steep: 담그다, 적시다.
- magic: 마법, 마술.
- lineup: 프로그램, 출전 선수들의 진용.
- list: 좋아하다(= like).
- taste: 기호, 취미.
- big: 현저한, 열중하는.
- lap: 에 열심히 귀 기울이다, 좋아하다.
- schmaltz: 극단적인(과장된) 감상주의,
- tie: (복수) 인연, 유대.
- soap opera: 멜로 드라마.
- mysticism: 신비주의.
- slapstick: 왁자지껄한 (희극).
- right: 고치다, 바로 잡다.
- veer: 방향을 바꾸다.
- scrutinize: 면밀히 검사하다.
- brim: 가득차다, 넘치다.

구문설명

"the + 형용사"는 "형용사 + 명사(단수/복수)"는 바꾸어 쓸 수 있는데 해당 명사는 문맥에서 결정된다. 위의 "Asian tastes also veer toward the emotional."에서 "the emotional"은 "emotional productions/shows"가 될 수 있다.

Reading 13

All their lives, they've known hardship. Everything they have, they've had to work for. They've had to develop a strict moral code and depend on each other. They have few comforting illusions. They will relate to all the people, and work for reforms if given the power to do so. Their leadership must be mixed with that of the nobles if there's to be any progress on Shanji." "They hate the very idea of an Emperor," said Kati. "They will not hate the one who replaces him." Mengmoshu's eyes were locked on hers, and they sat silently for a long moment. Kati looked at him from behind her steepled hands, and sighed. "You want me to be the Empress of Shanji." "Yes." "Mandughai said as much." **"It's Her decision, Kati,** and the Moshuguang supports it. We're doing all we can to prepare you for the responsibility."

/James C. Glass. Shanji

Word Bank

- know: 경험하다.
- comforting: 환영, 환상.
- noble: 고귀한 사람, 귀족.
- lock: 자물쇠를 채우다, 움직이지 않게 하다.
- hardship: 고난, 고초.
- relate: 관계되다, 잘 어울리다.
- as much: 바로 그만큼.
- steepled: 뾰족탑 모양의, 뾰족한.

구문 설명

Everything they have, they've had to work for. = They've had to work for everything they have. "everything they have"을 주제화하기 위해 전치시킨 표현이다. 자세한 설명은 주제화 구문 참조.

Reading 14

As I sat next to his hospital bed, my eyes fastened to the face I had been so afraid I would never see again, Dan told me his story. Immediately after his slide down the canyon, when he realized the seriousness of his predicament, Dan said that he thought of me and how much he would miss me if he didn't make it back. As he lay at the bottom of the rough cliff, he groped around until he found a suitable rock. Using the rock, which was sharply pointed, he managed to carve a message to me in a large rock near where he lay. If the worst should happen, he hoped I would eventually see the rock and know that I had been with him always, held close in his heart. I started weeping all over again. I knew how deeply I loved my husband, **but I was unprepared for this, the depth of his love for me.**

/Jack Canfield, et al. Chicken Soup for the Couple's Soul

Word Bank

- fasten: 얽어 매다, 고정시키다.
- canyon: 협곡.
- make it: 성공하다, 시간에 대다.
- rough: 울퉁불퉁한, 거칠한.
- grope: 손으로 더듬다.
- carve: 새기다, 조각하다.
- weep: 울다.
- slide: 미끄러지기, 활주.
- predicament: 곤경, 처지.
- cliff: 벼랑, 절벽.
- pointed: 뾰족한, 신랄한.
- close: 아주 가까이, 친밀하게.
- over again: 다시 한번.

Unit 2 외 치 (外置: Extraposition)

주어나 목적어가 절, 부정사, 혹은 동명사 형태의 긴 요소로 되어있을 때에 그 자리에 예비의 "it"(preparatory "it")을 남겨두고 그 요소를 문미로 옮겨가는 경우가 있는데 이를 외치(Extraposition)라고 한다. 흔히 말하는 "가주어-진주어" 또는 "가목적어-진목적어" 구문이 여기에 해당된다.
외치는 흔히 구문상의 이유 때문에 적용된다고 한다. 다시 말해서 영어에서는 주어나 목적어가 긴 문장은 좋지않다. 그래서 이런 경우에는 외치를 시킨다. 이런 제약이 목적어가 긴 경우에는 잘 맞는다. 그러나 주어가 긴 경우에는 문맥에서 이미 언급된 구정보 이거나 선행 문맥으로부터 추론이 가능한 경우에는 외치를 시키지 않고 주어자리에 그대로 두어도 문제가 되지않는다. 이 경우에는 주제역할을 한다. 그러나 긴 주어가 신정보일 때에는 외치를 시키는 것이 좋다.
정리하자면 외치가 일어나는 경우는 흔히 세가지 이유와 관련이 있다. 하나는 술어(형용사나 동사)의 특성상 외치를 해야 되는 경우와, 또 하나는 목적어가 너무 길어 동사와 보어 혹은 동사와 목적어 뒤의 전치사구와 관계가 너무 멀어질 때에 적용되고 그리고 나머지 하나는 주제는 문두에 놓이고 초점은 문미에 놓이는 속성 때문이다.

1 외치될 수 있는 요소

1.1. 부 정 사

01 a. To read many magazines is a waste of time. (주어)

b. It is a waste of time to read many magazines.
(잡지를 많이 읽는 것은 시간 낭비이다.)

02 a. For the odor to wear away takes at least one month. (주어)

b. It takes at least one month for the odor to wear away.
(그 냄새가 없어지는 데는 적어도 한 달이 걸린다.)

03 a. *I took to settle their quarrel upon myself. (타동사+부정사목적어+전치사+목적어)

b. I took it upon myself to settle their quarrel.
(나는 그들의 싸움을 해결하기로 했다.)

04 a. *I thought to find fault with him useless. (타동사+부정사목적어+보어)

b. I thought it useless to find fault with him.
(나는 그를 비난해보아야 아무 소용이 없다고 생각했다.)

예문 (3)과 (4)의 구조에서는 외치가 적용되는 것이 적절한 표현이다. 외치가 적용되지 않으면 많은 경우에서 적절치 못한 표현으로 간주된다. 그러나 일부 표현은 관용적으로 용인된다. “think fit (good, proper, right) to R,” “see fit (good, proper, right) to R” (~ 하는 것이 좋다고 생각하다) 은 예외적으로 예비의 “it”을 쓰지 않는다. I think fit to refuse his offer to help. (나는 도와주겠다는 그의 제안을 거절하는 것이 적절하다고 생각한다.). If our teacher thinks proper to join the club, I'll do so. (선생님이 클럽에 가입하는 것을 좋게 생각하신다면 나는 그렇게 하겠다.)

05 a. *He never gave that they are human beings a thought. (타동사+간접목적어+직접목적어)

b. He never gave it a thought that they are human beings.
(그는 결코 그들을 사람이라고 생각해본 적이 없다.)

1.2. 절

06 a. That politicians are not reliable bothers me very much. (주어)

b. It bothers me very much that politicians are not reliable.
(정치인들을 믿을 수 없다는 것이 나는 정말 괴롭다.)

07 a. Whether or not Tom will succeed in the work does not matter.

b. It does not matter whether or not Tom will succeed in the work.
(Tom이 그 일에 성공을 하느냐 하지 못하느냐 하는 것은 중요하지 않다.)

08 a. I wouldn't guarantee that he would arrive on time.

b. I wouldn't guarantee it that he will arrive on time.
(나는 그가 정시에 도착하리라고 장담하지 않으려 했다.)

09 a. *He made why he had to resign his post as chairman clear. (타동사+절 목적어 +보어)

b. He made clear why he had to resign his post as chairman. (복합명사구 이동)

c. He made it clear why he had to resign his post as chairman.
(그는 의장으로서의 직책을 왜 그만두어야 하는지를 분명히 했다.)

예문(8a)에서 보는 바와 같이 보어가 뒤따를 때에 절 목적어는 반드시 복합명사구 이동이나 외치가 적용되어야 한다.

1.3. 동명사

10 a. Complaining about it now is no use.

b. It is no use complaining about it now.
(이제 그것에 대해 불평해보아야 아무 소용이 없다.)

2 보충 설명

11 a. To keep our promise is important.

b. It is important to keep our promise.
(약속을 지키는 일은 중요하다.)

12 a. *That he is happy seems.

b. It seems that he is happy.
(그는 행복한 것 같다.)

예문 (1, 2, 6, 7, 10)에서처럼 주어로 쓰이는 부정사나 절은 선택적으로 적용하는 것이 가능하지만 예문 (12)에서처럼 seem, appear, happen, chance, likely, unlikely 등은 반드시 적용해야 된다.

13 a. *Is where the accident happened not fully clear?

b. Is it not fully clear where the accident happened?
(그 사고가 어디에서 일어났는지 아주 분명하지 않습니까?)

14 a. *In none of the cases does **whether the rumor is true or not** really matter.

b. In none of the cases does **it** really matter **whether the rumor is true or not.**
(그 소문이 사실인지 아닌지는 결코 중요치 않다.)

(13)과 (14)에서처럼 의문문과 부정요소가 전치된 구문에서 이들이 주어일 때에는 반드시 외치 되어야 한다.

15 a. Bill resents that people are always comparing him to Mozart.

b. Bill resents **it that people are always comparing him to Mozart.**
(Bill은 사람들이 항상 그를 Mozart와 비교하는 것을 불쾌하게 생각한다.)

16 a. Bill claims that people are always comparing him to Mozart.

b. Bill claims **it that people are always comparing him to Mozart.**
(Bill은 사람들이 항상 그를 Mozart와 비교한다고 주장한다.)

17 a. *The caretaker promised me to see to that the windows are properly shut.

b. The caretaker promised me to see to **it that the windows are properly shut.**
(관리인은 나에게 창문이 잘 닫혀있도록 조처를 취하겠다고 약속했다.)

위 예문 (15), (16), 그리고 (17)에서처럼 "that"절이 목적어로 쓰일 때에 그리고 주절의 동사(타동사나 자동사+전치사) 뒤에 다른 요소가 뒤따르지 않을 때에 "that"절 앞에 예비의 "it"을 앞에 둘 수 있다. 주절의 동사가 "타동사"일 때에는 외치를 적용할 수도 있고 하지 않을 수도 있다. 반면에 동사구가 "자동사+전치사"일 때에는 외치를 반드시 적용시켜야 한다. 그 이유는 전치사가 "that"절을 목적어로 취할 수 없기 때문이다. 이런 부류의 외치를 모든 동사에 다 적용할 수 있는 것은 아니고 일반적으로 그 주절의 동사가 취하는 목적절이 사실로 전제되는 사실동사에만 가능하다. 이런 사실 동사(factive verb)에는 "resent, regret, deplore, comprehend, forget, ignore, mind, guarantee, rely on, depend on, insist on, answer for, see to" 등이 있고 비사실 동사(nonfactive verb)에는 "believe, claim, assert, deem, figure, suppose" 등이 있다. 사실 동사와 비사실 동사를 구별하는 간단한 방법으로는 다음과 같이 접속사 "but"을 사용하여 논리적으로 대립시켜 보면 알 수 있다. 사실 동사인 경우에는 "but"을 첨가하면 앞 문장과 논리적으로 모순이 생기게 된다.

18 a. #John **regretted** that Mary had left, **but** in fact she had not left. (사실 동사)
(#John은 Mary가 떠난 것을 아쉬워했다. 그러나 사실 그녀는 떠나지 않았다.)

b. John **believed** that Mary had left, **but** in fact she had not left. (비사실 동사)
(John은 Mary가 떠났다고 믿고 있었다. 그러나 사실 그녀는 떠나지 않았다.)

동사 "regret"은 목적절 "Mary가 떠났다"는 것을 사실로 전제하고 있다. 반면에 동사 "believe"는 "Mary가 떠났다"는 것을 사실로 전제하고 있는 동사가 아니다.

19 a. *I take that we are to come early.

b. I take **it that we are to come early.**
(나는 우리가 일찍 와야 된다고 믿는다.)

20 a. *The enemy will have that we are defeated.

b. The enemy will have **it that we are defeated.**
(적은 우리가 패배했다고 주장할 것이다.)

"take(믿다, 생각하다)"와 "have(주장하다, 말하다)"는 관용적으로 외치를 시켜서 사용한다.

Practice Examples

Reading 01

Do not allow yourself to remain a vacillating creature, swayed half by reason and half by infantile folly. Do not be afraid of irreverence towards the memory of those who controlled your childhood. They seemed to you then strong and wise because you were weak and foolish; now that you are neither, **it is your business to examine their apparent strength and wisdom, to consider whether they deserve that reverence that from force of habit you still bestow upon them.**

/Bertrand Russell. The Conquest of Happiness

Word Bank

- vacillating: 흔들리는, 결단력이 없는.
- sway: 흔들다, 움직이다.
- infantile: 어린애 같은, 유치한.
- irreverence: 불경, 불손.
- now that: 이기 때문에(= since).
- apparent: 외관상의, 표면상의.
- bestow: 주다, 수여하다.

구문 설명

1. ~ now that you are neither, = ~ now that you are neither weak nor foolish,.
2. ~ it is your business to examine their apparent strength and wisdom, = ~ it is your business to examine why they are apparently strong and wise,

Reading 02

For many years it was easy for farmers to boost their harvests merely by dumping more fertilizer, pesticides and irrigation water on their land. Now, however, they are running up against the law of diminishing returns. Insects are increasingly developing resistance to pesticide. Reliance on chemical fertilizer, rather than on organic nutrients such as manure or compost, makes the soil more compact and thus more likely to dry out and eventually erode. Improper irrigation techniques can result in the evaporation of too much water from fields, leaving behind salts that build up in the soil and ultimately leave the land infertile. That's why vast areas of Pakistan have turned into salt flats.

/Time.

Word Bank

- boost: 을 증대 시키다, 을 밀어 올리다.
- harvest: 수확, 작물.
- dump: 을 부리다, 을 아무렇게나 내던지다(= let fall in or as if in a heap or mass).
- pesticide: 살충제.
- irrigation: 관개, 관수.
- run up against: 에 부딪치다, 만나다.
- return: 수입, 수익.
- nutrient: 자양물, 영양물.
- manure: 비료 거름.
- compost: 혼합물, 퇴비.
- compact: 빽빽한, 조밀한(= having a dense structure or parts or units closely packed or joined).
- erode: 침식하다, 좀먹어 들어가다.
- evaporation: 증발.
- build up: 모이다, 쌓이다.
- infertile: 비옥하지 않은, 불모의.
- flat: 평지, 습지.

Reading 03

Such reforms would not even be thinkable without the IMF's provisions. **It would have been very difficult to achieve them because the chaebol would have resisted.** So I am determined to utilize the IMF's reform provisions to transform our economic system so we can prepare to rebound in the 21st century. This is a blessing in disguise for us.

/Time.

Word Bank

- IMF: 국제 통화 기금(= International Monetary Fund).
- provision: 제공, 조항.
- transform: 바꾸다, 변화시키다.
- rebound: 되 튀다, 다시 일어서다.
- disguise: 위장, 은폐.
- a blessing in disguise: 모습을 바꾼 하늘의 은총, 모습을 바꾼 행운.

Reading 04

As change accelerates in society it forces a parallel acceleration within us. New information reaches us and we are forced to revise our image-file continuously at a faster and faster rate. Older images based on past reality must be replaced, for, unless we update them, our actions become divorced from reality and we become progressively less competent. **We find it impossible to cope.**

/Alvin Toffler. The Third Wave

Word Bank

- accelerate: 을 촉진하다, 가속하다.
- parallel: 대응하는, 평행의.
- revise: 을 바꾸다, 수정하다.
- file: 서류 정리함, 목록.
- reality: 사실, 현실.
- update: 을 최신정보로 바꾸다, 갱신하다(= bring up to date).
- divorce: 와 이혼하다, 와 분리하다.

구문 설명

~, our actions become divorced from reality and we become progressively less competent (for reality). We find it impossible to cope (with reality).

Reading 05

Since Americans often lay their silverware down during the meal, certain customs have developed. **It is not considered good manners to leave a spoon in a soup bowl or coffee cup or any other dish.** It is put where it will lie flat but not on the tablecloth. By doing this, one is less likely to knock the silverware onto the floor or spill the food. Another difference in custom is that the American uses the side of the soupspoon, not the tip.

/Gladys Doty & Janet Ross. Language and Life in the U.S.A.

Word Bank

- silverware: 식탁용 은 그릇. 은 식기류 (포크, 나이프, 스푼 등).
- tablecloth: 식탁 보.
- knock: 치다. 두드리다.
- spill: 엎지르다. 흘리다.

Reading 06

Rather than hiding his family history Kamiya talked about it in his classroom and around Japan. At first he referred to his father obliquely, as an "acquaintance." But in 1995, a young Diet member declared that her generation bore no responsibility for wartime atrocities. That alarmed Kamiya. So he began speaking openly. **"It's not just a matter of telling the truth," he said. "It's more important how and why a warm-hearted person like my father got involved in a situation where he couldn't say 'No.'" Kamiya has made it his mission to teach Japanese children to think and act more independently to avoid repeating the mistakes of his father's generation.** But he sees worrying signs of a revival of the same kind of nationalistic thinking that motivated men like Minoru. Says Kamiya: "The ghosts of Unit 731 are still alive." /TIME.

Word Bank

- obliquely: 비스듬히, 완곡하게.
- Diet: (덴마크, 스웨덴, 일본 등의) 국회, 의회
- declare: 선언하다, 밝히다.
- warm - heated: 마음씨 따뜻한, 인정 많은.
- mission: 임무, 사명.
- independently: 독립하여, 자유롭게.
- revival: 부활, 재생.
- nationalistic: 국가주의적인, 민족주의적인.
- motivate: 동기를 부여하다, 자극하다.
- acquaintance: 알고 있는 사람.
- bear: 지다, 떠맡다.

Reading 07

It doesn't take an Einstein to recognize that Albert Einstein's brain was very different from yours and mine. The gray matter housed inside that shaggy head managed to revolutionize our concepts of time, space, motion-the very foundations of physical reality-not just once but several times during his astonishing career. Yet while there clearly had to be something remarkable about Einstein's brain, the pathologist who removed it from the great physicist's skull after his death reported that the organ was, to all appearances, well within the normal range-no bigger or heavier than anyone else's.

/Time.

Word Bank

- take: 필요로 하다, 걸리다.
- matter: 물질, 내용.
- house: 을 넣어두다, 저장하다.
- shaggy: 털이 텁수룩한.
- revolutionize: 을 근본적으로 바꾸다, 에 혁명을 일으키다.
- foundation; 기초, 토대.
- pathologist: 병리학자.
- skull: 두개골, 머리.
- organ: 기관.
- to all appearances: 어느모로 보나, 언뜻 보기에는.
- well: 완전히, 전적으로.

구문 설명

an Einstein: a great scientist like Einstein. "a + 고유명사 / the + 고유명사 + 한정어/고유명사 복수"는 "고유명사와 같은 사람(것)"의 뜻을 나타낸다. an Edison = an inventor like Edison; a Shakespeare = a dramatist like Shakespeare. He was the Edison of the age. (그는 당대의 에디슨과 같은 발명가였다.). There are many Shakespeares in his study. (그의 서재에는 세익스피어의 작품이 많다.).

Reading 08

I have just returned from a visit with my older brother. It was the first time we had seen each other in years. Thank God he had the integrity to call me as soon as he realized how much he had hurt and offended me during our last meeting. An aunt had told him how I felt after I cried on her shoulder. He called, told me how sorry he was, and thanked me for taking the call. When we got together, I discovered that he, too, was angry about something I had completely forgotten. I didn't even remember what it was that he had said or done that angered me; I just knew I was angry. We lost many years because of our lack of communication. Abby, please tell your readers to pick up the phone and call the one with whom they are angry and talk about it. Start with, "I am sorry and I miss you." **It doesn't matter who did or said what to whom. If you love the person with whom you are angry, make the call and work it out.**

/Dear Abby.

Word *Bank*

- Thank God that 절: 고맙게도.
- integrity: 성실, 정직.
- hurt: 다치게 하다, 상하게 하다.
- offend: 감정을 해치다, 불쾌감을 주다.
- cry on a person's shoulder: 괴로움을 하소연하다.
- get together: 모이다, 만나다.

Reading 09

Francesca Johnson set her brandy glass on the wide oak windowsill and stared at an eight-by-ten black-and -white photograph of herself. **Sometimes it was hard for her to remember how she looked then, twenty-two years ago.** In tight faded jeans, sandals, and a white T-shirt, her hair blowing in the morning wind as she leaned against a fence post.

/Robert James Waller. The Bridges of Madison County

Word Bank

- oak: 참나무.
- tight: 꼭 끼는, 째는.
- lean: 기대다.
- window sill: 창턱, 창 받침.
- fade: 희미해지다, 바래다.
- fence: 울타리.

구문 설명

"In tight faded jeans, sandals, and a white T-shirt, ~"에 주어와 동사 "She was"가 생략된 것으로 생각할 수 있다.

Reading 10

One day, climbing on Great Gable, he noticed a girl waving excitedly from a dangerous-looking ledge. Thinking she was in difficulties, he hastened toward her, but in doing so slipped himself and wrenched his ankle. **But it turned out she was not in difficulties at all.**

/James Hilton. Goodbye, Mr. Chips

Word Bank

- ledge: 돌출부, 암초.
- wrench: 삐게 하다.

구문 설명

1. "Thinking she was in difficulties, ~" = "As he thought she was in difficulties, ~."
2. "it turned out she was not in difficulties at all." = "it turned out (that) she was not in difficulties at all."

Reading 11

By observing sharks repeatedly over the years, Klimley was able to solve the long-standing mystery of why hammerheads gather in schools. It's clearly not for protection, since nothing preys on what Klimley calls "the big tough guys of the ocean." It turns out that they gather, at least in part, for an elaborate mating ritual, in which large, dominant females fight their way to the center of the school. The males know which females are most desirable by their position in the pack.

/TIME.

Word Bank

- long-standing: 오랫동안 계속되어온, 여러 해의.
- hammerhead: 귀상어, 해머의 대가리.
- school: 떼, 무리.
- prey: 잡아먹다(on).
- elaborate: 정교한, 정성들인.
- mating: 교미, 교배.
- ritual: 의식.
- dominant: 유력한, 지배적인.
- pack: 무리, 떼.
- desirable: 바람직한, 호감이 가는.

구문 설명

fight one's way: (이와 같은 표현은 "TOUGH"이동 연습문제 (6)에서 설명되고 있다)

Reading 12

Where the pundits contradict each other so flagrantly the field is open to enquiry. I hope that I am sufficiently up-to-date to recognize that anything written in the 1890's must be nonsense. But I am not yet advanced enough to be committed to the view that anything written in the 1950's necessarily makes sense. **Indeed, it may already have occurred to you that this enquiry is liable to stray into something even broader than the nature of history.**

/Edward Hallett Carr. What Is History?

Word Bank

- pundit: 박식한 사람, 전문가.
- flagrant: 언어도단의, 현저한.
- open: 받기 쉬운, 노출되어 있는 (to).
- enquiry: 조사, 연구.
- up-to-date: 최신의, 현대적인.
- make sense: 뜻이 통하다, 이치에 맞다.
- commit: 전념 시키다, 빠지게 하다.
- liable: 하기 쉬운(= apt).
- stray: 잘못 들어서다.

Reading 13

From the mid-1950's it became increasingly apparent that these industries were backward and waning in the industrial nations.
In the United States, for example, while the labor force grew by 21 percent between 1965 and 1974, textile employment rose by only 6 percent and employment in iron and steel actually dropped 10 percent. A similar pattern was evident in Sweden, Czechoslovakia, Japan, and other Second Wave nations.

/Alvin Toffler. The Third Wave

Word Bank

- wane: 이울다, 작아지다.
- labor force: 노동력, 노동인구.
- textile: 섬유(의), 직물(의).
- employment: 고용, 직업.

Reading 14

The main difficulties in fluent reading in a foreign language are vocabulary and sentence structure. To help you overcome these barriers, the materials in this volume are graded. **It is assumed that you already have a basic vocabulary of some three thousand English words and know something about the structure of the language.** Less commonly used words are introduced gradually and are repeated. The complexity of sentence structure gradually increases throughout the readings.

/Gladys Doty & Janet Ross. Language and Life in the U.S.A.

Word Bank

- barrier: 장벽, 장애.
- grade: 등급화 하다, 분류하다.
- volume: 책, 서적.

구문설명

~ and know something about the language. = ~ and know something about English.

Reading 15

It should also be remembered that writing only what is true is as important to a news story as good writing. The best writing in the world is of no value if the facts are wrong. A newspaper can get into trouble with the law if it prints things which are not true.

/M. L. Stein. How to Be a Journalist

Word Bank

- get into trouble: 말썽을 일으키다.

Reading 6

One particular group of postpartum women intrigued Jeanne and me. Though their initial complaints had to do with anxiety and over-concern about their baby, **it puzzled us that the dread these women described on the phone did not match the emotional state we observed once they came into the office.** On the phone they seemed overwrought with distress. "It's urgent," they would tell us. "I have to come in." Then they made frantic statements such as "I'm afraid to be alone with my baby," "I'm frightened of dropping or falling with the baby."

/Deborah Sichel & Jeanne Watson Driscoll. Women's Mood

Word *Bank*

- postpartum: 출산후의.
- intrigue: 흥미를 돋구다, 호기심을 자극하다.
- over-concern: 지나친 근심.
- puzzle: 당황케 하다, 혼란케 하다.
- dread: 근심, 불안.
- overwork: 과도하게 일을 시키다, 지나치게 흥분 시키다.
- distress: 고민, 고통.
- frantic: 정신 없는, 미쳐 날뛰는.
- urgent: 절박한, 긴급한.

Reading 6

One particular group of postpartum women intrigued Jeanne and me. Though their initial complaints had to do with anxiety and over-concern about their baby, **it puzzled us that the dread these women described on the phone did not match the emotional state we observed once they came into the office.** On the phone they seemed overwrought with distress. "It's urgent," they would tell us. "I have to come in." Then they made frantic statements such as "I'm afraid to be alone with my baby," "I'm frightened of dropping or falling with the baby."

/Deborah Sichel & Jeanne Watson Driscoll. Women's Mood

Word Bank

- postpartum: 출산후의.
- intrigue: 흥미를 돋구다, 호기심을 자극하다.
- over-concern: 지나친 근심.
- puzzle: 당황케 하다, 혼란케 하다.
- dread: 근심, 불안.
- overwork: 과도하게 일을 시키다, 지나치게 흥분 시키다.
- distress: 고민, 고통.
- frantic: 정신 없는, 미쳐 날뛰는.
- urgent: 절박한, 긴급한.

Reading 17

In general, the better the communication, the better your chance to exert influence. If questions of personal safety can be resolved, **it makes sense to establish a dialogue with terrorists,** whether they are holding hostages or threatening some act of violence. If you have a good case, you are more likely to influence them than they are to influence you.

/Roger Fisher & William Ury. Getting To Yes

Word Bank

- communication: 의사소통, 통신.
- chance: 가능성, 기회.
- exert: 행사하다, 발휘하다.
- resolve: 해결하다.
- make sense: 이치에 맞다, 뜻이 통하다.
- establish: 수립하다, 맺다.
- terrorist: 폭력주의자, 테러리스트.
- hostage: 인질.
- influence: 영향을 끼치다, 움직이다.

Reading 8

We are apt to think it inevitable that a man in Marner's position should have begun to question the validity of an appeal to the divine judgment by drawing lots; but to him this would have been an effort of independent thought such as he had never known; and he must have made the effort at a moment when all his energies were turn into the anguish of disappointed faith. If there is an angel who records the sorrows of men as well as their sins, he knows how many and deep are the sorrows that spring from false ideas for which no man is culpable.

/George Eliot. Silas Mariner

Word Bank

- apt: 경향이 있는, 하기 쉬운.
- validity: appeal: 간청, 호소.
- divine: 신의, 신성한.
- lot: 제비, 추첨.
- spring: 생기다.
- culpable: 비난할 만한.

구문 설명

"~ and he must have made the effort at a moment ~."에서 "must"는 추측(~임에 틀림없다)의 의미로 쓰이고 있다. 현재의 추측과 과거의 추측을 나타낼 때 쓰인다: 현재추측 : must R = It is certain that S + 현재동사 ~임에 틀림없다. 과거추측 : must have p.p = it is certain that S + 과거동사 ~이었음에 틀림없다. The rumor must be false.= It is certain that the rumor is false. The trip must have been very interesting. = It is certain that the trip was very interesting.

Reading 19

On April 25, 1985, the telephone rang at the offices of Texas Instruments in Dallas, Texas. A voice with a foreign accent asked for a meeting with a company security executive. A Syrian electrical engineer who sought political asylum in the United States, Sam Kuzbary had once worked at TI before being fired as a security risk. **Rumor had it that the CIA had helped him get out of Syria, where he had once worked for the Syrian military.** Kuzbary carried a gun in his car. Now, he said, he wanted to ingratiate himself with TI and get his job back. He had information, he said, about important secrets that had been stolen from TI.

/Alvin Toffler. Power Shift

Word Bank

- executive: 간부, 이사.
- asylum: 망명, 보호.
- fire: 해고하다.
- security risk: (국가 안전에 위협이 되는) 위험 인물.
- get out of : 도망치다.
- ingratiate::~의 비위를 맞추다.

구문 설명

Rumor had it that the CIA had helped him get ~ = According to rumor, the CIA had helped ~.

Reading 20

When the guests saw it that she fell down over the floor, they burst into shouts of mocking laughter. She was so ashamed that she would gladly have sunk into the earth. She rushed to the door and tried to escape, but on the stairs a man stopped her and brought her back.

/Brothers Grimm. King Thrushbeard

Word Bank

burst into: 갑자기 ~ 하다. mock: 비웃다, 업신여기다.

Reading 21

They now seemed quite at home in our presence, **so it astonished us that on the two following evenings Elsa left them at an open salt lick about a hundred yard away,** and we were also puzzled to know how she trained them to stay put while she enjoyed a good meal in full view of them. /Joy Adamson, Living Free

Word Bank

- at home: 편안한.
- presence: 존재, 출석.
- salt lick: 암염지, 함염지(동물이 소금을 핥으러 모이는 곳).
- puzzle: 당황케 하다.
- stay put: 움직이지 않고 있다, 변하지 않다.
- in view of: 이 보이는 곳에.

Reading 22

I find it wholesome to be alone the grater part of the time. To be in company, even with the best, is soon wearisome and dissipating. I love to be alone. I never found the companion that was so companionable as solitude. We are for the most part more lonely when we go abroad among men than when we stay in our chambers. A man thinking or working is always alone, let him be where he will. Solitude is not measured by the miles of space that intervene with a man and his fellows.

/Henry David Thoreau: Walden

Word Bank

- wholesome: 건전한, 유익한.
- in company: 함께(with).
- wearisome: 싫증나는, 지루한.
- dissipate: 낭비하다, 흩어지게 하다.
- companion: 친구, 동료.
- companionable: 사귐성이 좋은, 사교적인.
- solitude: 고독.
- chamber: 방. 회의실.
- intervene: 사이에 있다, 개입하다.

구문 설명

"~ let him be where he will. = wherever he will. "let + 목적어 + 동사원형 + 의문사 + 주어 + 조동사"는 양보구문을 만든다. Let him say what he will, I don't mind. = Whatever he may say, I don't mind; Let the work be what it may, you must do your best. = Whatever the work may be, you must do your best.

Reading 23

The judge then issued an order for Springsteen to be brought to the courtroom. Springsteen was brought up and the testimony of Jeffrey Harlow, a psychologist who treated Springsteen in West Virginia, was read back to them. The testimony included a portion about Springsteen seeking help for impulsive anger. Springsteen appeared more confident in the courtroom this morning. He winked at his wife who was seated in the front row. If the jury is unable to reach a decision by Friday night they will be sequestered again Judge Mike Lynch said; but **it is not clear whether they will come back on Monday or work through the weekend.**

/News 8 Austin

Word Bank

- issue: 내리다, 공포하다.
- courtroom: 법정.
- bring up: 기르다, 제기하다, 출두 시키다.
- testimony: 증언.
- psychologist: 심리학자, 정신과 의사.
- read back: 소리 내어 읽다.
- portion: 일부, 부분.
- impulsive: 충동적인.
- sequester: 물러나게 하다, 압수하다.

Reading 24

In the second part of the experiment, Lowe puts a sensor-equipped shark into the open bay and follows it as it darts back and forth. After two days of nonstop tracking, he and his exhausted crew have a precise record of where the baby has gone and, by counting its tail beats, how much energy it has used. "We still have a lot of data to gather," he says, "but once we really understand what role the hammerhead pups play here, we can use that to begin understanding how adults fit into the ecosystem of the open ocean." Back in Honolulu, on the other side of Oahu, the tiger-shark tagging is another high-tech effort to understand a different aspect of shark behavior. In 1992 two people were killed by tiger sharks in Hawaiian waters, the first such deaths there in three decades. **An earlier spate of killings had provoked an all-out program to eradicate tiger sharks, but it was never clear whether that slaughter had been really effective.**

/TIME.

Word Bank

- sensor: 감지 장치, 센서.
- bay: 만.
- dart: 날쌔게 움직이다, 돌진하다.
- tracking: 추적.
- exhausted: 기진맥진한, 지친.
- crew: 승무원, 조.
- beat: 고동, 치기.
- hammerhead: 귀상어.
- ecosystem: 생태계.
- fit: 적응하다.
- tag: 에 꼬리를 달다.
- high-tech: 첨단 기술의.
- water: 바다, 해역.
- spate: 대량, 다수.
- provoke: 자극하다, 유발하다.
- all-out: 총력을 기울인, 철저한.
- eradicate: 근절시키다, 전멸시키다.

Reading 25

In 1950, TIME named Winston Churchill Man of the Half-Century, saying "he launched the lifeboats" that saved liberty. You cited Churchill's unmatched career: 50 years of international prominence, the only person to hold high office in both World Wars, the only one to write of his experiences in language that will live as long as words are read. As the first person to proclaim publicly the Soviet threat, Churchill became the architect of the century's triumph over it. The twin victories over two great evils are this century's dominating achievements. Great movements still in progress--civil rights, gender equality, democratization, market capitalism--would be impossible, or at least retarded, in fascist or Marxist societies. **It is beyond imagination what life would be like today had Churchill not lived, acted, written and spoken as he did.**

/Time.

Word Bank

- name: 부르다, 지명하다.
- launch: 진수 시키다.
- lifeboat: 구명정, 구조선.
- cite: 을 입에 올리다, 치하하다.
- unmatched: 비할 데 없는, 무적의.
- career: 생애, 경력.
- prominence: 현저함, 탁월.
- proclaim: 공언하다, 선언하다.
- publicly: 공공연히, 대중의 이름으로.
- architect: 건축가, 설계자.
- triumph: 승리.
- twin: 쌍둥이의.
- two great evils = both World Wars. achievement: 업적, 공적.
- gender: 성.
- equality: 평등.
- democratization: 민주화.
- capitalism: 자본주의
- retard: 늦추다, 방해하다.
- fascist: 파시즘의.
- Marxist: 마르크스 주의의.

구문설명

" ~ what life would be like today had Churchill not lived, acted, written and spoken as he did. = ~ what life would be like today if Churchill had not lived, acted, written and spoken as he did." "if"가 생략되면서 주어와 조동사가 도치됨. 주어 조동사 도치편 참조.

Reading 26

The bodies, most found in and around their cars, were still in the tunnel Friday evening, left in place so investigators could conduct their inquiry. **It wasn't known when the bodies would be removed.** The fire raised questions about the emergency systems in the tunnel, which is equipped with ventilation equipment and 17 shelters, each of which can hold dozens of people. The shelters are designed to resist heat and poisonous fumes for two hours. Only a handful of the victims managed to reach the shelters. Many felt security measures were not enough.

/ABC News.

Word Bank

- in place: 적소에, 같은 곳에(≠out of place).
- investigator : 조사원.
- inquiry: 질문, 조사.
- equip: 갖추다, 설비하다.
- ventilation: 환기, 통풍.
- equipment: 설비, 장치.
- shelter: 피난처, 은신처.
- poisonous: 유독한, 유해한.
- fume: 연기, 연무.
- victim: 희생자, 피해자.
- handful: 소량, 소수.

구문 설명

The bodies, most found in and around their cars, were still in the tunnel ~ = The bodies, most of which were found in and around their cars, were still in the tunnel

Reading 27

At an evening news conference in Oslo, Steinar Killi said there had been no contact between the traffic managers and the engineers just before the crash, **although it was not clear why.** He also said no technical problems were found on the line today, so one of the trains apparently missed a stop signal. "It should not have happened," he said. "We have to find out whether this was a technical fault or human error."

/ABC News.

Word Bank

- news conference: 기자회견(press conference).
- crash: 충돌, 불시착.
- technical: 기술적인, 전문의.
- miss: 놓치다, 타지 못하다.

구문 설명

1. "~ although it was not clear why." = "~ although it was not clear why there had been no contact between traffic managers and the engineers just before the crash."
2. "It should not have happened. = I wish it had not happened." "should + have p.p."는 과거의 행위나 상태에 대해 바라는 대로 이루지 않은 것에 대한 비난 후회를 나타냄. You should have seen the movie. = You had to see the movie but you didn't. = I wish you had seen the movie.

Reading 28

It may seem like a dream come true - being able to buy things without having the money. But racking up debt by using credit cards is no way to ensure a good financial future. Credit cards are fairly easy to get, but you have to be disciplined and responsible to use them wisely. "Credit cards are a good way to establish credit and show you're responsible enough" to manage payments, said Paul Lavoie, a credit counselor with American Consumer Credit Counseling. "But if young people don't get their education on how to use credit cards responsibly, bad things happen."

/CNN.

Word Bank

- credit: 신용.
- rack up: 달성하다, 올리다.

구문 설명

Credit cards are fairly easy to get, but ~ = It is fairly easy to get credit cards, but ~. 주어인 Credit cards가 get의 목적어로부터 전치된 것임. 자세한 설명은 "TOUGH" 이동 참조.

Reading 29

It is no use being a writer if one is not in sympathy with the world in which one is living. The pen can be used for different purposes: for instance, either in support of prevailing tendencies or in opposition to them. But to be effective for any purpose in the writer's own day, the written word must reach the minds and touch the feelings of the writer's contemporaries. If a writer cannot do that, he might as well lay his manuscripts away in a safe, in the hope that, some day, there may be a generation for whom his words will come alive.

/Arnold Toynbee, Mankind the Inevitable

Word Bank

- sympathy: 동감, 조화, 공명(共鳴).
- prevailing: 일반적인. 보통의.
- tendency: 경향, 추세.
- touch: 감동시키다.
- might as well: 하는 편이 낫다(= had better).
- manuscript: 원고.
- safe: 금고.

Unit 3 탈명사구 외치 (Extraposition from Noun Phrase)

관계절, 동격절, 전치사구, 혹은 부정사구의 수식을 받는 명사구를 복합명사구라고 하는데, 이런 명사구로부터 수식하는 관계절, 동격절, 전치사구, 혹은 부정사구를 분리하여 문미로 이동하는 규칙을 탈명사구 외치(脫名詞句 外置) 라고 한다. 탈명사구 외치는 명사구가 너무 길어지는 것을 막기 위하여 후치시키는 것이다.

1 명사구로부터 분리되는 요소

1.1. 동 격 절

01 a. The thought that he had been lying occurred to me.

b. **The thought** occurred to me **that he had been lying.**
(그가 거짓말 하고 있다는 생각이 들었다.)

02 a. The question whether the earth will collide with another star arises.

b. **The question** arises **whether the earth will collide with another star.**
(지구가 다른 별과 충돌할 것인지에 대한 문제가 생긴다.)

1.2. 관 계 절

03 a. He found the boy whom he had hired waiting in his office.

b. He found **the boy** waiting in his office **whom he had hired.**
(그는 그가 고용했던 소년이 사무실에서 기다리고 있다는 것을 알았다.)

04 a. The boss whom the staff respect much is very generous.

b. **The boss** is very generous **whom the staff respect much.**
(직원들이 대단히 존경하는 그 사장님은 아주 관대한 분이시다.)

1.3. 부 정 사 절

05 a. Permission for her to leave early was granted.

b. **Permission** was granted **for her to leave early.**
(그녀가 일찍 떠나도 된다는 허락이 떨어졌다.)

06 a. The time to decorate the house for Christmas has come.

b. **The time** has come **to decorate the house for Christmas.**
(크리스마스를 맞이해 집을 장식할 때가 왔다.)

1.4. 전치사구

07 a. A student with long hair came to see me yesterday.

b. **A student** came to see me yesterday **with long hair.**
(머리가 긴 학생이 어제 나를 만나러 왔다.)

2 보충 설명

08 a. A student of physics came to see me yesterday.
(물리학을 공부하는 학생이 어제 나를 만나러 왔다.)

b. ***A student** came to see me yesterday **of physics.**

예문 (7)과 예문 (8)은 겉으로 보기에 같은 구조로 보이지만 후자에서의 전치사구 "of physics"는 "student"의 의미상의 목적어 역할을 하고 있다. 즉, "a person who studies physics"라고 바꿔 쓸 수 있지만 예문 (7)에서는 그럴 수 없다. 이처럼 목적어 관계를 이루는 전치사구는 후치시킬 수 없다.

Practice Examples

Reading 01

Although the Chinese government has invested considerable political capital--and won plaudits from around the world--with repeated pledges not to devalue the renminbi, there are strong pressures to do so. Beijing knows the dangers: it has watched as devaluations in Thailand, South Korea, Indonesia and, most recently, neighboring Russia have gutted those countries' economies. **But signs are growing that Beijing has reached its pain threshold** and, according to a private economist with sources close to the leadership, the government is considering a devaluation of the renminbi early next year to stop further erosion of exports. The devaluation could amount to as much as 30%, depending on external factors, in particular the value of the Japanese yen.

/Time.

Word Bank

- renminbi: 인민폐(중국의 통화).
- plaudit: 칭찬, 박수갈채.
- pledge: 공약, 언질.
- watch as 주어 + 술어: 주어가 술어 하는 것을 지켜보다.
- devaluation: 평가 절하.
- threshold: 문지방, 입구.
- gut: 의 내부를 파괴하다, 의 내장을 꺼내다.

Reading 02

The water was cold and in flood and **many things passed that had been floated off the banks when the river rose.** I was lucky to have a heavy timber to hold on to, and I lay in the icy water with my chin on the wood, holding as easily as I could with both hands. I was afraid of cramps and I hoped we would move towards the shore. I went down the river in a long curve. It was beginning to be light enough so I could see the bushes along the shoreline.

/Earnest Hemingway. A Farewell to Arms

Word Bank

- float: 떠다니다, 표류하다.
- hold on to: 을 꼭 잡고 있다, 에 매달리다.
- hole: 버티다, 견디다.
- in a long curve: 긴 곡선을 그리며.
- timber: 목재, 통나무.
- cramp: 경련

구문 설명

"and I lay in the icy water with my chin on the wood, holding on as easily~" 에서 "with my chin on the wood"은 "my chin"과 "on the wood"가 주술관계. (WITH 주술관계 참조)

Reading 03

On the day of Mama's return to the village, most of its inhabitants were out in the fields. She walked into a hut she knew to be empty on the outskirts of the village-no one wanted to live there because it was remote and cramped - and began cleaning it up. She was beyond caring what would happen; all she wanted to do was rest. When people returned from the day's work, **word spread quickly that the village's firebrand was back.** But while no one offered hostility at first, no one offered welcome either. She was tolerated but not embraced. Her family wouldn't visit her. Whatever friends she may have had couldn't risk the disgrace of being seen with her. From that moment on, she remained on the periphery of village life. No one said anything when she quietly returned to her old place in the rice field. No one spoke to her at all.

I don't know how Mama managed when the time came for my birth. Perhaps the village midwife decided to ignore Mama's dishonorable status in return for payment. Perhaps Mama was left to her own devices. At any rate, I was born healthy. Mama now had a child and an ally. Now there was someone who didn't care about her status or her past sins. There was someone who needed her, loved her, and wanted to spend every moment with her.

/Elizabeth Kim. 2000. Ten Thousand Sorrows. p. 15

Word Bank

- inhabitant: 살고있는 사람, 주민.
- field: 들판, 분야.
- hut: 오두막, 임시가옥.
- outskirt: 교외, 변두리.
- cramped: 경련하는, 비좁고 갑갑한.
- firebrand: 횃불, 선동자.
- hostility: 적의, 적개심.
- disgrace: 불명예, 망신.
- periphery: 원조, 외부.
- midwife: 조산원, 산파.
- dishonorable: 불명예스러운, 창피한.
- device: 궁리, 계획.
- leave a person to his own devices: (조언도 도움도 주지 않은 채)남에게 제 마음대로 하게 하다.
- ally: 동맹국, 연합국.

Reading 04

What Chun will do about the two Kims is not clear. **Rumors have been circulating around Seoul that Chun plans to do away with the last vestiges of political ban before he travels to Washington in April.** But analysts in Seoul believe it unlikely that Chun will allow Kim Dae Jung back into politics any time soon. Even so, his rival's return has clearly put the president in a quandary. If Chun lets Kim go, he risks igniting the opposition and suffering a greater loss of authority. But as long as he keeps him muzzled, it may be hard to convince many South Koreans-and much of the international community-that he is genuinely interested in bringing democracy to South Korea.

/Newsweek.

Word Bank

- circulate: 퍼지다, 돌다.
- do away with: 죽이다.
- vestige: 흔적, 자국.
- ban: 금지, 규제.
- ignite: 점화하다, 에 불을 붙이다.
- quandary: 궁지, 곤혹.
- let go: 자유롭게 해주다, 석방하다.
- suffer: 입다, 받다.
- authority: 권위, 위신.
- muzzle: 에 재갈을 물리다.

구문 설명

"But analysts in Seoul believe it unlikely that Chun will allow Kim Dae Jung back into politics any time soon."에서 "it"은 "that"이하 절을 받고 있다. (외치 구문 참조)

Reading 05

As a matter of fact the sense of sin, so far from being a cause of a good life, is quite the reverse. It makes a man unhappy and it makes him feel inferior. Being unhappy, **he is likely to make claims upon other people which are excessive and which prevent him from enjoying happiness in personal relations.** Feeling inferior, he will have a grudge against those who seem superior. He will find admiration difficult and envy easy. He will become a generally disagreeable person, and will find himself more and more solitary.

/Bertrand Russell. The Conquest of Happiness

Word Bank

- as a matter of fact: 사실.
- far from ~ing: ~이기는커녕.
- inferior: 열등한.
- grudge: 원한, 유감.
- disagreeable: 마음에 들지 않는, 사귀기 어려운.

Reading 06

To put the proportions of the epidemic in perspective, consider that more people have died from AIDS over the past 20 years than from any other disease in human history, and more than 25 million Africans are infected. The cruel implication is that the virus is undermining the continent's prospects for emerging from poverty. And that poverty, in turn, functions as a virtual catalyst for the epidemic by limiting the continent's ability to contain it. **The question remains, however, what should be done?** Some governments have done a courageous and laudable job of acknowledging and dealing effectively with their AIDS crisis. Uganda, for example, has succeeded in lowering infection rates from 14 percent in 1989 to 8 percent by 1997, mostly by employing a public-awareness campaign.

/Washington Times.

Word Bank

- epidemic: 유행병(여기에서 the epidemic은 문맥상 AIDS를 나타낸다).
- in perspective: 올바른 균형으로, 진상을 올바르게.
- AIDS: 후천성 면역 결핍증(Acquired Immunodeficiency Syndrome).
- infect: 전염시키다, 감염시키다.
- cruel: 잔인한, 가혹한.
- implication: 함축, 암시.
- undermine: 의 밑을 파다, 해치다.
- emerge: 나타나다, 부상하다.
- poverty: 가난, 빈곤.
- virtual: 사실사의, 실제의.
- catalyst: 촉매.
- contain: 포함하다, 억제하다.
- courageous: 용기있는, 용감한.
- laudable: 칭찬받을 만한.

구문설명

"The question remains, however, what should be done?"와 같은 문장에서 "The question"과 의문사절/구가 나란히 놓이거나 떨어져 사용된다.

때로는 사이에 "of," "as to," "about"등이 함께 쓰이기도 한다. I have been asked to speak on the question (as to) how to make the best of life. (나는 인생을 어떻게 해서 가장 선용할 것인지에 관한 문제를 놓고 연설을 해달라고 요청을 받았다.)

Reading 07

Great history is written precisely when the historian's vision of the past is illuminated by insights into the problems of the present. **Surprise has often been expressed that Mommsen failed to continue his history beyond the fall of the republic.** He lacked neither time, nor opportunity, nor knowledge. But, when Mommsen wrote his history, the strong man had not yet arisen in Germany. During his active career, the problem of what happened once the strong man had taken over was not yet actual. Nothing inspired Mommsen to project this problem back on to the Roman scene; and the history of the empire remained unwritten.

/E. H. Carr. What is history?

Word Bank

- illuminate: 비추다, 조명하다.
- career: 생애, 활동.
- take over: 이어받다.
- beyond: 한 후에.
- strong man: 독재자, 실력자.
- inspire: 이끌다, 부추기다.

Reading 08

He waited, expecting that she would call out to him to bring it in to her. But she did not. She came to the door and through the crack her hand reached out and took the reed. She said no word, but he heard her panting as an **animal** pants **which has run for a long way.**

/Pearl Buck. The Good Earth

Word Bank

- call out: 큰 소리로 외치다.
- reach out: 손을 뻗다.
- pant: 숨차다, 헐떡거리다.
- crack: 문의 틈.
- reed: 갈대.

Reading 09

Slowly, painfully, over the next weeks, Nachum shook off his paralysis. He became fully able to move his hands and his legs. Not every day was a good one. There were setbacks. **The muscles often malfunctioned that controlled his ability to swallow, and he developed infections in his lung.** We redoubled our prayers, and with the help of medication this threat was banished.

/Guideposts

Word Bank

- shake off: 고치다, 떨쳐버리다.
- paralysis: 마비, 중풍.
- setback: 패배, 좌절.
- malfunction: 정상적으로 움직이지 않다. 제대로 돌지 않다.
- develop: 발현시키다, 발병시키다.
- infection: 감염, 전염.
- lung: 폐.
- redouble: 배가하다, 증가하다.
- medication: 약물치료, 투약.
- banish: 추방하다, 몰아내다.
- threat: 협박, 조짐.

Reading 10

The subway car was empty except for two women sitting across from me. We rattle along, making several stops. Then at Thirty-fourth Street, as the doors opened and closed, **the thought occurred to me that I was no longer concerned about my next step.**

/Guideposts.

Word Bank

- across from: 의 바로 맞은 편에.
- rattle: 덜걱덜걱 소리 내며 가다.
- occur: 문득 생각나다, 떠오르다.

Reading 11

In ecosystems as in social systems, causes and effects are often widely separated in both time and space. Accordingly, our interventions often yield unexpected consequences. **We find the horrible truth after years of spraying persistent pesticides to kill insects that we have come close to wiping out a national symbol, the bald eagle:** concentrated through food chain, pesticides accumulate in the tissues of eagles and certain other birds to the point of impairing reproduction.

/William Bowen. What is Ecology?

Word Bank

- ecosystem: 생태계.
- intervention: 개입, 중재.
- yield: 산출하다, 가져오다.
- pesticide: 살충제.
- persistent: 집요한, 지속적인, 분해하기 어려운.
- come close to ~ing: 하마터면 ~할 뻔하다.
- wipe out: 일소하다, 없애다.
- bald eagle: 흰머리 독수리.
- concentrate: 집중하다, 농축하다.
- tissue: 조직.
- impair: 손상시키다, 악화시키다.

Reading 12

The rush to offshore oil drilling, meanwhile, has obscured the possibility of "growing oil" in the sea. Dr. Lawrence Raymond at the Battelle Memorial Institute has demonstrated that it is possible to produce algae with a high oil content, and **efforts are under way to make the process economically effective.**

/Alvin Toffler. The Third Wave

Word Bank

- offshore: 앞바다의, 근해의.
- drill: 구멍을 뚫다.
- obscure: 희미하게 하다, 어둡게 하다.
- demonstrate: 논증하다, 설명하다.
- alga: 해조(= seaweed).
- under way: 진행중인.

Reading 13

On Sept. 5, 1972, the Olympic Games in Munich became the scene of a horrifying tragedy: 11 Israeli athletes were assassinated by a Palestinian terrorist group which called itself "Black September," a covert unit of the Palestine Liberation Organization. Could such an atrocity happen again? Yes. **The odds are high it could happen at the 2004 Olympic Games with this difference:** This time the target would be American athletes. Incredible? In Greece, scene of the 2004 Olympics, assassinations of an American diplomat, three American military officers, and the wounding with intent to kill of 30 U.S. officials has occurred over the last 25 years. Even more incredible is that during this reign of terror, there have been no arrests, no suspects, no convictions, no serious police investigations. The Greek government has done nothing yes, nothing to apprehend the criminals, let alone to identify them. In Greece, assassination of Americans has become established routine. Most recently terrorists bombarded the U.S. Embassy in central Athens and assassinated the British defense attache. Earlier, attempts on the lives of the Dutch and German ambassadors were made. No arrests, no suspects, no convictions, no serious investigations.

/Washington Times.

Word Bank

- horrifying: 소름 끼치는, 무서운.
- athlete: 운동선수, 경기자.
- assassinate: 암살하다.
- covert: 은밀한, 숨은.
- unit: 단위, 부대, 조직.
- atrocity: 포악, 잔혹.
- odds: 차이, 가능성.
- incredible: 믿어지지 않는
- scene: 장소, 현장.
- diplomat: 외교관.
- military: 군의, 군인의.
- reign of terror: 공포의 순간, 무서운 일이 일어나는 기간.
- arrest: 체포, 검거.
- suspect: 용의자, 수상쩍은 사람.
- conviction: 확신, 유죄의 판결.
- yes: 게다가, 더구나.
- apprehend: 이해하다, 염려하다, 체포하다.
- let alone: 은 말할 것도 없이.
- routine: 틀에 박힌 일, 관례.
- established: 확립된, 기정의.
- bombard: 폭탄을 투하하다.
- embassy: 대사관.
- attache: 수행원, 대사관원.

구문 설명

1. The odds are high it could happen at the 2004 Olympic Games with this difference. = The odds (that) it could happen at the 2004 Olympic Games with this difference are high.
2. "Even more incredible is that ~."에서 주어는 "that ~."이며 비교 요소가 문두에 오면서 주어 동사가 도치되어 있음. (주어 조동사 도치 참조)

Reading 14

"High-definition TV" is to today's home video screen what the compact disc is to the scratchy platter played on great-grandma's gramophone. High definition can put **pictures** on the TV screen **that match the quality of the best big-screen movies.** It can make an image blast off the computer monitor looking as bright and sharp as the finest printed page.

/Alvin Toffler. Power Shift

Word Bank

- high-definition: 고화질의, 고선명도의.
- scratchy: 긁히는 소리가 나는.
- platter: 큰 접시, 음반.
- great-grandma: 증조 할머니(= great-grandmother).
- match: 에 필적하다.
- image: 화상.
- blast: 망쳐놓다, 해치우다.

구문 설명

"High-definition TV" is to today's home video screen what the compact disc is to the scratchy platter played on great grandma's gramophone."의 구문은 "A is to B what C is to D."의 구문임. "A의 B에 대한 관계는 C의 D에 대한 관계와 같다."로 주로 옮긴다. 비슷한 표현으로는 다음과 같은 표현이 있다. A is to B as C is to D. = A is that to B which C is to D. = As C is to D, so is A to B.(so A is to B) = What C is to D, that is A to B. 이들 표현에서 전치사 "to"는 "related to"의 의미이다.

Reading 15

Every Friday five crates of oranges and lemons arrived from a fruiterer in New York--every Monday these same oranges and lemons left his back door in a pyramid of pulpless halves. **There was a machine in the kitchen which could extract the juice of two hundred oranges in half an hour** if a little button was pressed two hundred times by a butler's thumb.

/F.Scott Fitzgerald. The Great Gatsby

Word *Bank*

- crate: 나무 상자, 대바구니.
- fruiterer: 과일 장수.
- pulpless: 과육이 제게된.
- extract: 짜내다, 추출하다.
- butler: 집사, 식당 관리인.

Reading 16

Have you ever wondered what happened to the 56 men who signed the Declaration of Independence? Five signers were captured by the British as traitors and tortured before they died. Twelve had their homes ransacked and burned. **Two lost their sons who served in the Revolutionary Army.** Another had two sons captured. Nine of the 56 fought and died from wounds or hardships of the Revolutionary War. They pledged their lives, their fortunes and their sacred honor. What kind of men were they? Twenty-four were lawyers and jurists. Eleven were merchants. Nine were farmers and plantation owners. All were men of means and well-educated, but they signed the Declaration of Independence, knowing that the penalty would be death if they were captured.

/Ann Landers.

Word Bank

- Declaration of Independence: 미국 독립선언(서).
- capture: 붙잡다, 체포하다.
- traitor: 반역자, 매국노.
- torture: 괴롭히다, 고문하다.
- ransack: 샅샅이 뒤지다, 철저히 찾다.
- burn: 불태우다.
- serve: 복무하다.
- Revolutionary War: 미국 독립 전쟁(= American Revolution).
- hardship: 고난, 고초.
- pledge: 걸다, 맹세하다.
- sacred: 신성한, 종교의.
- jurist: 법학자.
- means: 재산.
- penalty: 형벌, 벌금.

Reading 17

"Every company must have the ability to innovate and improve its products," Gates said from the company's Redmond, Wash., headquarters. But the world's richest man conceded, "The legal process can be hard on anyone who goes through it." As for settlement talks, Gates said: "It's absolutely worth making an effort there." The Justice Department and state attorneys generals who brought the case also found victory in the conclusion that Microsoft operated an illegal monopoly. But the government and states might still appeal to the Supreme Court, try to negotiate a settlement or go back to the lower court to seek new penalties. **Political pressure mounted for the Bush administration to seek a settlement.**

/Associated Press.

Word Bank

- innovate: 혁신하다, 쇄신하다.
- headquarters: 본부, 본사.
- concede: 인정하다, 승인하다.
- go through: 겪다, 경험하다.
- settlement: 정착, 해결.
- bring: 제기하다, 제출하다.
- attorney general: 법무 장관, 검찰총장.
- operate: 운전하다, 경영하다.
- monopoly: 전매, 독점.
- appeal: 항소하다, 상고하다.
- Supreme Court: 대법원, 최고 법원.
- penalty: 형벌, 벌금.
- mount: 오르다, 늘다.

구문 설명

the world's richest man = Gates

Reading 18

First lady Laura Bush ignores television comedy attacks on her husband, shrugs off tabloid gossip about her daughters and concentrates her energy where she thinks she can do the most good: promoting education.
"I miss teaching. I love teaching. And **I have the opportunity, because I visit schools all the time, to still read with children and work with children,"** Bush said during an interview on CNN's Larry King Live. She said she was surprised and thrilled about the forum she gained by moving into the White House. She plans to use that extra influence to encourage more people to consider teaching as a profession. She especially likes two programs. "Troops to Teachers" helps pay tuition for retired military to get a teaching certificate or a master's in education. "Teach for America" benefits young recent college graduates who commit to teaching at least two years in rural or inner city areas.

/CNN.

Word Bank

- attack: 공격, 비난.
- shrug: 움츠리다, 무시하다(off).
- gossip: 험담, 뜬 소문.
- tabloid: 타블로이드 신문.
- good: 이익, 효용.
- forum: 공개 토론의 장, 비난. (여기에서는 "that extra influence"와 관계를 볼 때에 "influence"라는 의미로 쓰임).
- profession: 직업, 전문 직업.
- tuition: 수업료.
- troop: 무리, 부대, 군대.
- certificate: 증명서, 자격증.
- master: 주인, 석사.
- benefit: 혜택을 주다.
- graduate: 졸업생.
- commit: 전념하다, 헌신하다.

구문 설명

"I have the opportunity, because I visit schools all the time, to still read with children and work with children,"에서 후치는 목적어가 길어서 라기 보다는 부사절의 삽입에 의해서 이루어진 것이다.

Reading 9

Dr. Tim Oliver, professor of medical oncology at St. Bartholomew's Hospital and the Royal London Hospital, has found that although men are more likely to seek help than they were 15 years ago, around a third of those finding a symptom still wait at least three months before they see a doctor. Experiencing the trauma of cancer has given me a special bond with my patients. At least once a fortnight in my work as a gynecologist, I have to break the news to a woman that she has cancer of the ovary, womb or cervix.

/Reader's Digest.

Word Bank

- oncology: 종양학.
- symptom: 증후, 증상.
- trauma: 정신적 상처.
- bond: 유대, 결속.
- fortnight: 2주간, 14일.
- gynecologist: 부인과 의사.
- break: 알리다, 전하다.
- ovary: 난소.
- womb: 자궁.
- cervix: 경부.

Reading 20

There is a street in Copenhagen with a very strange name. It is called "Hysken" street. Where the name came from, and what it means is very uncertain. It is said to be German, but that is unjust to the Germans, for it would then be called "Hauschen," not "Hysken." "Hauschen," means a little house; and for many years it consisted only of a few small houses, which were scarcely larger than the wooden booths we see in the market places at fair time. They were perhaps a little higher, and had windows; but the panes consisted of horn or bladder-skins, for glass was then too dear to have glazed windows in every house. This was a long time ago, so long indeed that our grandfathers, and even great-grandfathers, would speak of those days as "olden times;" indeed, many centuries have passed since then.

/Hans Christian Andersen. The Old Bachelor's Nightcap

Word Bank

- consist of: 으로 구성되다.
- booth: 오두막, 판자집.
- pane: 창유리, 창틀.
- bladder: 방광, 부레.
- wooden: 목재의, 목재로 만든.
- fair: 박람회, 정기적으로 서는 장.
- horn: 뿔.
- glaze: 에 유리를 끼우다.

Unit 4 복합명사구 이동 (Complex Noun Phrase Shift)

관계절, 동격절, 전치사구, 혹은 부정사구의 수식을 받는 명사구를 복합명사구(複合名詞句) 라고 한다. 이런 복합명사구가 해당 문장 내에서 목적어 역할을 하고 그 목적어 뒤에 다른 문장 성분이 있을 때 그 명사구 전체를 문미로 이동하는 규칙을 복합명사구 이동이라고 한다. 복합명사구 이동은 동사와 목적어 뒤에 놓여 있는 보어나 전치사구와 긴밀성을 유지하기 위함이며 때로는 문장의 중의성(ambiguity)을 없애줄 수 있다. 이런 명사구는 일반적으로 문미로 옮기는 것이 더 좋은 표현이며, 반드시 후치시켜야 되는 경우도 많다.

1 복합 명사구 이동이 일어나는 구조

1.1. 동사+목적어+전치사구/부사

01 a. He explained all the terrible problems that he had encountered to her.

b. He explained to her **all the terrible problems that he had encountered.**
(그는 그가 접했던 모든 끔찍한 문제들을 그녀에게 설명해주었다.)

02 a. He says that the meeting was in Seoul yesterday expressly.

b. He says expressly **that the meeting was in Seoul yesterday.**
(그는 그 모임이 어제 서울에서 있었다고 분명하게 말하고 있다.)

1.2. 동사+목적어+보어

03 a. *He made that he was interested in the peaceful use of atomic energy clear.

b. He made **it** clear **that he was interested in the peaceful use of atomic energy.** (외치 구문)

c. He made clear **that he was interested in the peaceful use of atomic energy.**
(그는 원자력을 평화적으로 사용하는데 관심이 있다는 것을 분명히 했다.)

04 a. He thought most of the women in the room desirable.

b. He thought desirable **most of the women in the room.**
(그는 방안에 있는 여자들 대부분이 매력이 있다고 생각했다.)

2 보충 설명

05 a. He understood what I said perfectly.
(그는 내가 말한 것을 완벽하게 이해했다. 그는 내가 완벽하게 했던 말을 이해했다.)

b. He understood perfectly **what I said.**
(그는 내가 말한 것을 완벽하게 이해했다.)

예문 (5a)와 같은 경우에는 중의성(ambiguity)이 있을 수가 있다. 다시 말해 부사 "perfectly"가 바로 앞에 놓인 동사 "said"를 수식할 수도 있고, "understood"를 수식할 수도 있기 때문이다. 반면에 예문 (5b)에서는 "perfectly"가 "understood"만을 수식할 수 있다.

06 a. He made his position clear.
(그는 그의 입장을 분명히 했다.)

b. *He made clear his position.

예문 (6b)에서처럼 목적어가 짧은 경우에는 복합명사구가 아니기 때문에 후치시키지 않는다.

Practice Examples

Reading 01

The Dutch senate voted this week on euthanasia, passing into law **a bill that had been approved by the lower house of parliament last fall.** With the vote, the Netherlands becomes the first country in the world to legalize voluntary euthanasia. Though the law outlines strict criteria that must be followed before the request for euthanasia is granted, many critics voiced their concern about allowing one person to kill another, the role of physicians, and how the policy might be abused. **Passage of the law brings into the public arena a practice that has been going on for many years in the Netherlands,** although it until now has not been formally endorsed by the government. It rekindles the debate about how far individuals should be allowed to control their life and death, and who if anyone should be allowed to help them. Should the Dutch be proud or ashamed of their historic first, and what will it mean for the rest of Europe and the world?

/CNN.

Word Bank

- senate: 상원.
- euthanasia: 안락사(= easy and painless death).
- vote: 찬반 투표를 하다.
- pass: 가결하다, 통과하다.
- legalize: 합법화하다, 법률화 하다.
- outline: 의 윤곽을 그리다, 의 개요를 말하다.
- passage: 통행, 통과.
- arena: 활동장소, 무대.
- go on: 일어나다.
- endorse: 승인하다, 배서하다.

구문 설명

"~ about how far individuals should be allowed to control their life and death, and who if anyone should be allowed to help them."에서 "who"와 "if"사이에 앞에서 언급된 "should be allowed to control their life and death"가 생략되어 있다.

Reading 02

It is a terrible thing to be sixteen and never to have shaved. **On my birthday I received as a gift the most modern razor on the market.** "You will be needing it soon," my father said, with a confident wink. Every morning I searched the mirror, but the new year began without the slightest shadow on my face.

/Reader's Digest.

Word Bank

- terrible: 끔찍한, 무시무시한.
- razor: 면도기.
- confident: 확신하는, 자신 있는.
- search: 수색하다, 유심히 살피다.
- shadow: 그림자, ~한 기미.
- shave: 면도하다.

Reading 03

Life expectancy estimates, however, are just that -- estimates. Atlanta-based geriatrician Dr. Jeff Lesesne advised caution when trying to predict how long a patient may survive after diagnosis. "The course of events can be variable in the patient, and so **it's hard to predict exactly what someone is going to experience,"** he said. Alzheimer's disease attacks the nerve cells of the brain and impairs a person's memory, coordination and control over emotions. In its last stages, the disease robs its victims of all mental functioning.

/CNN.

Word Bank

- life expectancy: 평균 여명(餘命).
- estimate: 견적, 견해.
- geriatrician: 노인병학자, 노인병전문의.
- diagnosis: 진단, 진찰.
- nerve: 신경.
- impair: 손상시키다, 약화시키다.
- coordination: 조정, 공동작업.

Reading 04

When we compare the overall pace of First Wave or agrarian systems of wealth creation with that of Second Wave or industrial systems, it makes clear that smokestack economies run faster than traditional agricultural economies. Wherever the industrial revolution passed, it shifted economic processes into a higher gear.

/Alvin Toffler. Powershift

Word Bank

- overall : 전반적인, 종합적인.
- or: 말하자면, 즉.
- gear: 기어, 전동 장치.
- agrarian: 농지의, 농업의.
- smokestack: 공장 굴뚝.

Reading 05

The Human Genome Project is an international consortium supported mostly by the U.S. National Institutes of Health and the Wellcome Trust, a philanthropic organization based in London. Celera Genomics is a private company in Rockville, Maryland. The high level of international cooperation was instrumental in accomplishing so much of the project so quickly, the NIH's Collins said Monday. Although the public and private groups are using different methods in their human genome projects, they both have as a goal the discovery of the chemicals of the approximately 80,000 genes that make up the human body.

/CNN.

Word Bank

- genome: 30억쌍의 유전정보가 담겨 있는 46개의 인간 염색체 집합(gene + chromosome).
- consortium: 자본 연합, 공동체.
- philanthropic: 박애주의의, 자선 사업의.
- instrumental: 도움이 되는, 유익한.

Reading 06

No man can shave every morning for twenty or thirty years without learning something. Even if he is too lazy to shave himself, and submits himself to barbers, he cannot escape learning something about human nature by the time he is middle-aged. **For barbers contain in their ranks every variety of human nature.**

/Robert Lynd: A Sermon on Shaving

Word Bank

- shave: 면도하다.
- 부정어 + can + A + without B: B 하지 않고는A할 수 없다, A하면 반드시 B하게 된다.
- submit: 순종하게 하다, 복종시키다.
- barber: 이발사.
- escape: 피하다.
- rank 신분, 지위, 부류.

구문 설명

No man can shave every morning for twenty or thirty years without learning something. = No man can shave every morning for twenty or thirty years but he learns something.

Reading 07

Books are to mankind what memory is to the individual. They contain the history of our race, the discoveries we have made, the accumulated knowledge and experience of ages; **they picture for us the marvels and beauties of nature;** help us in our difficulties, comfort us in sorrow and in suffering, change hours of weariness into moments of delight, store our minds with ideas, fill them with good and happy thoughts, and lift us out of and above ourselves. There is an Oriental story of two men: one was a king, who every night dreamt he was a beggar; the other was a beggar, who every night dreamt he was a prince and lived in a palace.

/Lord Avebury: The Use of Life

Word Bank

- contain: 내포하다, 포함하다(= include).
- accumulate: 축적하다, 쌓다.
- marvel: 경이, 경탄.
- comfort: 위로하다.
- store: 저장하다, 공급하다.
- Oriental: 동양의, 동양풍의(Occidental).

구문 설명

A is to B what C is to D: "탈명사구 외치" 연습문제 14번 참조

Reading 08

Adolescent pregnancy and childbirth are current issues of great concern to citizens and policymakers. **They made clear that experiencing sexual abuse as an adolescent puts girls at higher risk for pregnancy.** An average of 29 Missouri teens gave birth each day in 1993. High pregnancy and birth rates are creating a generation of young people who are ill-equipped to meet the demands of parenthood.

/http://www.aecf.org/kidscount

Word Bank

- policymaker: 정책 입안자.
- abuse: 남용, 학대.
- be equipped to ~: ~할 수 있다.
- parenthood: 부모임.

Reading 09

Perhaps it is only in childhood that books have any deep influence on our lives. In later life we admire, we are entertained and we may modify some viewers we already hold, but **we are more likely to find in books merely a confirmation of what is in our minds already.**

/Graham Green. The Lost Childhood

Word Bank

- in later life: 만년(晩年).
- admire: 감탄하다, 찬양하다.
- entertain: 을 재미나게 하다, 을 즐겁게 하다.
- modify: 바꾸다, 수정하다.
- confirmation: 확인.

구문 설명

"Perhaps it is only in childhood that books have any deep influence on our lives." 에서는 전치사구 "only in childhood"를 강조하기 위해 분열 구문을 사용하고 있다. 자세한 설명은 "분열 구문"편에서 다루어진다.

Reading 10

I pulled from my bag photographs of the aftermath. The executive to my left looked through them with an expression of horror. Then he said, "I don't want these." He slid the pictures over to the Colonel, who looked at them and gently returned them to me.

/Harper's.

Word Bank

- aftermath: 여파, 결과.
- executive: 간부, 이사.
- slide: 슬그머니 주다.
- colonel: 대령.

Reading 11

In fact, U.S. and Western intelligence sources have confirmed that several hundred Russian engineers and technicians travel regularly to missile facilities outside Teheran, helping the Iranians draw up missile-production blueprints. **Russia may have transferred to Iran a supercomputer made by a U.S. company to complete the work.** And when the Iranians run into technical snags, they fly to top-secret military institutes in Russia to see how the Russians solved similar problems.

/Reader's Digest.

Word Bank

- intelligence: 정보, 첩보.
- source: 소식통, 출처.
- draw up: 작성하다.
- blueprint: 설계도, 청사진.
- transfer: 옮기다, 전하다.
- run into: 에 부딪치다, 을 우연히 만나다.
- snag: 장애, 곤란.
- top-secret: 극비의.

Reading 12

It was nine o'clock --almost immediately afterwards I looked at my watch and found it was ten. Mr. McKee was asleep on a chair with his fists clenched in his lap, like a photograph of a man of action. **Taking out my handkerchief I wiped from his cheek the remains of the spot of dried lather that had worried me all the afternoon.**

/F. Scott Fitzgerald. The Great Gatsby

Word Bank

- fist: 주먹.
- clench: 을 단단히 쥐다, 을 악물다.
- a man of action: 활동가.
- lather: 비누 거품. 땀.
- worry: 의 속을 태우다.

구문설명

"~ with his fists clenched in his lap, ~"은 "with + 목적어 + 과거분사"형태를 취하고 있다. 자세한 설명은 "WITH" 주술관계 참조.

Reading 13

Dorian worked for ten years as a computer programmer in Johannesburg and London. In his spare time he read books about the sea and wondered if he'd ever return to it. At 32, with a failed marriage behind him, he quit his job and headed for Asia, looking for a new start. **He thought advisable what he did in that way.** On a flight from Colombo to Singapore, he gazed out the window at the sparkling waters far below and felt the tug at his heart.

/Reader's Digest.

Word Bank

- spare: 여분의, 당장 쓰지 않는.
- quit: 떠나다, 사직하다.
- head: 향하다, 나아가다.
- sparkling: 거품이 일고 있는(= bubbling).
- tug: 끌기, 잡아 당기기.

구문설명

with a failed marriage behind him: 실패로 끝난 결혼 생활을 뒤에 두고 (= when he failed in marriage). 이 표현은 "with" 다음의 목적어와 뒤따르는 전치사구가 주술관계를 이루고 있다. 자세한 설명은 "WITH" 주술관계 참조.

Reading 14

Thus a sad but important hope would be held out to the refugees, the unhappy orphans and exhausted widows. Hope is important, especially to those who are deprived of it. It is up to us to persuade our own leaders to prevent these people from being massacred or deported. **We must tell victims, loud and clear, that we are with them in their suffering.** If they feel abandoned, then we are diminished. If they feel humiliated, we are the ones who should be ashamed.

/Time.

Word Bank

- hold out: 주다, 제공하다.
- exhausted: 지친, 기진 맥진한.
- up to ~: ~에게 달린, 의 의무인.
- massacre: 을 대량 학살하다.
- deport: 추방하다, 유배하다.
- diminish: 위신을 떨어뜨리다.
- humiliate: 굴욕감을 느끼게 하다.
- refugee: 피난자, 난민.
- deprive: 빼앗다, 박탈하다.
- abandoned: 버림받은, 유기된.

Reading 15

Ultimately, say critics, Hong Kong needs to admit to itself that such radical change is necessary. "There is a false pride in Hong Kong that makes us think we can make money without working hard," says Peter N.S. Lee, a politics professor at the Chinese University of Hong Kong. "We think all we have to do is invest in the stock market or get a business degree." Already, the territory faces a shortage of engineering and computer-science students, and the specialists it does produce face stiff competition from their mainland counterparts. "WTO will force Hong Kong to prove it's on a world-class level," says Mok. "It cannot survive as just another Chinese city." Unless Hong Kong can reinvent itself quickly, the enclave may succumb to a flaw worse than hubris: irrelevancy.

/Time.

Word Bank

- admit: 시인하다, 인정하다.
- radical: 철저한, 급진적인.
- stiff: 경직된, 힘든.
- territory: 지역, 영토.
- mainland: 본토, 대륙.
- counterpart: 상대, 한 쌍의 한 쪽.
- enclave: 고립 영토(한 나라에 둘러싸여있는 남의 나라의 영토).
- succumb: 굴복하다, 복종하다.
- flaw: 결함.
- hubris: 오만, 자만.
- irrelevancy: 부적절함. 엉뚱함.

구문 설명

1. "all we have to do is invest in the stock market or ~ = all we have to do is (to) invest in the stock market or"는 준분열 구문으로서 "We have to invest in the stock market or ~."의 문장에서 동사구를 강조한 표현이다. (분열 구문 참조).
2. 이 지문에서 "Hong Kong", "the territory", "it", 그리고 "the enclave"는 모두 같은 것을 나타내는 말인데 영어에서는 어떤 대상에 대해서 한가지의 표현만 쓰기 보다는 이와 같이 다른 어휘로 대체(lexical replacement)해서 쓰는 표현이 아주 발달되어있다.

Reading 6

Seventy percent of the 34 million people infected with HIV live in sub-Saharan Africa, where more than two million people died of AIDS last year. It is estimated that one in four sub-Saharan Africans will die of AIDS, now the region's leading cause of death. More than two million people in the region died in 1999 alone. Experts say that AIDS is wiping out an entire generation that is a major portion of the national work force, including doctors, teachers and engineers. **Parental deaths leave behind orphans who cannot afford to go to school or who cannot find someone to educate them.** "There will be, for the first time, more people in their 60s and 70s than people in their 30s and 40s," said Dr. Peter Piot, director of UNAIDS, the United Nations AIDS program.

/CNN.

Word Bank

- HIV: 인간 면역 결핍 바이러스(Human Immunodeficiency Virus).
- sub-Saharan: 사하라 사막 이남의.
- estimate: 평가하다, 짐작하다.
- leading: 주요한, 주된.
- wipe out: 일소하다, 파괴하다.
- work force: 노동력, 노동인구.
- afford: 할 여유가 있다, 할 수 있다.

구문 설명

"~ will die of AIDS, now the region's leading cause of death."에서 "AIDS"와 그 이하는 동격.

Reading 17

When they reached the meadow, the Princess sat down on the grass and let down her hair. It shone like pure gold, and when little Conrad saw it he was so delighted that he wanted to pluck some out. But he couldn't seize her hair. **He attributed to the wind his miss for getting her hair.**

/Eric A. Kimmel, et al. The Goose Girl

Word Bank

- meadow: 초원, 목초지.
- let down: 내리다, 실망시키다.
- pluck: 잡아채다. 잡아당기다.
- miss: 실패, 헛방.

Reading 18

With Suharto's leadership pushed to the brink, all eyes were on Indonesia's mighty military leaders, who ordered their troops to take over the streets. Tanks rolled through the streets and plumes of thick smoke billowed across the skyline of Jakarta. **Mobs set afire cars, tires, shops and houses.** Rock-throwing teens and children smashed hundreds of windows in a frenzy of destruction that sent foreigners and minorities fleeing. "Jakarta is on fire. We'll go anywhere," said Siaumei Wen, a 27-year-old ethnic Chinese woman trying to buy plane tickets out for her family.

/ABC News.

Word Bank

- brink: (낭떠러지, 벼랑의) 가장 자리.
- mighty: 강력한, 힘센.
- take over: 떠맡다, 접수하다.
- roll: 굴러 다니다, 구르다.
- plume: 깃털, 기둥.
- billow: 소용돌이 치다, 굽이치다.
- skyline: 지평선, (건물 등의) 윤곽.
- mob: 폭도. afire: 불타는(= on fire).
- smash: 때려부수다, 깨뜨리다.
- frenzy: 격분, 격앙.
- flee: 도망치다, 달아나다.
- ethnic: 인종의, 소수 민족의.

구문 설명

With Suharto's leadership pushed to the brink, ~ = While/As Suharto's leadership was pushed to the brink, ~. (With 주술관계 참조)

Reading 19

Schools Minister Segolene Royal announced on Sunday that from January, doctors and nurses working in state secondary schools will be authorized to hand out the pills on request. The decision is part of a nationwide sex education campaign being launched to combat a rise in teenage pregnancies. More than 10,000 French teens become pregnant each year, of which 6,700 choose abortions.

/BBC.

Word Bank

- authorize: 인가하다, 허락하다.
- pill: 알약, 피임약.
- combat: 와 싸우다, 에 저항하다.
- abortion: 낙태, 유산(= miscarriage)
- hand out: 나주어 주다, 분배하다.
- campaign: 운동, 선거운동.

Reading 20

The Korean Veterans' Association in Seoul officially endorsed the South Korean Defense Ministry's decision to cancel the anniversary parade, including battle reenactments, and replace them with photo exhibits and dinner parties for veterans. But the feeling of conciliation was not unanimous. Some veterans were angry at what they saw as conceding too much to North Korea. "It's as if the government were telling the people to forget the war without even getting an apology from North Korea for starting the war," a leader of a group of decorated war veterans, told The Associated Press. **Such comments indicate the difficulties that probably lie ahead as the two Koreas try to keep alive the spirit of reconciliation kindled at the summit.**

/CNN.

Word Bank

- veteran: 재향 군인, 퇴역 군인.
- battle: 전쟁, 전투.
- anniversary: 기념일(의).
- conciliation: 화해, 위로.
- unanimous: 만장일치의, 이의가 없는.
- concede: 양보하다.
- decorated: 훈장을 받은, 훈장을 단.
- Associated Press: 미국 연합 통신사, AP 통신.
- reconciliation: 화해, 조화.
- kindle: 을 밝게 하다.
- endorse: 승인하다, 지지하다.
- reenactment: 재연(再演).
- parade: 행렬, 열병식.

Reading 21

I have among my clippings a story that I know never happened, but it illustrates a truth, so I'll repeat it: According to this silly story, **a farm woman, at the end of a heavy day's work, set before her men folks a heaping pile of hay.** And when they indignantly demanded whether she had gone crazy, she replied: "Why, how did I know you'd notice? I've been cooking for you men for the last twenty years and in all that time I ain't heard no word to let me know you wasn't just eating hay."

/Dale Carnegie. Dale Carnegie's Lifetime Plan for Success

Word Bank

- clipping: 오려내기, 신문 따위에서 오려낸 것.
- illustrate: 명확히 하다, 을 설명하다.
- menfolk: 남자.
- heap: 수북이 쌓다.
- indignantly: 격분하여, 분개하여.
- ain't: "is not, are not, has not, 혹은 have not"의 단축형.

Reading 2

The Oak Brook, Ill.-based restaurant chain is monitoring closely a marketing test that lets its patrons use a tiny, gray plastic wand to pay for meals, instead of cash. The concept, while novel, is by no means new, but McDonald's, which is testing it in 26 locations in Boise, thinks it might be a good idea. More than 2,000 people have signed up for the program, which, essentially, gives them the convenience of waving the wand in front of an electronic sensor to pay for a meal. There's no fumbling for loose change or looking for smaller bills. "Fast food is not fast anymore," says Jerry McVety, the president of McVety & Associates, a Farmington Hills, Mich.-based food service consulting group. If the concept sounds familiar, it is. The same technology is increasingly used to let commuters breeze through toll plazas. A version called E-ZPass has garnered more than 6 million users in and around New York City. The system, much like the one McDonald's is testing, lets users roll through toll plazas at 5 mph. E-ZPass transponders, which deduct tolls from a prepaid account, are affixed to the windshield behind a vehicle's rearview mirror. /Associated Press.

Word Bank

- chain: 연쇄점, 체인점.
- monitor: 조사하다, 관찰하다, 감시하다.
- patron: 후원자, 단골손님.
- wand: 지팡이, 막대.
- by no means: 결코 ~않다.
- sign: 서명하다, 사인하다.
- electronic: 전자의, 전자공학의.
- fumble: 손으로 더듬다, 더듬어 찾다.
- loose change: 잔돈.
- associate:
- technology: 과학 기술, 전문용어.
- breeze: 산들바람이 불다, 잽싸게 움직이다.
- toll: 통행요금, 사상자수.
- version: 변형, 다른 형.
- roll: transponder: 자동 응답 장치.
- windshield: 자동차의 방풍유리.
- rearview mirror: 백미러.
- deduct: 빼다, 공제하다.
- tiny: 소ㅗ바한.
- novel: 새로운, 신기한.
- location: 위치, 소재.
- wave: 흔들다, 휘두르다.
- sensor: 감지기, 감지장치.
- commuter: 통근자.
- consult: 상의하다, 참고하다.
- plaza: 광장, 서비스 지역.
- garner: 저장하다, 모으다.

구문 설명

1. The concept, while novel, is by ~. = The concept, while it is novel, is by ~.
2. If the concept sounds familiar, it is. = If the concept sounds familiar, it is familiar.

Reading 23

My father always reminded me that I should enjoy life, and he practiced what he preached. **No matter how hard he worked, he always made sure to leave enough room to have a good time.** He loved bowling and poker as well as good food, drink, and especially good friends. He always made friends with my colleagues at work. During my career at Ford, I think he knew more people there than I did.

/Lee Iacocca. The Autobiography of Lee Iacocca

Word Bank

- preach: 설교하다. 설득하다.
- practice: 실천하다.
- room: 여유, 여지.
- make friends with: 과 친해지다, 와 친구가 되다.
- career: 직업, 활동.

구문 설명

make sure of ~ (to ~, that ~):확인하다, 확신하다. "make sure"에서 "to ~"나 "that ~"은 "make"의 목적어가 아니다. 따라서 위 예문은 복합명사구 후치가 적용된 문장이 아니다.

English Special Constructions

English Special Constructions

Chapter 03
도 치 / Inversion

Chapter 03 도치(到置) Inversion

도치란 무엇인가?

영어에서 도치란 글자 그대로 어떤 요소들의 순서가 뒤집혔다는 뜻이다. 규범적인 문형들은 일반적으로 주어가 조동사나 동사 앞에 놓여 있는데 역으로 주어가 조동사나 혹은 동사 뒤에 놓여 순서가 바뀐 경우를 도치라고 한다. 도치에는 주어 조동사 도치(Subject-Aux Inversion)와 주어 동사 도치(Subject-Verb Inversion)구문이 있다.

01 a. A country had never achieved so much development in so short a time in history.

b. Never in history **had a country** achieved so much development in so short a time.
(역사적으로 단기간에 그렇게 많은 발전을 이룬 나라는 없었다.)

02 a. Two young women called Mary and Lisa worked on the third floor.

b. On the third floor **worked two young women called Mary and Lisa.**
(삼층에서 Mary와 Lisa라는 이름의 젊은 두 여자가 일을 했다.)

도치는 언제 쓰이는가?

주어 동사의 도치와 주어 조동사의 도치는 하나로 묶어서 설명할 수는 없다. 먼저 주어 동사 도치구문에서 전치되는 요소는 구정보에 해당된다. 그리고 동사 뒤로 후치되는 요소는 신정보에 해당되거나 주어가 긴 경우에 해당된다.

03 a. She is a nice woman, isn't she? Our next guest is also a nice woman.

b. She is a nice woman, isn't she? Also a nice woman **is our next guest.**
(저 여자분은 좋은 분이시지? 우리의 다음 손님 역시 좋은 분이시다.)

04 a. They dragged a burning coach, and the lord of the manor who had ruled there one hundred years before sat within it.

b. They dragged a burning coach, and within it **sat the wicked the lord of the manor who had ruled there one hundred years before.**
(그들은 불에 타고 있는 마차를 끌었습니다. 그리고 그 마차 안에는 백년 전에 그곳을 지배했던 사악한 장원 영주가 앉아 있었다.)

주어 조동사의 도치는 문장의 종류에 따라서 혹은 주변 요소의 전치에 의하거나 혹은 생략에 의하는 등 여러 가지 이유 때문에 일어난다.

05 a. **Can you** solve the problem? (의문문)
(당신은 그 문제를 풀 수 있습니까?)

b. **May you** succeed! (기원문)
(당신의 성공을 빕니다.)

06 a. I little dreamed that he was there.

b. **Little did I** dream that he was there. (부정요소의 전치)
(나는 그가 거기에 와 있으리라고는 꿈에도 생각 못했다.)

07 a. If it were not for water, no living things could survive.

b. **Were it** not for water, no living things could survive. (if의 생략)
(물이 없다면 어떤 생물도 살아 남을 수 없을 것이다.)

Unit 1 주어 동사의 도치 (Subject-Verb Inversion)

영어에서 동사가 자동사(be, sit, stand, lie, hang, go, come, fly, roll, 등)이거나 수동형을 취하고 있는 문장에서 일부 요소가 문두에 놓이게 되면 주어와 동사 도치가 자주 일어난다. 이런 구문에서 주어는 동사 뒤로 이동하고 동사 뒤에 있는 요소는 동사 앞으로 이동한다. 주어 조동사의 도치와 달리, 주어 동사의 도치구문에서 동사라 함은 조동사를 포함한 모든 동사를 말한다.
여기에서 어떤 요소가 앞으로 이동되는 이유중의 하나는 구정보(Old Information)가 신정보(New Information) 보다 앞에 놓이려는 속성때문이며, 이때 전치된 요소는 주제 역할을 한다. 다시 말해 전치된 구성요소는 일반적으로 구정보이고 후치되는 구성요소는 신정보이다. 그러나 만약 두 요소가 모두 구정보라면 전치된 요소가 더 친숙한 정보이어야 한다. 여기에서 더 친숙하다는 말은 전치되는 구성 요소와 후치되는 구성 요소 둘 다 선행 문맥에서 명시적으로 언급된 정보에 해당될 때에는 보다 더 최근에 언급된 정보를 말한다. 또 하나의 이유는 너무 긴 주어가 놓이는 것을 꺼려 주어를 뒤에 놓는 과정에서 도치가 일어난다.

1 도치가 일어나는 경우

1.1. 장소 부사 뒤에서

01 a. A beautiful young girl lay on the bed.

b. **On the bed** lay a beautiful young girl.
(침대 위에는 아름다운 처녀가 누워 있었습니다.)

02 a. Beautiful flowers stood here and there over the grass.

b. **Here and there over the grass** stood beautiful flowers.
(여기 저기 잔디 위에는 아름다운 꽃이 있었습니다.)

1.2. 방향 부사 뒤에서

03 a. A baby carriage rolled down the street.

b. **Down the street** rolled a baby carriage.
(그 거리에서 유모차가 굴러 떨어졌습니다.)

04 a. Many curiosities are gathered here.

b. **Here** are gathered many curiosities.
(이곳에 많은 골동품들이 모여있습니다.)

1.3. 분사 뒤에서

05 a. A number of school children are waiting for the bus.

b. **Waiting for the bus** are a number of school children.
(버스를 기다리고 있는 사람들은 많은 초등 학생들 이었습니다.

06 a. My father was examined today and found in good health.

b. **Examined today and found in good health** was my father.
(아버지는 오늘 진찰을 받으셨는데 건강이 좋은 것으로 밝혀졌다.)

1.4. 비교 표현 뒤에서

07 a. The country's economic growth has been still more remarkable.

b. **Still more remarkable** has been the country's economic growth.
(훨씬 더 주목할만한 것은 우리 나라의 경제 성장이었다.)

08 a. His behavior toward his son was equally inexplicable.

b. **Equally inexplicable** was his behavior toward his son.
(그와 마찬가지로 설명할 수 없었던 것은 그의 아들에 대한 그의 행동이었습니다.)

1.5 허사 "there" 뒤에서

09 a. A policeman is at the door.

b. There is a policeman at the door.
(한 경관이 문에 있습니다.)

10 a. A stranger came late in the evening.

b. There came a stranger late in the evening.
(낯선 사람이 밤 늦게 왔습니다.)

여기에서 전치된 요소 "there"는 상대방이 아는 곳을 가리키는 경우이기 때문에 구정보에 해당되지만 주어와 동사가 도치되는 이유는 신정보인 주어를 뒤로 놓기 위함이다. 이런 문장에서 신정보인 주어를 동사 앞에 두는 표현은 좋지 않다.

1.6. 직접 화법의 피전달문 뒤에서

11 a. Tom said, "The children had better go to bed early."

b. "The children had better go to bed early," said Tom.

c. "The children had better go to bed early," Tom said.
(아이들은 일찍 자는 것이 좋다고 Tom은 말했다.)

1.7. 주어가 너무 길 때

12 a. The man who can say that he is content with his life is happy.

b. Happy is the man who can say that he is content with his life.
(자신의 삶에 만족하고 있다고 말할 수 있는 사람은 행복하다.)

2 보충 설명

13 a. She comes here. (그녀가 이쪽으로 오고있다.)

b. *Here comes she.

c. Here he comes. (이쪽으로 그녀가 오고 있다.)

주어 동사의 도치구문에서 문미의 위치는 초점이 놓이는 자리이다. 일반적으로 대명사는 초점으로 사용되지 않기 때문에 주어가 대명사인 경우에는 주어와 동사가 도치되지 않는다. 문미에는 일반적으로 초점의 위치로서 신정보(New Information)가 놓인다. 1인칭 대명사와 2인칭 대명사는 상황 속에서 이미 화자와 청자가 서로 알고 있는 구정보(Old Information)이고, 3인칭 대명사는 이미 앞에서 언급된 명사를 다시 반복하는 것으로 구정보(Old Information)이기 때문에 문미에 놓일 수 없다.

14 a. The boy ran into the house.

b. Into the house ran the boy.

c. Into the house the boy ran.
(그 집으로 소년은 달려들어갔습니다.)

여기에서 주어 "the boy"는 이미 앞에서 언급된 구정보이다 이와 같이 대명사가 아닌 명사구인 주어를 초점으로 만들고자 하는 경우에는 주어를 문미에 두지만 그렇지 않은 경우에는 전치된 요소와 동사구 사이에 놓인다. 특히 이와 같이 전치된 구성요소와 후치된 구성요소 둘 모두가 구정보에 해당될 때에는 보다 더 최근에 언급된 정보가 전치되고 그렇지 않은 정보가 후치된다. 따라서 예문 (14b)와 (14c)에서는 "the house"가 "the boy"보다 더 최근 정보임을 알 수 있다.

15 a. Our local congressman will be speaking at today's lunch.

b. Speaking at today's lunch will be our local congressman.

c. *Speaking at today's lunch will our local congressman be.
(우리 지역 국회의원이 오늘 점심때에 연설을 할 예정이다.)

주어 동사의 도치구문에서 동사라 함은 조동사를 포함한 전부를 말한다. 위 예문 (15c)에서는 주어와 동사의 도치가 아닌 주어와 조동사의 도치가 일어난 경우인데 이런 구문은 적절치 못하다.

Practice Examples

Reading 01

Thousands of secret CIA missives and other previously classified materials, many documenting the internal foreign policy debate in the Kennedy administration, have been made public for the first time. **Among the documents are memos between President Kennedy and former National Security Council Adviser McGeorge Bundy, cables sent from the U.S. Embassy in Laos to the State Department during the early days of the Vietnam War and efforts at political subversion in Cuba.** Hundreds of historians are expected to scrutinize the 4,500 pages made public Wednesday at the John F. Kennedy Library and Museum. "The puzzle of the Kennedy administration is almost complete, but there are definitely holes," said Maura Porter, an archivist at the library.

/CNN.

Word Bank

- missive: 서한, 공문서.
- document: 에 문서를 첨부하다, 을 문서로 제공하다(= supply with documents)
- adviser: 조언자, 고문.
- cable: 전신. 전보.
- subversion: 전복, 타도.
- scrutinize: 을 면밀히 검사하다(= examine thoroughly).
- archivist: 기록 보관자, 공문서 보관자.

구문설명

~, many documenting the internal foreign policy debate in the Kennedy administration, = ,many of which document the internal foreign policy debate in the Kennedy administration,

Reading 02

The windows on the sunny side of the street were shuttered. The taxi stopped at the curb. I saw the sign HOTEL MONTANA on the second floor. The taxi-driver carried the bags in and left them by the elevator. I could not make the elevator work, so I walked up. **On the second floor up was a cut brass sign:** HOTEL MONTANA. I rang and no one came to the door. I rang again and a maid with a sullen face opened the door.

/Ernest M. Hemingway. The Sun Also Rises

Word Bank

- shutter: 의 덧문을 닫다.
- work: 작동하다.
- brass: 놋쇠, 황동.
- curb: 연속, 제갈.
- cut: 깎아 다듬은, 세공의.
- sullen: 시무룩한, 골 난.

Reading 03

This holds true for music, for medicine, for carpentry and for love. And, maybe, **here lies the answer to the question of why people in our culture try so rarely to learn this art,** in spite of their obvious failurcs: in spite of the deep-seated craving for love, almost everything else is considered to be more important than love: success, prestige, money, power--almost all our energy is used for the learning of how to achieve these aims, and almost none to learn the art of loving.

/Erich Fromm. The Art of Loving

Word Bank

- carpentry: 목수일, 목공.
- deep-seated: 뿌리 깊은.
- prestige: 명성, 위신.

구문 설명

1. Keep/continue/lie/hold/remain/stand/stay/rest + 보어: 계속해서 보어하다. 여전히 보어하다. 예를 들면, She kept silent. (그녀는 여전히 말이 없었다.) He continues obdurate. (그는 여전히 완고하다.) The door lay open. (그 문은 계속해서 열려있었다.) The visa holds good for three months. (그 비자는 계속해서 3개월 동안 유효하다.) I remained his friend all my life. (나는 평생 그의 친구로 남아있었다.)
2. ~ and almost none to learn the art of loving. = ~ and almost none is used to learn the art of loving.

Reading 04

Just north of San Francisco, where we start, are large forests of ancient redwood trees, famed for their size. South of San Francisco, along the Pacific coast, is a procession of cities whose names reflect the early Spanish settlement of this area: San Jose, Santa Barbara, San Diego. The old mansions and other white stucco buildings with red tile roofs also show the Spanish influence. As you leave San Francisco on your trip east, you cross the central area of California, which produces much of the citrus fruit and vegetables for the entire nation. A mild climate and irrigation make this a productive area all through the year.

/Gladys Doty & Janet Ross. Language and Life in the U.S.A.

Word Bank

- redwood: 삼나무.
- coast: 연안, 해안.
- procession: 행렬, 행진.
- settlement: 식민, 정착.
- mansion; 저택.
- irrigation: 관개 (시설).
- stucco: 치장 벽토(= kinds of plaster or cement used for covering and decorating wall surfaces).
- citrus: 감귤류(= genus of trees that includes the lemon, lime, citron, and orange).

Reading 05

In a religious point of view, it may be permitted to endeavor to improve our temporal condition, by the use of lawful and just means, but it is never proper to repine. Christ, in the parable of the vine dressers, has taught us a sublime lesson of justice, by showing that to the things which are not our own, we can have no just claim. **To this obvious truth may be added the uncertainty of the future, and the ignorance in which we exist of what is good, or what is evil, as respects our own wants.**

/James Fenimore Cooper. The American Democrat: On Religion

Word Bank

- point of view: 관점, 견해(= viewpoint).
- temporal: 시간의, 속세의(= of this physical life).
- repine: 불평하다, 투덜거리다.
- parable: 우화, 비유.
- vinedresser: 포도 재배자, 포도 경작자.
- sublime: 고상한, 숭고한.
- claim: 요구, 권리.
- as respects: 에 대해서는, 에 관하여(= as regards).

구문 설명

1. ~ by showing that to the things which are not our own, we can have no just claim. = ~ by showing that we can have no just claim to the things which are not our own. 자세한 설명은 주제화 구문 참조.
2. and "the ignorance in which we exist of what is good, or what is evil, as respects our own wants."에서 "of what is good, or what is evil, as respects our own wants."은 명사구 "the ignorance"의 바로 뒤에 있는 요소인데 그것으로부터 분리되어 뒤로 후치된 구문이다. 자세한 설명은 탈명사구 외치편 참조.

Reading 06

During the last year of his life his friends got him a job as a clerk in the Denver post office, which his money had built. When he died in 1899, his last words to Baby Doe were, "Hang on to the Matchless. It will make you a fortune." Baby Doe did what Tabor told her, and she moved into a little shack at the entrance to the mine. The shack is still there and is much as it was when she lived there. There is a cot, a table, and one or two chairs. A small coal stove sits in one corner. On the walls are a few pots and pans. **There is a Catholic altar against one wall, with some candles and a cross on it.** Letters of Baby Doe, which are preserved in a case at one side of the room, indicate that in her last years she seldom left the shack for fear that someone would try to enter the mine. Friends brought her food and coal. To keep track of time, she marked off the days on her calendar, which still hangs on the wall. In the middle of March 1935, the marking stopped. The frozen body of the 73-year-old woman was found a few days later, still guarding the Match Mine.

/Gladys Doty & Janet Ross. From Language and Life in. the U.S.A.

Word Bank

- clerk: 사무원, 점원.
- hang on to ~: ~을 꼭 붙들다.
- shack: 오두막, 판자집.
- cot: 간이 침대.
- altar: 재단.
- keep track of: 의
- guard: 지키다.

구문 설명

~ is much as it was when she lived there.

Reading 07

The nurse opens the dressing-room door, and although it is a room no bigger than a bathing-box, her voice sounds as if she were bending down and talking to something under the seat. "Come on, Beale," she says, "Come with me." And **out comes Beale with his trousers collapsing and his braces on the floor, lost in a huge dressing-gown.**

/V. S. Pritchett. X-ray

Word *Bank*

- dressing-room: (침실에 붙어있는) 화장실, 분장실.
- bathing-box: 해수욕장의 탈의실.
- bend: 몸을 구부리다.
- collapse: 무너지다, 흘러내리다.
- braces: 바지 멜빵(= suspenders).
- be lost in: 에 몰두하다, 속에 모습을 감추다.
- dressing-gown: 실내복, 화장옷

구문 설명

~ with his trousers collapsing and his braces on the floor, ~ 자세한 설명은 "WITH" 주술관계 참조.

Reading 08

Francesca stepped off the porch and walked unhurriedly through the grass toward the gate. **And out of the pickup came Robert Kincaid, looking like some vision from a never-written book called *An Illustrated History of Shamans*.**

/Robert James Waller. The Bridges of Madison County

Word *Bank*

- porch: 현관.
- pickup: 소형 트럭(= pickup truck)
- vision: 예견, 모습.
- illustrate: 에 삽화를 넣다.
- shaman: 무당, 마술사.

Reading 09

The struggle intensified at the end of the war when Britain's occupation of Palestine became a mandate ultimately sanctioned by the League of Nations. **Incorporated into the mandate was the Balfour Declaration, issued in late 1917 by British Foreign Secretary Arthur Balfour,** who endorsed the idea of a Jewish homeland in Palestine (but not, the declaration stipulated, at the expense of the Palestinian Arabs). The British also had promised to help Arab leaders create their own independent states in return for their support against the Ottoman Empire. But a misunderstanding arose that would have longstanding implications: The Arabs thought Palestine would be among the newly independent Arab states. The British said that was not what they intended, but neither did they intend for Palestine to be exclusively a Jewish state. Rather, they said, a Jewish state would exist within Palestine.

/CNN.

Word Bank

- intensify: occupation: mandate: sanction:
- League of Nations: 국제 연맹.
- incorporate: 넣다, 포함하다.
- homeland: 고국, 모국.
- endorse: 승인하다, 확인하다.
- stipulate: 명기하다, 규정하다.
- longstanding: 오랫동안에 걸친, 오래 계속되는.
- implication: 함축, 암시.

구문설명

1. But a misunderstanding arose that would have longstanding implications = But a misunderstanding that would have longstanding implications arose. "misunderstanding"을 수식하는 "that"절이 주어가 너무 길어 분리된 문장. 자세한 설명은 탈명사구 외치 참조.
2. "~ but neither did they intend for Palestine to be exclusively a Jewish state."에서는 부정요소 'neither"가 앞에 놓임로써 주어와 조동사가 도치되어있다. "~ but they did not intend for Palestine to be exclusively a Jewish state, either."로 바꾸어 쓸 수 있다. 자세한 설명은 주어 조동사 도치편 참조.

Reading 10

Fueling this child-sex industry are tens of thousands of pedophile tourists from the United States, Canada, Britain, Germany, Sweden, Japan, Australia and New Zealand. Often assisted by clandestine pedophile networks, they fly to southern Asia for child sex, knowing they face little risk of being caught and small penalty if they are. The lure of tourist dollars leads government and law-enforcement officials in these countries to look the other way.

/Reader's Digest.

Word *Bank*

- fuel: 에 연료를 공급하다, 을 자극하다.
- pedophile: 아이들에게 성욕을 갖는.
- clandestine: 은밀한, 비밀의.
- lure: 미끼, 매력.
- penalty: 형벌, 벌금.
- law-enforcement: 법 집행의.

구문 설명

"~, knowing they face little risk of being caught and small penalty if they are." = "~, as they know they face little risk of being caught and small penalty if they are caught."

Reading 11

Closely related to this factor is another feature characteristic of contemporary culture. Our whole culture is based on the appetite for buying, on the idea of a mutually favorable exchange. Modern man's happiness consists in the thrill of looking at the shop windows, and in buying all that he can afford to buy, either for cash or on installments. He (or she) looks at people in similar way. For the man an attractive girl and for the woman an attractive man are the prizes they are after.

/Erich Fromm, The Art of Loving

Word Bank

- feature: 특징, 특색.
- appetite: 욕구, 욕망.
- thrill: 전율, 설렘.
- contemporary: 현대의.
- favorable: 유리한, 호의적인.
- installment: 할부.

Reading 12

Under wartime-level security, President Bush arrived Friday afternoon to survey the hellish scene that was once the gleaming World Trade Center. "This conflict was begun on the timing and terms of others," Bush said earlier in the somber, sodden day. "It will end in a way and at an hour of our choosing." Fighter jets flew overhead to ensure security as Bush's helicopter slowly circled the wreckage. **Awaiting him on the ground was an army of search and rescue workers.** Some placed small American flags on their earth-moving equipment; one strapped Old Glory to the back of his heavy work jacket.

/USA Today.

Word Bank

- security: 안전, 방어.
- hellish: 지옥의, 소름 끼치는.
- somber: 어두컴컴한, 음산한.
- overhead: 머리 위에, 하늘 높이.
- wreckage: 파괴, 잔해
- Old Glory: 미국 국기, 성조기(= the Stars and Stripes).
- survey: 개관하다, 조사하다.
- gleaming: 반짝 빛나다.
- sodden: 흠뻑 젖은.
- circle: 돌다, 선회하다.
- strap: 묶다, 달다.

Reading 13

Enclosed is a poem my late father wrote in 1951 for Mother's Day. I thought you might like to print it. Absolutely! Your father's poem carries a strong message for children who live at a distance from their mothers. If the message is taken to heart, it should brighten Mother's Day for many a mother.

/Universal Press Syndicate. Dear Abby.

Word Bank

- enclose:
- print: 인쇄하다, 게재하다.
- absolutely: 물론(= quite so).
- at a distance: 떨어져서.
- take(lay) ~ to heart: 을 깊이 마음속에 새기다, 을 깊이 생각하다.

Reading 14

In its 158-page petition, CSPI pointed to such well-known brands as Odwalla juices, Snapple and Arizona teas, Fresh Samantha and Golden Temple Cereals containing added herbal ingredients that are not "generally recognized as safe" by the FDA nor are approved as food additives. **Also cited were products that make unlawful claims on their labels and are thus considered "adulterated and/or misbranded under the Federal Food Drug and Cosmetic Act," the consumer group said.** CSPI asked the FDA to take "appropriate enforcement action" to ensure that these products are no longer marketed.

/Washington Post.

Word Bank

- petition: 탄원(서), 진정(서).
- CSPI: 미 공익과학 센터 (= The Center for Science in the Public Interest).
- brand: 품질, 상표.
- herbal: 풀의, 약초의.
- ingredient: 성분, 요소.
- additive: 첨가물, 첨가제.
- label: 꼬리표, 표찰.
- adulterate: 에 불순물을 섞다.
- misbrand: 에 잘못된 상표를 붙이다.
- cite: 인용하다, 언급하다.
- FDA: 연방식품 의약품국 (= Food and Drug Administration).
- appropriate: 적절한.
- enforcement: 시행, 집행.
- market: 을 시장에 내놓다, 을 팔려고 내놓다.

Reading 15

At roughly 9,000 years of age, Kennewick Man is one of the oldest remains ever found in North America. Accidentally discovered in the summer of 1996 by boat-race spectators in the shallows of Oregon's Columbia River, he presented scientists with a thrilling find: the well-preserved remains of a battle-scarred man thought to have been in his 40s, who, perhaps until an arrowhead in his hip brought him down roughly 90 centuries ago, stood about 5 feet 10 inches tall. **Even more intriguing was his surprisingly long face and large, protruding nose, facial features that do not resemble those of any known American Indian tribe.**

/Washington Times.

Word Bank

- remain: 나머지, 유해, 유골.
- accidentally: 우연히, 뜻하지 않게.
- boat-race: 조정대회, 보트레이스.
- spectator: 구경꾼, 관객.
- shallow: 물이 얕은 곳, 여울.
- present: 제출하다, 내놓다.
- thrilling:오싹하게 하는, 소름이 끼치는.
- find: 발견, 발견물.
- battle-scarred: 전상을 입은, 전쟁의 상처가 남은.
- arrowhead: 화살 촉.
- bring down: 죽이다.
- intriguing: 흥미를 자아내는, 호기심을 자극하는.
- protrude: 내밀다, 튀어나오다.
- tribe: 부족, 종족.

구문 설명

"Even more intriguing was his surprisingly long face and large, protruding nose, facial features that do ~."에서 "facial features ~"는 앞에 나온 "his surprisingly long face and large, protruding nose"를 부연 설명하고 있다. "facial features"앞에 "which are"가 생략된 표현으로 볼 수 있다.

Reading 6

The report, requested by U.S. Rep. Charles Rangel, an opponent of sanctions, says: "U.S. wheat exports to Cuba could total between $32 million and $52 million annually, representing about 1 percent of recent U.S wheat exports." **More instructive are the experiences of other countries:** "With Mexico," according to the Wall Street Journal, "Cuba is in arrears on about $400 million of commercial credits. France recently withheld a shipment of wheat and canceled $160 million in credits because Mr. Castro hasn't paid for earlier shipments. Chile is attempting to establish "a payment plan" for $20 million worth of fish shipped to Cuba last year. South Africa, according to the Johannesburg Sunday Times, is "frustrated" by Havana's failure to settle a $13 million debt and will not approve new credit guarantees until the debt is settled.

/Washington Times.

Word *Bank*

- Rep.: 국회의원, 하원의원 (= Representative).
- opponent: 적수, 반대자.
- sanction: 재가, 제재.
- wheat: 밀
- export: 수출, 수출품.
- instructive: 교훈적인, 유익한.
- arrear: 지연, 지체.
- commercial: 상업상의, 통상의.
- credit: 신용, 외상, 대부.
- withhold: 보류하다, 억제하다.
- shipment: 선적, 수송.
- ship: 배에 싣다, 수송하다.
- frustrated: 실망한, 좌절감을 느낀.
- settle: 해결하다, 청산하다.
- guarantee: 보증.
- Havana: 하바나(쿠바의 수도), 쿠바 정부.

Reading 17

Alcoholism and drug addiction are the forms which the individual chooses in non-orgiastic culture. In contrast to those participating in the socially patterned solution, such individuals suffer from guilt feelings and remorse. While they try to escape from segregateness by taking refuge in alcohol or drugs, they feel all the more separate after the orgiastic experience is over, and thus are driven to take recourse to it with increasing frequency and intensity. **Slightly different from this is the recourse to a sexual orgiastic solution.** To some extent it is a natural and normal form of overcoming separateness, and a partial answer to the problem of isolation.

/Erich Fromm. The Art of Loving

Word Bank

- alcoholism: 알코올 중독(증).
- drug: 약, 마약.
- addiction: 탐닉, 중독.
- isolation: 고립, 고독.
- orgiastic: 주신제의(같은), 술 마시고 법석대는, 감정을 절제하지 못하는.
- guilt: 죄를 범하고 있음, 죄가 있음.
- remorse: 양심의 가책, 자책.
- segregate: 분리하다, 격리하다.
- refuge: 피난처, 도피처.
- drive: 몰다, 억지로 하게 하다.
- recourse: 의지, 의뢰.
- frequency: 빈발, 진도, 주파수.
- intensity: 강렬, 강.도.
- partial: 부분적인, 불공정한.

구문 설명

1. with increasing frequency and intensity = more and more frequently and intensively.
2. "같다"나 "다르다"의 의미를 갖는 형용사나 부사들은 "~와 같다"나 "~와 다르다"의 의미로서 잠재적으로 비교 대상을 필요로 하기 때문에 비교요소로 간주한다. 예를 들면 similar, different, equal 등이 여기에 해당된다.

Reading 18

In 1996, more than half a million American teens gave birth. Most of these adolescents were unmarried, and many were not ready for the responsibilities and demands of parenthood. For a good share of these new mothers, premature parenting will foreshorten their schooling, narrow their personal development, and greatly increase the likelihood that they will be poor and dependent as young adults. **Equally predictable is that the hardship of too-early parenting will be visited upon the next generation.** The children of teenagers are far more likely than other babies to be below average in weight at birth, to be deprived of adequate learning opportunities, and to be poor. And as they grow up, these kids are more likely to drop out, get into trouble, and end up as teen parents themselves.

/http://www.aecf.org/kidscount/teen/foreword

Word Bank

- adolescent: 젊은이(남자는 14-25세; 여자는 12-21세).
- parenthood: 부모임.
- good: 상당한.
- share: 몫, 할당량.
- premature: 시기 상조의, 너무 이른.
- parenting: 임신, 출산.
- foreshorten: 단축하다.
- schooling: 학교 교육, 교실 수업.
- young adult: 10대 후반의 청소년.
- visit: 에 주다, 에게 가하다.
- deprive: 빼앗다, 박탈하다.
- drop out: 낙제하다, 중퇴하다.
- end up: 결국 마지막에는 ~이 되다.

Reading 9

Measured in terms of traffic deaths per 10,000 vehicles, Korea was the world's third worst country in 1992 (after Botswana and Morocco). With concerted campaign, it managed to improve in three years to ninth place, but it is still scary. Thirty-five people die a day on the roads, seventeen are permanently disabled, and over 950 are treated for injuries. **Similar to the unsure drivers are the unsure pedestrians.** The next five minutes should be spent observing them. As a modern country, Korea has traffic lights and pedestrian crossings as we do. But many back streets have neither pedestrian crossings nor pavements. Old women, especially, often seem to cross roads without looking, just hoping that they won't be knocked down.

/Michael Breen. The Koreans: Who They Are, What They Want, Where Their Future Lies

Word Bank

- measure: 측정하다, 평가하다.
- in terms of: 에 의하여, 의 관점에서.
- death: 죽음,
- vehicle: 탈것, 매개물.
- concerted: 협정된, 합의된.
- campaign: 전쟁, 운동, 유세.
- improve: 개선하다, 향상시키다.
- scary: 무서운, 겁 많은.
- disabled: 불구가 된, 신체 장애자들.
- injury: 부상, 상해.
- unsure: 불안정한, 불확실한.
- pedestrian: 보행자.
- back street: 뒷골목, 뒷길.
- crossing: 건널목, 횡단보도.
- pavement: 포장 도로, (美) 차도, (英) 인도, 보도.
- knock down: 치어 넘어뜨리다.

Reading 20

The seven North Koreans entered the UNHCR office in the morning of June 26 and refused to leave, said a witness who followed the family into the building. Three women were among the seven, including a 17-year-old artist whose drawings depicting the hardships under Pyongyang's rule could expose her to punishment, said Redmond. "We believe that these people deserve asylum and we are seeking assistance to find a solution for them with all concerned authorities," he added. UNHCR officials were in contact with Chinese authorities and with governments that may be willing to take in the family. **"We assume that they are safe in our office," said Redmond.**

It was the first time that North Korean asylum-seekers had sought help from the UNHCR's office in Beijing. But Redmond said many more North Koreans had entered China to flee repression, famine and dire living conditions in the communist-ruled country. "This is just the tip of the iceberg. **There have been reports of large numbers of North Koreans entering China, but we have limited access to them because they remain in border areas," Redmond said.** The UNHCR estimates that tens of thousands of North Koreans have fled their country to China.

/Associated Press.

Word Bank

- UNHCR: 유엔 난민 고등판무관(United Nations High Commissioner for Refugees).
- witness: 목격자, 증인.
- drawing: 그림, 뽑기.
- depict: 묘사하다, 서술하다.
- hardship: 곤란, 결핍.
- expose: 드러내다, 노출시키다.
- asylum: 도피처, 망명.
- take in: 섭취하다, 받아들이다.
- flee: 달아나다, 도망치다.
- repression: 억압, 억제.
- famine: 식량 부족. 기근.
- dire: 무시무시한, 비참한.
- the tip of the iceberg: 빙산의 일각.

Reading 21

Once upon a time there lived a sweet little girl. She was loved by everyone. But no one loved her so much as her grandmother. One day the grandmother gave the little girl a red velvet cap. It fitted her so well that she was wearing it all the time. So she was called Little Red-Cap.

/J. & W. Grimm. Little Red-Cap

Word Bank

- velvet: 벨벳, 우단.
- fit: 에 들어맞다, 적합하다.

구문 설명

But no one loved her so much as her grandmother. = But no one loved her so much as her grandmother did.

Reading 22

In a unified market, such as the United States or Europe, **there should be a single agency** that is responsible for ensuring that consistently high standards assuring the safety of the food supply are being applied. **There needs to be a pan-European food safety agency** that has the capability and independence to make high-quality and publicly credible food safety decisions. The current dioxin crisis that started in Belgium and spread across much of Europe illustrates the need to have an effective system to manage food safety problems that cross national borders.

/Time

Word Bank

- ensure: 보장하다, 안전하게 하다.
- assure: 보장하다, 확보하다.
- high-quality: 고급의.
- credible: 믿을 수 있는, 확실한.

Reading 23

I was named "Margaret" after my mother's beloved Aunt Madge. I have a first cousin who is a year older than me who was also named Margaret, but has always been "Madge." (Her father was my mother's brother.) My mother and my uncle were neglected by their widowed, alcoholic father. It was Aunt Madge who gave my uncle a loving home after my mother left home to attend college and later marry. For this reason she was very special to my uncle. **There may have been some resentment toward my mother for giving me the same name,** but if so, I never heard about it. We were called by variations of the same name, and there is no animosity.

/Universal Press Syndicate. Dear Abby.

Word Bank

- beloved: 사랑하는.
- cousin: 사촌, 친사촌(= first cousin, full cousin, cousin-german).
- neglect: 내버려두다, 소홀히 하다(= to give no or not enough care to).
- widow: 의 남편을(아내를) 잃게 하다.
- resentment: 원한, 분노.
- variation: 변화, 이형(= something as an individual or group that exhibits variation).
- animosity: 원한, 적개심.

Reading 24

The most dangerous flashpoint in the Middle East sits at the edge of a chain-link fence just beyond the southern Lebanese village of Kfar Shuba. A chill wind whistles over rocky hills covered with pale grass and speckled with cypress trees. **"Danger, death, minefield," warn white signs.** From a hilltop observation post just over the fence, Israeli soldiers closely follow the movements of a Land Cruiser as it rumbles toward the border. **"Last week someone lingered here too long and they took a shot at his car," warns Khaled Khadry, 25, a farmer who lives in Kfar Shuba.** Khadry gestures to an abandoned shack beside the fence that served as a base for Hizbullah guerrillas - until the group kidnapped three Israeli soldiers in a daring operation last November.

/Newsweek.

Word *Bank*

- flashpoint: 폭발점, 일촉즉발의 위기.
- edge: 가장자리, 가.
- chill: 차가운, 쌀쌀한.
- whistle: 휘파람 불다, 씽씽 불다.
- pale: 창백한, 빛깔이 엷은.
- speckled: 얼룩덜룩한, 반점이 있는.
- cypress: 싸이프러스.
- minefield: 광석 매장 구역, 지뢰밭.
- sign: 기호, 신호, 간판.
- hilltop: 언덕(작은 산) 꼭대기.
- observation post: 감시초소, 관측소.
- closely: 면밀히, 바싹.
- rumble: 덜거덕거리며 달리다.
- linger: 남아 있다, 꾸물거리다.
- shot: 발포.
- take a shot at:을 겨누다, 저격하다.
- gesture: 몸짓을 하다, 손짓을 하다.
- shack: 오두막집.
- serve: 근무하다, 역할을 하다.
- base: 기초, 기지.
- kidnap: 납치하다, 유괴하다.
- daring: 대담한, 무모한.
- operation: 운전, 작전.

Reading 25

He considered calling the police but decided it wouldn't be wise to stir trouble in the neighborhood. He resigned himself to suffering in silence--until he moved. Unfortunately such situations are far from unusual. Most of us have had a conflict, great or small, with a neighbor. Many local organizations that track quarrels between neighbors say such conflicts?about tumbledown fences, loud stereos, parties, undisciplined children?are on the rise. **Sometimes, says Jay Folberg, law-school dean at the University of San Francisco, such disputes wind up in court.** Some cases are serious, but others border on the ludicrous.

/Reader's Digest

Word Bank

- stir: 불러일으키다, 자극하다.
- trouble: 근심, 분쟁.
- resign oneself to: 체념하고 ~하기로 하다.
- far from: 조금도 ~않다, 이기는커녕.
- unusual: 드문, 별난.
- track: 추적하다, 찾아내다.
- tumble-down: 넘어질 듯한.
- stereo: 입체음향.
- undisciplined: 규율 없는.
- on the rise: 증가하는, 상승추세에 있는.
- law school: 법과 대학원, 법학부, 법학 대학.
- dean: 학장, 주임 사제.
- dispute: 논쟁, 분쟁.
- wind up: 끝을 맺다, 결말을 내다.
- court: 코트, 법정.
- case: 경우, 사건
- border: 인접하다, 가깝다.
- ludicrous: 어이없는, 우스운.

Unit 2 주어 조동사의 도치 (Subject-Auxiliary Inversion)

주어 조동사의 도치(Subject Auxiliary Inversion) 는 주어 동사의 도치(Subject-Verb Inversion)와 구별되어야 한다. 주어 조동사의 도치 구문은 조동사가 여러 개 있다고 하더라도 첫번째 조동사만이 주어 앞으로 이동되어 둘 사이의 위치가 바뀌게 되는 경우를 말한다. 단 조동사가 없는 경우는 인칭과 시제에 맞게 활용된 "Do"를 사용한다.

1 도치가 일어나는 경우

1.1. 의문문에서

01 a. **Have you** seen John anywhere?
(너 어디에선가 존을 본 적 있니?)

b. Where **are the president and his family** staying?
(대통령과 가족들이 어디에 머무르고 있습니까?)

c. He's the new secretary, **isn't he**?
(그가 바로 새로 온 비서지요?)

1.2. 감탄문에서

02 a. **Hasn't she** grown!

b. She has grown a lot.
(그 애 정말 많이 컸구나!)

03 a. **Did he** look annoyed!

b. He looked very annoyed.
(그는 정말 곤혹스러워 보였다.)

04 a. What **have I** not suffered!

b. I have suffered a lot.
(나 정말 혼났다.)

부정어 "not"은 부정(否定)의 의미 없이 허사(虛辭)로 쓰이며 감탄의 정도를 높이는 역할을 한다. 형태는 부정 의문문이지만 질문이라기보다는 경이(驚異)의 표현이나 동의를 구하는 표현이다.

1.3. 기원문에서

05 a. **May God** bless you!

b. God bless you!
(하나님의 축복이 있기를!)

06 **May the new year** bring you happiness!
(새해 복 많이 받으십시오. = I wish you a happy new year.)

주어가 3인칭인 경우에 조동사 "may"가 생략되어 나타나는 경우가 많으나 그 경우에도 동사는 여전히 원형을 사용한다.

1.4. 부정 명령문에서

07 a. **Don't you** talk like that.

b. Don't talk like that.
(그렇게 말하지 마라.)

08 **Don't anybody** move.
(아무도 움직이지 마라.)

명령문은 대화의 현장에 있는 상대방에게 명령하는 문장이다. 따라서 사용된 주어가 형태상 2인칭인 "you"가 아니더라도 상황을 고려해볼 때에 대화의 현장에 있는 2인칭이다. 예문 (8)에서의 "anybody"는 "any of you present here"의 의미이다. 일반적으로 주어를 생략하지만 강한 명령이나, 분노, 특정인을 지칭할 때에는 주어를 사용한다.

1.5. "if"를 생략한 가정법에서

09 a. If I had known what was going to happen, I would never have left her alone.

b. **Had I** known what was going to happen, I would never have left her alone.
(무슨 일이 일어날 지 알았더라면 나는 그녀를 혼자 내버려 두지 않았을 것이다.)

10 a. If I were rich, I could help all of you.

b. **Were I** rich, I could help all of you.
(내가 부자라면 너희들 모두들 도와줄 수 있을 텐데.)

11 a. If I should fail this time, I would try it again.

b. **Should I** fail this time, I would try it again.
(혹시라도 이번에 실패한다면 나는 그것을 다시 한번 해볼 것이다.)

가정법 과거, 과거완료, 미래를 포함하여 "if"가 이끄는 부사절에서 "if"를 생략하면 주어와 조동사가 도치가 된다.

1.6. 부정 요소 전치 구문에서

12 a. We don't know the values of health until we lose it.

b. **Not** until we lose health **do we** know its value.
(우리는 건강을 잃고 나서야 비로소 건강의 가치를 안다.)

13 a. We can transform those obsolete power structures that threaten our future only when this is understood.

b. **Only** when this is understood **can we** transform those obsolete power structures that threaten our future.
(이점을 이해할 때에만 우리는 우리의 미래를 위협하는 그런 낡은 권력구조를 바꿀 수 있다.)

부정(否定) 요소를 문두에 놓는 이유는 부정의 의미를 강조하기 위한 것이며 초점으로서 강한 억양을 받는다. 그리고 이런 요소들이 문두에 놓이면 반드시 주어와 조동사는 도치되어야 한다. 이런 종류의 부정어에는 not~ , never, no~, nothing, hardly, scarcely, rarely, seldom, only, at no time, under no circumstances, in no way, on no account 등이 있다.

1.7. So / Nor / Neither 다음에서

14 a. He is an honest fellow. **So is his brother.**
(그는 정직한 사람이다. 그의 동생도 마찬가지이다.)

b. I caught a cold and **so did my wife.**
(나는 감기에 걸렸다. 그리고 나의 아내도 마찬가지이다.)

c. I must leave now. **So must I.**
(나는 지금 떠나야 한다. 나도 그래.)

"So + 조동사 + 주어"는 "주어도 그래"의 뜻으로 쓰이는데 이런 경우에 선행문장은 긍정문이어야 하고 선행문장에서 쓰인 조동사와 같은 조동사가 사용되어야 한다.

15 a. I am not tired. **Neither (Nor) am I.**
(난 피곤하지 않아. 나도 그래.)

b. He did not go and **neither (nor) did I.**
(그는 가지 않았다. 나도 안 갔어.)

c. I can't swim. **Neither (Nor) can I.**
(나는 수영을 못해. 나도 그래.)

"Nor/Neither + 조동사 + 주어"는 "주어도 (안)그래"의 뜻으로 쓰이는데 이런 경우에 선행문장은 부정문이어야 하고 선행문장에서 쓰인 조동사와 같은 조동사가 사용되어야 한다.

1.8. 비교 접속사 "as"나 "than" 뒤에서

16 a. She respects him far more **than does her son.**

b. She respects him far more than her son does.
(그녀는 아들이 존경하는 것보다 훨씬 더 그를 존경한다.)

17 a. She traveled a great deal, as **did most of her friends.**

b. She traveled a great deal, as most of her friends did.
(그녀는 그녀의 대부분의 친구들과 마찬가지로 여행을 많이 했다.)

비교접속사 "as, than" 다음에서 주어가 대명사가 아닌 경우에 주어와 조동사가 도치될 수 있다.

1.9. 강조 요소 뒤에서

18 a. So absurd did he look that everyone stared at him.

b. He looked so absurd that everyone stared at him.
(그가 너무 우스워 보였다. 그래서 모든 사람들이 그를 쳐다보았다.)

19 a. To such an extreme did they go that all moderate solutions became impossible.

b. They went to such an extreme that all moderate solutions became impossible.
(그들이 너무 극단으로 치달았기 때문에 모든 온건한 해결책은 불가능하게 되었다.)

20 a. Especially did we enjoy the life of the beaches.

b. We especially enjoy the life of the beaches.(특히 우리는 광장 생활을 즐겼다.)

"so, such, especially, well"등과 같은 강조 요소가 문두에 놓이면 주어와 조동사가 도치된다.

2 보충 설명

21 a. A story for children, whether it be written or spoken, should have a great deal of action.

b. A story for children, be it written or spoken, should have a great deal of action.
(어린이들을 위한 이야기는 글로 쓰든 혹은 말로 하든 많은 몸 동작이 있어야 한다.)

22 a. Let it be ever so humble, there is no place like home.

b. Be it ever so humble, there is no place like home.

c. However humble it may be, there is no place like home.
(집이 아무리 초라하다 해도 집만한 곳은 없다.)

접속사 "if"와 마찬가지로 양보절을 이끄는 "Whether"와 "Let"이 생략될 때에도 조동사가 "be"일 때에는 주어와 조동사가 도치된다.

23 a. Allen can speak English better than I can.
(Allen은 나보다 더 영어를 더 잘 할 수 있다.)

b. *Allen can speak English better than can I.

접속사 "than"뒤의 주어가 명사가 아닌 대명사인 경우에는 주어 조동사의 도치가 일어나지 않는다.

24 a. Not all economists agree with you.
(모든 경제학자가 너와 의견을 같이하고 있는 것은 아니다.)

b. Not a single word passed his lips.
(단 한 마디 말도 그의 입에서 나오지 않았다.)

25 a. Not long ago he went to America.
(얼마 전에 그는 미국으로 갔다.)

b. *Not long ago did he go to America.

c. In no time at all they had routed the enemy.
(그들은 즉시 적을 물리쳤다.)

d. *In no time at all had they routed the enemy.

예문 (24)와 (25)에서와 같이 부정요소가 문두에 와도 주어와 조동사의 도치가 일어나지 않은 경우가 있다. 부정요소가 주어를 부정하거나 문장의 동사를 부정하지 않고 바로 뒤따르고 있는 단어를 부정하는 경우에는 도치가 일어나지 않는다. "not long ago"는 "안 오래 전에" 다시 말해서 "얼마 전에"라는 뜻으로 부정어가 뒤따르는 단어를 부정하고 있으며, 만찬가지로 "in no time"은 "전혀 시간이 걸리지 않고" 다시 말해 "즉시, 곧"의 의미를 갖는다.
그리고 이렇게 전치된 요소는 초점으로서 역할을 하지않으며 강한 스트레스를 받지도 않는다.

26 a. For no money, she would dance naked.
(돈이 없어서 그녀는 벌거 벗고 춤을 추곤 했다.)

b. For no money would she dance naked.
(아무리 많은 돈을 주어도 벌거벗고 춤은 추지 않을 것이다.)

예문 (26a)와 (26b)는 부정요소가 전치되어 있다. 하지만 주절의 주어와 조동사가 도치된 문장도 정문이고 도치가 되지 않은 문장도 정문이다. 주어와 조동사가 도치가 된 경우에는 부정어가 뒤따르는 단어를 부정하지 않고 문장을 부정하지만, 반면에 주어와 조동사가 도치가 되지 않은 경우에는 부정어가 뒤따르는 단어를 부정하는 국부부정을 하고 있다.

Practice Examples

Reading 01

My father, the poet Su Jinsan, was criticized in 1957 as one of the most notorious "rightists" in Henan province. My mother was labeled an "extreme rightist" because she refused to divorce him. They were both attacked again during the Cultural Revolution. In 1989 I worried about my children, especially my elder son. In May I sent him to my hometown on the pretext that my father was ill. **Little did I imagine that my younger son, Zhao Long, would die.** At 4 a.m. on June 4, Zhao Long still hadn't returned home, so I set out to find him. I headed toward the square, but it was overrun with soldiers. I went to the nearby hospitals, carrying his photo. I worked my way through the sick rooms to the morgue. The bodies were in drawers. We pulled out one after another looking for him. My husband and I finally found Zhao Long on June 6 at the No. 3 Hospital.

/Time.

Word Bank

- criticize: 비난하다, 혹평하다.
- notorious: 악명 높은, 유명한.
- rightist: 우익파, 보수주의자.
- divorce: 이혼하다.
- hometown: 고향.
- pretext: 구실, 핑계
- set out: 착수하다, 시작하다.
- head: 나아가다, 향하다.
- overrun: 짓밟다, 범람하다.
- morgue: 시체 공시장(公示場),
- body: 몸, 시체. drawer: 서랍, 장롱.
- work one's way: 고생하며 나아가다, 고학하다. (이와 같은 표현은 "TOUGH"이동 연습문제 (6)에서 설명되고 있다.)

Reading 02

"It is the last one," said Johnsy. "I thought it would surely fall during the night. I heard the wind. It will fall today and I shall die at the same time." "Dear, dear! " said Sue, leaning her worn face down to the pillow, "think of me, if you won't think of yourself. **What would I do?**"

/O. Henry. The Last Leaf

Word Bank

- lean: 기울이다, 의지하게 하다.
- worn: 지친, 수척한.
- pillow: 베개.

Reading 03

The next morning before the plane came to get us, I asked my mother if she would like to come back and live with me in England or the United States. "But what would I do?" "That's precisely it. I don't want you to do anything. You've done enough work. It's time to rest." "No. Your father's getting old and he needs me. Besides, I can't just sit around. If you want to do something, get me a place in Somalia that I can go to when I'm tired. This is my home. This is all I've ever known." I gave her a big hug. "I love you, Mama. **I'm coming back for you, don't you forget that.**"

/Reader's Digest.

Word Bank

- That's it. 그것이 문제다. 네 말이 맞다.
- place: 주거, 집.

Reading 04

Before we turn to these new possibilities, we need to press our analysis of the dying system. We need to X-ray our obsolete political system to see how it fitted into the frame of Second Wave civilization, how it served the industrial order and its elites. **Only then can we understand why it is no longer appropriate or tolerable.**

/Alvin Toffler. The Third Wave

Word Bank

- press: 추진하다, 실행하다.
- dying: 죽어가는, 사라져 가는
- obsolete: 사라진, 시대에 뒤떨어진.
- X-ray: 의 엑스선 사진을 찍다, 엑스선으로 검사하다.
- fit: 적합하다, 어울리다.
- frame: 틀, 액자.
- serve: 기여하다.
- elite: 엘리트, 정예.
- tolerable: 지탱할 수 있는.

Reading 05

Mr. Arafat is a revolutionary terrorist. And so long as he commands the Palestinian Authority, there will be no peace in the Middle East. At Camp David, Israeli Prime Minister Ehud Barak and President Clinton offered Mr. Arafat the most generous terms. Mr. Arafat flatly rejected the offer. **Had he accepted, occupation would be at an end and there would be a Palestine state today.** There would be no need for violence. It should be clear to the international community, the Palestinians and the Israeli public that so long as Yasser Arafat heads a terrorist organization, there will be no Palestine state. Mr. Arafat is not a partner for peace, and he must go. Obviously, it is up to the Palestinians to bring a revolutionary change to their government.

/Washington Times.

Word Bank

- revolutionary: 혁명의, 혁명적인.
- authority: 권한, 정부.
- term: 조건, 협정.
- occupation: 점령.
- up to: 에 달려있는, 의 책임은.
- command: 지휘하다, 지배하다.
- Prime Minister: 수상, 총리.
- flatly: 평평하게, 단호하게.
- head: 의 장이 되다, 을 지도하다.

구문 설명

"Had he accepted, occupation would be at an end and there would be a Palestine state today." = "If he had accepted, occupation would be at an end and there would be a Palestine state today." 이 문장은 조건절에서는 가정법 과거완료와 귀결절에서는 가정법 과거가 섞인 형태를 취하고 있다.

Reading 06

I do not deny that the feeling of success makes it easier to enjoy life. A painter, let us say, who has been obscure throughout his youth, is likely to become happier if his talent wins recognition. **Nor do I deny that money up to a certain point, is very capable of increasing happiness;** beyond that point, I do not think it does. What I do maintain is that success can only be one ingredient in happiness, and is too dearly purchased if all the other ingredients have been sacrificed to obtain it.

/Bertrand Russell: The Conquest of Happiness

Word Bank

- let us say: 이를테면, 말하자면(= say, shall we say).
- obscure: 애매한, 무명의.
- recognition: 인정, 인식.
- ingredient: 요소, 성분.

구문 설명

1. I do not think it does. = I do not think it increases happiness.
2. What I do maintain is that success can only be one ingredient in happiness, and is too dearly purchased if ~ = I maintain that success can only be one ingredient in happiness, and is too dearly purchased if ~. "maintain"의 목적어절을 준 분열 구문을 이용해 초점화 하고 있다. 자세한 설명은 분열 구문 참조.

Reading 07

In coping with international crises, coherent diplomacy is indispensable. So is political and economic pressure. But they are rarely sufficient, if it seems certain that they will almost never be backed by force. **Nor should it be assumed that force can always be limited to air power.** What if bombing does not settle a conflict--does the U.S. then just walk away? The use of ground forces simply cannot be ruled out if the U.S. wants to be taken seriously. American politicians of all shades keep talking about the need for U.S. leadership, but leadership is expensive-in money and sometimes in lives. If we really mean to lead, and to bring about a world more or less congenial to itself, we should stop pretending that we can do the job on the cheap and by remote control. In many situations, if they want a peace to keep, we will have to go beyond peacekeeping.

/Time.

Word Bank

- cope: 대처하다(with).
- coherent: 응집성의, 일관성 있는.
- diplomacy: 외교.
- rarely: 좀처럼 ~않다(= seldom).
- back: 후원하다, 지지하다.
- force: 군사력, 무력.
- walk away: 떠나다.
- rule out: 제외하다, 제쳐놓다.
- all shades: (문맥상) 의견의 다양함(= all shades in opinion).
- keep ~ing: 계속해서 ~하다.
- lead: 이끌다, 앞장서다.
- congenial: 마음이 맞는, 적합한.
- pretend: ~인 체하다, 이라고 속이다.
- on the cheap: 싸게.
- go beyond: 을 능가하다, 을 넘다.

구문 설명

1. So is political and economic pressure. = In coping with international crises, political and economic pressure is also indispensable. 자세한 설명은 주어 조동사 도치 구문 참조.
2. "Nor should it be assumed that force ~"에서 "it"은 "that"이하의 절을 받는다. 자세한 설명은 외치 참조.
3. What if bombing does not settle a conflict? = What will happen if bombing does not settle a conflict?

Reading 08

During his long career as an agitator, Hitler had studied the effects of herd poison and had learned how to exploit them for his own purposes. He had discovered that the orator can appeal to those hidden forces which motivate men's action, much more effectively **than can the writer.** The writer speaks only to individuals, sitting by themselves in a state of normal sobriety.

/Aldous Leonard Huxley. Propaganda Under a Dictatorship

Word Bank

- agitator: 선동가.
- exploit: 이용하다, 착취하다.
- sobriety: 취해있지 않음, 진지함.
- herd: 군중, 대중.
- orator: 연설자, 웅변가.

구문 설명

much more effectively than can the writer. = much more effectively than the writer can appeal to them.

Reading 09

Miss Bennet's astonishment was soon lessened by the strong sisterly partiality which made any admiration of Elizabeth appear perfectly natural; and all surprise was shortly lost in other feelings. She was sorry that Mr. Darcy should have delivered his sentiments in a manner so little suited to recommend them; but still more was she grieved for **the unhappiness which her sister's refusal must have given him.**

/Jane Austen. Pride and Prejudice

Word Bank

- astonishment: 놀람, 경악.
- lessen: 감소시키다, 줄이다.
- sisterly: 자매의, 자매다운.
- partiality: 편견, 편애.
- recommend: 추천하다, 의 호감을 사다.

구문 설명

~ the unhappiness which her sister's refusal must have given him. = ~ the unhappiness which he must have because of her sister's refusal.

Reading 10

A woman walked into the shoe store, tried on a dozen pairs of shoes, without finding a proper fit. Finally, the bored assistant told her, "Madam, we can't fit you because one of your feet is larger than the other." The woman walked out of the store without buying anything. In the next store, the fitting proved equally difficult. At last, the smiling assistant explained, "Madam, **do you know that one of your feet is smaller than the other?**" The woman left the store with two new pairs of shoes under her arm.

/Reader's Digest.

Word Bank

- try on: 입어 보다, 착용해보다.
- assistant: 조수, 점원(= clerk).
- fit: 몸에 맞는 것.

구문 설명

~ with two new pairs of shoes under her arm. 자세한 설명은 "WITH" 주술관계 참조.

Reading 11

Parents need to be especially vigilant not to say something casually that they may be alarmed to hear later in the mouths of their children. A wife who tells her husband to shut up and a father who calls a neighbor a jerk are likely to hear their children speak the same way to them. "If we aren't practicing good manners, how can we expect our children to?" notes etiquette author and "Ms. Demeanor" columnist Mary Mitchell. Prompt and Praise. "You're such a mess; you never clean up your room." "You'd better write that thank-you note or you're not watching TV." **"Don't you raise your voice to me."** Most parents have said these things to their children. They're meant to correct behavior. Why, then, do they fail so miserably? Because rude behavior in children is more often the result of thoughtlessness than of deliberate aggression. Criticism, name-calling and orders only make a child angry and defensive. They reinforce the notion that the child is incapable of good behavior whout coercion.

/Reader's Digest.

Word Bank

- vigilant: 조심성 있는, 자지않고 주의하는.
- casually:우연히, 무심코.
- jerk: 얼간이, 멍청이.
- etiquette: 예의, 예법.
- alarmed: 깜짝 놀란.
- practice: 을 늘 행하다, 연습하다.
- columnist: 기고가.

- prompt: 자극하다, 재촉하다.
- aggression; 공격, 침략.
- reinforce: 강화하다, 보강하다.
- thank-you: 감사의, 사례의.
- coercion: 강제, 강압.

구문 설명

1. "~ not to say something casually that they may be ~"에서 "that"절은 "something"을 수식하는 관계 대명사절이다. 부사 "casually"때문에 선행사로부터 분리된 것이다. 탈명사구 외치편 참조.
2. "~, how can we expect our children to?" = "~, how can we expect our children to practice good manners?". "to"는 대부정사.
3. Why, then, they fail so miserably? = Why, then, they fail so miserably to correct behavior?

Reading 12

He knows his mother well and how irritating she can be to everybody. But so far we haven't been able to come up with any good solution. I do respect his mother. **Never have I talked back to her or argued with her, no matter how wrong I think she is.** Part of the reason is also that if you try to tell her something while she's lecturing you, she'll get louder and louder until your ears finally explode and give up. Can you give me some advice on how to deal with someone who you absolutely cannot stand, but have to learn to get along with? I am very worried about our future in this aspect.

/http://www.loveadvice.com/

Word Bank

- irritating: 화나게 하는, 약 올리는.
- come up with: 을 내놓다. 제안하다.
- lecture: 에게 강의하다, 에게 설교하다.
- explode: 폭발하다, 파열하다.
- give up: 체념하다. stand: 참다.
- get along with: 와 사이 좋게 지내다.

구문 설명

get + 보어: 보어 되다. It is getting warmer and warmer day by day. (날씨가 하루하루 더 더워지고 있다)

Reading 13

Take a walk. A Swiss study showed that one hour outdoors during the daytime-even when the sun is not shining-provides enough light to lift the spirit significantly. Have Fun. In summer, families can clear the dinner dishes and still have plenty of time for a back-yard catch or Frisbee throwing. **Come winter, we stay indoors.** Despite the weather there are enjoyable ways to get the physical activity we need.

/Reader's Digest.

Word Bank

- clear: 명백히 하다, 치우다.
- backyard: 뒤뜰.
- catch: 캐치볼.
- Frisbee: (원반 던지기 놀이의) 플라스틱 원반.
- come: ~이 오면.

구문 설명

"Come winter, we stay indoors." = "When winter comes, we stay indoors."
일반동사는 "if"를 생략하게 되면 드물게 조동사 "do"를 사용해 주어 조동사를 쓰는 경우가 있으나 잘 쓰지 않는 표현이다. 특이하게 "come", "go", "fare" 등이 도치되어 주어 앞에 놓이는 경우가 있다. How goes it with you? = How does it go with you? (요즈음 경기는 어떻습니까?); How fares it with you? = How does it fare with you? (어떻게 지내십니까?)

Reading 14

It must been about two in the morning when I returned home. I tried to wake up my wife by ringing the doorbell, but she was fast asleep, so I got a ladder from the shed in the garden, put it against to the wall, and began climbing towards the bedroom window. I was almost there when a sarcastic voice below said, "I don't think the windows need cleaning at this time of the night." I looked down and nearly fell off the ladder when I saw a policeman. I immediately regretted answering in the way I did, but I said, "I enjoy cleaning windows at night." **'So do I,'** answered the policeman in the same tone. "Excuse my interrupting you. I hate to interrupt a man when he's busy working, but would you mind coming with me to the station?" "Well, I'd prefer to stay here," I said. "You see, I've forgotten my key." "Your what?" he called. "My key," I shouted. Fortunately, the shouting woke up my wife who opened the window just as the policeman had started to climb towards me.

/L. G. Alexander. Practice and Progress

Word Bank

- fast: 푹, 깊게.
- ladder: 사다리.
- shed: 헛간, 광.
- sarcastic: 빈정대는, 비꼬는.
- excuse: 용서하다.
- interrupt: 방해하다, 중단하다.
- forget: 을 두고 오다, 을 가지고 나오는 것을 잊다(= leave behind).

구문 설명

I don't think the windows need cleaning at this time of the night. = I don't think the windows need to be cleaned at this time of the night.

Reading 15

In the fall, Vanessa happily discovered she was pregnant. **No sooner had she and Robert begun to celebrate and plan, though, than she miscarried.** For months she and Robert mourned the loss. It seemed a bitter winter. But with the arrival of spring the couple began thinking of trying again.

/Reader's Digest.

Word Bank

- pregnant: 임신한.
- though: 그러나(= however).
- no sooner A than B: A하자마자 B하다(= hardly/scarcely A when/before B).
- celebrate: 축하하다, 의식을 거행하다.
- plan: 계획을 세우다.
- miscarry: 유산하다(= abort)

구문설명

1. Vanessa happily discovered she was pregnant. = She was happy to discover she was pregnant. 문장 부사는 형용사로 바꾸어야 이해하기 좋은 경우가 많다. 이런 문장부사는 확신(certainly, surely, absolutely, evidently, etc)이나 추측(presumably, probably, possibly, etc)을 나타내는 말들이거나 그리고 어미가 ~ably(understandably, conceivably, reasonably, undeniably, etc)나 ~edly(reportedly, admittedly, supposedly, allegedly, etc)가 붙은 단어가 많다. Understandably, he bitterly attacked Communism. = It is understandable that he bitterly attacked Communism. (그가 공산주의를 신랄하게 공격하는 것은 이해가 된다.). The criminal is reportedly still at large. = According to reports, the criminal is still at large. = It is reported that the criminal is still at large. = Reports have it that the criminal is still at large. (보도된 바에 의하면 그 범인은 아직 붙잡히지 않았다.).
2. But with the arrival of spring the couple ~. = But when spring arrived, the couple ~. (WITH 주술관계 참조)

Reading 16

A unanimous federal appeals court on June 28 overturned the court-ordered breakup of Microsoft but ruled that the software giant violated antitrust laws. In a rare rebuke, the appellate judges said the trial judge seriously tainted the case with his derogatory comments about Bill Gates and his empire. In a 7-0 ruling, the U.S. Court of Appeals for the District of Columbia Circuit set aide the breakup order, narrowed the antitrust case and sent it to a new judge to decide whether a breakup or some other penalty is warranted for the software giant. Although U.S. District Judge Thomas Penfield Jackson engaged in serious misconduct, the appeals judges said, "We agree with the District Court that the company behaved anti-competitively and that these actions contribute to the maintenance of its monopoly power." **Though its legal troubles aren't behind it yet, Microsoft's stock shot up, as did the spirits of company executives.** They pressed ahead with plans for their new Windows XP operating system and Internet services with a promise to pursue settlement talks.

/Associated Press.

Word Bank

- unanimous: 만장일치의.
- appeal: 항소, 상고.
- overturn: 전복하다, 뒤엎다.
- antitrust: 독점 금지의.
- appellate judge: 항소 판사.
- ruling: 판결.
- circuit: 순회 재판구,
- set aside: 제쳐놓다, 취소하다.
- misconduct: 비행, 직권 남용.
- district court: 지방 법원.
- competitively: 경쟁적으로.
- behind: 을 지원하여, 지지하여.
- shoot up: 급등하다, 우뚝 솟다.
- press ahead with: 추진하다.
- federal: 연방의.
- court: 법원.
- breakup: 분할, 분해.
- rebuke: 질책, 비난.
- trial judge: 예심 판사

Reading 17

These days, people who do manual work often receive far more money than clerks who work in office. People who work in offices are frequently referred to as 'white collar workers' for the simple reason that they usually wear the white collar and tie to go to work. **Such is human nature, that a great many people are often willing to sacrifice higher pay for the privilege of becoming white collar workers.**

/L.G. Alexander. Developing Skills

Word Bank

- refer to A as B: A를 B라고 부르다.
- nature: 본성, 천성.
- sacrifice: 을 바치다, 을 희생물로 하다.
- privilege: 특권, 특전.

Reading 18

"Are you English?" I asked, perhaps tactlessly. "Rather. **You don't think I look like an American, do you?** British to the backbone, that's what I am." To prove it, Mr. Kelada took out of his pocket a passport and airily waved it under my nose. King George has many strange subjects. He spoke with a fluency in which there was nothing English. I felt pretty sure that a closer inspection of his passport would have betrayed the fact that Mr. Kelada was born under a bluer sky than generally seen in England.

/W. Somerset Maugham. Mr. Know-All

Word Bank

- tactlessly: 재치 없이.
- rather: 물론이죠, 그렇고 말고요.
- to the backbone: 철저하게, 완전히.
- passport: 여권, 증명서.
- George: 영국 왕의 이름.
- inspection: 조사, 검사.
- airily: 가볍게.
- subject: 백성, 국민.
- betray: 드러내다.

구문 설명

1. ~ a closer inspection of his passport would have betrayed the fact ~ = ~ if I had inspected his passport more closely, it would have betrayed the fact ~.
2. ~ Mr. Kelada took out of his pocket a passport ~ = ~ Mr. Kelada took a passport out of his pocket ~. 자세한 설명은 복합명사구 이동 참조.

Reading 19

Man is gifted with reason; he is life being aware of itself; he has awareness of himself, of his fellow man, of his past, and of the possibilities of his future. This awareness of himself as separate entity, the awareness of his own short life span, of the fact that without his will he is born and against his will he dies, that he will die before those whom he loves, or they before him, the awareness of his aloneness and separateness, of his helplessness before the forces of nature and of society, all this makes his separate, disunited existence an unbearable prison. **He would become insane could he not liberate himself from this prison and reach out, unite himself in some form or other with men, with the world outside.**

/Erich Fromm. The Art Of Loving

Word Bank

- gift: 을 선물로 주다, 을 천부적으로 부여하다.
- separate: 분리된, 독립된, 개개의.
- life span: 수명.
- helplessness: 무력, 무능.
- liberate: 해방하다, 석방하다.
- against: 에 반하여.
- disunite: 분리하다.
- unite: 결합시키다, 합병시키다.

구문 설명

"~ that he will die before those whom he loves, or they before him, ~" = " ~ that he will die before those whom he loves, or they will die before him, ~"
He would become insane could he not liberate himself ~ = He would become insane if he could not liberate himself ~.

Reading 20

However, the accusations of rudeness being made against the owners of cellular telephones are often unfair. "They're just showing off," is the charge hurled at people who use their cell phones to do what everybody else is legitimately doing-talking on the bus, making calls from the sidewalk, chatting while driving a car. An expensive telephone might be considered a status symbol-but **so are a lot of other things that are less obviously useful and yet don't arouse public ire.** It should be recognized that the cell phone is just a tool. What determines rudeness is how it is used. People who need to shout into their cell phone probably just need a better phone, but shouting itself is already an etiquette violation.

/Time.

Word Bank

- accusation: 비난.
- rudeness: 무례함, 버릇없음.
- show off: 과시하다, 허세부리다.
- charge: 비난, 고소.
- hurl: 을 던지다, 퍼붓다.
- legitimately: 합법적으로, 정당하게.
- sidewalk: 인도, 보도.
- ire: 화, 분노.

구문설명

1. but so are a lot of other things that are less obviously useful and yet don't arouse public ire. = but a lot of other things that are less obviously useful and yet don't arouse public ire are considered a status symbol.
2. "What determines rudeness is how it is used."은 "How it is used determines rudeness."에서 주어절을 포커스화 시킨 준 분열구문 이다. 자세한 설명은 분열구문 참조.

Reading 21

Is the United States a free country? Not by traditional measures. In the history of Western civilization, freedom has an economic meaning and a legal meaning. The U.S. fails both measures of freedom. April 15 Tax Day which confronted us this week has come to symbolize America′s lack of economic freedom. **Americans have no more claim to their incomes than did medieval serfs.** The most successful Americans are comparable to slaves. The long struggle for freedom was a struggle to own oneself and the value of one′s labor. European serfs did not own their labor. Consequently, they were not free to sell their labor in markets for wages.

/Washington Times.

Word Bank

- measure: 기준, 조치.
- fail: 의 도움이 되지않다, 기대에 어긋나다.
- confront: 직면하다, 들이 닥치다.
- claim: 주장, 청구.
- medieval: 중세의.
- serf: 농노, 노예.

구문 설명

A is no more B than C is D. = A is not B any more than C is D. = A is not B, just as C is not D. (C가 D가 아닌 것처럼 A는 B가 아니다.)

Reading 2

Just as Socrates felt that it was necessary to create a tension in the mind so that individuals could rise from the bondage of myths and half-truths to the unfettered realm of creative analysis and objective appraisal, so must we see the need for nonviolent gadflies to create the kind of tension in society that will help men rise from the dark depths of prejudice and racism to the majestic heights of understanding and brotherhood. The purpose of our direct-action program is to create a situation so crisis-packed that it will inevitably open the door to negotiation. I therefore concur with you in your call for negotiation. **Too long has our beloved Southland been bogged down in a tragic effort to live in monologue rather than dialogue.**

/Martin Luther King, Jr. Letter from Birmingham Jail

Word Bank

- create: 일으키다, 야기하다.
- tension: 긴장, 불안.
- bondage: 노예의 신분, 속박.
- myth:신화, 잘못된 통념(an unfounded or false belief).
- half-truth: 일부만 진실인 말(a statement that is only partially true, a statement that mingles truth and falsehood with deliberate intent to deceive).
- unfettered: 족쇄가 풀린, 속박에서 벗어난.
- appraisal: 평가, 감정.
- gadfly: 쇠파리, 끈질기게 주장하는 사람(= a person who stimulates or annoys especially by persistent criticism)
- concur: 동의하다, 일치하다.
- beloved: 사랑하는, 귀여운.
- bog: 꼼짝 못하게 하다, 빠뜨리다.
- monologue: 독백.

구문 설명

just as A, so B: "just"은 "바로"나 "꼭"의 뜻으로 "as"를 강조. 그리고 "so"는 생략 가능하며 "so"가 있을 때는 종종 주어와 조동사가 도치된다. As food nourishes our body, so books nourish our mind/so do books nourish our mind. (음식이 우리 몸에 영양분을 공급해주는 것처럼, 책은 우리 마음에 영양분을 공급해준다).

Reading 23

In England, landlords and businessmen who had any surplus money began to deposit it for safety with the goldsmith. And he would lend the money at a high interest. **Gradually his lending department became so profitable that not only did he stop charging the depositors for safeguarding their wealth. but he actually paid them for doing it.** He would of course pay them less than he charged those borrowing from him. The difference between what he paid depositors and what he charged borrowers constituted his profits. The modern bank has shed its goldsmith's business and has specialized in this receiving and loaning of money.

/Victor Cohen. The Origin of Modern Bank

Word Bank

- landlord: 지주.
- surplus: 잉여의, 여분의, 나머지의.
- deposit: 맡기다.
- interest: 이자.
- lending department: 대출부.
- profitable: 이익이 되는, 유익한.
- safeguard: 막다, 보호하다.
- charge: 청구하다, 에게 부담시키다.
- constitute: 을 구성하다.
- shed: 버리다. 떨어뜨리다.
- specialize in: 을 전문으로 하다.

구문설명

"paid them for doing it"에서 "doing it"은 앞의 "safeguarding their wealth"를 받는다.

Reading 24

Democracy, we are told, brings not merely political responsibility and maturity but happiness and prosperity. See it bring joy to those who once labored under communism. **Pity the victims of African dictatorships, whose societies would resemble our own could they enjoy its benefits.** Bewail the absence of democracy in both Yugoslavia and Iraq. If these countries could cast off the dictator's yoke they would become as fair and decent, as just and reasonable, as NATO's members.

/Time.

Word Bank

- labor: 열심히 일하다, 고생하다.
- pity: 에 동정하다, 불쌍히 여기다.
- bewail; 을 몹시 슬퍼하다.
- cast off: 버리다.
- yoke: 멍에, 속박.
- decent: 품위있는, 꽤 좋은.
- NATO: 북대서양 조약기구(= North Atlantic Treaty Organization).

Reading 25

He didn't stay in touch. **Neither did she.** He signed the divorce papers when they arrived a year later and caught a plane for Australia the next day. She had asked for nothing except her freedom.

/Robert James Waller. The Bridges of Madison County

Word Bank

- touch: 접촉.
- divorce: 이혼.

Reading 26

Matt got permission to go to a movie with two friends, freshman Cory Engen and senior Lee Grandt. But the boys headed instead for the apartment of 18-year-old Amy Pestor. **Amy's sister Karin, 12, was there, as were two of Matt's classmates, David Milbrandt and Ross Raymond.** The seven kids talked and watched TV. No one touched the beer in the refrigerator.

/Reader's Digest.

Word Bank

- head: 향하다, 나아가다.

구문 설명

instead = instead of going to a movie

Reading 27

The new role of woman in American life outside the home has brought about changes in the social structure and in the way the American family lives. **No longer is the family property solely in the hands of the husband, and no longer is the husband's consent necessary if a woman is to transact business.** Increasingly women have become joint owners of property with their husbands or owners in their own right. Increasingly they have been transacting business by themselves. With women owning a share in the family property, women have more say in determining how the family income shall be spent. Family decisions in matters of finance, religion, politics, policies of raising the children, health, and recreation are generally the result of discussions between husband and wife.

/Gladys Doty Janet Ross. Language and Life in the U.S.A.

Word Bank

- bring about: 일어나게 하다, 생기게 하다.
- property: 재산, 자산.
- transact: 행하다, 처리하다.
- in one's own right: 당연히, 자기만으로.
- In matters of: 에 관해서는.
- consent: 동의, 승낙.

구문 설명

1. 무생물 주어는 자주 부사적으로 옮기는 것이 좋다. "The new role of woman in American life outside the home has brought about changes in the social structure and in the way the American family lives." = "Because of the new role of women in American life outside of the home, there have been changes in the social structure and in the way the American family lives."
2. "and no longer is the husband's consent necessary if a woman is to transact business."에서 "if" 절 안의 "be to"는 "intent to/wish to"의 의미이다.
3. With women owning a share in the family property, women have more say in ~ = As women own a share in the family property, women have more say in ~. (WITH 주술관계 참조)

Reading 8

In 1872 he married Marian Hooper, an heiress and a woman of remarkable character. She killed herself in 1885. Adams loved only two women in his life, his sister and his wife, and both died tragically. **Nowhere in his autobiographical writings does he so much as mention his marriage; the wound was too deep to probe.**

/Stanley J. K. American Authors

Word Bank

- heiress: 여자 상속인.
- autobiographic: 자서전의.
- remarkable: 주목할 만한, 비범한.
- probe: 엄밀히 조사하다, 규명하다.

Reading 29

They were within twenty yards of each other, and **so abrupt was his appearance, that it was impossible to avoid his sight.** Their eyes instantly met, and the cheeks of each were overspread with the deepest blush. He absolutely started, and for a moment seemed immovable from surprise; but shortly recovering himself, advanced towards the party, and spoke to Elizabeth, if not in terms of perfect composure, at least of perfect civility.

/Jane Austin. Pride and Prejudice

Word Bank

- overspread: 을 온통 덮다.
- blush: 불그레함, 홍조.
- in terms of : 의 말로, 의 관점에서.
- composure: 냉정, 침착.
- deep: 짙은.
- party: 일행, 당.
- civility: 공손, 예의 바름.

구문 설명

1. ~ and so abrupt was his appearance that his sight was impossible to avoid. = ~ and he appeared so abruptly that it was impossible to avoid his sight. ("TOUGH" 이동 참조).
2. ~, if not in terms of perfect composure, ~. = ~, if he did not speak in terms of perfect composure, ~.

Reading 30

It is never too late to increase the love in your life. You only need to learn a new way. Whether you are in therapy or not, if you want to have more fulfilling relationship with the opposite sex, this book is for you. It is a pleasure to share with you Men are from Mars, Women are from Venus. May you always grow in wisdom and in love. **May the frequency of divorce decrease and the number of happy marriages increase.** Our children deserve a better world.

/John Gray. Men are from Mars, Women are from Venus

Word Bank

- therapy. 치료, 요법.
- frequency: 주파수, 빈도.
- fulfill: 수행하다, 만족시키다.
- deserve: 받을만하다, 가치가 있다.

Reading 31

On this national day of prayer and remembrance, we ask almighty God to watch over our nation and grant us patience and resolve in all that is to come. We pray that He will comfort and console those who now walk in sorrow. We thank Him for each life we now must mourn, and the promise of a life to come. As we've been assured, neither death nor life nor angels nor principalities, nor powers nor things present nor things to come nor height nor depth can separate us from God's love. **May He bless the souls of the departed. May He comfort our own. And may He always guide our country.**

/President Bush's Prayer Service Address

Word Bank

- remembrance: 추억, 회상.
- almighty: 절대적인 힘을 가진, 전능의 (= omnipotent).
- watch over: 지키다, 돌보다.
- grant: 주다, 허락하다.
- resolve: 결의, 불굴의 의지.
- comfort: 위로하다, 격려하다.
- console: 위로하다, 달래다.
- mourn: 슬퍼하다, 애도하다.
- principality: 군주의 지위, 권품 천사.
- departed: 죽은. (명사적으로 the departed: 고인).

구문 설명

"As we are ~ from God's love"는 성경 로마서 8장 38절을 인용한 것임.

Reading 32

Not until I came across a report on sleep deprivation did I finally find out something was wrong. The report included a sleepiness quiz, and I flunked it miserably. The results suggested severe sleep disorder. **Only then, once I started following some basic tips for a good night's sleep, did I get on the road to recovery.**

/Reader's Digest.

Word Bank

- come across: 우연히 만나다.
- deprivation: 박탈, 상실, 결핍.
- flunk: 낙제하다, 실패하다(= fail in).
- miserably: 비참한 정도로, 불행하게.
- disorder: 무질서, 병, 질환.
- tip: 조언, 충고.

Reading 33

About five years ago, I received a letter from my birth mother, and we have met a few times. Although she and her family are nice people, and want to continue a relationship - I do not. I have hinted about the way I feel, but they don't seem to understand. I want to tell them outright, but my wife says I will hurt their feelings, and I should leave "the door open" in case I change my mind. I am sure of my feelings and disagree with my wife. I learned that my birth mother was going through a bitter divorce while she was pregnant with me. Money was scarce and she felt she could not afford a third child. **She later remarried-as did my birth father.** I met him once, and he has been more considerate of my feelings. He respects my privacy.

/Universal Press Syndicate. Dear Abby.

Word Bank

- outright: 솔직한
- pregnant: 임신한
- considerate: 사려 깊은
- in case: 에 대비하여
- scarce: 부족한

구문 설명

Although she and her family are nice people, and want to continue a relationship-I do not. = Although she and her family are nice people, and want to continue a relationship-I do not want to continue a relationship.

Reading 34

"We can merge science with herbalism," Duke said. "This will give us better drugs than if we rely on manufactured drugs alone. We can use science to test plants, to find what works best. The issue is not nature versus science; rather it is how to use science to get the best medicine, **be it natural or synthetic.**"

/National Geographic.

Word Bank

- herbalism: 약초학.
- manufacture: 제조하다.
- rely on: 의존하다.

구문 설명

best medicine, be it natural or synthetic. = best medicine, whether it be natural or synthetic.

English Special Constructions

English Special Constructions

Chapter 04

기 타

Chapter 04

기타

Unit 1 분열 구문과 준분열 구문 (Cleft & Pseudo-Cleft)

분열 구문이란 흔히 강조구문이라 하는데, 문장의 어떤 요소를 강조(Emphasis)하기 위하여 다른 요소들과 분리시켜 놓은 문장을 말하며 분열 구문(Cleft)과 준분열 구문(Pseudo-cleft)으로 나눈다. 아래 예문(1b)는 분열 구문이고 (1c)는 준분열 구문인데, 굵은 글씨가 강조되는 요소이고 그 곳이 강조되는 위치이다.

01 a. He read a book yesterday.

b. It was **a book** that he read yesterday.

c. What he read yesterday was **a book**.

분열 구문은 초점(Focus)과 긴밀한 관계가 있다. 초점은 말하는 사람이 아직 상대가 알지 못하고 있다고 가정하는 정보로서 발화를 통해서 듣는 사람에게 알려지는 정보이며, 강조의 일종으로서 문장에서 가장 중요한 정보이다. 그래서 말하는 사람은 자신이 전달하고자 하는 중요한 정보 부분을 다른 부분보다 두드러지게 하게 된다. 그런 방법으로 영어에서는 초점에 강한 스트레스를 부여하거나 초점을 문장 뒷부분에 둔다. 그리고 필요에 따라서는 분열구문 혹은 준분열구문을 사용하게 된다.
분열 구문에서는 강조되는 요소가 초점인 경우가 대부분이지만 "that"절 이하가 초점인 경우도 있다. 우선 강조되는 요소가 초점이 되는 경우에는 문맥에서 신정보이거나 "that"절 보다 덜 친숙한 정보에 해당된다. 혹은 강조되는 요소가 대립되는 정보로 채워지기도 한다. 그러나 후자의 경우에서는 "that"절이 신정보이거나 강조되는 요소 보다 덜 친숙한 정보이어야 한다.
이와 마찬가지로 준분열 구문 역시 강조되는 요소가 초점이 되는 경우가 대부분이지만 "what"절이 초점이 되는 경우도 있다. "what"절이 초점인 경우에는 "what"절이 강조되는 요소 보다 신정보 이거나 덜 친숙한 정보이어야 한다.

1 분열 구문

[It be 강조되는 요소 that ~]의 분열 구문에서는

① 강조어는 주어와 목적어(명사, 대명사와 동명사), 부사(전치사구, 부사, 부사구/절)가 될 수 있으며 보어(명사와 형용사)는 강조어가 될 수 없다.

② "It" 다음의 "be" 의 시제는 종속절의 시제에 따른다.

③ 강조어가 복수가 되어도 "be" 는 "is" 나 "was" 이지, "are" 나 "were" 가 되지 않는다.

1.1. 분열 구문의 유형

1.1.1. 강조되는 요소가 초점인 경우

02 But U.S. collaboration with police and military forces that don't share their concern for civilian lives has marred America's image in the region. This undermines U.S. interests, and bolsters anti-American demagogues, such as Hugo Chavez, the president of Venezuela. This does not mean, however, that the United States should withdraw from the war on drugs in Latin America. **It is primarily America's drug habit that is causing so many of these problems.** So the United States must help other countries contain drug production and its consequences.

(그러나 민간인의 목숨에 미국 당국처럼 관심을 기울이지 않는 경찰 및 군대와 미국정부가 협조함으로써 그 지역에서 미국의 이미지가 손상되고 있다. 이는 미국의 국익을 해치고 Hugo Chavez 베네주엘라 대통령과 같은 반미적인 선동정치가의 입지를 굳혀준다. 그러나 이런 상황이 미국이 라틴아메리카에서 현재 벌이고 있는 마약과의 전쟁에서 손을 떼야 한다는 것을 뜻하는 것은 아니다. 상당수의 이런 문제가 발생하는 원인은 일차적으로 바로 미국인들의 마약 사용 습관이다. 따라서 미국은 다른 국가들의 마약 생산과 그 생산에 따르는 결과를 막는 것을 도와주지 않으면 안 된다.)

여기에서 분열구문의 "that"절 내에 있는 "these problems"는 앞에서 언급된 내용이다. 즉 미국의 이미지 손상, 미국 국익 배치, 그리고 반미 선동가들의 입지 강화" 등을 나타내고 있다. 반면에 강조되고 있는 요소 "primarily America's drug"는 신정보이며 초점 역할을 한다.

1.1.2. "That"절 이하가 초점인 경우

03 In the days when coffins were actually carried, it required strong men to lift them. However, today the coffin is placed on a church "truck," and it's perfectly acceptable for women to be pallbearers. In early America, **it was the women who cared for the dead. It was they who bathed and shrouded the body for burial. In a sense, women are now taking their rightful place again by acting as pallbearers.**

(관을 실제로 들고 운반했던 시대에는 힘센 남자들이 들어야만 했다. 그러나 오늘날에는 관이 교회의 차에 실린다. 그래서 여자들이 관을 메는 것도 완전하게 받아들여지고 있다. 초기 미국에서는 바로 여자들이 시신을 돌보았다. 그리고 바로 그들이 시신의 몸을 씻고 장례를 치르기 위해 수의를 입혔었다. 어떤 의미에서 지금 여자들이 관을 멤으로써 그들의 당연한 위치를 되찾고 있는 것이다.)

이런 구문에서는 강조된 요소가 앞에서 언급된 구정보이며 대명사, 장소 부사, 시간 부사, 이유를 나타내는 말이 자주 삽입된다.

1.1.3. 대립되는 요소가 초점이 경우

04 And if I do what I do not want to, I agree that the law is good. As it is, **it is no longer I myself who do it, but it is sin living in me.** I know that nothing good lives in me, that is, in my sinful nature.

(그리고 만약 내가 하고 싶지 않은 일을 하고 있다면 내가 율법이 선하다는 것에 동의하는 것입니다. 그러나 실제로 그와 같은 일을 하는 것은 내가 아니라, 내 속에 자리를 잡고 있는 죄입니다. 나는 내 속에, 다시 말해 사악한 내 본성 속에는 선한 것은 아무것도 들어 있지 않다는 것을 알고 있습니다.)

1.2. 강조 위치에 놓일 수 있는 요소

1.2.1. 명사구(주어, 목적어)

05 a. The burglar broke the window.

b. **It was** the burglar **that/who** broke the window.
(바로 그 도둑이 유리창을 깨뜨렸다.)

삽입되는 요소가 사람일 때에는 "that"대신에 "who"나 "whom"을 쓸 수 있는데 "who"는 삽입되는 요소가 "that"이하 절에서 주어역할을 할 때에 사용하고 "whom"은 목적어역할을 할 때에 사용한다. 그리고 삽입되는 요소가 사물일 때에는 "that" 대신에 "which"를 사용하기도 한다.

06 a. I desire your happiness as well as my own

b. **It is** your happiness as well as my own (**that/which**) I desire.
(내가 바라는 것은 나 자신의 행복뿐만 아니라 바로 너의 행복이다.)

분열 구문에서 관계 대명사(that / which / whom)는 강조되는 요소가 초점으로 쓰이며 "that / which / whom"절에서 주어기능을 하지않을 때에는 생략할 수 있다. 생략되는 경우에는 "that / which / whom"절이 초점이 아니다.

07 a. I can't bear the fact that Mary hates me.

b. **It is** the fact that Mary hates me (**that**) I can't bear.
(바로 Mary가 나를 미워한다는 사실을 참을 수가 없다.)

08 a. What made you so angry?

b. What was **it** (**that**) made you so angry? (직접 의문문)
(도대체 무엇 때문에 당신은 그렇게 화가나 있습니까?)

의문사가 들어 있는 의문문에서는 의문사만을 강조할 수 있다.

09 a. I'd like to know what troubles you so much.

b. I'd like to know what **it is that** troubles you so much. (간접 의문문)
(나는 너를 그렇게 괴롭히는 것이 무엇인지를 알고 싶다.)

1.2.2. 전치사구와 부사구/절

10 a. My mother threw an egg at him yesterday.

b. **It was** yesterday **that/when** my mother threw an egg at him.

강조되는 부사(구)가 "때"를 나타내는 말일 때에는 "that" 대신에 "when"을 쓸 수도 있다.

11 a. We found the money under the mattress.

b. **It was** under the mattress **that/where** we found the money.

강조되는 부사(구)가 "장소"를 나타내는 말일 때에는 "that"대신에 "where"을 쓸 수도 있다.

12 a. They are fighting for their independence.

b. **It is** for their independence **that** they are fighting.

c. **It is** their independence **that** they are fighting for.
(바로 그들의 독립을 위해 그들은 싸우고 있다.)

"전치사 + 명사"를 강조할 때에는 전치사구 전체가 삽입될 수도 있고 명사만 삽입될 수도 있다.

13 a. They took a plane so that they could get there.

b. **It was** so that they could get there early **that** they took a plane.
(바로 그들은 그곳에 일찍 도착하기 위해서 비행기를 탔다.)

14 a. He likes them because they are always helpful.

b. **It is** because they are always helpful **that** he likes them.
(바로 그들이 항상 도움이 되기 때문에 그는 그들을 좋아한다.)

15 a. Why does he like them?

b. **Why is** it that he likes them? (직접의문문)
(도대체 왜 그는 그들을 좋아하는가?)

16 a. I don't know why he likes them.

b. I don't know **why it is** that he likes them. (간접의문문)
(나는 도대체 왜 그가 그들을 좋아하는지 모르겠다.)

1.2.3. 동명사

17 a. I enjoyed buying a new hat.

b. **It was** buying a new hat **that** I enjoyed.
(내가 즐기는 것은 바로 새 모자를 사는 것이다.)

18 a. Explaining your motives was important.

b. **It was** explaining your motives that **was** important.
(바로 너의 동기를 설명하는 것이 중요하다.)

1.3 보충 설명

19 a. I met the girl in the bus yesterday.

b. It was I/me who met the girl in the bus yesterday.
(어제 버스 안에서 그 소녀를 만난 사람은 바로 나였다.)

강조되는 요소가 "that"절에서 주어 기능을 하는 대명사일 때에는 동사 "be" 뒤에서 주격 대명사나 목적격 대명사가 사용될 수 있다.

20 a. It must have been his brother that you saw.
(네가 보았던 사람은 그의 동생임에 틀림없다.)

b. It might be his father that you're thinking of.
(네가 생각하고 있는 사람은 아마 그의 아버지일 것이다.)

분열 구문의 "It is ~, It was ~, 혹은 It's ~" 대신에 "It must be ~, It might be ~," 등이 쓰이는 경우도 있다.

21 a. John is a conductor.

b. #It is a conductor that John is.

22 a. Bill is very happy.

b. #It is very happy that Bill is.

분열 구문에서는 보어를 강조할 수 없다.

23 a. You should blow up some buildings.
(당신은 건물 몇 채를 폭파시켜야 합니다.)

b. *It is blow up some buildings that you should do.

24 a. I wanted to buy a new hat.
(나는 새 모자를 사고 싶었다.)

b. *It was to buy a new hat that I wanted.

25 a. For Mary to drive carelessly upsets Ann.
(Mary가 차를 부주의하게 몰아 Ann이 당혹스러워 하고 있다.)

b. *It is for Mary to drive carelessly that upsets Ann.

26 a. The defendants are questioned so closely only to discover these relationships.

b. **It is** only to discover these relationships **that** the defendants are questioned so closely.
(바로 이런 관계를 규명하기 위해서 피고인들이 아주 면밀하게 심문을 받고있다.)

예문 (23), (24) 그리고 (25)가 보여주는 바와 같이 분열 구문에서 원형 부정사와 "To"부정사는 강조할 수 없다. 단 (26)에서와 같이 부정사가 부사기능을 하는 경우에는 강조할 수 있다.

27 a. That you explain your motives was important.
(네가 너의 동기를 설명하는 것이 중요하다.)

b. ***It was** that you explain your motives **that** was important.

28 a. Bill realizes that John has come too late.
(Bill은 John이 너무 늦게 왔다는 것을 잘 알고 있다.)

b. ***It is** that John has come too late **that** Bill realizes.

29 a. They took a plane that they could get there early.

b. **It was** that they could get there early that they took a plane.
(바로 그들은 그곳에 일찍 도착하기 위하여 비행기를 탔다.)

예문 (27)과 (28)에서 보여주는 바와 같이 분열 구문에서 명사적으로 사용되는 "that"절은 강조할 수 없다. 단 "that"절이 (29)에서 처럼 부사 기능을 하는 경우에는 강조 위치에 놓일 수 있다.

30 a. John noticed the boy taking the apple.
(John은 그 소년이 사과를 집는 것을 알고 있었다.)

b. ***It was** taking the apple **that** John noticed the boy.

c. She kept smoking in spite of the warnings
(그녀는 경고에도 불구하고 담배를 계속 피웠다.)

d. ***It was** smoking in spite of the warnings **that** she kept.

분열 구문에서 동명사와 달리 현재분사는 강조할 수 없다.

31 a. Since they are always helpful, he likes them.
(그들이 늘 도움이 되기 때문에 그는 그들을 좋아한다.)

b. ***It is** since they are always helpful **that** he likes them.

이유절을 이끄는 "since"는 강조위치에 놓일 수 없다. 그러나 시간 접속사로서 "~이래로"의 뜻으로 쓰일 때에는 강조 위치에 놓일 수 있다.

32 a. Who made this table? **Was it** the teacher **that** made it?

b. Who made this table? **Was it** the teacher?
(이 테이블을 누가 만들었습니까? 바로 그 선생님이 그것 만드셨나요?)

분열 구문에서 강조된 요소가 초점이고 선행하는 문맥에서 "that"이하 절을 추론 가능할 때에는 생략할 수 있다.

2 준분열 구문

[What ~ be 강조되는 요소]의 준분열 구문에서는 강조어는 주어와 목적어(명사구/절, 대명사, 동명사, 그리고 부정사)와 동사구 그리고 보어가 강조될 수 있다.

2.1 준분열 구문의 유형

2.1.1. 강조되는 요소가 초점인 경우

33 I recently went to visit my widowed, elderly father in Florida. Like many elderly, his eyesight is not what it once was. He suffers from macular degeneration and has trouble reading small print. **What** disturbed me so **was** the fact that he could no longer go to restaurants because he couldn't read the menu.

(나는 최근에 플로리다에서 홀로 살고 계시는 연로하신 아버지를 뵈러 갔었다. 연세 드신 많은 분들과 마찬가지로 그분의 시력은 예전의 시력이 아니었다. 그분은 망막이 나빠져 고통을 받고 있으며 작은 글자를 읽는데 어려움을 겪고 계셨다. 나를 정말 당혹스럽게 했던 것은 그분이 식단표를 읽을 수 없어서 더 이상 식당에 갈 수 없다는 것이다.)

2.1.2. "What"절 이하가 초점인 경우

34 a. The answer is that you should definitely not offer criticism or advice unless he asks. Instead, you should try giving him loving acceptance. This **is what** he needs, not lectures.

(대답은 그가 먼저 청하지 않는 한 분명히 충고와 비판은 해서는 안 된다는 것이다. 그 대신 너는 사랑으로 그를 받아들이도록 노력해야 한다. 이런 것을 그가 필요로 하지 훈계를 필요로 하진 않는다.)

대부분 "what"절이 초점이 되는 경우에는 강조되는 요소로 "this," "that," 대명사, 혹은 앞에서 이미 언급된 요소가 주로 나타나고, [What ~ be 강조되는 요소]의 어순이 [강조되는 요소 be what ~]로 바뀐다.

2.2 초점 위치에 놓일 수 있는 요소

2.2.1 명사구(주어, 목적어)

35 a. The political campaign of our times is very interesting.

b. **What** is very interesting **is** the political campaign of our times.
(아주 흥미로운 것은 우리 시대의 선거 운동입니다.)

36 a. You need a good rest most.

b. **What** you need most **is** a good rest.
(네가 가장 필요로 하는 것은 충분한 휴식이다.)

37 a. The teacher requires that they all leave early.

b. **What** the teacher requires **is** that they all leave early.
(선생님께서 요구하시는 것은 그들 모두가 일찍 떠나야 한다는 것이다.)

2.2.2 형용사구

38 a. John is very brave.

b. **What** John is **is** very brave.
(John은 아주 용감하다.)

2.2.3 동사구

39 a. You should blow up some buildings.

b. **What** you should do **is** (to) blow up some buildings.
(John이 해야 될 일은 건물 몇 채를 폭파하는 것이다.)

준분열 구문에서 강조되는 요소가 동사구일 때에는 "to"를 쓸 수도 있고 생략할 수도 있다. 그리고 동사구를 강조할 때에는 "what"절에 "do"가 사용된다.

40 a. They are painting the house.

b. **What** they are doing **is** painting the house.
(그들은 집을 페인트 칠하고 있다)

진행형인 동사구를 강조할 때에는 "what"절에 "doing"이 사용된다.

2.2.4 부정사구

41 a. It was most important for them to give this boy a lifetime of love in the very short time.

b. For them to give this boy a lifetime of love in the very short time was most important.

c. What was most important was for them to give this baby a lifetime of love in the very short time.
(가장 중요했던 점은 그들이 이 소년에게 아주 짧은 시간에 평생동안의 사랑을 주었다는 것이다.)

2.2.5 동명사

42 a. He likes collecting stamps.

b. What he likes is collecting stamps.
(그가 좋아하는 일은 우표를 수집하는 것이다.)

3 보충 설명

43 a. The one/person who painted the house last week was Mary.
(지난 주 그 집을 페인트칠을 한 사람은 Mary였다.)

b. The thing which I need is a book.
(내가 필요로 하는 것은 책이다.)

c. The place where Ronald saw Ellen was Lotteria.
(Ronald가 Ellen을 본 곳은 롯떼리아였다.)

d. All I know is that I love him.
(내가 알고 있는 것은 바로 내가 그를 사랑하고 있다는 것이다.)

흔히 준분열구문은 [What ~ be 강조된 요소]와 [강조된 요소 be what ~]의 형태를 일컫는 말이지만 "what"대신에 "the one / person who," "the thing which," "the time when," "the place where," "all that" 등이 대신 쓰이기도 한다.

Practice Examples

Reading 01

It is generally the idle who complain they cannot find time to do that which they fancy they wish. In truth, people can generally make time for what they choose to do. **It is not really the time but the will that is wanting.**

/Lord Avebury: The Pleasure of Life

Word Bank

- the idle: idle people.
- make time: 시간을 내다.
- fancy: 생각하다, 상상하다.
- choose: 선택하다, 원하다.

Reading 02

In the second half of the sixth year the prisoner began zealously studying languages, philosophy, and history. He threw himself eagerly into these studies-so much so that the banker had enough to do to get him the books he ordered. In the course of four years some six hundred volumes were procured at his request. **It was during this period that the banker received the following letter from his prisoner.**

/Anton Chekhov. The Bet

Word Bank

- zealously: 열심히, 열광적으로.
- throw oneself into: 몰두하다, 헌신하다.
- • eagerly: 열심히, 열망하여.
- have enough to do to R: 하는 것이 고작이다, 하기도 힘겹다.
- in the course of : 중에, 동안에.
- procure: 획득하다, 구해주다.
- banker: 은행가, 은행업자.

구문 설명

"~so much so that ~."에서 앞의 "so"는 "that"와 상관 관계를 맺고 있으면 뒤에 있는 "so"는 앞에 나오는 형용사나 부사를 대신하는 대형태(代形態: Pro-form) 이다. 여기에서 뒤의 "so"는 "so eagerly"를 대신하는 표현이다.

Reading 03

Not long ago, I had a chance to watch surgeon perform a delicate brain operation. **A slight slip of his hand would have meant paralysis or death for the patient. What impressed me about the doctor was not his skill but his amazing calmness.**

/W. M. Martstom. Put Your Mind on the Spot

Word Bank

- surgeon: 외과 의사. (cf. physician: 내과 의사).
- delicate: 미묘한, 다루기 어려운.
- paralysis: 마비.

구문 설명

A slight slip of his hand would have meant paralysis or death for the patient.
= If his hand had slipped slightly, it would have meant paralysis or death for the patient.

Reading 04

Sheets did everything himself because at that time he couldn't afford not to. **Now, when his grown children visit, it's his labors of love they recall most fondly. "It wasn't the house or the lake that made that time so special."** Sheets says. "It was the fun we put into them as a family." Just as happy families value pleasures that involve personal effort, so they value possessions that have personal meaning, like Grandma's wedding ring. Unhappy people, however, are more likely to prize possessions because of their cost or utility-a car that handles well or an expensive necklace.

/Reader's Digest.

Word Bank

- afford: 할 수 있다, 할 여유가 있다.
- labor: 노력, 노동, 수고.
- fondly: 사랑스럽게, 다정하게.
- value: 평가하다, 소중히 하다.
- possession: 소유, 소유물.
- prize: 높이 평가하다, 소중히 하다.
- utility: 유용, 효용.
- necklace: 목걸이.

구문 설명

~ because at that time he couldn't afford not to. = ~ because at that time he couldn't afford not to do everything himself.

Reading 05

What amazed her was how quickly their relationship changed. Jim became much more attentive and interested in her. Within a couple of weeks, Jim started to come back to his old self again. He was wanting to do fun things with her and started planning dates. He got his motivation back.

/John Gray. Men are from Mars, Women are from Venus

Word Bank

- attentive: 주의 깊은, 친절한.
- self: 자기, 자신.
- motivation: 자극, 동기부여.

구문 설명

What amazed her was how quickly their relationship changed. = How quickly their relationship changed amazed her. = What amazed her was that their relationship changed very quickly.

Reading 06

I do not deny that the feeling of success makes it easier to enjoy life. A painter, let us say, who has been obscure throughout his youth, is likely to become happier if his talent wins recognition. Nor do I deny that money up to a certain point is very capable of increasing happiness; beyond that point, I do not think it does. **What I do maintain is that success can only be one ingredient in happiness, and is too dearly purchased if all the other ingredients have been sacrificed to obtain it.**

/Bertrand Russell. The Conquest of Happiness

Word Bank

- let us say: 이를 테면, 말하자면(shall we say).
- obscure: 애매한, 무명의.
- recognition: 인식, 인정.
- ingredient: 성분, 요소.
- dearly: 비싸게, 애정을 가지고.

Reading 07

"I've been in love with you for years," she said, "since the first time I saw you from the Addisons' living room window. **Yes-it was me they wanted you to meet.** But you wouldn't let anyone introduce us. You wouldn't let the Addisons set us up; you wouldn't take Karen's word for it that we would like each other. I thought I was never going to meet you."

/Jack Canfield, et al. Chicken Soup for the Couple's Soul

Word Bank

- introduce: 소개하다, 대면 시키다.
- set up: 보이다, 내걸다.
- take one's word (for it): 남의 말을 곧이 듣다, 남의 말을 그대로 믿다.

구문설명

"you wouldn't take Karen's word for it that we would like each other."에서 "it"은 "that"이하 절을 가리킨다. 자세한 설명은 외치구문 참조.

Reading 08

Questions of education are frequently discussed as if they bore no relation to the social system in which and for which the education is carried on. This is one of the commonest reasons for the unsatisfactoriness of the answers. **It is only within a particular social system that a system of education has any meaning.** If education today seems to deteriorate, if it seems to become more and more chaotic and meaningless, it is primarily because we have no settled and satisfactory arrangement of society, and because we have both vague and diverse opinions about the kind of society we want. Education is a subject which cannot be discussed in a void: our questions raise other questions, social, economic, financial, political. And the bearings are on more ultimate problems even than these: to know what we want in education we must know what we want in general, we must derive our theory of education from our philosophy of life. The problem turns out to be a religious problem.

/T. S. Eliot. Selected Essays

Word Bank

- bear: 나르다, 가지다.
- carry on: 경영하다.
- deteriorate: 나쁘게 하다, 타락시키다.
- chaotic: 대혼란의, 무질서한.
- settled: 고정된, 확립된.
- arrangement: 배열, 준비, 제도.
- vague: 모호한, 불명확한.
- subject: 주제, 제목.
- void: 공간, 허공.
- bearing: 몸가짐, 관계.
- derive: 이끌어 내다, 얻다.

구문 설명

1. ~ as if they bore no relation to the social system in which and for which the education is carried on. = ~ as if they bore no relation to the social system though the education is carried on in it and for it.
2. This is one of the commonest reasons for the unsatisfactoriness of the answers. = This is one of the commonest reasons why the answers are unsatisfactory.
3. And the bearings are on more ultimate problems even than these. = And they (= our questions) have bearing on more ultimate problems even than these.

Reading 09

I am grief-stricken. Yesterday my husband and I faced the awful experience of putting our 3-year-old chocolate Labrador to sleep. For two or three days, he wouldn't eat or drink, and was lethargic and vomiting. We took him to the emergency vet hospital. The vet examined him and found "something" in his abdomen, which would require surgery to remove. **What they found in his intestines was part of a kitchen towel.** Unfortunately, the tissue around the towel was infected and dead from the lack of blood supply to his intestines. The damage was worse than anticipated, and he began bleeding internally. He was too weak to make it, and we had to put him to sleep. To say that we're devastated is an understatement.

/Universal Press Syndicate. Dear Abby.

Word Bank

- grief-stricken: 슬픔에 젖은, 비탄에 잠긴.
- put ~ to sleep: 을 재우다, 을 죽이다.
- lethargic: 혼수상태의, 졸리는.
- vomit: 음식을 토하다, 게우다.
- emergency: 돌발 사태, 긴급 사태.
- vet: 수의(獸醫) (veterinarian (수의) 이나 veterinary(수의의) 의 약어).
- abdomen: 복부.
- surgery: 외과, 수술.
- intestine: 장.
- tissue: 조직.
- infect: 감염시키다, 전염시키다.
- damage: 손해, 손상.
- bleed: 피를 흘리다.
- make it: 성공하다, 시간에 대다.
- devastate: 유린하다, 압도하다.
- understatement: 억제해서 말하기, 삼가는 말.

Reading 10

Even before the rise of today´s many social activist movements, T.S. Eliot understood such people and their priorities. Writing in 1950, he said: "Half the harm that is done in this world is due to people who want to feel important. They don´t mean to do harm but the harm does not interest them. Or they do not see it, or they justify it because they are absorbed in the endless struggle to think well of themselves."There is little hope of changing such people. **But what the rest of us can do is stop gullibly accepting their ego trips as idealistic efforts for others.**

/Washington Times.

Word Bank

- activist: 적극적인 행동주의자, 운동가.
- priority: 우선권, 우선 해야 하는 일.
- harm: 해, 해악.
- due to: 에 기인하는, 때문에.
- important: 중요한, 영향력 있는.
- do: 끼치다, 입히다.
- justify: 옳다고 하다, 정당화 하다.
- absorb: 흡수하다, 열중 시키다.
- trip: 망상, 도취감.
- endless: 끊임없는, 무한한.
- struggle: 몸부림치다, 분투하다.
- gullible: 잘 속는.
- ego: 자아, 자기.

Reading 11

You made some good points in your reply to "Used in North Carolina," who married his pregnant girlfriend and nine years later learned that his son was "not his own." This father resented that he was expected to take care of a child "who isn't even mine." However, you missed an important point. Because your column is so widely read, **it's important to call attention to what it is that really makes a child "one's own."** I am a pediatrician. I interact with children from all sorts of families day in and day out. **From a child's perspective, what makes a child "belong" to a parent is the emotional-psychological bond between parent and child. What makes a child emotionally healthy is the stability of that social bond.** This emotional bond is essential for the child, regardless of biological relatedness. For the sake of our children, this cannot be left unsaid.

/Universal Press Syndicate. Dear Abby.

Word Bank

- resent: 분개하다, 불쾌하게 생각하다.
- call: 을 불러 일으키다.
- call attention to: 에 대하여 주의를 환기시키다.
- pediatrician: 소아과 의사.
- interact: 상호 작용하다, 서로 영향을 주다.
- day in and day out = day in, day out: 날이면 날마다, 매일.
- bond: 결속, 유대.
- stability: 안정, 안정성.
- relatedness: 관련성, 혈연관계.
- unsaid: 말하지 않은, 입 밖에 내지 않은.

Reading 12

As the year progressed, the class became more aware of the good fortune in having a genius in the art of humanity in their midst. I have asked this question to countless groups in seminars and the reply is always the same: When you see someone crying, you go up to them and usually say something. **What is it you say?** Everyone replies, "What's wrong?" Jimmy never said that. His question was always, "Can I help?"

/Canfield, J. & M. V. Hansen. Chicken Soup for the Soul

Word Bank

- art: 예술, 인문과학.
- humanity: 인류, 인문학.
- midst: 한복판, 한가운데.
- countless: 셀 수 없는, 무수한.

구문 설명

What is it you say? = What is it that you say?

Reading 13

It was Bell who first remembered the explosion behind them and turned around to see what had caused it. What he saw was Sgt. Keck lying on his back with his eyes closed, in a strangely grotesque position, still holding the ring and safety pin of a hand grenade in his right hand. Bell called out, and rushing to him, they rolled him over gently and saw that there was nothing they could do for him. His entire right buttock and part of his back had been blown away. Some of his internal organs were visible, pulsing busily away, apparently going about their business as if nothing had happened. Steadily, blood welled in the cavity. Gently they laid him back.

/James Jones. The Thin Red Line

Word Bank

- explosion: 폭발, 폭발음.
- turn around: 뒤돌아 보다. 방향을 바꾸다.
- Sgt: 중사(= sergeant).
- hand grenade: 수류탄, 소화탄.
- buttock: 엉덩이, 둔부.
- internal organs: 내장.
- well: 솟아나다, 분출하다.
- grotesque: 괴상한, 우스꽝스러운.
- gently: 친절하게, 서서히.
- organ: 기관.
- go about: 착수하다, 열심히 하다.
- cavity: 구멍, 강.

구문설명

What he saw was Sgt. Keck lying on his back with his eyes closed, = He saw Sgt. Keck lying on his back with his eyes closed,. "saw"이하의 요소를 준분열 구문을 이용해 강조하고 있다. (분열 구문 참조)

Reading 14

To live with ideal is a successful life. **It is not what one does, but what one tries to do, that makes a man strong.** Unceasing effort is the price of success. If we do not work with all our might, others will; and they will defeat us in the race, and pick the prize from our grasp. Success grows less and less dependent on luck and chance. Self-distrust is the cause of most of our failures. The great and indispensable help to success is character. Character is crystallized habit, the result of training and conviction. The worst fool in the world is the man who will admit nothing that he cannot see or feel or taste, who has no room for imagination or vision or faith. Man is capable of various kinds of education. He is possessed of physical, social, religious, intellectual and moral capabilities. Each requires education. The education of all makes him complete; the education of part only leaves him deficient. The educated man is the man who can do something, and the quality of his work marks the degree of his education. The best investment a young man make is in good books, the study of which broadens the mind.

/Earnest Hemingway: Advice to a Young Man

Word Bank

- might: 힘, 완력.
- grasp: 세게 쥐기, 보유
- indispensable: 없어서는 안 되는, 꼭 필요한.
- character: 인격, 품성.
- crystallize: 을 구체화하다, 을 결정시키다.
- conviction: 확신, 신념.
- capability: 능력, 용량.
- defeat: 에 이기다, 을 꺾다.
- self-distrust: 자기 불신, 자신 부족.
- room: 공간, 여지
- deficient: 부족한, 결핍된.

구문 설명

If we do not work with all our might, others will. = If we do not work with all our might, others will work with all their might.

Reading 15

She may not like this response, but she will respect it. Of course she wants him to be his usual loving self, but if he needs to pull away, then that is his valid need. He cannot give what he doesn't have. **What he can do is avoid making things worse.** The solution lies in respecting his needs as well as hers. He should take the time he needs and then go back and give her what she needs.

When a man can't listen to a woman's hurt feelings because he needs to pull away, he can say "I understand you feel hurt and I need some time to think about it. Let's take a time-out." For a man to excuse himself in this way and stop listening is much better than trying to explain away her hurt.

/John Gray. Men are from Mars, Women are from Venus

Word Bank

- pull: 끌리다, 움직이다.
- pull away: 이탈하다, 감정적으로 멀어지다, 떨어지다.
- valid: 타당한, 유효한.
- explain away: 둘러대다, 발뺌하다.
- time-out: 중간 휴식.

구문 설명

1. if he needs to pull away = if he needs to pull away from her (그가 감정적으로 그녀와 멀어져야 한다면, 그가 그녀에게 많은 관심을 표하기 어려운 상황이라면).
2. "~ but if he needs to pull away, then that is his valid need."에서 "that"은 "he needs to pull away"를 가리키는 말이다.

Reading 16

The reality of Communist China must not be obscured by fairy-tales. China, which has the largest standing army in the world, is re-arming at an extraordinary rate its defense budget increases 8 percent annually in a region where there simply is no war threat from any other country or combination of countries now or long into the future. Taiwan and China are going to negotiate again and again over reunification but the cross-straits meetings will lead to nothing except Beijing's frustration or worse. As ex-President Lee Teng-hui once put it: **"It's not that Taiwan does not want reunification. It's just that the Taiwanese people do not want to live under a communist system."**

/Washington Times.

Word Bank

- communist: 공산주의자(의).
- obscure: 가리다, 애매하게 하다.
- fairy-tale: 동화, 꾸민 이야기.
- standing: 서 있는, 상비의.
- rearm: 재무장하다, 신무기를 갖추다.
- rate: 비율, 속도.
- budget: 예산, 경비.
- simply: (부정문에서)전혀, 절대로.
- combination: 결합, 연합
- reunification: 재통일.
- cross-strait: 양안(兩岸)의.
- nothing but: 단지(= only).
- frustration: 좌절, 낭패.
- put: 말하다, 진술하다.

Reading 17

So she called softly after it, "Mouse dear! Do come back again, and we won't talk about cats, or dogs either, if you don't like them!" When the Mouse heard this, it turned round and swam slowly back to her: its face was quite pale, and it said, in a low, trembling voice, "Let us get to the shore, and then I'll tell you my history, and **you'll understand why it is I hate cats and dogs.**"

/Lewis Carroll. Alice's Adventures in Wonderland

Word Bank

- call after: 을 뒤에서 부르다. 을 부르며 뒤쫓다.
- tremble: 떨다.

Reading 18

The letters from "Grieving Grandmother" and Anne Coakley were tragic reminders of the problem of guns in our nation. Unfortunately, such episodes get little attention from the media except on a local newscast or in the back pages of the local paper. They aren't "news." It happens all too often. It takes a school massacre to get the national notice the situation deserves. **Perhaps what needs to be done is to have a running "scoreboard" set up in New York's Times Square:** a continuing count of the gun deaths in the entire nation since the start of every year. The count could even be categorized by accidental deaths and murders. Running messages could give the particulars of the latest death as to date, location and the victim's age.

/Universal Press Syndicate. Dear Abby.

Word Bank

- reminder: 생각나게 하는 것(사람), 조언.
- unfortunately: 불행하게도
- all too: 너무나 …한.
- deserve: 을 받을 가치가 있다.
- attention: 주의, 주목.
- massacre: 대학살.
- take: 필요로 하다, 들다.

- notice: 주목, 통지.
- running: 가동중인, 연속적인.
- scoreboard: 득점 게시판
- set up: (제도를) 만들다, 시작하다
- entire: 전체의, 완전한
- categorize: 분류하다
- accidental: 우연한, 우발적인
- murder: 살해하다, 살인
- particular: 상세, 명세서.
- victim: 희생자, 피해자.

Reading 9

I'd decide to speak those lines and see what happened. I was always disappointed. Usually the man would look at me blankly and change the subject, or say "Oh, what's that?" and I'd tell him and he'd say, "Hmm. And you memorized it. Why?" It never lived up to my fantasy. **What I wanted was for someone to feel the same way I felt about the lines.**

/Elizabeth Kim. Ten Thousand Sorrows

Word Bank

- line: 시구(詩句), 일행.
- blankly: 멍하니, 우두커니.
- live up to: 에 합당한 생활을 하다, 에 부응하다.
- fantasy: 상상, 환상.

구문설명

What I wanted was for someone to feel the same way I felt about the lines. = I wanted someone to feel the same way I felt about the lines. 규범적인 문장이 준분열구문으로 바뀌면서 "for"가 삽입되었음에 주의해야 한다.

Reading 20

It is not what we say that hurts but how we say it. Quite commonly when a man feels challenged, his attention becomes focused on being right and he forgets to be loving as well. Automatically his ability to communicate in a caring, respectful, and reassuring tone decreases. He is aware neither of how uncaring he sounds nor of how hurtful this is to his partner. At such times, a simple disagreement may sound like an attack to a woman; a request turns into an order. Naturally a woman feels resistant to this unloving approach, even when she would be otherwise receptive to the content of what he was saying.

A man unknowingly hurts his partner by speaking in an uncaring manner and then goes on to explain why she should not be upset. He mistakenly assumes she is resisting the content of his point of view, **when really his unloving delivery is what upsets her.** Because he does not understand her reaction, he focuses more on explaining the merit of what he is saying instead of correcting the way he is saying it.

/John Gray. Men are from Mars, Women are from Venus

Word Bank

- caring: 배려하는, 봉사하는.
- respectful: 공손한, 정중한.
- reassuring: 안심시키는, 위안을 주는.
- disagreement: 의견 차이, 논쟁.
- receptive: 잘 받아들이는, 감수성이 풍부한.
- unknowingly: 모르고서.
- mistakenly: 잘못하여, 실수로
- delivery: 배달, 말투, 분만.
- merit: 장점, 시비.

구문설명

~ when really his unloving delivery is what upsets her. = ~ when really his unloving delivery upsets her.

Reading 21

I am a 14-year-old girl with a big problem. Today, when my father and I went to the supermarket, I saw a book that looked interesting. It was called "How to Win at Love." I picked it up not because I was having a problem with my love life but I am curious about "love," so I read a few pages and decided to buy it. My dad saw the title and got mad at me. Then one of my sisters started treating me like I was a freak. Now, I'm scared my dad and sister will tell my mom, and then Mom will be mad, too. My mom has told me I shouldn't have a boyfriend until I'm finished with school. How am I supposed to tell her I was only curious? I know they both think I'm too young to have a boyfriend, but that's not it. The book isn't about guys and marriage. It's about changing yourself and being in charge of your own life. It's not my fault I'm curious about love. It's because my parents won't talk about it with me. Every time I ask something about it, they say, "Why do you want to know? Do you have a boyfriend?" I hate that. **What hurts most is knowing if I can't talk to my parents about love, what can I talk to them about?**

/Universal Press Syndicate. Dear Abby.

Word Bank

- pick up: 집다.
- mad: 미친, 노발대발 하는(= angry).
- freak: 변덕, 성적 도착자.
- scared: 겁에 질린, 두려운.
- be supposed to R: 하기로 기대(요구)되다.

구문 설명

~ if I can't talk to my parents about love, what can I talk to them about? = ~ if I can't talk to my parents about love, I can't talk to them about anything. 이 문장은 수사 의문문을 이루고 있다.

Reading 22

As she improved, the two began playing card games to help Karen's concentration. Even small progress required playing for long stretches of time, sometimes up to eighteen hours a day. Karen was improving, but the pace was slow. The strain was becoming too much for both of them. What was a father to do? While in the shower one morning, it hit him. True, he wasn't a doctor. He wasn't even a professional therapist. But he was a computer scientist. **And perhaps that was what could help Karen the most!**

/Canfield, J. & M. V. Hansen. Chicken Soup for the Soul

Word Bank

- concentration: 집중, 전념.
- up to: 까지, 의무인.
- too much: 못 견딜, 감당 못 할.
- professional: 직업적인, 전문적인.
- therapist: 치료전문가, 의사.
- stretch: 범위, 한도.
- strain: 정신적 긴장, 과로.
- hit: 때리다, 떠오르다.

구문 설명

While in the shower one morning, it ~. = While he was in the shower one morning, it ~.

Reading 23

At the seminar Sandra said, "I have spent twenty years trying to get Larry to talk. I wanted him to open up and be vulnerable. **I didn't realize that what I was missing was a man who would support me in being open and vulnerable. That is what I really needed.** I have shared more intimate feelings with my husband this weekend than in twenty years. I feel so loved. This is what I have been missing. I thought he had to change. Now I know nothing is wrong with him or me. We just didn't know how to support each other."

/John Gray. Men are from Mars, Women are from Venus

Word Bank

- open up: (생각, 기분 등을) 털어놓다.
- open: 솔직한, 숨김없는.
- vulnerable: 상처 입기 쉬운, 약점이 있는.
- intimate: 친밀한, 마음속으로부터의.

Reading 24

Kerr, a writer and teacher who has lived in Japan for more than 35 years, finds fault with almost every aspect of today's Japan. The educational system is rigid and uninspiring; teaching obedience to authority is its highest goal. No wonder students are anxious and increasingly prone to bullying and attacking each other in school. The press colludes with the authorities to cover up unpleasant truths. Foreigners and foreign ideas are widely distrusted and disparaged. "No matter how much lip service is paid to internationalization, the country's basic policies have been to keep Japan closed," Kerr writes. All are valid points, but "Dogs and Demons" seems a little too alarmist. **It isn't until the end of the book that Kerr acknowledges Japan's continuing strengths, and he does so almost always in a backhanded manner.**

/Newsweek.

Word Bank

- obedience to: 복종(= submission).
- find fault with: 을 흠잡다(= pick on), 비판하다
- no wonder = it is no wonder that it is natural that. anxious: 걱정하고, 염려하는.
- bully: 골탕먹이다, 못살게 굴다.
- collude 공모하다(= conspire).
- cover up: 은폐하다.
- disparage: 폄하하다. 깔보다.
- lip service: 입에 발린 말.
- alarmist: 소란을 피우는, 공연히 소란을 피우는 사람(= scaremonger).
- strength: 힘, 강점.
- backhanded: (언동이) 성의가 없는, 모호한, 비꼬는.

구문 설명

"Dogs and Demons"는 Ales Kerr가 쓴 책명이다. 원제는 "Dogs and Demons : Tales from the Dark Side of Japan"이다.

Reading 25

On the day of my departure I was given a cotton dress, bordered in red and white checks, and ankle socks. Those clothes, which like my maroon trousers and shirt came from castoffs sent to us by American churches, felt uncomfortable and alien. The dress was too big. I wore green rubber shoes with tiny red flowers painted on them, and I had pictures of my new parents in my hand. I had been taught a few words, including "Mom" and "Dad" and **all I knew was that those words connected with the strange people in the pictures.**

/Elizabeth Kim. Ten Thousand Sorrows

Word Bank

- departure: 출발, 이탈.
- border: 접하다, 단을 대다.
- ankle: 발목
- maroon: 밤색, 고동색.
- castoff: 버림받은 물건, 입지않은 헌 옷.
- alien: 외국의. 이질의.
- rubber: 고무.
- cotton: 목화, 무명.
- check: 점검, 체크무늬.
- sock: 양말.

구문 설명

~ all I knew was that those words connected with the strange people in the pictures. = ~ what I knew was that those words connected with the strange people in the pictures.

Reading 26

But after that Sunday, Gretchen never felt quite so alone again. Gradually the truth seemed to come upon her-that an ordinary child, no matter how charming, would not have been able to lift her spirits in that mysterious and welcome way. Instead, the child had been sent by someone who understood her suffering and was reaching out to comfort and heal her. **Perhaps it was Fred.**

/Canfield, J. et al. Chicken Soup for the Couple's Soul

Word Bank

- lift: 들어 올리다, 돋우다.
- spirit: 정신, 기분.
- welcome: 환영 받는, 기쁜.

구문설명

1. in a/the + 형용사 + way = 부사.
2. Perhaps it was Fred. = Perhaps it was Fred who understood her suffering and was reaching out to comfort and heal her. 분열구문에서 삽입된 요소가 신정보이고 "that"절이 구정보일 때에는 자주 생략되어 나타난다.

Reading 27

Twenty-four years ago Jim Kilter was a typical, active high school student. He was captain of the high school football and wrestling teams, played baseball, and was gifted on the trampoline, He could do triple flips and one-and-a-half twists. At age sixteen his life changed forever. Jim was working at his father's logging business one summer in the small town of Montesano, Washington. **It was on a Friday.** Jim usually never went in on Fridays, but his dad woke him at 4:30 A.M. and asked if he would go in with him. After helping his father run the loader, work the power saw and drive the logging truck, Jim crawled into the grapple that picks up the logs for an after-lunch snooze. **He laid in it like a hammock, with his feet on one side and his head resting against the other.**

/Canfield, J. & M. V. Hansen. Chicken Soup for the Soul

Word Bank

- typical: 전형적인, 대표적인,
- active: 활동적인, 적극적인.
- captain: 대위, 주장.
- gift: 선물로 주다, 부여하다.
- trampoline: 트램폴린(캔버스로된 스프링 달린 도약용 운동용 용구).
- flip: 공중제비.
- logging: 재목 벌채.
- run: 움직이다. 돌리다.
- loader: 김을 싣는 사람, 적하기.
- work: 움직이다, 운전하다.
- power: 동력, 전기.
- saw: 톱.
- snooze: 선잠, 낮잠.
- grapple: 갈고랑 쇠(= grapnel).
- hammock: 해먹(달아매는 그물 침대)

구문 설명

It was on a Friday that/when Jim was working at his father's logging business one summer in the small town of Montesano, Washington.

Reading 28

Friendship is above reason, for, though you find virtues in a friend, he was your friend before you find them. **It is a gift that we offer because we must;** to give it as the reward of virtue would be to set a price upon it, and those who do that have no friendship to give. If you choose your friends on the ground that you are virtuous and want virtuous company, you are no nearer to true friendship than if you choose them for commercial reasons.

/A. Clutton-Brock. On Friendship

Word Bank

- virtue: 미덕, 장점.
- reward: 보답, 보상.
- set a price upon: 에 값을 매기다.
- virtuous: 덕이 있는, 고결한.
- on the ground that: 하다는 이유로.
- company: 일단, 동료.
- commercial: 상업적인, 돈벌이 위주의.

구문 설명

1. "It is a gift that we offer because we must ~."는 분열 구문이 아니다. 이 문장에서 "It"은 앞의 "Friendship"을 받는다.
2. ~ on the ground that you are virtuous and want virtuous company ~. = ~ on the ground that you are virtuous and want to be in company with virtuous people ~.

Reading 29

My dad taught teachers, and he became a master teacher. My rich dad always taught young people his way of doing business. In retrospect, it was their generosity with what they knew that made them smarter. There are powers in this world that are much smarter than we are. You can get there on your own, but it's easier with the help of the powers that be. **All you need to be is generous with what you have,** and the powers will be generous with you.

/Robert T. Kyosaki & Sharon L. Lechter. Rich Dad Poor Dad

Word Bank

- master: 주인, 교사.
- retrospect: 회상, 추억.
- generosity: 너그러움, 마음이 후함.
- powers that be: 당국, 유력자(= those who hold effective power in a system or situation).
- on one's own: 독립하여, 혼자 힘으로.

Reading 30

The inability of scientists to produce precise answers to such questions contributes to the public's anxiety. Making regulatory decisions when all the data is available is not difficult. **What is hard is making the correct decisions in the face of such uncertainty.** Only a strong system of food safety regulation that is focused on public health and has public credibility can navigate these uncertainties successfully.

/Time.

Word Bank

- contribute to: 기부하다, 원인이 되다.
- regulatory: 규정하는, 조절하는.
- available: 이용할 수 있는, 쓸모 있는.
- in the face of: 에 직면하여, 에 불구하고.
- uncertainty: 확신이 없음, 불명확.
- regulation: 규칙, 규제.
- credibility: 진실성, 믿을 수 있음.
- navigate: 항해하다, 조종하다.

Reading 31

Only belatedly did some major media figure Ted Koppel on "Nightline" actually confront Mitch Snyder and ask the source of his statistic. **Mr. Snyder then admitted that it was something he made up, in order to satisfy media inquiries.** Moreover, homeless advocates defended what Mr. Snyder had done and called it "lying for justice." People have been lying for centuries. **What makes their statistical lies so dangerous today is that so many people in the media are ready to accept and broadcast statistics turned out by activist groups with an ax to grind when those groups share the liberal-left orientation of the media.** False statistics are only part of the problem. Even accurate statistics can be given misleading emphasis.

/Washington Times.

Word Bank

- belatedly: 뒤늦게.
- figure: 모습, 인물, 숫자.
- confront: 마주보다, 직면하다.
- source: 출처, 자료.
- statistic: 통계치.
- make up: 작성하다, 날조하다.
- inquiry: 질문, 조사, 연구.
- advocate: 옹호자, 주창자.
- defend: 방어하다, 옹호하다.
- broadcast: 방송하다, 방영하다.
- turn out: 만들어 내다, 생산하다.
- have an ax(e) to grind: 속셈/딴마음이 있다
- orientation: 방향, 지향.
- misleading: 사람을 잘 못하게 하는, 오해 시키는.

구문 설명

"Mr. Snyder then admitted that it was something he made up ~," "it"은 앞에서 언급된 "his statistic"을 가리킨다. 문장구조는 분열구문과 비슷하지만 분열구문이 아니다.

Unit 2 Though 이동 ("Though" Movement)

접속사 'Though'나 'As'절에 있는 일부 요소가 이들 접속사 앞으로 이동되어 문두에 놓이는 경우가 있는데 이를 흔히 'THOUGH'이동이나 "THOUGH"도치라 한다.

1 "Though" 이동되는 요소

1.1. 명 사

01 a. Though he was a hero, he was killed at last.

b. *A hero as/though he was, he was killed at last.

c. **Hero as/though he was,** he was killed at last.
(그는 영웅이었음에도 불구하고 결국에는 죽었다.)

02 a. Though I am a woman, I shall be of help in time of need.

b. **Woman as/though I am,** I shall be of help in time of need.
(제가 여자이기는 하지만 어려운 때에 도움은 될 것입니다.)

"THOUGH"이동이 일어난 구문에서는 보어인 명사가 "as / though"앞에 올 때에는 관사를 생략한다.

1.2. 형용사(구)

03 a. Though the house is expensive, we have decided to buy it.

b. **Expensive as/though the house is,** we have decided to buy it.
(그 집이 비싸기는 하지만 우리는 사기로 했다.)

04 a. Though he is fond of Mary in some ways, he doesn't really love her.

b. **Fond of Mary in some ways as/though he is,** he doesn't really love her.
(그가 몇 가지면에서 Mary를 좋아하기는 하지만 그녀를 정말 사랑하고 있는 것은 아니다.)

05 a. As she was careless, she could never pass an examination.

b. **Careless as she was,** she could never pass an examination.
(그녀는 주의력이 부족해서 시험에는 도저히 합격할 수 없었다.)

1.3. 과거분사

06 a. Though Fred was intimidated by Mary, he stood his ground.

b. **Intimidated by Mary as/though Fred was,** he stood his ground.
(Fred는 Mary에게 협박을 받았음에도 불구하고 자기의 주장을 굽히지 않았다.)

07 a. Although John is gone, his charisma is still influential among the followers.

b. **Gone as/though John** is, his charisma is still influential among the followers.
(John은 가버리고 없지만 그의 카리스마는 아직도 지지들 사이에서는 영향력이 있다.)

1.4. 부사(구)

08 a. Though he loved his native land dearly, he loved liberty even more.

b. **Dearly as/though he loved his native land,** he loved liberty even more.
(그는 그의 조국을 정말로 사랑했지만 자유를 훨씬 더 사랑했었다.)

09 a. Though she wanted to show her sympathy much, Lucy did not know what to say.

b. **Much as/though she wanted to show her sympathy,** Lucy did not know what to say.
(Lucy는 그녀의 동정을 많이 표하고 싶었지만 뭐라고 말해야 좋을지 몰랐다.)

1.5. 동사(구)

10 a. Though John ate the meat nude, nobody thought he was crazy.

b. **Eat the meat nude though John did,** nobody thought he was crazy.
(John은 벌거벗고 고기를 먹었지만 아무도 그가 미쳤다고 생각하지는 않았다.)

11 a. Though Andy will attack Clinton, he won't vote against the government.

b. **Attack Clinton though Andy will,** he won't vote against the government.
(Andy가 Clinton을 공격은 하겠지만 정부에 대해 반대표를 던지지는 않을 것이다.)

2 보충 설명

12 a. As he is poor, he works overtime in the factory every day.

b. **Poor as he is,** he works overtime in the factory every day.
(그는 가난해서 공장에서 매일 잔업을 하고 있다.)

"명사/형용사/부사/동사 though 주어 + 동사"는 "~이기는 하지만, ~이라고는 하나" 의 뜻으로 양보를 나타내고 규범적인 문장어순으로 바꾸어 쓸 때에는 "though, although, even though"를 사용한다. 반면에 "명사/형용사/부사/동사 as 주어 + 동사"는 "~이기는 하지만, ~이라고는 하나" 의 뜻으로 양보를 나타내기도 하지만 "~하여서, ~때문에"의 뜻으로 이유를 나타내기도 한다. 이 경우에는 규범적인 어순으로 바꾸어 쓸 때에 "as, because, since"등을 사용한다.

13 a. Though he was poor, he had won the general respect of the neighborhood.

b. **Poor as / though he was,** he had won the general respect of the neighborhood.

c. **As poor as he was,** he had won the general respect of the neighborhood.
(그는 가난하기는 했지만 전반적으로 이웃 사람들의 존경을 받았다.)

d. ***As poor though he was,** he had won the general respect of the neighborhood.

"형용사/부사 as 주어 + 동사"의 표현은 "as 형용사/부사 as 주어 + 동사"의 표현으로도 쓰인다.

14 a. Though the concert is in June, we decided to buy the tickets now.
(콘서트가 6월에 있지만 우리는 지금 표를 사기로 했다.)

b. ***In June as/though the concert is,** we decided to buy the tickets now.

15 a. Although the book is of interest, it doesn't sell well.

b. **Of interest as/though the book is,** it doesn't sell well.

c. **Interesting as/though the book is,** it doesn't sell well.
(그 책은 재미는 있는데 잘 팔리지 않고 있다.)

일반적으로 전치사구는 (14b)에서와 같이 "as"나 "though"앞에 놓일 수 없다. 단 (15)에서처럼 전치사구가 형용사 기능을 할 때에는 가능하다.

16 a. Even though I was naked, I braved the storm.

b. **Naked as/that I was,** I braved the storm.
(나는 벌거벗은 몸이었지만 폭풍우에 용감히 맞섰다.)

17 a. Jim, since he was a fool, completely ruined the dinner.

b. Jim, **fool as/that he was,** completely ruined the dinner.
(Jim이 바보였기 때문에 저녁식사를 완전히 망쳐놓았던 것이다.)

문어체에서 "명사/형용사 as/though 주어 + 동사"표현에서 "as/though"대신에 "that"을 쓰는 경우가 있다.

18 a. Although it may sound strange, yet it is quite true.

b. **Strange as/though it may sound,** yet it is quite true.
(이상하게 들릴지 모르지만 그것은 전적으로 사실이다.)

c. ***Strange although it may sound,** yet it is quite true.

"although"는 'though"와 의미상으로 같지만 "THOUGH" 이동이 일어나지 않는다.

19 a. **Standing as it does on the hill,** his house commands a fine view.

b. As it stands on the hill, his house commands a fine view.
(그의 집은 언덕 위에 있기 때문에 전망이 좋다.)

c. *Standing as it is on the hill, his house commands a fine view.

20 a. Although the book is interesting, it doesn't sell well.

b. **Interesting though the book is,** it doesn't sell well.
(그 책은 재미있음에도 불구하고 잘 팔리지는 않는다.)

현재분사는 예문 (19c)에서 보여주는 바와 같이 "as"나 "though"앞에 놓일 수 없다. 예문 (20b)에서처럼 현재분사 형태인 "~ing" 어미가 붙은 단어가 분사가 아닌 형용사일 때에는 가능하다. 단 현재분사가 앞에 놓일 때에는 예문 (19a)에서처럼 동사 "do"가 사용된다.

Practice Examples

Reading 01

It is both logical and fundamentally right that Australia should have an Australian head of state. It is illogical and wrong that the Queen of Great Britain and Northern Ireland, **excellent woman though she is,** should continue to be our head of state. I believe that the overwhelming majority of Australians accept these propositions and, indeed, I believe that almost every Australian would accept them given the opportunity to gain access to all of the facts related to this issue.

/Australian Republican Movement. Address to the Constitutional Convention.

Word Bank

- logical: 논리적인, 이치에 맞는.
- United Kingdom: 영국(Great Britain + Northern Ireland).
- head: 장, 지배자.
- proposition: 제안, 주장.

Reading 02

These findings, **egalitarian though they may be,** do not bode well for the brave new world originally engineered in the name of feminism. They suggest that there is a steep, possibly prohibitive, cost in the so-called "liberated" life of countless American women, who, for reasons ranging from desperation to desire, have seen fit to warehouse a whopping 75 percent of the nation's youngsters in some form of child care to further or maintain full-time professional careers. Indeed, it is to these mothers that this study most plaintively speaks, given that the kids most prone to scientifically quantified meanness were those who've effectively made a childhood career out of day care, spending 30 or more hours a week there.

/Washington Times.

Word Bank

- finding: 발견, 조사결과.
- egalitarian: 평등주의의.
- brave: 용감한, 화려한.
- bode: 징조이다, 조짐이다.
- engineer: 설계하다, 꾀하다.
- feminism: 여권주의, 여성 해방론.
- steep: 가파른, 터무니 없이 비싼.
- prohibitive: 금지의, 터무니 없이 비싼.
- liberate: 자유롭게 하다, 해방하다.
- desperation: 자포자기, 절망.
- meanness: 비열함, 비열한 행동.
- warehouse: 창고에 보관하다, 창고 같은 곳에 수용하다.
- whopping: 엄청난, 굉장한.
- plaintively: 구슬프게, 하소연 하듯이.
- prone: 경향이 있는, 쉬운.
- quantify: 수량화 하다.

구문 설명

1. "~ from desperation to desire, have seen fit to warehouse a whopping 75 percent of the nation ′ s youngsters ~"에서 "seen" 다음에 오는 "fit"는 목적보어로 쓰이고 있고 "to ~"이하는 목적어로 쓰이는데 복합명사구 이동이 일어난 구문이다. 이 경우에는 관용적으로 외치는 적용되지 않는다. 자세한 설명은 "외치"편 참조.
2. Indeed, it is to these mothers that this study most plaintively speaks, given ~. = Indeed, this study most plaintively speaks to these mothers, given ~. "to these mothers"를 강조한 분열구문.

Reading 03

At a rich merchant's house there was a children's party, and the children of rich and great people were there. The merchant was a learned man, for his father had sent him to college, and he had passed his examination. His father had been at first only a cattle dealer, but always honest industrious, so that he had made money, and his son, the merchant, had managed to increase his store. **Clever as he was, he had also a heart;** but there was less said of his heart than of his money. All descriptions of people visited at the merchant's house, well born, as well as intellectual, and some who possessed neither of these recommendations.

/Hans Christian Andersen. Children's Prattle

Word Bank

- description: 묘사, 종류.
- well born: 집안이 좋은, 태생이 좋은.
- recommendation: 추천, 추천하는 말.

Reading 04

On the moment, Presley had risen from the table and, clapping on his hat, had hurried into the streets, where the lamps were already beginning to shine. But **search though he would,** Presley could not again come upon the young woman, in whom he fancied he had seen the daughter of the unfortunate German. At last, he gave up the hunt, and returning to his club at this hour almost deserted smoked a few cigarettes, vainly attempted to read from a volume of essays in the library, and at last, nervous, distraught, exhausted, retired to his bed.

/Frank Norris. The Octopus

Word Bank

- clap on: 후딱 쓰다.
- search: 찾다, 수색하다.
- come (up)on: 우연히 만나다, 급습하다.
- fancy: 생각하다, 상상하다.
- hunt: 사냥, 추적.
- desert: 버리다, 비우다.
- volume: 다수, 다량.
- essay: 수필, 에세이.
- read from: 띄엄띄엄 읽다, 드문드문 빼먹고 읽다.
- distraught: 정신이 혼란하여, 마음이 산란해진.
- retire: 은퇴하다, 자다.

구문 설명

"~ the young woman, in whom he fancied he had seen the daughter of the unfortunate German."에서 관계대명사 앞에 있는 전치사 "in"은 동격을 나타낸다. 예를 들면, "I have found a friend in Mary. (나는 메리라는 친구를 발견했다) In him you have a fine leader. (당신에게는 그 사람이라는 훌륭한 지도자가 있다.)

Reading 05

This time, our baby did not make it through. Soon after the surgery, he died. **As devastating as it was to lose this child, my husband and I remain united in our relationship.** It was as though Derian gave us a gift of deeper love for one another. Despite the pain, together we still believe in prayer, miracles, a mighty God-and most of all, the divine guidance we now receive from a little angel named Derian.

/Jack Canfield, et al. Chicken Soup for the Couple's Soul

Word Bank

- make it: 잘 해내다, 시간에 대다.
- devastating: 파괴적인, 통렬한.
- united: 연합한, 일치하는.
- mighty: 힘이 있는, 엄청난.
- divine: 신의, 신성의.
- guidance: 지도, 안내.

구문 설명

"our baby did not make it through."는 문맥상 "our baby did not make it through the surgery."를 의미하고 있다.

Reading 06

A few days later he was installed provost of the chapter of Geneva. He took up his duties with an ardor that never abated. He ministered lovingly to the poor and in the confessional devoted himself to the needs of the humblest with special care. His style of preaching was so simple that it charmed his hearers; **scholar though he was,** he refrained from filling his sermons with Greek and Latin quotations and theological subtleties, in the prevailing fashion.

/St. Francis de Sales. Introduction to the Devout Life

Word Bank

- install: 설치하다, 임명하다.
- provost: 주임사제, 성당 참사회장.
- chapter: 참사회, 총회.
- take up: 착수하다, 처리하다.
- abate: 줄다, 경감되다.
- minister: 성직자로서 임무를 다하다, 봉사하다.
- confessional: 고해(실).
- humble: 겸손한, 낮은.
- preaching: 설교, 전도.
- refrain: 자제하다, 삼가다(from).
- sermon: 설교, 강론.
- quotation: 인용, 인용문.
- subtlety: 섬세함, 미묘함.
- prevailing: 우세한, 널리 행해지는.

Reading 07

My wife, Bonnie, says this experience of "going down" is like going down into a dark well. When a women goes into her "well" she is consciously sinking into her unconscious self, into darkness and diffused feeling. She may suddenly experience a host of unexplained emotions and vague feelings. She may feel hopeless, thinking she is all alone or unsupported. But soon after she reaches the bottom, if she feels loved and supported, she will automatically start to feel better. **As suddenly as she may have crashed, she will automatically rise up and again radiate love in her relationships.**

/John Gray. Men are from Mars, Women are from Venus

Word Bank

- well: 우물.
- radiate: 발산하다, 방사하다.
- unconscious: 무의식적인, 부지불식간의.
- diffused: 널리 흩어진, 산란한.
- host: 많은 무리, 다수.
- vague: 분명치 않은, 막연한.
- hopeless: 절망적인, 희망이 없는.
- unsupported: 지지를 받지 못하는, 후원이 없는.
- reach the bottom: crash: 무너지다, 실패하다.

Reading 08

As of April 17, the day when Secretary of Health and Human Services Tommy Thompson launched his organ donation initiative, there were 75,863 people waiting to receive organs. Last year, more than 5,500 Americans died waiting for transplants. There is an urgent need for more donors, and simple awareness of how to donate could save thousands of lives this year. The secretary's initiative aims to increase knowledge about organ donation in places such as schools and businesses. He is also partnering with transplant surgeons to increase research to help those needing organs. **Worthy as the cause is, however, Mr. Thompson's initiative has been controversial, mainly due to misinformation about what the plan involves.**

/Washington Times.

Word Bank

- as of: 현재.
- Secretary of Health and Human Services: 보건-인간 봉사부 장관(미국).
- launch: 착수하다, 일으키다.
- organ: 기관, 장기.
- donation: 기부, 기증.
- initiative: 시작, 주도.
- transplant: 이식(하다).
- urgent: 긴급한, 급박한.
- partner: 제휴하다, 짝이 되다.
- surgeon: 외과 의사.
- worthy: 가치 있는, 훌륭한.
- cause: 목적, 대의 명분.

4장 기타

Reading 09

When he left me I went to my room. After a little while, not hearing any sound, I came out and went up the stone stairs to where I could look out towards the south. There was some sense of freedom in the vast expanse, **inaccessible though it was to me,** as compared with the narrow darkness of the courtyard. Looking out on this, I felt that I was indeed in prison, and I seemed to want a breath of fresh air, though it were of the night. I am beginning to feel this nocturnal existence tell on me. It is destroying my nerve. I start at my own shadow, and am full of all sorts of horrible imaginings.

/Bram Stoker. Dracura

Word Bank

- vast: 광막한, 막대한.
- expanse: 팽창, 넓게 퍼진 장소.
- courtyard: 안마당, 안뜰.
- nocturnal: 밤의, 야행성의.
- existence: 존재, 생활.
- tell on: 고자질 하다, 영향을 주다.
- destroy: 파괴하다, 망치다.
- nerve: 신경, 뻔뻔함.
- start: 놀라다, 움찔하다.
- shadow: 그림자, 환영.

Reading 10

Formerly, when going into action, Rostov had felt afraid; now he had not the least feeling of fear. He was fearless, not because he had grown used to being under fire (one cannot grow used to danger), but because he had learned how to manage his thoughts when in danger. He has grown accustomed when going into action to think about anything but what would seem most likely to interest him-the impending danger. During the first period of his service, **hard as he tried and much as he reproached himself with cowardice,** he had not been able to do this, but with time it had come of itself.

/Tolstoy. War and Peace

Word Bank

- action: 전투, 교전.
- go into action: 전투를 시작하다.
- not the least: (least에 강세를 두어) 조금도 ~않다, (not에 강세를 두어) 적잖은, 막대한.
- used to ~ing: ~에 익숙해 있는.
- under fire: 포화의 세례를 받고, 공격을 받고.
- impending: 임박한, 절박한.
- reproach: 질책하다, 비난하다.
- service: 봉사, 복무.
- cowardice: 겁, 소심.

Reading 11

During that time the flower has stood in the window, withered and forgotten, till at length cast out among the sweepings into the street, on the day of the lodgers' removal. And this poor flower, **withered and faded as it is,** we have added to our nosegay, because it gave more real joy than the most beautiful flower in the garden of a queen.

/Hans Christian Andersen. Fairy Tales: The Angel

Word Bank

- wither: 시들다, 말라죽다.
- till: (결과를 나타내어) ~하여 마침내.
- at length: 마침내, 상세히.
- sweeping: 청소, 쓰레기.
- removal: 제거, 이사.
- fade: 시들다, 쇠퇴하다.
- cast: 던지다.
- lodger: 숙박인, 하숙인.
- nosegay: 꽃다발.

구문 설명

"And this poor flower, withered and faded as it is, we have added to our nosegay, because ~"에서 "this flower"는 동사 "add"의 목적어 역할을 하는데 문장의 주제가 되어 문두에 놓여있다. 자세한 설명은 주제화 구문 참조.

Reading 12

In other parts of Europe consumers are hearing ever more spooky stories of what goes into animal feed, **isolated and unproved though some of these claims are.** In the Netherlands last week it was reported that swill--edible waste from restaurants and hospitals--is still being used in some pig feed despite being banned there since 1986. In Spain last week, one television station reported a claim that in Andalucia dead pets from animal homes are recycled into feed.

/Time.

Word Bank

- taker: 수취인, 소비자.
- spooky: 유령 같은, 무시무시한.
- feed: 먹이, 사료(= fodder).
- swill: 구정물, 밥찌끼.
- edible: 먹을 수 있는, 식용의.
- ban: 금지하다.
- station: 서, 소, 국.
- recycle: 재생하여 이용하다, 재순환시키다.

Reading 13

Her parents were equally perturbed, because they presumed she would return to live with them. **Much though they loved their daughter, they felt it would now be a mistake to share the same roof: she had changed more than ever.** But Margaret was determined to be independent, and stayed a dutiful week with her parents before finding rooms in a somewhat run down boarding house in Notting Hill Gate. The rent was cheap, however, and Margaret knew this was important. On advice from her friend Julia, she then registered with an employment agency near the tube station.

/Sue Jackson. Making Waves

Word Bank

- convent: 수도회, 수녀원.
- hue and cry: 고함소리, 대소동.
- label: 라벨을 붙이다, 부르다.
- perturb: 당황하게 하다, 불안하게 하다.
- presume: 추정하다, 간주하다.
- dutiful: 본분을 다하는, 예의 바른.
- hue: 외침, 소리.
- nun: 수녀.
- asset: 자산, 정보제공자.
- run-down: 피로한, 황폐한.
- tube: 관, 지하철.

Reading 14

The ability to see the situation as the other side sees it, **as difficult as it may be,** is one of the most important skills a negotiator can possess. It is not enough to know that they see things differently. If you want to influence them, you also need to understand empathetically the power of their point of view and to feel the emotional force with which they believe in it. It is not enough to study them like beetles under a microscope; you need to know what it feels like to be a beetle. To accomplish this task you should be prepared to withhold judgment for a while as you "try on" their views. They may well believe that their views are "right" as strongly as you believe yours are. You may see on the table a glass half full of cool water. Your spouse may see a dirty, half-empty glass about to cause a ring on the mahogany finish.

/Roger Fisher & William Ury. Getting To Yes

Word Bank

- negotiator: 협상하는 사람.
- influence: 영향을 주다, 움직이다.
- empathically: 단호하게, 분명하게.
- study: 공부하다, 자세히 보다.
- beetle: 풍뎅이, 딱정벌레.
- withhold: 억제하다, 보류하다.
- judgment: 판단.
- mahogany: 마호가니제 식탁, 적갈색(의).
- ring: 둥근 모양, 고리.
- try on: 시험해보다.
- finish: 마무리, 겉칠.

구문설명

They may well believe that their views are "right" as strongly as you believe yours are. = They may well believe that their views are "right" as strongly as you believe yours are right.

Reading 15

I recently acquired a Gateway computer and it is running Windows ME. The problem is this: From time to time the A key and the Caps Lock key get "linked" together so that typing an A turns on the Caps Lock and typing another A turns the Caps Lock off. Typing a series of A's looks like this: AaAaAaAa. **As strangely as it started, it then stopped.** This has happened several times now. We tried a new keyboard and have reinstalled the Windows operating system. What now?

/Chicago Tribune.

Word Bank

- acquire: 취득하다, 입수하다.
- run: 움직이다, 돌리다.

구문설명

일반적인 키보드에는 Lock 키가 세 개 있다. Caps Lock, Scroll Lock, Num Lock 키가 그것이다. 이러한 키는 자판에 불이 들어오거나 나가게 함으로써 현재의 상태를 알려준다. 이들 중에서 영문 대문자를 입력하려면 Caps Lock키를 누른다. 다시 한 번 Caps Lock 키를 누르면 영문 소 문자를 사용할 수 있게 해주는 키다.

Reading 16

Yet, even Theseus, **great hero as he was,** could not retain control of the turbulent Athenians when he succeeded his father on the throne. In his old age he was driven from the city and died in exile. Then his countrymen remembered all his services and brought his body back in honor, and ranked him among the gods.

/Edward S. Ellis & Charles F. Horne. The Story of the Greatest Nations and the World's Famous Events

Word Bank

- retain: 보유하다, 유지하다.
- succeed: 계승하다,
- drive: 몰아내다, 쫓겨나다.
- body: 몸, 시체.
- turbulent: 휘몰아치는, 난폭한.
- throne: 왕위, 옥좌.
- exile: 망명, 유배.
- rank: 나란히 세우다, 평가하다.

구문 설명

~ and ranked him among the gods. ~ and ranked him as a god.

Reading 17

But **rescued though she was from one peril,** it seemed as if she had only fallen into another. The Sultan commanded a horse to be given her, and conducted her to his own palace, where he led her to a beautiful apartment, and selected female slaves to wait on her, and eunuchs to be her guard. Then, without allowing her time to thank him for all he had done, he bade her repose, saying she should tell him her adventures on the following day.

/Andrew Lang. Arabian Night Entertainments: The Enchanted Horse

Word Bank

- Sultan: 술탄, 회교국 군주.
- wait on: 시중을 들다, 응대하다.
- guard: 파수꾼, 수호자.
- bid: 명령하다, 말하다 (bid + 目 + do).
- conduct: 행동하다, 안내하다.
- eunuch: 환관, 내시.
- repose: 쉬다, 휴식하다.

Reading 18

I was acutely aware of my many flaws. In Korea I was subhuman. Now I was sub-Christlike. I knew I wasn't good enough for anyone, and I felt complete despair. I couldn't measure up to anyone's standards. My parents told me I was saved from Korea to be re-created into God's image, but I wasn't a malleable enough piece of clay. **As repetitive as all this sounds, it's impossible to do justice to the stultifying monotony of my life in that household.** I was trapped on a wheel that turned endlessly on the same theme.

/Elizabeth Kim. Ten Thousand Sorrows

Word Bank

- acutely: 날카롭게, 예리하게.
- flaw: 결점, 결함.
- subhuman: 인간 이하의, 인간답지 못한,
- sub-Christlike: 이교도의.
- despair: 절망, 자포자기.
- measure up to: 에 달하다, 에 부합되다.
- malleable: 단련할 수 있는, 유순한.
- repetitive: 반복적인, 되풀이하는(= repetitious)
- do justice to: 올바르게 평가하다.
- stultify: 바보처럼 보이게 하다.
- monotony: 단조로움, 한결같음.
- trap: 덫을 놓다, 함정에 빠뜨리다.
- theme: 주제, 선율..

Reading 19

Last year, my parents celebrated their 60th wedding anniversary. Trying to find the right gift was a real challenge. My younger sister suggested a scrapbook filled with memories. Each sibling (there are eight of us) was given three pages to fill with anything we chose. **Try as I might,** I could think of nothing to put on my pages. I finally wrote them this letter, which I hope you will print for all those who have parents they love and cherish.

/Ann Landers.

Word Bank

- celebrate: 거행하다, 경축하다.
- challenge: 도전.
- sibling: 형제, 자매.
- anniversary: 기념일, 기념제.
- scrapbook: 스크랩북.

구문 설명

1. Try as I might, = Try as hard as I might, = However hard I may try,.
2. I finally wrote them this letter, which I hope you will print for all those who have parents they love and cherish. = I finally wrote them this letter, and I hope you will print it for all those who have parents they love and cherish.

Reading 20

This convinced me that there was no going on shore for us in the night upon that coast; and how to venture on shore in the day, was another question, too; for to have fallen into the hands of any of the savages, had been as bad as to have fallen into the paws of lions and tigers; at least, we were equally apprehensive of the danger of it. **Be that as it would,** we were obliged to go on shore somewhere or other for water, for we had not a pint left in the boat; when or where to get it was the point.

/Daniel Defoe. The Life and Surprising Adventures of Robinson Crusoe

Word Bank

- convince: 확신 시키다, 납득시키다.
- there is no ~ing: ~할 수 없다 (= it is impossible to ~).
- shore: 뭍, 육지.
- coast: 해안, 해변.
- venture: 위험을 무릅쓰고 ~에 가다.
- savage: 야만인, 미개인.
- paw: 발.
- apprehensive: 염려하는, 두려워하는.
- oblige: 강제로 ~하게 하다.
- be obliged to: 해야하다.
- pint: 파인트(약 0.4리터).
- point: 주안점, 요점.

Reading 21

Yet **scientist and philosopher as he was,** with the unquenchable faith in the inevitability of socialism, Marx was no mere man of the study. He took part in the German revolution of 1848, was active in the preparation of the revolution of that year, and to the end of his days participated, whenever possible, in the workers struggles against capitalism which he always knew as preparation for social revolution. In 1871, when the workers of Paris established the Commune, Marx hailed it as one of the greatest events in human history.

/C.L.R. James. Labor Action. 1946. 3. 18. They Showed the Way to Labor Emancipation

Word Bank

- unquenchable: 억제할 수 없는, 막을 수 없는.
- inevitability: 필연성, 불가피.
- take part in: ~에 참여하다. ~에 조력하다.
- to the end of: capitalism:
- establish: 수립하다, 설립하다.
- Commune: 지방자치구, 코뮌(파리 코뮌(the Paris Commune): 세계 최초의 사회주의 정권).
- hail: 환영하다, 부르다.

Reading 22

Perhaps you are wondering why I am quoting the mighty Zeus from Clash of the Titans and talking about Perseus since obviously this is a son of Hercules movie, and Perseus, **great Greek hero that he was,** was not a son of Hercules. Sure there are some connections. After all, Hercules was born of a mortal woman and a horny Zeus. So was Perseus. Because of his father's infidelity, Hercules drew the ire of Zeus's pissed off wife, Hera.

/Keith Allison. Review about the movie Medusa against the Son of Hercules

Word Bank

- mighty: 힘이 있는, 강력한.
- Hercules: 헤라클레스(= Heracles).
- Perseus: 페르세우스(Zeus와 Danae사이에서 태어난 영웅).
- after all: 아무튼, 결국.
- mortal: 죽음을 면할 수 없는, 이 세상의.
- horny: 뿔의, 호색의.
- infidelity: 불성실, 부정(不貞).
- ire: 노여움, 분노.
- piss off: 화나게 하다, 애를 먹이다.

구문 설명

So was Perseus. = Perseus was born of a mortal woman and a horny Zeus, too. 자세한 설명은 주어조동사편 참조.

Unit 3 'WITH' 주술관계 ('WITH' Nexus)

두 요소 A와 B가 있을 때 A가 주어 역할을 하고 B가 술어 역할을 할 때 그 둘을 주술관계(Nexus)에 있다고 한다. 이런 관계는 주어와 술어 사이에서 그리고 목적어와 목적보어 사이에서 주어와 전치사구 사이에서 그리고 목적어와 전치사구 사이에서 나타난다.

① The dog (A) barks (B). (A와 B는 주술관계)

② The event made him (A) a hero (B). (A와B는 주술관계: He was a hero)

③ I (A) saw him (B) walking by the bank (C).
= I was walking by the bank when I saw him. (A와 C가 주술관계)
= He was walking by the bank and he saw it. (B와 C가 주술관계)

④ He completed the task in a week (A), a remarkable achievement (B).
= He completed the task in a week, which was a remarkable achievement.

위에서 본 바와 같이 시제절(finite clause)에서 뿐만 아니라 비시제절(nonfinite clause)에서도 주술관계가 나타나는데, 특히 비시제절에서의 주술관계에 대한 이해는영어구문을 보고 사용하는데 많은 도움이된다.
이와 마찬가지로 전치사 "with"를 뒤따르는 목적어와 목적어 뒤에 있는 요소 사이에서도 주술관계가 나타난다. 여기에서 전치사 "with"는 "having"의 뜻으로서 주절과의 관계에서 다양한 기능을 가지며 시간(when, while), 이유(as, since), 조건(if), 양보(though), 부대상황(as, while)의 의미를 갖는다.

1 'WITH' 주술 관계 유형

1.1. With+목적어+형용사

01 a. Don't speak **with your mouth full.**

b. Don't speak when your mouth is full.
(입안에 음식물이 가득 차있을 때에는 말하지 말아라.)

02 a. She sleeps **with one eye open.**

b. She sleeps while/as one eye is open. (그녀는 한쪽 눈을 뜨고 잔다.)

1.2. With+목적어+부사/전치사구

03 a. I shall be lonely **with you away.**

b. I shall be lonely if you are/get away. (네가 떠나고 나면 나는 외로울 꺼야.)

04 a. He stood **with his back against the wall.**

b. He stood while his back was against the wall.
(그는 벽에 등을 기대고 서있었다.)

05 a. **With the police on all sides of them and ready to shoot,** the bank robbers finally surrendered.

b. As the police were on all sides of them and ready to shoot, the bank robbers finally surrendered.
(경찰이 그들을 사방에서 포위하고 총을 쏠 준비가 되어 있어서 은행 강도는 마침내 항복을 했다.)

1.3. With+목적어+현재분사(~ing)

06 a. She came to see me, **with a heavy rain failing.**

b. She came to see me, though/when a heavy rain was falling.
(그녀는 폭우가 내리고 있었음에도 불구하고 나를 만나러 왔다.)

07 a. The ocean looks very beautiful **with the moonlight glimmering on its surface.**

b. The ocean looks very beautiful while the moonlight was glimmering on its surface.
(달빛이 수면위로 아른거린 가운데 바다는 아주 아름다워 보입니다.)

08 a. **With everybody insisting on going there,** I don't know whom I should send.

b. As everybody insists on going there, I don't know whom I should send.
(모두가 그곳에 가겠다고 고집을 부려 나는 누구를 보내야 할 지 모르겠다.)

목적어와 분사간에 능동이나 진행의 주술관계가 이루어진다.

1.4. With+목적어+과거분사(~ed)

09 a. He fell asleep, **with his radio turned on.**

b. He fell asleep, while his radio was turned on.
(그는 라디오를 켜놓고 잠이 들었다.)

10 a. **With half the work still unfinished,** she became frantic about the lack of time.

b. As half the work was still unfinished, she became frantic about the lack of time.
(일의 절반이 아직 끝나지 않아 그녀는 시간이 부족해 허둥지둥 서두르게 되었다.)

목적어와 분사간에 수동이나 완료의 주술관계가 이루어진다.

1.5. With+목적어+절

11 I can't live on my wages with prices what they are.
(물가가 현 상태라면 내 월급으로는 살 수가 없다.)

2 보충 설명

12 a. He stood there, hat in hand and pipe in mouth.

b. He stood there, with a hat in his hand and a pipe in his mouth.
(그는 모자를 손에 들고 파이프를 입에 문 채 그곳에 서있었다.)

13 a. Her eyes full of tears, she explained why she had to give up the idea of going to college.

b. With her eyes full of tears, she explained why she had to give up the idea of going to college.
(그녀는 눈에 눈물이 가득한 채 왜 대학 가려는 생각을 단념해야 했는지를 설명했다.)

'With' 주술관계 구문에서 "with," 관사, 그리고 소유격이 생략되어 나타나거나 "with"만 생략되어 나타나는 경우가 많다.

14 a. With the arrest and imprisonment of the prowler, everyone in the neighborhood felt relieved.

b. With the prowler arrested and imprisoned, everyone in the neighborhood felt relieved.
(그 도둑이 체포되어 감금이 되어서 이웃의 모든 사람들이 안도감을 느꼈다.)

'With+명사+전치사구'의 구조는 위에서 다루어진 'WITH' 주술관계 유형으로 바꾸어 쓸 수 있는 경우가 많다.

15 a. He carried out the plan without his friends knowing anything about it.
(그는 그의 친구들은 그것에 대해 아무것도 모르게 그 계획을 수행했다.)

b. They lived in the same house nearly a year and a half without a single word spoken between them.
(그들은 서로 아무 말도 하지 않고 거의 1년 반 동안을 한 집에서 살았다.)

"Without"도 "With"와 마찬가지로 주술관계 구문을 형성한다.

Practice Examples

Reading 01

In the accord that followed, the Palestinians agreed to remove language from their founding charter that called for the dismantling of the Jewish state, and the Israelis agreed to cede an additional 13 percent of the West Bank. At the same time they set a deadline of September 13, 2000, to reach a final peace accord. By mid-year 2000, **with the deadline approaching and no agreement in sight,** Clinton invited Barak and Arafat to a three-way summit at Camp David, the presidential retreat in Maryland. **The talks began July 11 and ended 15 days later with no agreement in sight,** the two sides at an impasse largely over the sovereignty and control of Jerusalem.

/CNN.

Word Bank

- accord: 동의, 협정.
- remove: 제거하다, 삭제하다.
- charter: 조항, 헌장.
- call for: 요구하다.
- dismantle: 제거하다, 파괴하다.
- cede: 양도하다, 양보하다.
- set: 정하다, 설정하다.
- deadline: 원고 마감 시간, 최종 기한.
- three-way: 세 가지 방법의, 3자간의.
- summit: 정상, 정상 회담.
- retreat: 은퇴, 피난처, 요양소.
- impasse: 막다른 골목, 난국.
- sovereignty: 주권, 통치권.

구문설명

1. "~ language from the founding charter that called for the dismantling of the Jewish state, ~ = ~ language that called for the dismantling of the Jewish state from the founding charter, ~". 자세한 설명은 "탈명사구 외치" 참조.
2. ~ 15 days later with no agreement in sight, the two sides at an impasse largely over the sovereignty and control of Jerusalem. = ~ 15 days later with no agreement in sight, with the two sides at an impasse largely over the sovereignty and control of Jerusalem.

Reading 02

Eight months later, on November 26, 1994, 71-year-old Margaret Garrish, **with Kevorkian present,** died of carbon monoxide poisoning. Garrish was the 21st person to receive Jack Kevorkian's assistance. Since then, he says, he has helped more than a hundred others die, either by inhaling carbon monoxide or by intravenous poisoning. His work culminated in the death of Thomas Youk on September 17, 1998, as Kevorkian videotaped himself injecting the 52-year-old man with a lethal dose of chemicals, then played the tape for Mike Wallace on CBS's "60 Minutes."

/Reader's Digest.

Word Bank

- carbon monoxide: 일산화탄소(CO).
- poisoning: 중독.
- inhale: 흡입하다, 들이 마시다.
- intravenous: 정맥내의, 정맥 주사의.
- culminate: 절정에 이르다. 최고조에 달하다.
- videotape: 을 테이프에 녹화하다.
- inject: 주사하다, 주입하다.
- lethal: 치사의, 치명적인.

Reading 03

I am having problems with our neighbors and their child. My husband and I are energetic, outgoing and like to get things done--yard work, gardening, etc. These neighbors are the exact opposite. They hold down the couch most weekends and are proud to boast how lazy they are. If they see we are out playing with our children, they send their child over uninvited and unwanted. I've never disliked a child before in my life, but she is rude, disrespectful, has no manners, and quite honestly, is not the kind of kid I want my children playing with. I know that she has no parental supervision, so I can't help but feel sorry for her but I don't want her at my house. I don't know what to say to the parents because I don't want to start a "hate thy neighbor" relationship. **My husband is able to tolerate it to keep the peace, but with summer coming, I know it will only get worse.**

/Universal Press Syndicate. Dear Abby.

Word Bank

- energetic: 원기 왕성한, 힘이 넘치는(= virile, vigorous)
- outgoing: 사교적인(= showing eagerness to mix socially with others).
- opposite: reverse: 반대
- hold down: 누르다, 억제하다, 유지하다.
- couch: 소파.
- disrespectful: 존경심 없는, 무례한, 예의 바르지 못한.
- supervision: 감독, 통제
- can't help but: 하지 않을 수 없다(= can't help ~ing: ~).
- thy: thou의 소유격, 너의, 그대의
- tolerate: 견디다, 허용하다

Reading 04

With all these groups making up the American people, it may seem surprising that American society is as uniform as it is. American culture has typical features, and perhaps one of the most characteristic is the blending of all of the diverse strains to produce American customs and ideals.

/Gladys Doty Janet Ross. Language and Life in the U.S.A.

Word Bank

- make up: 을 구성하다, 형성하다.
- uniform: 한결 같은, 획일적인.
- typical: 전형적인, 대표적인.
- blend: 섞다, 혼합하다.
- strain: 혈통, 기질.

구문설명

as uniform as it is = very uniform.

Reading 05

Rudy grabbed the edge of the bridge, the water lapping at his chin, and tried to lift himself onto the solid surface. He couldn't move. He was unaware that his left leg had become entangled in the thick yellow towrope he had used to secure the trolling motor. The weight of the boat and motor was like an anchor, pulling his lower body underneath the bridge while he fought to keep his head above the surface. Complicating matters, the other half of the boat had folded behind Rudy's back **with a large tackle box wedged in between,** pounding against his head and shoulders.

(Reader's Digest 41)

Word Bank

- grab: 움켜지다, 잡아채다.
- chin: 아래턱.
- towrope: 예선 밧줄(= towline).
- secure: 묶다, 고정시키다.
- complicate: 복잡하게 하다, 곤란하게 하다.
- tackle: 연장, 낚시도구.
- wedge: 을 쐐기로 고정시키다, 을 박아넣다.
- lap: 잔물결이 찰싹찰싹 치다.
- entangle: 얽히게 하다, 걸리게 하다.
- troll: 견지낚시질을 하다.
- pound: 두드리다.

Reading 06

The object departed silently, and Delgado returned to his patrol car where, he says, the ignition, lights, and police radio all started up again without his assistance. At 3:56 a.m., four minutes after Delgado made his distress call, three patrol cars roared up. Sergeant H.L. Bartley found Delgado sitting in his cruiser **with the door open,** shaking. Later that morning Delgado underwent both a physical and a psychological examination, neither of which found any evidence of injury or mental abnormality. Sgt. Bartley, now retired from the force, vouches for Delgado's credibility. "I don't doubt he saw something strange out there that morning."

/Reader's Digest.

Word Bank

- depart: 떠나다, 출발하다.
- ignition: 점화, 점화장치.
- radio: 무선 통신기.
- distress call: 구조 요청 신호, 조난 신호(= distress signal).
- roar: 요란한 소리를 내다.
- sergeant: 상사, 경사.
- cruiser: 순찰차(= patrol car).
- shake: 떨다.
- undergo: 을 받다, 경험하다.
- psychological: 심리적인, 정신적인.
- abnormality: 이상, 변칙.
- retire: 은퇴하다, 퇴직하다.
- force: 부대, 경찰.
- vouch: 보증하다, 단언하다.
- credibility: 진실성

Reading 07

There was a shepherd who was fond of playing practical jokes. He would drive his flock some distance from the village and then shout to the villagers for help, saying that wolves had attacked his sheep. Two or three times the inhabitants came rushing out in alarm and then went back **with the shepherd laughing at them.** Eventually, however, some wolves really came. They got between the shepherd and his flock and he called the neighbors to aid him. But they thought he was up to his usual trick and did not bother their heads about him. So he lost his sheep.

/Aesop's Fables. Crying Wolf Too Often

Word Bank

- practical joke: 짓궂은 장난, 못된 장난.
- drive: 몰다, 몰아대다.
- rush: 달리다, 돌진하다.
- trick: 속임수.
- up to ~: 에 종사하여, 을 꾀하여.
- bother: 괴롭히다. 썩히다.
- bother one's head about something: 일로 골치 앓다.

Reading 08

The day after his death all the ladies prepared to call at the house and offer condolence and aid, as is our custom. Miss Emily met them at the door, dressed as usual and with no trace of grief on her face. **She told them that her father was not dead. She did that for three days, with the ministers calling on her, and the doctors trying to persuade her to let them dispose of the body.** Just as they were about to resort to law and force, she broke down and they buried her father quickly.

/William Faulkner. A Rose for Emily-Great Short Stories

Word Bank

- call at + 장소/call on + 사람: 을 방문하다.
- condolence: 문상, 조의.
- trace: 흔적, 자취.
- minister: 목사, 장관.
- dispose: 처리하다, 처분하다(of).
- body: 몸, 시체.
- resort: 호소하다(to).
- break down: 굴복하다, 울음을 터뜨리다.

Reading 09

Tom had stood during the speech **with his hands raised, and his eyes dilated,** like a man in a dream. Slowly and gradually, as its meaning came over him, he collapsed, rather than seated himself, on his old chair, and sank his head down upon his knees.

/Harriet Stowe: Uncle Tom's Cabin

Word Bank

- dilate: 크게 하다, 넓히다.
- collapse: 무너지다, 쓰러지다.
- sink: 숙이다, 수그리다.

구문 설명

with his hands raised, and his eyes dilated, = raising his hands and dilating his eyes,

Reading 10

The water was cold and in flood and many things passed that had been floated the banks when the river rose. I was lucky to have a heavy timber to hold on to, and I lay in the icy water **with my chin on the wood,** holding on as easily as I could with both hands. I was afraid of cramps and I hoped I would move towards the shore. I went down the river in a long curve. It was beginning to be light enough so I could see the bushes along the shoreline.

/Earnest Hemingway. A Farewell to Arms

Word Bank

- float: 떠다니다, 표류하다.
- hold on to: 을 꼭 잡고 있다, 에 매달리다.
- cramp: 경련
- timber: 목재, 통나무.
- in a long curve: 긴 곡선을 그리며.

Reading 11

Mrs. Anne Sterling did not think of the risk she was taking when she ran through a forest after two men. They had rushed up to her while she was having a picnic at the edge of a forest with her handbag. In the struggle, the strap broke and, **with the bag in their possessions, both men started running through the trees.** Mrs. Sterling got so angry that she ran after them. She was soon out of breath, but she continued to run. When she caught up with them, she saw that they had sat down and were going through the contents of the bag, so she ran straight at them. The men got such a fright that they dropped the bag and ran away. 'The strap needs mending,' said Mrs Sterling later, 'but they did not steal anything.'

/L. G. Alexander. Practice and Progress

Word Bank

- strap: 가죽 끈, 혁대.
- catch up with: 을 따라 잡다.
- go through: 조사하다, 검사하다.
- out of breath: 숨을 헐떡이며.
- fright: 공포, 놀라움.

구문 설명

The strap need mending. = The strap needs to be mended.

Reading 12

In the introduction on "How to Read in a Foreign Language," the authors indicated that you should develop the ability to pick out grammatical patterns and read by these word groups rather than word by word. In this way you will read more rapidly and with greater comprehension. **To help develop this ability, listen with your books closed while your instructor reads aloud the following sentences.**

/Gladys Doty & Janet Ross. Language and Life in the U.S.A

Word Bank

- introduction: 도입(부), 소개.
- indicate: 가리키다, 언급하다.
- pick out: 고르다, 선별하다.

Reading 13

All went well until 1893, the year of the silver panic. The United States no longer used silver as a standard for coinage. **With the price of silver down,** Tabor could not afford to operate the Matchless Mine. He had spent all his money in extravagant living and had to go to work as a day laborer in Denver. It is reported that one time when he and Baby Doe had nothing in the house to eat, his first wife, living comfortably on her $1,200,000, sent them a wagonload of food, enough to keep them all winter.

/Gladys Doty & Janet Ross, Language and Life in the U.S.A.

Word Bank

- go: 진행되다.
- standard: 표준, 본위.
- extravagant: 사치스러운, 낭비하는.
- wagonload: 마차 1대분의 짐.
- panic: 당황, 공황.
- coinage: 경화, 화폐.

Reading 14

The silence was suddenly broken when a large car, with its headlights on and its horn blaring, roared down the arcade. It came to a stop outside the jeweler's. One man stayed at the wheel while two others **with black stockings over their faces** jumped out and smashed the window of the shop with iron bars. While this was going on, Mr. Taylor was upstairs. He and his staff began throwing furniture out of the window. Chairs and tables went flying into the arcade. One of the thieves was struck by a heavy statue, but he was too busy helping himself to diamonds to notice any pain. The raid was all over in three minutes, for the man scrambled back into the car and it moved off at a fantastic speed. Just as it was leaving, Mr. Taylor rushed out and ran after it throwing ashtrays and vases, but to stop the thieves was impossible. They had got away with thousands of pounds worth of diamonds.

/L.G. Alexander. Developing Skills

Word Bank

- horn: 뿔, 경적. roar: 큰 소리를 내며 움직이다.
- arcade: 아케이드, 상가.
- smash: 을 때려 부수다.
- help oneself to ~: ~을 마음껏 먹다, ~을 훔치다.
- raid: 기습, 습격.
- scramble: 바삐 서두르다. 기어 오르다.
- move off: 떠나다.
- get away with: 을 가지고 도망치다.
- worth: 가치, 어치.
- at the wheel: 핸들을 쥐고.
- statue: 상, 조상.
- ashtray: 재떨이.

구문설명

It came to a stop outside the jeweler's. = It came to a stop outside the jeweler's (shop). 명사의 소유격 다음에 오는 장소나 건축물(house, shop, store, office, church, cathedral, palace) 등이 자주 생략 된다. 해당 장소나 건축물은 문맥에서 결정된다.

Reading 15

Firefighters say a child started a south Austin house fire Wednesday night. Crews got the fire under control quickly, but it did cause $70,000 worth of damage. **A 36-year-old man is in fair condition with second-degree burns on his hands.** His six-year-old daughter is in good condition, and is being treated for smoke inhalation. Three other children had to get treatment at the scene.

/FOX 7.

Word Bank

- firefighter: 소방대원(= fireman).
- crew: 승무원, 조원.
- inhalation: 흡입. scene: 상년, 현상.

Reading 16

They set off, He was in front this time. And when they were once more in the little sitting room, she saw that he was putting his linen and slippers in a sack that she knew well. **Desperately but respectfully, she followed all his movements, with his complexion pale.** He laid his hand on her neck to reassure her.

/Animal Sleep. Freshman English. 외대 출판사

Word Bank

- set off: 출발하다.
- sitting room: 거실.
- linen: 속옷, 내의.
- sack: 부대, 쇼핑백.
- respectfully: 정중하게, 예의 바르게.
- complexion: 얼굴, 용모.
- reassure: 안심시키다, 기운 차리게 하다.

Reading 17

Witnesses said more than 200 looters died when they were trapped inside a mall set ablaze by other rioters. **With relatives wailing around them,** residents banded together to take away the bodies, which were burned and blackened beyond recognition. Police and rescue officials were nowhere in sight at the mall, located near slums in the Kelender section of eastern Jakarta. Unrest intensified last week after Suharto introduced new austerity measures under a $43 billion rescue plan imposed by the International Monetary Fund to overcome Indonesia's worst economic crisis in decades.

/ABC News.

Word Bank

- looter: 약탈자, 강탈자.
- mall: 쇼핑센터, 몰.
- relative: 친척, 일가.
- band: 단결하다, 모이다.
- recognition: 인식, 알아봄.
- slum: 빈민가.
- intensify: 격렬해지다, 강해지다.
- austerity: 긴축, 내핍.
- measure: 대책, 조치.
- trap: 덫을 놓다, 가두다.
- rioter: 폭도.
- wail: 울부짖다, 통곡하다.
- unrest: 불안, 동요.

Reading 18

It was a small window with narrow pieces of paper pasted across it to prevent it from breaking during the heavy air raids. In the small space at the center that remained, a little man with glasses was carefully setting out his display of clocks and watches. He paid no attention to the many Londoners hurrying to begin another day.

/Howard Breslin. Clock Work

Word *Bank*

- paste: 바르다, 붙이다.

Reading 19

The bishops said that Milingo had betrayed his vows because he was still under his priestly commitments. Bishop Dennis Dejong, spokesman for Zambia's Roman Catholic Church, said Milingo turned his back on the church by marrying. ``By doing this, the former archbishop has put himself outside the Catholic Church," Dejong said. ``We feel sympathy for the many people who put their trust in the former archbishop and now feel betrayed and abandoned." Milingo has long been at odds with the Roman Catholic hierarchy. While archbishop of Lusaka, he ran afoul of the Vatican over his ministry of faith healings and exorcisms. **He resigned under pressure in 1983, a very rare occurrence with an archbishop below normal retirement age and in good health.** He then was brought to Rome as a functionary in the Pontifical Council for Pastoral Care of Migrants and Itinerant Peoples, but continued public meetings of healing and exorcism. Last year, he was quietly retired from the post.

/Associated Press.

Word Bank

- bishop: 주교.
- priestly: 성직자의, 사제의.
- commitment: 의무, 언질.
- turn one's back on: ~에서 등을 돌리다
- archbishop: 대주교.
- at odds: 사이가 좋지 않아.
- hierarchy: 계급 제도, 교회 정치.
- run afoul: 충돌하다, 상반하다.
- ministry: 성직자의 직무.
- exorcism: 귀신 쫓아내기, 굿.
- pontifical: 교황의, 주교의.
- functionary: 직원, 공무원

구문 설명

1. while archbishop of Lusaka = while he was archbishop.
2. He resigned under pressure in 1983, a very rare occurrence ~ = He resigned under pressure in 1983, which was a very rare occurrence.

Reading 20

The South is a land of contrasts. Here you may still find a few plantation mansions, relics of a past century. Characteristic of these buildings is a porch supported by white pillars. The house is often surrounded by a garden beautiful in spring with masses of flowering shrubs. **In the South also are unpainted shacks of white or black sharecroppers, with little tobacco or cotton fields beside them.**

/Gladys Doty and Janet Ross. Language and Life in the U. S. A.

Word Bank

- contrast: 대조, 대립.
- plantation: 농장, 농원.
- mansion: 큰 저택.
- relic: 유물, 유적.
- porch: 현관.
- shack: 오두막, 판자집.
- sharecropper: 소작인.

구문 설명

Characteristic of these buildings is a porch supported by white pillars. = A porch supported by white pillars is characteristic of these buildings. In the South also are unpainted shacks of white or black sharecroppers, = Unpainted shacks of white or black sharecroppers are also in the South,. 이들 문장은 주어와 조동사가 도치되어 있다. 자세한 설명은 주어 조동사 도치편 참조.

Reading 21

My grown children try to work out their own problems and hardly ever come to me for help. When my wife's kids have problems with their marriages, they stay at our home. One has been with us for several months now. Another thinks we should baby-sit two or three times a week. When I say anything to my wife, she gets upset. I'm retired now and would like to have my home back for my wife and me to enjoy our retirement. I worked for more than 40 years to enjoy retirement - now I hate every day of it. I've considered leaving, but **with the laws as they are, she would get half of my retirement,** and she never worked to put anything into it. Not a day goes by that I don't wish I had not remarried. I would have been happier living by myself.

/Universal Press Syndicate. Dear Abby

Word Bank

- upset: 전복한, 엉망진창이 된, 불편한.
- baby-sit: 애를 봐주다.

Reading 22

As the century ends, the challenges of the next are already hovering on the horizon. **With the fall of the Soviet Union in 1989, former Communist countries became eager to embrace the sense of identity and nationhood that had been suppressed for so long.** Over twenty countries have since gained their independence, ushering in a new nationalism that, while admirable, has proven itself to be a significant source of instability and local conflict in the last decade - and a wellspring of unrest for decades to come.

/PBS.

Word Bank

- hover: 날다, 떠돌다.
- on the horizon: 수평선상에, 조짐이 보이는.
- embrace: 받아들이다.
- identity: 정체성, 주체성.
- suppress: 억압하다, 억누르다.
- usher: 의 도래를 알리다(in).
- instability: 불안정, 우유부단.
- wellspring: 수원, 원천(= wellhead).

구문 설명

With the fall of the Soviet Union in 1989, = As the Soviet Union fell in 1989,

Reading 23

Most of us have acquired the habit of wearing a hat, for instance, when we leave the house, and we go on doing this, not so much in order to protect our heads from the weather as because we have always done it since childhood, **Today there are many people who go about without a hat on,** but there is still a widespread prejudice against them.

/Robert Lynd. The Newsboy

Word Bank

- acquire: 얻다, 습득하다.
- not so much A as B: A라기 보다는 오히려 B인(= not A so much as B = B rather than A).
- go about: 돌아다니다.
- prejudice: 편견, 선입관.

Reading 24

If I believe I'm right, and you believe you're right, we can take advantage of this difference in beliefs. **We may both agree to have an impartial arbitrator settle the issue, each confident of victory.** If two factions of the union leadership cannot agree on a certain wage proposal, they can agree to submit the issue to a membership vote.

/Fisher, Roger & William Ury. Getting to Yes

Word Bank

- take advantage of: 을 이용하다(= use).
- impartial: 공정한, 편견이 없는.
- arbitrator: 중재인, 조정자.
- faction: 그룹, 파벌.

구문 설명

each confident of victory = with each confident of victory =if each of us is confident of victory

Reading 25

With the closets finished and the bureaus empty, the room emanated loneliness. Dad was gone. His things were going, and a new era in my life was beginning. **How do you go on without one that you loved so much, without that person being there when you most need him?** Who will answer the phone now when I call to say, "I love you, Dad?"

/Canfield, J. & M. V. Hansen. Chicken Soup for the Soul

Word Bank

- closet: 벽장, 사실.
- emanate: 발산시키다.
- go on: 계속하다, 지내다.
- bureau: 양복장, 침실용 장롱.
- go: 죽다, 사라지다.

Reading 26

I had the surgery and then went home to the little cabin for a long period of convalescence. During that time I had to remain either flat on my back or completely upright. Leigh did the cooking and cleaning and provided nearly around-the-clock nursing care for me, in her own unique style. She read aloud to me from Shakespeare. **She made tea for us and curled up on a bank of pillows, book in hand**-the same way I had read to her a few years earlier.

/Elizabeth Kim. Ten Thousand Sorrows

Word Bank

- surgery: 외과, 수술.
- cabin: 오두막집.
- convalescence: 회복, 요양.
- upright: 똑 바로 선, 직립의.
- around-the-clock: 24시간 꼬박의.
- nursing: 양육하는, 간호하는
- curl: 곱슬곱슬하게 하다, 웅크리다.
- bank: 은행, 저장소.
- pillow: 베개.

구문 설명

~ a bank of pillows, book in hand ~ = ~ a bank of pillows, with a book in her hand.

Reading 27

The year was 1991, and the real estate market in Phoenix was terrible. People were giving houses away. **I suggested to my classmate that he buy a house with some of the money in his mutual fund.** The idea intrigued him and we began to discuss the possibility. His primary concern was that he did not have the credit with the bank to buy another house, since he was so over-extended. I assured him that there were other ways to finance a property other than through the bank.

/Robert T. Kyosaki & Sharon L. Lechter. Rich Dad Poor Dad

Word Bank

- real estate: 부동산 (= real property).
- give away: 거저 주다, 선물로 주다..
- intrigue: 흥미를 끌다, 관심을 돋구다.
- credit: 신용, 신용대부.
- mutual fund: 뮤추얼펀드 (유가증권투자를 목적으로 한 회사의 주식을 투자가가 갖는 형태, 즉 회사형(會社型)을 택하여, 투자가는 수익자인 동시에 주주가 된다. 또한 오픈 엔드형(開放型)에서 수익증권에 해당하는 주식의 매입에 의한 자본금(신탁재산)의 감소가 인정되므로, 수익자인 투자가는 언제라도 주식을 매각할 수 있다).
- overextend: 지나치게 확대하다, 한도 이상의 것을 시키다.
- assure: 보증하다, 단언하다.
- finance: 자금을 공급하다, 출자하다.

구문 설명

"~ that he buy a house with some of the money in his mutual fund."에서 "WITH 주술관계"의 구조를 가지고 있지만 다른 표현으로 사용되고있다.

Reading 28

After beginning work, I came to find out just how benevolent and empathetic he truly was. **With house prices what they are in Washington, I had trouble finding one I could afford.** So I rented a small room. That meant an eight-hour drive home on weekends to visit my family.

/Transport Topics.

Word *Bank*

- benevolent: 호의적인, 인정 많은.
- empathetic: 공감할 수 있는.
- afford: (경제적으로 혹은 시간적으로) 할 여유가 있다.

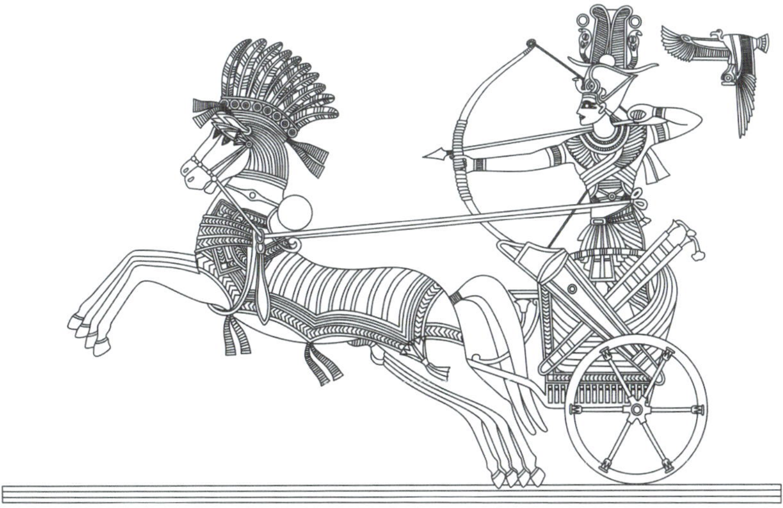

English Special Constructions

English
Special
Constructions

05

전문 해석

Chapter 1. 전 치 (Preposing)

Unit 1 주제화 (Topicalization)

01 나는 세계에서 가장 큰 도시의 자랑스런 아들로서 내가 바로 지금 다루고자 하는 문제를 다루어야만 한다는 것이 몹시 괴롭다. 그러나 나는 이 문제를 꼭 다루어야만 하겠다. 이상하고 무책임한 아주 많은 소문들이, 물론 새빨간 거짓말이지만, 최근 우리가 존경하는 시장과 관련해서 떠돌고 있다. 결국 그 유언비어가 사실이 아님을 증명해서 우리 시의 명예를 지켜야만 하겠다. 뉴욕을 제외한 나머지 미국과 세계는 그 진실을 알아야만 할 것이다. 뉴욕의 Rudolph Giuliani, 그는 강하고 헌신적인 사람이며 두려움이 없는 사람이다. 그는 또한 새로운 생각들을 터트리는 혁신자이다. 물론 그러한 사람에게는 적이 있다. 물론 그는 언론 매체의 보수주의자들과 허무주의자들, 야당, 그리고 이 도시의 기존 이익 단체들의 신랄한 반대를 불러일으키고 있다. 그러나 소문일 뿐! 그 터무니없는 거짓말을 여러분들은 읽고 듣고 있는 것이다. 나는 여기 저기 퍼지고 있는 우스운 거짓말 몇 가지만 싣고자 한다. 그 거짓말들은 곧 사실들에 의해서 거짓으로 밝혀지게 될 것이다.

02 옛날 한 불행한 소녀가 살았습니다. 그녀는 정말 불행했습니다. 왜냐하면 그녀의 엄마가 돌아가시고, 그녀의 아버지가 딸이 둘 달린 과부와 결혼을 했는데 그녀의 계모가 전혀 그녀를 사랑해주지 않았기 때문입니다. 좋은 일들, 친절한 배려 그리고 애정어린 손길은 모두가 그녀 자신의 딸들만을 위한 것이었습니다. 그런 친절한 배려, 그리고 사랑만이 아니라 옷, 신발, 숄, 맛있는 음식, 편안한 침대 그리고 집에서 모든 안락함도 마찬가지였습니다.

03 양배추와 감자는 정원에서 재배되는 유일한 식물이었습니다. 그러나 울타리 밖에는 버드나무 한 그루가 자라고 있으며 이 버드나무 아래에는 한 어린 소녀가 앉아 있었습니다. 그리고 그녀는 앉아서 시선을 오두막집 사이에 있는 오래된 참나무에 고정시키고 있었습니다.

04 부모님은 내가 두려움을 극복하고 신에 대한 믿음을 갖도록 하기 위해 끊임없이 다양한 방법들을 강구해내고 계셨습니다. 예를 들어 그분들은 어둠에 대한 내 걷잡을 수 없는 두려움을 극복하도록 하기 위해 내게 약간의 연습을 시키셨습니다. 긴 복도 끝에 제 방은 있었습니다. 그 복도 바닥에는 부모님들께서 호랑이 인형을 놓아 두었습니다. 복도는 캄캄했고 부모님과 저는 응접실에 서 있었습니다. "이제 저 복도를 내려가 호랑이 인형을 가져 오너라. 그 바보 같은 두려움을 없애야 해."라고 부모님은 제게 말씀을 하셨습니다. 저는 호랑이 인형이 필요했지만 캄캄한 복도와 그리고 어두운 방안에서 기다리고 있을 지도 모를 무언가가 너무 무서웠습니다. 부모님은 불을 켜 주시지도 않았고 함께 가주시지도 않으셨습니다. 왜냐하면 그분들이 제게 말씀하신 바와 같이 저 자신을 위해 저에게 무언가를 가르쳐주려고 하셨기 때문입니다. 결국 저는 가지 않으려고 한참 동안 울며 애원을 한 후 마음을 굳게 먹고 복도를 따라 내려갔습니다. 왜냐하면 어둠 속에 호랑이 혼자 있다고 생각하니 호랑이가 너무 가여웠기 때문이었습니다.

05 최근까지만 해도 도구를 만들 수 있는 능력은 인간과 그들 조상들을 모든 다른 동물들과 구별해주는 특징들 중의 하나로 생각되었다. 1964년 Goodall 박사는 그녀가 아프리카 숲속의 침팬지가 흰개미를 잡는데 쓸 간단한 도구를 자주 만드는 것을 관찰하면서 이런 생각을 깨게 되었다. 이 원숭이(침팬지)는 먼저 적당한 재료를 찾는다. 다음 알맞은 크기와 모양의 잔가지를 조심스레 선택하고는 잎을 뜯어내어 버린다. 이것을 원숭이는 흰개미 집에 있는 구멍 속에 집어넣는다. 그리고 나서 이 잔가지를 뽑아내면 그 가지는 맛있는 흰개미들로 덮여 있다.

06 1963년 봄 졸업식이 카네기홀에서 거행되었다. 나는 의학(박사) 학위를 받으러 단상 위를 걸으면서 눈물이 어머니의 눈과 Lottie이모의 눈에 고여 있는 것을 보았다. 그리고 자부심이 아버지의 미소 속에 서려있음을 보았다. 나는 그분들을 모두 껴안았다. 그분들의 도움으로 나는 해낼 수 있었다. 그러나 내가 왜 그렇게 열심히 공부를 해야만 했었는지 그것은 여전히 풀리지 않는 수수께끼로 남아있다.

07 여자들이 점수를 주는 방식은 자기가 더 좋아하는 것에 점수를 줄 뿐만 아니라 자기가 진정으로 필요로 하는 것을 받았을 때 점수를 준다. 여자들은 사랑 받고있다는 관계 속에서 많은 사랑의 표현을 원한다. 한 두 차례의 사랑 표현으로는 아무리

탁월한 것이라도 그녀를 만족시킬 수없다. 이러한 것은 남자들이 이해하기 극히 어려운 일일 수도 있다. 그것을 이해할 수 있는 한 가지 방법은 여자들의 사랑의 탱크가 어쩌면 자동차의 연료 탱크와 비슷하리라는 상상을 해보는 것이다. 그것은 자꾸자꾸 채워 넣어야 할 필요가 있다. 작은 일들을 많이 해서 점수를 따는 것이 여자가 지닌 사랑의 탱크를 가득 채우는 비결이다. 여자들의 사랑의 탱크가 가득 차게 되면 여자는 사랑 받고 있다고 느낀다. 그러면 그녀는 보다 큰 사랑, 신뢰, 수용, 칭찬, 감탄, 승인과 격려를 그에게 되돌려 줄 수 있다. 그녀의 사랑의 탱크를 가득 채우기 위해서는 작은 일들을 많이 할 필요가 있다.

08 이런 감정은 아이들에게 만큼이나 어른들에게도 일반적이다. 예를 들어 하녀들의 경우를 보자. 내 기억으로 우리 집 하녀들 중에 결혼한 여자가 하나 있었는데 임신 중이어서 무거운 물건은 들지 않아도 된다고 했더니, 바로 나타난 결과는 다른 하녀들 중 어느 누구도 무거운 것은 들지 않으려 했다는 것이다. 그래서 하녀들이 마땅히 해야 될 일들을 우리가 직접 해야만 했다.

09 안개가 걷힌 정확한 순간을 나는 기억할 수 있다. 그때 작은 산을 등반하는 여행을 할 때였다. 그 산을 오르는 것은 내 생각이 아니었다. 나는 높은 곳을 무서워 했고, Matthew도 그가 꼭대기에서 경치를 구경하기 전까지는 마찬가지였다. "엄마, 너무 아름다워요. 왜 말해주지 안으셨어요?" 라고 그가 헐떡거리며 말했다.

10 텔레비전과 언론에 보도된 사진들은 참혹한 충격을 가져 다 주었다. 그 카메라를 검은 젖은 눈의 병들어 죽어가고 있는 바다 표범들이 원망의 눈초리로 바라보고 있었던 것이다. 그 바다 표범들은 알 수 없는 전염병에 걸린 약 7천 마리 중의 일부였다. 이 전염병은 지난 4월 덴마크 연안 앞바다에서 처음 발견되었는데, 그 후 독일 서쪽 영해로 퍼져 지금은 영국에 있는 2만 마리의 점박이 바다 표범까지 위협하고 있다. 이런 영상들은 서유럽인들의 뇌리에서 떠나지 않았다. 대기 오염과 같은 문제들도 그리 많은 분노를 자극하지 못했던 영국에서 바다 표범이 처한 이 곤경에 대한 반응은 그야말로 어마어마한 것으로 묘사되었다.

11 인간은 생산하지 않고 소비하는 유일한 피조물이다. 인간은 우유를 생산하지 않으며, 알을 낳지도 않으며, 너무 나약해서 쟁기를 끌 수도 없으며, 그리고 토끼를 잡을

만큼 그렇게 빨리 달리지도 못한다. 그러나 인간은 만물의 영장이다. 그래서 인간은 그들에게 일을 하도록 해서, 그들이 굶어죽지 않을 만큼 최소한의 것을 되돌려주며, 그리고 그 나머지는 그 자신을 위해 보관해둔다. 우리의 노동으로 땅을 경작하고 우리의 배설물로 땅을 비옥하게 한다. 그러나 우리들 중 자신의 벌거벗은 피부 외에 더 많은 것을 가지고 있는 자는 아무도 없다.

12 맞아. 그것은 소라껍질이야. 전에 그와 같은 것을 본 적이 있어. 어떤 누군가의 집의 뒷담에서. 그런데 그는 그것을 소라라고 불렀어. 그 애가 그것을 불곤 하면 그의 어머니가 오시곤 했었지. 그것은 굉장히 귀중한 것이었어.

13 만약 넉넉한 생활을 하는 것과 관련해 딸이 엄마만큼 걱정을 했다면 그녀는 오래 전에 Arnie를 버렸을 것이라고 저는 생각합니다. 저는 딸과 의논해야 한다고 엄마에게 해주는 당신의 충고에 강한 이의를 가지고 있습니다. Abby 선생님, 충고를 들어야 할 사람은 바로 엄마입니다. 그분의 의도가 선의에서 나온 것이겠지만 저는 그분이 사랑과 부는 다정하게 나란히 가는 것만은 아니라는 것을 깨달았으면 좋겠어요.

14 사실 이상한 행동의 몇 가지 예가 그런 소문을 낳기는 했었지만 그들이 겉으로 마음 아픈 척 했던 일은 일어나지 않았었다. 평범한 인간 본성의 특징들 중에서 시기심이 가장 불행한 것이다. 시기심이 강한 사람은 다른 사람에게 불행을 주고 싶어하고 그리고 처벌 받지 않고 할 수 만 있다면 언제든지 남에게 불행을 줄 뿐만 아니라, 그 자신 역시 시기심으로 불행하게 된다. 그는 자기가 가지고 있는 것으로부터 기쁨을 얻지 못하고, 다른 사람들이 가지고 있는 것으로부터 고통을 끌어온다.

15 그리고 우리가 영위하는 이 비참한 생애마저도 수명대로 누리지 못하게 되어 있습니다. 내 자신은 운이 좋은 사람들 중의 한 사람이었기 때문에 불평하지 않습니다. 나는 열 두 해를 살았고 자식이 사백도 넘으니까요. 이런 것이 바로 돼지의 자연스러운 생애입니다. 그러나 어떤 짐승도 결국엔 잔인한 칼날을 피하지 못합니다. 내 앞에 앉아 있는 젊은 식용돼지 여러분, 여러분도 모두 1년 안에 비명을 지르며 도마 위에서 목숨을 잃게 될 것입니다. 그런 끔찍한 일을 우리 모두 필연적으로 당하게 됩니다. 암소, 돼지, 닭, 양 모두가 말입니다. 말이나 개라고 해서 더 좋은 운명을 타

고 난 것은 아닙니다. Boxer, 당신도 그 건장한 근육이 힘을 잃은 바로 그 날 Jones가 당신을 도살자에게 팔아 넘길 것이며 그리고 그 도살업자는 당신의 목을 따서 삶아 여우사냥개의 먹이로 만들 것입니다. 개들의 경우에도 늙어 이가 빠지면 Jones는 그들 목에 벽돌을 매달아 제일 가까운 연못에 빠뜨려 죽일 것입니다.

16 우리는 율법이 신령한 것인 줄 압니다. 그러나 나는 욕정에 매인 존재로서, 죄 아래에 팔린 몸입니다. 나는 내가 하는 일을 도무지 알 수가 없습니다. 내가 해야겠다고 생각하는 일은 하지 않고, 도리어 해서는 안 되겠다고 생각하는 일을 하고 있으니 말입니다. 그런 일을 하면서도 그것을 해서는 안되겠다고 생각하는 것은, 곧 율법이 선하다는 사실에 동의하는 것입니다. 그렇다면, 그와 같은 일을 하는 것은 내가 아니라, 내 속에 자리를 잡고 있는 죄입니다. 나는 내 속에, 곧 내 육신 속에 선한 것이 깃들어 있지 않다는 것을 압니다. 선을 행하려는 의지는 나에게 있으나, 그것을 실행하지 않으니 말입니다.
(성경. 표준새번역. 로마서 7:14-18)

17 네덜란드 사람들은 바로 그들 의사들을 죽음의 의사로 임명했다. 네덜란드 상원은 의사들로 하여금 환자들이 말기에 '감당할 수 없는 고통'을 겪는다면 환자들의 목숨을 끊을 수 있도록 허용하는 법안을 지난 주에 통과시켰다. 그렇게 함으로써 네덜란드는 자살 방조를 합법화하고 의학을 치료의 목적에서 살인 목적으로 바꾸는 최초의 국가가 되었다. 유럽의 경우에서는 이런 모든 일들이 망령처럼 되살아 나는 몇 가지 암시를 갖게 된다. 종교계로부터 정치계, 언론에 이르기까지 독일에서는 정부의 안락사 관행을 승인하는 것에 강력하게 반대하는 항의가 있었다. 나치는 1939년부터 1941년 사이에 신체적으로나 혹은 정신적으로 장애가 있는 남녀와 어린이 10만 명을 비밀리에 살해했었는데, 네덜란드 사람들은 지금 어린이, 고령자, 정신 장애인들을 죽이려는 일을 공공연히 받아들이고 있다. 나치체제의 희생자 가운데는 네덜란드 사람 자신들도 포함되어 있었다. 네덜란드 의원들은 그러한 교훈을 기억하지 않기로 결정했음을 보여준 것이었다. 이번 새 법률로 인해 네덜란드에서 생명의 가치가 떨어지게 되었다.

18 해리는 그 편지를 잡아챘습니다. 그러나 작은 아버지 Vernon이 그의 손을 쳐서 편지를 잡을 수 없었습니다. 그 여자는 응시하고 있었다. "내게 주세요" 라고 작은 아버지는 말씀을 하시면서 벌떡 일어나 식당에서 그녀를 뒤따라갔습니다.

여보 집으로 돌아가는 것이 더 좋지 않겠어요? 라고 Petunia숙모께서 몇 시간 후 조심스럽게 말씀하셨습니다. 하지만 작은 아버지는 숙모님의 말씀을 듣고 있지 않는 것 같았습니다. 작은 아버지가 정확히 무엇을 찾고 있는 지 그들 중에 알고 있는 사람은 아무도 없었습니다. 작은 아버지는 그들을 차에 태워 숲속으로 들어가더니 차에서 내려 여기저기를 살펴보며 고개를 갸우뚱거렸습니다. 그리고 자동차로 되돌아와서 다시 출발했습니다. 똑 같은 일이 일구어 놓은 들판 한 복판에서 그리고 현수교를 중간쯤 건너던 지점에서 그리고 복층 주차장 꼭대기에서도 일어났습니다.

19 내가 오늘 신문을 펼쳤을 때에 일면에는 Lucille Ball의 사진이 실려있었다. 그녀의 푸른 눈과 붉은 머리와 아름다운 미소는 나의 어머니를 생각나게 했다. 나의 어머니는 불과 40밖에 안되었는데 지난 달에 돌아가셨다. 어머니는 힘든 삶을 사셨다. 그분은 태어나면서부터 몸이 허약했다. 태어날 당시 1파운드였고 폐는 하나뿐이었다. 평생 그분은 의사에게 가는 것을 싫어했다. 나는 나의 계부의 마음을 위로하려고 한다. 왜냐하면 그분은 어머니가 처음 아픔을 느끼기 시작했을 때에 억지로라도 의사의 진찰을 받게 하지 못한 것을 자책하고 계시고 있기 때문이다.

20 우리가 그녀의 일생 동안에 일어났던 주요한 역사적이고 정치적인 많은 사건들에 대하여 그녀의 작품에서 증거를 찾아야 한다는 것은 헛된 일인 것 같다. 그녀는 불란서 혁명, 나폴레옹의 출세와 몰락, 미국의 독립 전쟁, 그리고 1812년 영국과의 전쟁을 보고 겪었다. 그녀는 워터루 전쟁(1815)과 페터루 전쟁(1819) 중간인 1817년에 죽었고, Thompson이 '영국의 일하는 계급의 형성'으로 묘사했던 것과 동시에 일어났던 많은 혼란을 겪으며 살았다. 그녀는 역시 불란서 혁명의 결과로 영국에서 일어났던 자코뱅당과 반자코뱅당원들의 싸움을 알고 있었음에 틀림없다. 그 싸움은 Edward Burke의 〈프랑스 혁명에 대한 회상〉과 Thomas Paine의 〈인간의 권리〉에서 피력되고 있는 견해에 대립된 것으로 적절하지 않지만 아주 쉽게 묘사되고 있는 싸움이다. 이러한 혼란스러운 혁명, 변화, 그리고 논쟁은 그녀의 소설에는 거의 흔적이 남아있지 않는 듯하다. 그러나 물론 그녀는 무슨 일이 일어나고 있는지는 알고 있었다. 이러한 모든 사건들이 그녀의 작품에, 설사 있었다면, 어떤 영향을 미쳤는지를 결국 우리는 고찰해보아야 할 것이다.

21 현재 미국인들은 저축과 투자의 60%을 주식 시장에 맡겨두고 있다. 이는 1982년에 비해 2배 증가한 것이다. 그래서 급격히 하락하는 주가는 실질적인 부의 상실

을 의미하게 된다. 신경제에 무슨 일이 일어나고 있는가? 우리는 그것을 되돌릴 수는 있는가? 신경제의 한 복판에는 장거리통신, 마이크로 전자, 소프트웨어, 경영관리 분야에서의 여러 가지 발전이 있었다. 이런 발전으로 인해 신제품이 만들어졌고, 일터와 기업의 공급 망의 혁신이 이루어졌으며, 이는 잠재적 생산성을 1960년대 이후 유래 없는 수준으로 제고 시켰다. 보다 좋은 제품과 생산성으로 미국의 경쟁력이 되살아나게 되었다. 1989년부터 1998년까지 수출이 미국의 성장에 25%을 차지했다.

22 당신의 시어머니가 당신에 대한 사랑과 관심을 보여주려 하고 있다는 사실을 받아들이고 그저 웃고, 그분 뜻에 머리를 조아리고 그리고 그분의 말씀에 너무 개의치 말도록 하세요. 일단 쌍둥이가 태어나면 시어머니께 애들은 훌륭한 의사의 보살핌을 받고 있다는 것을 말씀드려 안심케 해드리세요. 그러면 당신은 시어머니의 여러 가지 말씀을 의사 선생님께 말씀드리고 그 말씀이 당신이 이미 받고 있는 의사의 조언과 상충되지 않는다는 것을 확신하게 될 것입니다. 그리고 당신의 시누이와 관련해서는 그녀에게 당신이 기력을 회복하고 당신과 애들이 확정된 일정을 짠 후 아마 휴가 중에나 그녀를 보면 좋겠다고 상냥하게 말씀을 드리세요. 그렇게 하는 것이 그녀의 마음을 서운하게 하지않는 것입니다. 그리고 그것은 출산 후 회복할 당신의 권리를 주장하는 것입니다.

23 미국 정부, 환경보호 단체들, 안보 기관들이 있을 법하지도 않은 동맹을 맺었다. 다른 국가들이 자국의 핵폐기물을 재처리하지 않기를 바라고 1977년 (미국은) 핵폐기물 재처리를 일시적으로 유보하는 조치를 취했다. 이런 생각은 비핵국가들 사이에 핵이 확산되는 것을 막자는 취지였다. 반핵운동가들은 핵폐기물 처리에는 안전한 방법이 없다고 믿는다. 그래서 오늘날에도 석탄을 사용하는 화력 발전소냐 아니면 건설중인 핵발전소를 더 지을 것인가를 실제로 선택할 때면 핵폐기물 재처리보다는 원자력발전소를 폐쇄하는 방법을 선호한다. Ralph Nader의 '퍼블릭 시티즌'이 주도하는 여러 환경단체와 반핵단체들은 소량의 핵폐기물을 재처리하자는 제안에도 반대하고 있다.

24 내 생각으로는 당신이 쌍둥이를 임신한 여인에게, 즉 "공포의 9월"이라는 편지에 대한 답장이 좀 불충분했던 것 같습니다. 그 부인은 애들을(쌍둥이를) 낳은 직후 그녀를 휘어잡으려는 시어머니와 그리고 시누이 집 식구들의 있을 수 있는 방문

을 다루어야 하는 문제를 놓고 걱정을 하고 있는 것입니다. 당신은 그 부인에게 시어머니의 사랑을 받아들이고, 그 분을 안심시키고 그리고 그 분의 말에 너무 개의치 않도록 충고를 하셨습니다. 그리고 그 부인의 시누이와 관련해서 당신의 말은 그 부인이 확정된 일정을 갖을 때까지 시누이가 자기 가족들의 방문을 연기시켜야 한다는 것이었습니다. 좋은 충고입니다. 하지만 이 충고는 다른 사람한테 해당되는 것입니다.

Unit 2 좌향전이 (Left-Dislocation)

01 가난한 부모의 아들이었던 그는 선생님이 될 작정이었다. 사범 학교에 다니던 학생 시절에 그는 세균에 관심이 있었고 그는 일생동안 연구할 준비가 되어 있었다. 과학 선생님이 되어서도 그는 계속해서 연구를 해 나아갔고, 세균을 발견하고 무서운 질병들의 여러 가지 좋지 않은 영향들을 연구하였다. 그렇게 함으로써 그의 나라의 여러 환경을 개선하게 되었고 탄저병과 다른 질병들을 치료할 수 있게 되었다.

02 그 소녀들은 고기 계산대로 가서 McMahon에게 무엇인가를 묻고 있었다. 그가 어딘가를 가리켰고, 그들도 따라 가리켰다. 그리고 피라미드처럼 쌓여 있는 '다이엇 딜라잇' 복숭아더미 뒤로 가더니 보이지 않았다. 우리가 볼 수 있었던 것은 McMahon이 가볍게 입을 두드리며, 그리고 그들의 고기 무게를 재면서 그들을 바라보는 모습 이었다. 불쌍한 아이들, 난 그들에 대한 측은한 마음이 들기 시작했다. 그들은 어찌할 수 없었다. 이제 여기서부터 이 이야기의 슬픈 부분이 시작된다. 적어도 우리 가족은 슬프다고 이야기를 하지만 나는 슬프지 않다는 생각이 든다. 가게는 목요일 오후이었음에도 불구하고 텅 비어 있었다. 그래서 금전등록기에 기대어 그 소녀들이 다시 나타나기를 기다리는 것 외에 별로 할 일이 없었다.

03 이따금씩 평야를 가로질러 한 바탕 날리는 먼지는 저 멀리서 화물차가 다가오고 있음을 나타낸다. 사하마 화산은 계속해서 지평선에서 잠자코 있다. 길을 가다 보면 눈에 띄는 씨우다드 드 피에라를 지나간다. 거대한 석탑과 받침 없이 서있는 둥근 돌들은, 그들 중 어떤 것들은 버스만큼이나 큰데, 그것들이 풍경을 가득 채우고 있

다. 그 것이 주는 효과는 무시무시하며, 거의 달과 같다. 당신은 '뿌야 라이몬디'를 보게 될지도 모른다. 이 웅대한 선인장은 높이가 25에서 32 피트이고 세상에서 가장 큰 꽃이 피는데 백년에 단 한번 꽃이 핀다.

04 이 으리으리한 상업지역으로 소심한 캐리가 들어갔다. 그녀는 밴 뷰런가를 따라 별로 크지 않은 지역을 거쳐 동쪽으로 걸어갔다. 그리고 마침내 그 지역은 커다란 빈민촌과 저탄장으로 변했으며 강과 접하고 있었다. 그녀는 용감하게 앞으로 계속 걸어 나갔는데, 이것은 솔직히 일자리를 구하고자 하는 욕망 때문 이었으며, 사방에 펼쳐지는 광경에 대한 호기심과 그녀가 일찍이 알지 못했던 능력과 힘이 아주 역력하게 나타나고있는 것들 사이에서의 무력감 때문에 한 걸음 한 걸음 지연되기도 했다. 이 거대한 빌딩들, 그것들은 과연 무엇이었는가? 이 기이한 힘과 거대한 관심거리들, 이것들은 어떤 목적을 위해 그곳에 있었는가? 그녀는 개인적인 용도로 조그마한 대리석 조각들을 새기는 콜럼비아시 석공들의 조그마한 작업장의 의미는 이해할 수 있었다. 그러나 어떤 거대한 돌 공장의 작업장이 시야에 들어와 단거리 지선과 화차로 가득 차 있고, 강으로부터 도크로 관통되어 목재와 강철을 거대한 운반용 크레인을 이용해 머리위로 운반되고 있을 때, 그것은 그녀의 조그마한 체험 세상에서의 모든 의미를 잃게 했다(그녀의 조그마한 체험 세계 속에서는 도저히 납득이 가지 않는 일이었다.)

05 텔레비전, 그것은 학습과 성장 발달에 있어서 매우 긍정적인 잠재력을 가진다. 그것은 아이들에게 독서와 글짓기를 통해 개발되는 것들과는 다른 정신적 기술들을 제공해준다. 텔레비전은 일부 유형의 정보를 전달하기 위한 인쇄물 보다 더 나은 매체이며, 그리고 전통적인 학교 상황에서 공부를 잘 하지 못하는 아이들과 심지어는 읽지 못하는 아이들에게까지 학습을 가능하게 해준다.

06 David과 Ad는 Hall이 결정을 내릴 당시 그와 교신 중이었다. 이 유명한 안내자를 여러 해 동안 알고 지내온 영화 제작자이며 등반가인 그들은 그 보다 2,400m 아래에 있는 산중턱의 야영지에 비교적 안전하게 있었다. 반면에 홀은 세계 최고봉인 에베레스트 산의 8,848m 정상에서 120m 못 미치는 곳에 있었는데 갑작스럽게 눈보라가 산을 강타한 후 그날 밤을 보냈던 노두에서 꼼짝 못하고 있었다. 그 상황을 극복하고 산다는 것은 아마도 불가능했었다. 그럼에도 불구하고, 다른 등반 대원들은 홀이 그 상황을 극복하고 살 수 있도록 돕기로 했다.

07 한 소녀가 라사에 있는 한 뒷골목에서 그녀의 어린 남동생을 안고있다. 중국 군대가 주둔하고 있음에도 불구하고 사람들은 방해 받지 않고 그들의 일상 생활을 열심히 하려고 애쓰고 있다. 그러나 젊은 세대들은 그들의 삶을 즐기는 것이 너무 지나치다. 그들은 열심히 일은 하지 않고, 맥주를 마시며 항상 놀기만 하고 있다.

08 다시 여행과 같은 일을 예로 들어보자. 어떤 이는 여러 나라를 여행하되 항상 일류 호텔에 들르고, 집에서와 같이 똑같은 식사를 하고, 집에서와 같이 한가하고 부유한 사람을 만나고, 그리고 집의 식탁에서와 똑 같은 주제를 놓고 이야기를 나눈다. 이들이 집에 돌아와 느끼는 감정은 고작 비싼 여행의 지루함을 끝마쳤다는 안도감일 것이다. 또 다른 사람들은 가는 곳마다 그 특색을 보고, 그 지방을 대표하는 이들과 사귀고, 역사적으로나 사회적으로 흥미 있는 것은 모두 관찰하고, 그 지방음식을 먹고, 그곳 풍습과 언어를 배우고, 그리고 겨울 밤 새로 즐거운 사색에 잠길 수 있는 많은 것들을 가지고 돌아온다.

09 때로는 공공장소에 숨는 것이 가장 좋은 경우가 있다. 류장궈는 조용히 모임을 갖기 위해 지난 주 화요일 베이징의 한 스타벅스 커피숍에 모습을 나타냈다. 북 푸순시 출신의 공산당원인 류는 뉴스위크지에 왜 그가 파룬공을 지지하는 일에 기꺼이 목숨을 걸려고 하는지를 설명하고자 했다. 중국당국은 이른바 '사교 숭배'를 일소하려는 일환으로 수천 명에 이르는 그의 추종자들을 체포했었다. 류(50)는 파룬공이 불교, 도교, 기공이 신비롭게 혼합되어 있어서 그의 고혈압과 그의 아내의 심리적 장애가 치유될 수 있었다고 생각하고 있다. 파룬공 사범인 그는 당국의 탄압에 반대하는 대중집회에 참여하려던 참이었다. "내가 사느냐 죽느냐 하는 것은 중요치 않다,"고 그는 말했다. 이 부유층의 커피숍 주변을 가리키면서 다음과 같은 말을 덧붙였다. "우리가 다음에 파룬공에 대해서 이야기할 때의 장소는 이곳이 아닐 것이다. 아마도 나는 교도소에 수감되어있을 것이다. 우리의 얘기가 끝나면 나는 (천안문) 광장으로 나가서 체포될 생각이다.

10 Alfonso Orefice는 탐파에 알폰소 피자리아를 가지고 있는데 추가로 주문한 치즈의 가격을 3불로 인상했다. 이 가격은 1불 60센트의 다른 타핑들 가격의 거의 2배에 해당된다. Orefice는 치즈 가격이 계속해서 비싸게 되면 피자 가격 역시 인상할 것이라고 말한다. "점차 힘들어져 가고 있습니다. 소 때문에 미칠 지경입니다." 라고 그는 말을 했었다.

11 Tom과 나는 강도들이 동굴 속에 감추어 놓은 돈을 찾아 냈으며, 그것으로 우리는 부자가 되었다. 한 사람이 6천 달러씩 갖게 되었는데 이게 모두 금화였다. 그 돈은 쌓아 놓고 보니 엄청났다. 아무튼 Thatcher 판사 그가 그것을 맡아서 이자놀이를 해 주었고, 그로 인해 우리 각각에게 1년 내내 날마다 1달러씩 굴러들어왔다. 그것은 아무도 어떻게 해야 할지 모를 정도로 큰 돈이었다. Douglas 과부 아주머니는 나를 아들처럼 여겼으며 그녀는 나를 교화시켜 줄 생각이었다. 그러나 이 아주머니가 모든 면에서 정말로 무섭게 깔끔하고 고상하다는 점을 고려해볼 때, 밤낮 집안에 틀어박혀 산다는 것은 힘든 일이었다. 그래서, 더 참을 수 없게 되었을 때, 나는 도망쳐 버렸다. 다시 전에 입던 누더기 옷을 입고 커다란 설탕 통을 들고서야 나는 비로소 자유롭고 만족하게 되었다. 하지만 Tom Sawyer, 그가 나를 찾아내어, 자기가 강도단을 조직하는 중인데 만일 내가 과부 아주머니 댁에 다시 돌아와서 얌전하게 굴면, 가입할 수도 있을 것이라고 말했다. 그래서 나는 되돌아가게 되었다.

12 Captain John Smith(1580~1631)의 작품은 아마도 두 부류의 독자들을 모두 만족시켰던 것 같다. 진정한 모험가였던 그는 부상을 입어 포로가 되었던 헝가리에서 터키 족과 싸웠다. 그는 노예로 팔려가서 그의 주인을 죽이고 도망쳐 나왔다. 1607년 그는 아메리카에서 최초의 영국식민지인 Jamestown을 수립하는데 기여했다. 세부적인 내용들은 항상 정확한 것은 아니지만, 그의 작품 "True Relation of Virginia (1608)" 과 "Description of New England (1616)"은 독자들로 하여금 신세계에 정착하도록 설득하고 있는 매혹적인 "광고"가 되고있다. 예를 들어 청교도들은 그의 "Description of New England"라는 작품을 주의 깊게 연구하였고 그리고 나서 1620년에 그곳에 정착하기로 결심했던 것이다. 스미쓰는 그의 책에서 자신이 했던 모험을 자주 자랑하고 있었다.

13 여성화 되어가던 기독교 신자이며 도덕론자였던 그는 돈을 헤프게 쓰고 폭식하며 살았고, 유럽의 궁전에서 가져온 단자와 양탄자에 둘러싸여 Leonardo da Vinci의 비망록과 셰익스피어의 2절판 책들이 들어있는 금고를 옆에 두고 업무 회의를 열었다. Morgan은 유태인과 그 밖의 소수민족을 그의 커다란 코 아래로 경멸하듯 내려다보았고, 노동조합을 증오했고, 새 돈을 비웃었으며, 자기 시대의 다른 "강도귀족"들과 끊임없이 싸움을 벌였다.

14 지난 몇 주 동안에는 살인수법이 한층 더 대담해졌다. 6월 5일 일요일에는 일단의 무장 괴한들이 손님들이 다트 놀이를 하고 월드컵 경기를 시청하던 리치몬드 시의 한 술집에 들이 닥쳤다. 그 괴한들은 무차별 총격을 가해 8명을 살해했다. 그 다음 주말에는 한 여성과 그녀의 세 살배기 딸이 마고다에서 함께 총에 맞아 죽었다.

15 그녀는 혼자 야경을 서는 일과 같은 더 많은 책임을 요하는 일을 맡겨달라고 나를 졸라댔다. 그렇게만 할 수 있다면야 나의 생활은 좀 더 편해졌겠지만, 그녀가 근무를 설 때에는(배를 조종하는 동안) 깊은 잠을 이룰 수 없었다. 이 배는 특히 이렇게 폭풍우가 칠 것 같은 날씨에 그녀가 혼자 다룰 수 있을 거라는 것을 믿을 수가 없었다.

16 지금과 21세기 사이에 있는 30년이라는 짧은 기간 동안에 수많은 보통 사람들, 다시 말해 정신적으로 정상적인 수많은 사람들이 미래와 갑작스러운 충돌에 직면하게 될 것이다. 세계에서 가장 부유하고 기술적으로 앞선 나라들의 시민들, 그들 중 많은 이들은 우리 시대를 특징짓고 있는 변화에 대한 끊임없는 요구에 뒤지지 않고 따라가기가 점점 더 고통스러워 질 것을 알게 될 것이다. 그들에게는 미래가 너무 빨리 도달하게 될 것이다.

17 Bill은 누구에게 들이 보아도 인물다운 네가 있었다. 그는 여행사 직원이었는데 열렬한 골퍼이기도 했다. 그는 두 번이나 미주리 아마추어 선수권을 획득했고, 1955년에는 US Open대회에도 참가했다. 하지만 대부분의 사람들은 Bill Stewart를 그가 화려한 스포츠코트를 입었기 때문에 기억하고 있다.

18 단지 한 명만이 부상을 입었다는 것은 이상했다. 부상자가 더 많이 있을 거라는 확실한 느낌이 있었다. 그리고 물론 그들 주변의 다른 부대에서는 더 많은 부상자가 있었다 찰리의 머리 글자에 해당하는 C 소속의 한 부상자는 Pfc Marl 이었는데 그는 네브라스카주의 시골뜨기에 건조지대의 농사꾼이었다. 그는 꺽다리에, 일을 많이 해서 손에 마디가 많았으며, 아버지의 농장을 떠나기 싫어했던 징병군인 이었는데 어쨌든 군대를 그리 좋아해 본 적이 없었다.

19 "정말이야. 그녀는 매우 기뻐할 꺼야. Ruth은 시골 여자고 많은 필리핀 사람들을 만나보지 못했어. 나는 필리핀 사람들이 나보다 더 젊고 단정해 보인다고 말한 거야. 우리는 너도 알다시피 그저 가난한 농사꾼들이고 그렇게 자주 도시에 가지도 않아. Roger, 그 앤 내 아들인데 그 애는 도시로 학교를 다녀. 아침 일찍 버스타고 갔다가 오후에 돌아오지. 착한 아이 야."

Unit 3 동사구 전치 (Verb Phrase Preposing)

01 어스틴 경찰은 화요일 밤 Chuy's에서 술을 사기 위하여 가짜 신분증을 사용한 것과 관련해 부시 대통령의 쌍둥이 딸 (19)들을 소환했다. Barbara와 Jenna 그리고 친구인 Jesse는 모두 이 사건으로 경범죄 소환장을 발부 받았다. Jenna는 미성년자가 나이를 거짓 사용한 혐의로 소환되었으며, Barbara와 Jesse(20) 두 사람은 미성년자가 알코올을 소지한 혐의로 소환되었다. 어스틴 경찰국과 텍사스 주류 위원회는 술집에서 위조 신분증을 사용한 것과 관련하여 여러 가지 있을 수 있는 법률 위반을 놓고 이 사건을 수사하고 있다. 이 기사는 현직 대통령의 딸이 연루되어 있어서 전국적으로 중요 뉴스가 되고 있다. 하지만 부시 집안은 이번 일을 사사로운 것으로 취급하려 하고 있다. 그들은 이번 사건과 관련하여 아직 공식적인 발표는 하지않고 있고 그럴 의사가 있다는 것도 보이지 않으려 하고있다.

02 한 친구가 부랴부랴 집으로 들어와 급히 나를 불러내더니 이 해변으로 데리고 왔던 것이 거의 10년 전 일이었다 당황해서 멍했던 나는 그가 무슨 생각을 하고 있는지 물었다. 질문에 대한 반응으로 그는 수줍어 하며 그저 바다와 부서지는 파도만 바라보곤 했었다. 그리고 나서 약 한 시간이 지나서 바다를 보며 서서히 말문을 열었다. 그가 사랑에 빠졌다는 말을 했다. 그러나 그는 그 여자에게 그의 다정한 사랑을 고백하지 못했다는 것이었다. 그는 충고를 원하고 있었다. 나는 그에게 그녀에 대한 사랑을 즉각 표현하도록 했다. 그는 나의 충고를 따라 그렇게 했다. 그러나 그녀는 그의 사랑을 받아주지 않았다. 나중에 그가 다시 그 해변으로 나를 데리고 가서 그가 퇴짜 맞은 것에 대한 이야기를 해주며 자기는 기다릴 거라며 다시 바다를 향해 공언했다. 그리고 그는 기다렸다. 기나긴 7년 동안을 기다렸다. 나는 그와 함께

그 해변으로 갔다. 그곳에서 그는 그의 꿈이 실현되었다는 이야기를 했다. 그녀가 마침내 그의 사랑을 받아들였다는 것이었다. 그들은 바로 얼마 후에 결혼을 했다.

03 정치판은 과학을 하는 사람들이 기대하고 있는 윤리적 상화작용과는 반대로 돌아가고 있다. 정치인들은 기만적으로 이해갈등이 있는 유권자들을 결합해서 선출된다. 그들은 단지 당선되고 권력을 얻기 위해 지킬 수 없는 약속을 한다. 기업인이나 과학자들은 그와 유사한 상황윤리를 이용하게 되면 명예가 실추되거나 투옥될 것이다. 이것은 기업인이나 과학자들이 항상 윤리적이다라는 것, 즉 그들만이 인간적이다라는 것을 의미하는 것은 아니다. 그러나 정치인들에게 윤리적인 행동을 기대한다 것은 어려운 일이다. John, 바톤을 넘겨주어라. 당신은 열심히 일을 해서 많은 것을 이루었다. 그러나 네가 바톤을 넘겨야 한다면 누군가에게 혹은 그 일을 책임질 수 있는 단체에 넘겨주어라.

04 그 파티에 앞서 대통령은 그의 개인 변호사인 David Kendall을 만나 의견을 교환했다. 하루전날 Lewinsky가 Kenneth Starr특별검사와 협력하고 Clinton과의 성 관계를 가졌다는 말을 하기로 합의를 했었다. 이 문제와 Starr검사로부터 받은 소환장에 직면한 Clinton은 자기가 직접 조치를 취했다. 그는 8월 17일 백악관으로부터 실황으로 연결해서(폐쇄회로 TV를 통해) 연방 대배심에 '자발적으로' 증언하겠다는 것이었다. Kendall이 그런 합의 내용을 발표하고 Clinton은 이스트 룸으로 갔다. 그 후 백악관 법무실 변호사들은 뉴스를 보기 위해 TV채널을 여기 저기 돌리고 있었다.

05 구급차는 다음날까지 오지 않았다. 그날은 우리가 생환으로 행군하기 전날이었다. 그 차는 땅거미가 진 후에 도착했는데 Bell은 차가 오고있다는 말을 듣자마자 병원에서 살짝 빠져 나와 밀림으로 들어가 밤새도록 그곳에 있었다. 그 구급차는 결국 그를 두고 떠났다. 그곳 병사들은 마치 초등 학생들이 동료를 감싸주는 것처럼 그의 총과 탄띠, 그리고 침구류를 들어주며 그를 돌봐주었다. 나는 생환전투 아침에 그를 보았다. 그는 내게 어차피 죽어야 한다면 싸우다 죽고싶다는 말을 했다. 그래서 나는 그를 되돌려 보내고 싶지않았다. 그는 그날 그리고 그 이후에 참호에서 임무를 훌륭히 수행했다. 그 전투가 다시 두 번이 있었지만 그때마다 그는 구사일생해서, 위기를 모면하고 우리와 함께 미국으로 돌아왔다.

06 어떤 지역도 사람들이 전쟁터로 만들지 못 할 만큼 거칠거나 까다로운 곳은 없다. 숲속 저 군용 함정의 기슭에는, 물론 그곳에서 출구를 장악하고 있다면 일개 군을 굶주려 항복을 받아낼 수 있는 곳인데, 대략 연방 보병 5개 연대가 잠복해 있었다. 그들은 전날 온 종일 행군을 하고 휴식을 취하고 있었다. 해질 녘에 그들은 다시 도로로 나가서, 그 때 그들의 근무 태만한 초병이 졸고 있던 곳으로 올라간 다음, 다른 편 산등성이 비탈을 내려가 자정 무렵에 적진을 공격하게 될 것이다. 그들이 원하는 것은 적을 기습하는 것이었다. 왜냐하면 그 길이 적진의 후방으로 통하고 있었기 때문이었다. 실패할 경우 그들의 진지는 극도로 위험에 처하게 될 것이다. 그리고 우연한 사고나 경계 때문에 적에게 동태가 알려진다면 그들은 틀림없이 실패하게 될 것이다.

07 옛날에 한 가난한 왕자가 살았습니다. 그가 살던 왕국은 아주 작았습니다. 그렇지만 그가 결혼할 수 있을 만큼은 충분히 컸습니다. 그리고 그는 결혼을 하려고 했습니다. 황제의 딸에게 "나와 결혼을 해주겠소"라고 가서 청혼을 할 정도로 다소 대담했습니다. 하지만 위험을 무릅쓰고 그렇게 했던 것이다. 왜냐하면 그의 이름이 방방곡곡에 알려져 있었기 때문이었다. 기꺼이 그를 받아들이고자 했던 수많은 공주들이 있었다.

08 7월 4일 그들은 항복을 했다. 빅스버그와 미시시피 강은 빼앗겼다. 결국 그들은 같은 날 게티스버그에서 Lee가 대패했다는 것을 알게 될 것이다. 그러나 John Wright는 일단 동료 장교들과 함께 앞장서서 북부에 맞서 무기를 다시는 들지 않겠다는 서약에 서명을 했다. 그들은 며칠 후에 풀려났다. 그러나 그들은 집으로 가지 않았다. 전쟁 중에 남부의 의지와 사기와 관련해서 많은 글을 쓰고 많은 것을 생각했었다. 펨버튼의 병사들은 사방팔방으로 뻗쳐나갈 수 있는 기회가 충분했다. 물론 일부는 그렇게 했다. 그러나 John에게 있어서는 그것은 힘든 선택이었음에 틀림없었다.

09 Antony Yip은 고급 식당에서 음식을 주문하기에는 너무 어려 보인다. 하물며 미국 벤처 자본 기업으로부터 650만 달러를 끌어와 인터넷 기업을 차린다는 것은 두 말할 필요도 없다. 그러나 사실 그는 생선과 칩에 이어 아이스크림, 즉 딸기 두 스쿱과 초코렛 하나를 주문한 것이다. 그는 소년 티가 나는 스물 한 살에 헐렁한 바지와 스

니커즈 신발을 착용하고 있지만 그의 나이만이 이례적인 것은 아니다. Antony Yip은 중국어를 잘 쓰고 말할 수 없음에도 불구하고 그의 사이트 Myrice.com 아래에 모여있는 중국어로 된 열 다섯 개의 웹사이트 전체를 운영하고 있다. "그것은 정말 우스운 일이에요,"라고 그는 말하며, 천진스럽게 미소를 짓는다.

10 연극이 개봉된 후 Joan과 나는 여자 아이들을 데리고 플로리다로 갔다. 갑자기 절뚝거리는 증상이 다시 나타났다. Joan은 계단을 오를 때 난간을 붙잡고 거칠게 숨을 쉬면서 조금 천천히 움직였다. 며칠 후 고통은 더 심해졌고 그녀는 지팡이 없이는 더 이상 돌아다닐 수 없었다. 나는 그녀가 머지않아 죽게 될 것임을 알았었고, 그리고 얼마 후 그녀는 정말 죽었다.

11 세상의 여기저기 성숙한 민주주의 국가에서는 지위가 높은 사람들이 자신들의 좋은 명성이 오명으로 얼룩지지 않도록 '사임'을 한다. 그러나 이런 고상한 단어가 우리 나라와 정치용어 사전에서 오래 전에 사라졌다. 그렇다. 우리 정치인들이 마지막으로 사임한 것이 언제였던가? 당신들이 진정 사임하지 않으려면 우리 국민들을 위해 적어도 할 수 있는 일은 똑바로 서서 허심탄회하게 이야기를 하는 것이다. 우리가 들을 수 있도록 큰 소리로 허심탄회하게 이야기를 하는 것이다. 우리에게 당신들이 지도적인 역할을 할 것이라고 그리고 당신들 주변에 있는 무식한 사람들에게 이끌려 다니지 않을 거라고 말해주라.

12 바다 오리는 날 수는 있지만, 그들은 분명 세상에서 가장 훌륭한 "비행사"는 아니다. 사실, 그들이 바닷가에 도착하는 모습은 비행기가 불시착하는 모습과 비슷해 보일 수 도 있다. 게다가, 바다 오리는 이륙하는 모습이 다소 어색하며, 때때로 바다오리의 날개는 튼튼한 몸집을 지탱하지 못 할 것처럼 보인다. 일부 바다 오리는 바다에서 빠져 나오느라 고생하기도 한다. 그러나 일단 날개가 퍼덕거리면 1분에 400번 씩 이나 퍼덕거려 바다 오리는 시간당 50마일의 순항속도에 이를 수 있다. 바다 오리에게는 육지 보다는 바다가 더 편안한 것은 분명하다. 그렇지만 그들은 필연적으로 육지에 와야만 한다. 왜냐하면 바다 오리 부부는 그들 새끼들을 위해 둥지를 마련해야 하기 때문이다. 바다 오리 부부는 육지에 도착하는 즉시 그 둥지를 청소하게 되는데 그 둥지는 어디에서나 길이가 20인치에서 그 크기의 4배까지 된다. 바다 오리 부부는 그 둥지를 따라 풀과 가지 그리고 깃털로 만들어진 침구류를 놓는다. 일부 바다 오리는 둥근 돌 아래 틈새나 혹은 바위 틈새에 둥지를 튼다.

바다 오리는 부리를 이용해서 조심스럽게 흙을 헤쳐나간 다음 그 흙을 물갈퀴가 달린 발로 파낸다.

13 낮을 밤으로 그리고 빛을 어두움으로 바꾸고 좋은 일들을 단지 하찮은 어리석은 것들로 바꾸는 것은 무의미한 일이다. 더구나 무도회에 자주 가는 사람들은 자신이 허영심을 품게 되는 것은 거의 불가피하다. 그리고 허영심은 엉뚱한 욕망과 위험스러운 집착을 불러일으킨다. 무도회와 관련해서 나는 의사들이 버섯등과 같은 몇몇 식품에 대해 하는 이야기를 하고 싶다. 아무리 좋은 것이라도 그리 좋은 것만은 아니다. 그러나 여러분들이 꼭 그런 음식을 먹어야 한다면 적어도 적절하게 요리가 되었는지는 신경을 쓰도록 해라. 그래서 여러분들이 통제하기 어려운 상황으로 인해 그런 곳에 가게 되면 들어가기 전에 어떤 마음의 준비를 해야 하는지 주의를 기울이도록 해라. 요리의 맛은 절제, 품위, 그리고 선의로 돋구어야 한다. 여전히 버섯을 참고로 하자면 의사들은 그것들을 절제해서 먹되 그것도 어쩌다가 먹으라고 이야기를 한다. 왜냐하면 아무리 드레싱이 잘되어도 지나친 것은 좋지 않기 때문이다. 그래서 여러분들이 재미에 너무 빠져드는 위험을 무릅쓰지 않도록 하기 위해서는 춤도 조금만 그것도 어쩌다가 추도록 해라.

14 정치적 현실을 본다면 민주주의가 도래하리라 상상하는 일은 불가능한 것으로 보였다. 그러나 변화하고 있는 문화를 본다면 그런 일이 일어나리라는 것은 필연적인 것으로 보였다. 그 일은 1987년에 국민들의 힘이 거세게 분출하면서 일어났다. 그리고 이것으로 인해서 민주적인 대통령 선거가 있었다. 이렇게 전개되는 정세들은 모두가 기적이라는 느낌이 들었다. 개개의 지도자들이라기보다는 국민들의 힘으로 그런 일이 일어나게 되었던 것이다. 그 다음 해에 한국은 올림픽을 개최하게 되었다. 나는 이런 기적을 일구어낸 사람들이 올림픽을 주최하는 것을 볼 수 있길 정말 학수고대하고 있었다. 나는 한국인들이 망쳐놓으리라 기대하지는 않았다. 그러나 그들은 망쳐놓고 말았다.

15 그들(스페인 사람들의) 사회는 상층과 하층만 있고 중간층이 없는 엄격한 두 계급 사회였다. 그 사회는 또 정부의 정치적 절대주의를 강화해 주는 중상주의의 봉건적인 토지소유제도 및 정통주의적 종교 양식을 갖추고 있었다. 이와 대조적으로 북아메리카의 여러 식민지는 정복자들에 의해 생생하게 구현되는 구세계의 갖가지 봉건적 압제를 피해 탈출한 사람들에 의해 대부분 개척되었다. 17세기와 18세기에 주

민이 이주하여 식민지가 건설된 미국은 시작부터 현대세계에 속했다. 같은 반구에 위치해 있는 두 사회는 다른 원천에서 시작되어 다른 상태에 머무르고 있다. Wiarda는 라틴 아메리카의 사상에 영향을 미친 마르크시즘을 포함해 여러 가지 정치 독트린을 자세히 설명하고 있다. 미국적 사고방식과는 정반대로 라틴 아메리카의 각 개인만으로는 어떤 권리도 없지만 집단의 정체성을 통해 통치에 역할을 했다. Wiarda씨는 라틴 아메리카의 정서와 영혼을 탁월하게 설명하고 있으나 이 지역의 미래를 고찰하면서 대다수 경제학자들이 심오한 것으로 생각하고 있는 북미자유무역협정(NAFTA)이 멕시코에 미친 영향에 대해서는 논하지 않고 있다. NAFTA가 확장되면 그리고 그렇게 되겠지만 라틴 아메리카의 여러 나라에 여전히 존재하고 있는 많은 과두지배계급이 가지고있는 기득권을 휩쓸어 버릴 수 있을 것이다.

16 그리고 나서 그는 부엌으로 되돌아와서 두려움에 차 놀란듯한 아이의 손을 심각하게 잡고 그를 서재로 데리고 갔다. 그리고 그는 그를 앞에 두고 정직하다는 것이 얼마나 중요한지에 대해서 훈계를 시작했으며 자신이 믿는 모든 처벌의 전형으로 이런 결론을 내릴 작정이었다.--너는 스스로 이것을 기억할 능력이 없기 때문에 내가 너에게 약간의 고통을 가해서 기억할 수 있도록 해주어야겠다. 그렇게 해야 한다는 것과 또 내가 그렇게 하지않으면 네가 기억할 수 없다는 것은 유감스러운 일이다. 그러나 그가 바로 이런 적절하고 바람직한 결론에 이르기에 앞서서 그리고 엄숙할 정도의 슬픈 얼굴을 하고 있는 그 아이의 겁먹은 표정과 나무라는 말에 마음 아파하면서 그가 여전히 자기 생각대로 하고있는데 갑자기 Sally가 끼어 들었다. 그런데 Thurstan님, 당신이 엄선한 것을 보았는데 그 가느다란 회초리를 가지고 무얼 하시려고 그러세요? 라고 그녀는 물었다. 그때에 그녀는 적어도 그녀가 대답을 했더라면 틀림없이 나왔을 것으로 알고 있던 답에 화가 나서 눈이 번쩍거렸다.

17 얼마 안 가서 나는 다시 예전 버릇대로 돌아와 그가 어디에 있는지, 그리고 그가 무얼 하려 하는지 알아보려고 했다. 어느 날 나는 전화를 걸어 사람들이 웃고 시끄러운 음악이 뒤에서 연주되는 것을 들었을 때 내 상상력은 걷잡을 수 없게 되었다. 나는 질문을 퍼부어 대기 시작했다. "엄마는 아직 가벼운 얘기 하시는 법을 배우지 못하셨군요."라고 말을 하고는 전화를 끊었다. 나는 뒷문으로 달려나가 집 뒤에 있는 숲 속으로 가서 숨을 헐떡거리며 통나무 위에 앉아있었는데 가슴이 두근거리고, 토끼를 쫓는 사냥개들처럼 화나게 하는 여러 생각들이 나를 떠나지 않았다. 나는 나의 행동 방식이 싫었지만 나도 어쩔 수 없었다.

18 아마도 미친 사람이나 사막 한가운데 식당을 지을 것이다. 그러나 그런 일을 바로 Mike Dabour가 캘리포니아 베이커에 자신 소유의 식당을 내면서 했던 일이었다. 일부 아는 사람들은 Dabour씨에게 그가 문명으로부터 외진 곳에 그런 건물을 짓는 것을 보면 제정신이 아닌 사람이라고 했다. 그러나 Mike씨는 그 자신의 생각을 확고하게 품고 있었다. 그 식당은 완공되었고 그에 어울리게 "The Mad Greek Café"라는 이름을 붙였다. 이것이 처음은 아니었다. Michael씨는 다른 사람들이 그리스 식당은 성공할 수 없을 것으로 생각했던 인적이 드문 곳에다 이미 몇 채의 "Mad Creek Café's"를 지었었다. 그러나 그는 성공을 했다. 아마도 그것은 그 젊은 그리스인이 가지고 있던 불굴의 결단력 때문이었던 것 같다. Michael은 그의 아내 Angela와 함께 그리스 아테네에서 1968년에 미국으로 이주해왔다.

19 Barnard박사가 전극을 심장의 양쪽에 놓도록 지시하면서 전류가 흐르게 되었다. 심장은 그 충격으로 뛰었고 맥박이 빠르게 뛰기 시작했다. Barnard박사의 심장도 뛰었다. 마스크를 통하여 그는 외쳤다: 'Christ, 심장이 이제 작동하게 될 거야!' 사실 그것은 이미 작동하고 있었다.

20 대만은 지금 UN에 가입하고자 하는데 중국 본토는 대만의 가입을 꺼리고 있다. 마치 1949년부터 1971년까지 해왔던 쌍방간의 외교적 주도권 싸움을 단지 역할만 뒤바꿔 재연하는 것 같다. 당시로 거슬러 올라가면 UN에 가입을 원했던 것은 중국 본토였고 대만은 중국을 따돌리기 위해 가능한 모든 일을 하고 있었다. 중국 본토가 UN에 가입하는데 22년이 걸렸지만 결국 대만을 희생시키며 성공했다. 지금 대만의 조직적인 활동은 당시의 중국의 활동 보다 분명히 훨씬 더 위압적이다. 왜냐하면 당시에는 대만이 중국의 강적이었지만 지금은 중국이 대만에 훨씬 더 무서운 적이 되고 있기 때문이다. 그러나 대만이 지금 바라고 있는 것은 당시의 본토가 바랬던 것 보다는 훨씬 더 작다. 당시에 중국은 UN에 가입을 원하는 것 만이 아닌 안전보장 이사회에서 상임 이사국의 지위를 인정 받는 주요 강대국으로서 가입을 원했던 것이다. 게다가 중국은 자신들의 회원 가입에 앞서 어떤 명목에서라도 UN에서 대만의 모든 대표를 없앨 것을 주장했다. 대만은 국제 사회에서 고립되지 않기 위해서 어떤 명목에서라도 일반 회원국으로 UN에 가입을 원하고 있다.

Unit 4 "TOUGH" 이동 ("TOUGH" Movement)

01 돈 없이 물건을 살 수 있다는 것은 꿈이 실현되는 것처럼 보일지도 모르겠다. 하지만 신용카드를 사용해 빚이 늘어나는 것은 재정적으로 좋은 미래를 보장하는 방법은 아니다. 신용카드를 만들기는 아주 쉽다. 하지만 여러분들은 카드를 현명하게 사용하는데 익숙해져야 하며, 그리고 그것을 현명하게 사용해야 할 책임이 있다. 미국 소비자신용상담소의 상담원인 Paul Lavoie는 "신용카드는 신용을 쌓는데 좋은 수단이며, 여러분들이 지출을 조절할 수 있을 만큼 충분한 책임감이 있는지를 보여주는 좋은 방법이다. 하지만 젊은이들이 신용카드를 책임감 있게 사용하는 방법을 배우지 않으면 좋지않은 일이 생기게 된다"라고 이야기를 하고 있다.

02 시체로 인해 곰들이 몰릴만한 휴양지 같은 장소, 다시 말해 인기 있는 소풍장소와 도로가 혹은 오솔길과 같은 장소에서 큰 동물의 시체(말, 노새, 큰 사슴 등)를 제거하거나 없애는 일이 중요할 때가 있다. 큰 동물 시체들은 급경사 밑이나 외딴 곳에 있으면 특히 치우기가 더 어려울 수 있다.

03 젊은이, 아직 시간이 있으니 그 점에 대해서 좀 더 생각해보게나. 나에게는 200만 불이 별 것 아닐세. 하지만 자네는 자네 인생에서 가장 좋은 시기의 3-4년을 잃게 되네. 내가 3-4년이라고 말하는 것은 자네가 더 오래 머물지 못할 것이기 때문이네. 이봐 불쌍한 사람아, 자발적으로 감금되는 것은 강제로 감금되는 것 보다 훨씬 더 힘들다는 것도 잊지 말게. 자네가 아무 때에나 자유롭게 걸어 나올 권리가 있다는 생각도 자네의 모든 수감생활을 더 힘들게 만들 것일세. 자네가 참 가엾네.

04 나의 직장 동료 중에 한 사람이 다음 달 결혼할 예정인데 사무실 직원 대부분을 그녀의 결혼식에 초대했다. 나는 그녀에게 선물을 하나 사줄 계획을 하고 있지만 아마 참석하지는 않을 것이다. 우리는 친하지는 않다. 그녀와 함께 일한다는 것이 너무 힘들다. 아마도 그녀는 내가 지금껏 만난 사람 중에 가장 위선적인 사람일 것이다. 나는 이 여자가 함께 일해온 4년 반 동안 동료들, 고객들 그리고 판매원들에게 나의 험담을 하는 것을 우연히 엿들은 적이 있다. 나는 그녀 때문에 이 회사를 그만둘까 진지하게 고려하고 있는 중이다. 나의 상사는 여러 차례 나에게 그녀에 대해 신경 쓰지 말라고 이야기를 하고 있다.

05 물론 멕시코의 경험은 현명하고 상호 양립적인 경제 정책이 중요하다는 것을 다시 한 번 확인시켜 주었다. 그런 정책이 없다면 금융 혼란을 막기 힘들다. 그러나 멕시코는 역시 여러 가지 문제들이 위기로 변하는 것을 막을 수 있는 최상의 방법에 관한 책을 다시 쓰고 있다. 지금 이 책 속에는 주요한 교훈 두 가지가 들어있다.

06 사생활은 인간 생활의 필수적인 것들 중의 하나이다. 그래서 사생활을 잃게 되면 인생을 견뎌내기가 어렵게 된다. 이 점은 바로 불행하게도 왕족으로 태어난 사람들이 때로는 사생활로 도망쳐 나오기 위해 필사적인 노력을 하는 이유인 것이다. 왕족으로 태어난다는 것은 미리 공적인 삶을 살아야 할 운명이라는 것을 의미하는데, 이는 거의 참고 견딜 수 없는 노예 생활인 것이다.

07 이제는 산을 관통해 터널이 만들어져서 그 고개를 넘는 것이 덜 위험해졌지만, 아직도 매년 여행객들이 어려움에 처할 때마다 개들이 눈 속으로 파견된다. 터널이 새로 생겼음에도 불구하고, 아직도 무모하게도 걸어서 그 고개를 넘으려 하는 사람들이 일부 있다.

08 오직 변화의 물결만이 항상 주어진 사회에서 영향력을 갖는 다면, 미래의 발전 양상들을 식별하기는 비교적 쉬운 일이다. 작가, 화가, 저널리스트, 그리고 기타 다른 사람들은 미래의 물결을 감지한다. 그래서 19세기의 유럽의 많은 사상가들, 재계의 지도자들, 정치인들, 그리고 일반인들은 미래에 대해 분명하고도 기본적으로는 정확한 이미지를 가지고 있었다.

09 Aeh는 태국의 경제 붐이 절정을 이루고 있던 1993년에 신용카드를 처음으로 갖게 되었을 때에 방콕의 한 통신사에서 근무하는 22세의 비서였다. 그녀의 월급은 미화 360달러에 불과했지만 얼마 안 있어 값비싼 옷가지와 세인트 버나드 강아지를 사고 친구들에게 줄 고가의 많은 선물들을 구입하기 시작했다. 청구서들이 쌓이자 그녀는 신용카드 셋을 더 발급 받아 백화점에서 외상으로 화장품을 구입해서 이윤을 남기며 사무실 동료들에게 팔기 시작했다. (그들은 형편이 닿는 대로 그 대금을 치르기로 했었다.) 그 끝이 어떻게 되리라는 것을 예상하기는 어려운 일이 아니었다. 친구들은 대금을 지불할 수 없었고 Aeh 자신도 지불할 능력이 없어서 신용카드

는 취소되었으며, 그녀가 자취를 감춘 지 1년도 더 된다. 친구들은 그녀가 창녀로 전락했을까 봐 걱정하고 있다.

10 이 자료는 1960년부터 1963년까지 Kennedy 재직시절동안의 것으로 당시 정부의 외교 정책 결정을 보다 더 분명히 보여주는데 도움이 될 것이라고 버지니아대학의 Miller공공문제 연구소의 David Coleman 조교수는 말하고 있다. 그러나 이 사학자는 이들 문서의 공개를 학수고대해 왔었으면서도 놀랄만한 폭로가 있을 것으로는 기대하지 말라고 주의를 주고 있다. Coleman 교수는 Kennedy 대통령이 백악관에서 비밀리에 녹음을 해둔 테이프들을 책에 옮겨 쓰는 일을 하고 있는 중이다. 중앙정보국과 관련된 문서들이 특별히 귀중한 것은 입수하기가 가장 어렵기 때문이라고 그는 말했다. 이들 자료들 중에는 쿠바와 베트남에 관한 것들 외에도 미국의 대(對)도미니카공화국, 독일, 인도, 소련과의 관계에 관한 문서들도 포함되어 있다.

11 미국은 Veronica Bowers와 그녀의 딸 Charity가 살해된 4월 20일의 선교사 비행기 격추사건을 조사하기 위해 대표단을 페루에 파견했다. 사람들은 페루 공군의 제트기가 확인도 하기 전에 사고 비행기에 총격을 가할 때 사고지역에 있었던 미국 중앙정보국 비행기가 이를 막기 위해 어느 정도 적극적으로 개입했는지를 이번 조사단이 정확하고 정직하게 평가해 주기를 희망하고 있을 것이다. 사실 Bowers 모녀의 비극적인 죽음으로부터 배울 수 있는 교훈은 많다. 마약과의 전쟁은 선과 악의 싸움이다. 그러나 마약을 단속하기 위한 힘든 노력은 규정이나 협상이 대단히 어려운 애매모호한 영역을 만들어냈다. 사망자가 발생한 이번 페루 선교단 비행기 격추 사건처럼 이 회색지대의 위험성을 더 잘 보여주는 사례는 없다.

12 원칙적인 협상의 기본 요소는 객관적인 사실과 원칙에 의해 계속해서 설득당하는데 있다. 조심스럽게 객관적인 사실에 대한 자신의 견해를 정확하지 않을 수도 있는 것으로 간주하고 Jones여사에게 그것을 정정해달라고 요청함으로써 Turnbull은 이성에 입각해서 대화의 틀을 마련하게 된다. 그가 주어진 사실에 동의하거나 혹은 그런 사실들을 바로 잡아 주며 그녀를 대화에 참여하도록 한다. 그러면 대결 상황은 해소된다. 이런 식으로 접근하게 되면 그들 두 사람은 사실을 입증하려고 노력하게 된다. 만약 Turnbull이 단순히 사실을 사실이라고만 주장한다면 Jones여사는 위협을 느끼고 수세에 몰리는 느낌이 들 것이다. 그렇게 되면 그녀는 사실들을 받아들이지 않을지도 모르고 협상은 건설적으로 시작되지 못할 것이다. 만약

Turnbull이 정말로 잘 못 알고 있다면 미리 정정을 요청하는 것이 그런 사실을 보다 더 쉽게 받아들이도록 할 것이다. Jones여사에게 사실은 이런 것입니다라고 말을 했는데 그가 잘 못 했다는 것을 알게 되면 그는 체면을 깎이게 될 것이다. 설상가상으로 그녀는 그가 말하는 다른 모든 것들에 대해서 훨씬 더 많은 의심을 하게 될 것이고 결국 협상은 어렵게 될 것이다.

13 해양 생물학자들은 이 지역에 있는 다른 암초에 비해 Raja Ampats의 암초의 상태가 좋다는 것을 알아냈다. 그러나 그 과학자들은 현지인들과 태국과 필리핀의 상업용 어선들의 불법적인 어로행위의 증가로 인해 피해를 입을 수 있다는 징후에 특히 걱정을 하고 있었다. 점차적으로 많은 어부들이 물고기를 기절 시키기 위해 다이너마이트와 청산칼리 폭약을 이용하고 있다. 그러면 물고기가 수면 위에 떠올라 쉽게 잡아 팔 수 있게 된다. 다이너마이트와 청산칼리는 역시 산호를 죽이게 된다. 이들 산호를 생물학자들은 생물의 다양성의 독특함과 중요성에서 우림에 비유하고 있다. 인도네시아의 일부 지역에서는 폭발물로 고기를 잡는 바람에 산호 서식지가 80퍼센트나 줄어들었다고 말레이지아 Penang에 본부를 두고있는 세계 어류 센터는 말하고 있다.

14 나는 5형제 중의 막내이다. 형제들과 나는 나이 차이가 크다. 그리고 솔직히 말하자면 지금 내가 38살의 의사임에도 불구하고 그들은 나를 진지하게 대우해주지 않는 것 같다. 문제는 내 가족들이 내가 일하고 있는 동안에 전화를 계속 건다는 점이다. 나는 의사이다. 그리고 여러분들은 이런 일을 믿기 어렵다는 것을 어쩌면 알고 있겠지만 이들은 그들이 가족이기 때문에 하루 중 어느 때나 나와 통화를 해도 괜찮다고 생각하고 있다. 나는 근무 시간 중에는 환자들을 돌보는 일에 신경을 집중해야 한다는 것을 설명하려고 한다. 그러나 그들은 나의 사무실로 전화를 걸고 편지를 보내고 그리고 소포 꾸러미를 보낸다.

15 Del. 1에 살면서 델라웨어 3개군을 통근하는 사람들에게 통행료 혜택을 주려는 의회의 조치는 좋은 생각이다. 새로 생긴 주의 이 남북 유료도로는 환영 받고 있지만 New Castle군에 살면서 Kent나 Sussex에 직장을 갖고 있는 사람들에게는 재정적으로 다소 부담을 주고있다. 그리고 이런 의회의 조치는 새로 생긴 이 도로근처에 살면서 이 도로를 이용하는 것이 편리하다는 것을 알지만 비싼 통행료 지불을 꺼려하는 사람들을 특히 화나게 하고있다.

16 지금은 저 세상 사람이 된 아내와 나는 결혼을 하고 60년 넘도록 함께 살았다. 내가 글을 쓰는 이유는 나의 아내의 장례를 치른 이후 나의 친구들과 친척들이 나한테 쌀쌀 맞게 대하고 있다는 것을 알고 정말로 큰 충격이 되고 있다는 말을 하기 위함이다. 나는 왜 그러는지 이해가 안 된다. 살아가면서 도움과 격려가 필요할 때에 이러한 고독과 상실감에 맞선다는 것이 쉬운 일이 아니다. 장례비용과 수입 감소로 인한 활동을 제한해야 한다는 것은 받아들이기에 힘든 변화이다. 그러나 친구라고 생각했던 사람들의 거부반응은 훨씬 더 심하게 마음의 상처를 주고있다. 이런 냉대와 전화 연락이 없어지는 특별한 이유가 있는가? 오히려 그 반대의 것이 필요한 것이 아닌가? 이전의 몇몇 친구들은 신앙심이 강한 교인들이다. 나는 세계 2차 대전 때에 우리 나라를 위해 군복무를 했고 두 번이나 부상을 당했다. 나는 복무 기간 중에 내게 등을 돌리는 군인을 결코 만나본 적이 없었다.

17 몇 개의 항목은 모종의 대단한 헌신을 의미하기 때문에 위협적이다. 나는 죽기 전에 소설을 내고 싶고 영문학 분야의 철학 박사학위를 받고싶다. 나는 또한 그림 그리기와 현악 사중주단과 함께 피아노 연주하는 것을 배우고 싶다. 이런 것들은 내가 성취하기에 어렵다는 것을 알고 있다. 내가 이런 일들을 성취하려면 매일 글을 쓰고 피아노 실력을 갈고 닦는 일을 시작해야 한다.

18 그는 처음에 중금속성 소행성에 우주 탐사선을 금년에 쏘아 올려 채광 유망지들을 조사해보고 싶었었다. 하지만 이런 특정한 여정에 적합한 투자자들을 찾는다는 것은 마치 그곳에서 채굴한 금속을 지구로 가져오는 방법을 생각하는 것처럼 하나의 도전이었다. "1마일 높이의 철광산을 어떻게 깎아낼 것인가? 내 마음속에 품고 있는 그런 문제도 아직 풀지 못했다"라고 Bensen은 말했다. 그래도 전 인터넷계의 이 거물은 낙관적이다. "지구 근처의 우주에 널려있는 천연 자원의 양은 상상을 초월한다. 아울러 이들 소행성은 막대한 자원을 지니고 있고 그 곳에 접근하기도 쉽다." 먼저 소행성 탐사 파견단은 경제적인 가치를 가늠해보고, 그 다음 소유권을 분명히 하고, 이런 일에 5천만달러 이하로 비용을 산정할 것이라고 Bensen은 말했다.

19 최근에 나는 또 다른 여인 곁에 앉게 되었는데 그 여자의 문병을 간다는 것이 어려운 일이라는 생각이 들었다. 그 여인은 아주 흉측스러운 커다란 종양이 머리와 목에 나 있었다. 그녀는 혀가 뒤틀려 있어서 말을 할 수가 없었다. 나는 그녀를 건강

할 때부터 잘 알고 있었기 때문에, 그녀의 침실로 들어서자마자 가장 먼저 떠 오른 생각은 '어떻게 하면 그녀의 감정을 상하게 하지 않고 빨리 도망 나올 수 있을까?' 하는 것이었다.

20 나는 약속하나를 예정해 두고 있다. 의사와 약속이 있기 바로 하루 전에 몸 상태에 놀라운 새로운 부작용 두 가지를 감지하기 시작했다. 하나는 조그마하게 시작되던 종기가 발전되기 시작하고 있었다. 그리고 글자 그대로 이들 종기가 진행되면서 내 살을 잠식하며 점차 커지고 있었다는 것이다. 그것들이 내 발에만 있는 것 같았다. 그래서 그 점에 대해서 고맙게 생각했었다. 나머지 다른 부작용은 내 손에 관절염을 앓고 있었다. 그로 인해 손을 사용하기가 고통스러웠다. 나는 의사와 약속하기 전날에 이것을 처음으로 감지했다. 이문제가 진행되면서 내 손은 통증이 훨씬 더 심해졌고 사용하기가 훨씬 더 어려워졌다.

21 나는 캘리포니아에서 자란 젊은 여성으로서 자주 법을 집행하는 직업(경찰관)을 꿈꾸었다. 나는 항상 법을 많이 존중했었고 특히 제복 입은 여성 등을 동경했지만 여자들은 경찰관이 되는 것이 탐탁치 않게 여겨졌다. 사실 나는 그 일을 내가 할 수 있는 일로 생각하지 않았다. 고교 졸업 후에 독립해서 혼자 살기 시작했으며 현지 전문대학에서 수업을 받기 시작했다. 혼자 힘으로 생활해야 되었기 때문에 시어스에 취직해서 사탕가게 계산원에서부터 가구 판매원으로 까지 노력해서 올라갔다. 최소 임금으로 산다는 것은 힘든 일이었다. 나는 직업으로서 법 집행하는 일에 대해 다시 생각을 했었지만 소화기에 대해서는 아무것도 알지 못했다. 자동차 운전을 배운 적도 없었다. 그 일을 할 수 없을 것으로 생각했었다. 그래서 계속해서 저임금을 받고 일을 하며 살면서 보다 나은 일을 할 것을 생각했다.

22 이구아나는 아주 멋진 동물이다. 이것들은 미국인들이 좋아하는 파충류 애완동물에 속한다. 그것들을 돌보는 일은 약간 힘들 수가 있고 종종 초보자들이 키우기에 가장 좋은 파충류도 아니다. 나는 이구아나 몇 마리를 가지고 있다. 여러분들이 질문, 제안, 의견, 반응 등이 있다면 원하는 때에 언제든지 저에게 이메일을 보내시면 됩니다.

23 Watkins와 Pearce는 자신들의 사업에는 주의를 기울였지만 자신들의 새로운 삶의 다른 면들은 계획하지 않았었다. 이들 두 사람은 사업의 꿈을 품고 지난 유월에 산안토니오에 도착했는데 사회보장 번호, 보험, 교통 수단, 심지어는 주거지도 없이 왔었다. 사람들이 이 나라에 어떤 이력이 없다면 그런 세부적인 것 모두를 신경 쓴다는 것은 힘든 일이었다.

24 이민은 이런 저런 면에서 그녀의 모든 제자들의 마음에 영향을 주는 주제입니다. Kathleen는 학생들에게 그들 친척들과 그들의 가정이 어떻게 미국으로 이민 오게 되었는지 인터뷰를 하도록 했다. 그들은 사진과 메달과 같은 물품을 수집했고 그런 물품들과 이야기가 들어있는 웹사이트를 만들었다. 전에는 많은 학생들이 그 이야기를 들어본 적이 없었다. 왜냐하면 친척들이 그런 이야기를 하는 것이 고통스럽다는 것을 알고 있었기 때문이다.

25 부모가 눈과 귀 그리고 마음을 열고 아이들의 행동을 객관적으로 보고 그리고 질병이 진행되기 바로 전에 전문적인 도움을 구하는 것은 아주 중요한 일이다. 나는 다른 식구들과 전문가들에게 그 당시 나이 스물의 아들이 심하게 앓고 있다는 것을 납득시키기 위해 필사적인 노력을 했었다. 그는 하루에 16-20시간을 자곤 했으며 빛과 소음에 아주 민감했다. 불안해 하며 밤에 몇 시간동안 정처없이 돌아다니곤 했다. 그는 심한 두통을 하소연했고 그의 이상한 행동 때문에 그와 함께 살수가 없었다. 그는 환영과 망상이 있었고 신의 목소리를 포함해 여러 가지 소리를 들었고 사교적인 면에서 내성적으로 변하고 고립되어갔다. 그는 편집증에 시달리고 정신을 집중할 수 없었다. 그는 무언가가 TV에서 나와 그를 잡을까 봐 두려워 TV를 보지 못했다. 그는 자주 손과 얼굴을 씻으며 강박관념의 행동을 드러냈다. 그는 이상한 얼굴 표정을 지으면서 거울 속의 자신을 바라보곤 했다.

26 그리고 그곳에는 Bobby가 있었다. 그는 평생동안 복지원에서 살았으며 점자법을 배웠고 주어진 환경 내에서 잘 지낼 수 있었다. 그의 나이 서른 여섯에 나는 그를 알게 되었다. 그리고 나는 재활원 교사로 Bobby가 복지원을 떠나 직장도 구하고 더 많은 친구도 사귀고 그리고 간단히 말하자면 그에게서 본 큰 잠재력에 맞게 살 수 있도록 하기 위하여 그에게 필요한 훈련과 자신감을 줄 수 있다고 믿을 만큼 아주 젊었었다. 내가 처음 몇 차례 방문한 후 재활원 운영진들이 다시는 오지 말라고

부탁했다. Bobby는 잘 적응이 되어 마음이 편안해졌는데 갑자기 머리를 벽에 박으며 그를 다룰 수 없을 정도로 충동적인 행동을 하기 시작했다는 것이다. 그는 이제 나이가 들어 늙었지만 내 생각에는 아직도 그곳에 있는 것 같다. 그는 행복할까?

Chapter 2. 후　치 (Postposing)

Unit 1 우향전이 (Right-Dislocation)

01 그는 밝은 햇살 속에서 눈을 가늘게 뜨고 조그마한 배를 섬 쪽으로 움직여갔다. 그 섬은 그의 시선 앞에서 너울 거리며 춤을 추고 있었는데, 마치 넘실거리는 바다 조류 사이로 한 순간 사라졌다가 다시 마치 의기양양한 주먹처럼 솟아오르는 것 같았다. 이 곳은 육지 최후의 보루였다. 이곳 너머로 대서양이 먼 수평선 속으로 뻗쳐 있었다. 그들이 그 쓸쓸한 섬에 가까이 이르렀을 때에 밀려드는 파도소리가 마치 연거푸 치는 망치소리처럼 더 요란해졌다. 이런 파도는 석벽에 부딪쳐 요란한 소리를 내며 물보라를 비교적 높이 뿜어댔다.

02 콜로라도 아스펜의 한 공항 밖에는 몸이 몹시 안 좋은 일단의 아이들이, 그들 중 일부는 머리카락이 없고 또 일부는 목발을 짚고 있었는데 차가 와서 야회 파티장으로 태워다 주길 기다리고 있었다. 때는 1992년 이었다. Andrea가 그들을 일주일간의 캠핑에 초대했는데 이 캠프는 그녀의 비영리 단체인 Kids' Stuff Foundation이 후원하고 있었다. 이 곳 아스펜에서 그녀는 그 아이들이 질병으로 잃어버린 희망을 되찾길 바라고 있었다. Andrea는 모든 세세한 것에 대해 특히, 어떻게 그녀가 그 아이들과 잘 친해질 수 있을 지에 대해 걱정을 했다. 주변을 둘러보던 그녀는 검은 머리의 소녀가 한 손으로는 한 아이를 감싸고, 동시에 다른 아이와 장난치며, 다른 아이의 머리에 있는 야구모자까지 바로잡아 주고 있는 것을 보았다. 그녀는 Andrea가 감탄할 정도로 쉽게 아이들 사이를 돌아다니고 있었다. 그녀는 캠프 생활을 하는 사람들 중에서 나이가 가장 많은 사람이었는데 18세의 Rhea Olsen이었다. Andrea는 그 열 다섯 명의 아이들 앞에 서서 그들에게 하루 동안의 활동에 대해 격려사를 하면서 Rhea가 그녀의 두 손을 엉덩이에 대고 냉소적으로 쳐다보고 있는 것을 알았다. Andrea는 이런 회의적인 십대 아이를 찾아내는 것이 좋겠다는 결심을 했다.

03 내가 읽고 있던 이 책은 도서관에서 실수로 가져온 것이었다. 그들이 나에게 책을 잘 못 주었고, 그 사실을 알게 된 것은 방으로 돌아온 다음 이었다. 그들이 나에게 Isak Dinesen의 Out of Africa를 주었던 것이다. 나는 그 책이 그리 좋지 않을 것으로 생각했었는데, 그렇지가 않았다. 그것은 아주 좋은 책이었다. 나는 글을 잘 몰랐지만 많이 읽었다. 내가 가장 좋아하는 작가는 내 형 D.B.이고 그 다음으로 좋아하는 작가는 Ring Lardner이다. 내 형은 내가 Pencey로 가기 바로 전 Ring Lardner가 쓴 책 한 권을 나에게 생일 선물로 주었다. 그 책에는 너무 웃기는 이상한 여러 개의 극이 있었는데 그 중 하나는 항상 과속을 하는 한 매우 귀여운 여자와 사랑에 빠지는 교통 경찰에 관한 것이었다. 그 경찰은 결혼을 했고, 그래서 그는 그녀와는 결혼이든 뭐든 할 수 없다. 그리고 그 여자는 늘 과속을 하다 죽게 된다. 이 이야기는 정말 웃겼다. 내가 가장 좋아하는 책은 가끔 웃기는 책이다. 나는 Return of Native 등과 같은 고전들을 많이 읽었고 나는 그것들을 좋아했다. 그리고 나는 전쟁과 추리 서적들도 많이 읽었다. 그러나 그것들은 나에게 그리 큰 감명을 주지 못 한다.

04 Morkan자매가 매년 여는 댄스파티는 항상 대단한 모임이었다. 그들을 아는 모든 사람들 즉, 가족들, 그 가족의 오랜 친구들, Julia의 합창 단원들, 어른이 된 Kate의 제자들, 그리고 심지어는 Mary Jane의 몇몇 제자들까지도 그 파티에 참석했다. 결코 단 한번도 그 파티는 재미없어 본 적은 없었다. 여러 해 동안 그 파티는 모든 사람들이 기억하는 한 굉장하게 진행되었다. Kate와 Julia가 그들의 오빠인 Pat가 죽은 후에 스토니 배터에 있는 집을 두고, 하나 뿐인 그들의 조카 Mary Jane을 데리고 가서 어셔 섬의 어둡고 으스스한 집으로 들어가 살게 된 이후로 죽 그러했었다. 그들은 Fulham씨로부터 그 집의 위층을 빌려 살았는데 그 집 1층에는 곡물 도매상이 있었다.

05 "그녀가 말하는 독립은 그 가족의 특성상 그녀의 몫이다." 그녀의 아들이 그 문제에 대해 내린 판단은 보다 더 호의적이었다. "저 젊은 여성들의 숭고한 정신이 어떻든 간에, 그녀의 정신은 그것에 만만치 않다. 그녀는 모든 일을 그녀 스스로 하기를 좋아하고 그녀를 도와줄 어떤 이의 능력도 믿지 않았다. 그녀는 나를 접착제 없는 우표만큼이나 쓸모없다고 생각한다. 그리고 만약 내가 그녀를 만나러 리버풀에 간다고 하면 그녀는 나를 절대로 용서하지 않을 것이다."

06 온 세상 사람들이 그날 선생님의 말씀을 듣고 있었고 우리 모두는 네가 아빠가 안 계신다는 것을 알고 있었다. 이런 식의 무감각이 얼마동안 지속되었다. 나는 오랫동안 나 자신에 대해 측은함을 느끼며 지냈다. 그리고 나서 어느 날 나는 이 술꾼을 어떤 식당에서 만났다. (만나기에 앞서) 나는 신발을 닦고 신문을 팔면서, 온 종일 열심히 일하며 밖에서 지냈다. 그래서 나는 아주 많은 돈을 호주머니에 넣게 되었다. 나는 내가 먹으려고 15센트짜리 칠리 한 접시, 5센트짜리 치즈 버거 한 개, 그리고 10센트짜리 초콜릿 케□ 한 개를 먹으려고 샀다. 그것은 훌륭한 식사였다. 내가 이것들을 먹고 있을 때 바로 이 나이든 술꾼이 들어왔던 것이다. 나는 술꾼들을 좋아한다. 왜냐하면 그들은 자신들 외에는 어느 누구에게도 해를 끼치지 않기 때문이다.

07 다른 식구들과 마찬가지로 나는 내 나이를 모른다. 대충 짐작만 할 수 있을 뿐이다. 우리는 계절과 태양에 의존하며 살면서 비가 필요할 무렵에 이동을 계획하고 이용 가능한 일광 시간에 따라 하루를 계획했다. 우리집은 마치 텐트처럼 도움 구조를 하고 풀로 엮어진 움막이었으며 막대기로 된 틀 구조물 위에 지어져 있었다. 그 집은 직경이 약 6피트 정도 되었다. 이동할 때가 되면 우리는 그 움막을 철거해서 낙타 등에 붙들어 매었다. 그리고 나서 물과 낙엽이 무성한 곳을 찾게 되면 우리는 다시 움막을 짓곤 했다. 그 움막은 우리에게 한 낮의 태양으로부터 피난처와 신선한 우유를 보관할 저장 공간을 제공해주었다. 밤에 우리 아이들은 멍석 위에서 서로 바싹 다가 붙어 별을 보며 밖에서 잠을 잤고, 아버지는 우리를 지키며 한 쪽에 기대어 수부셨다.

08 핵미사일을 상대방에게 겨누며 각자의 직장 생활을 해왔던 이 사람들은 콜로라도 피터슨 공군기지의 창문 없는 방안에 서로 나란히 앉아 있었다. 미 우주군 장교들과 러시아의 장교들이 지구의 종말을 막기위해 12월 31일 모여있었다. 그들은 함께 조기 경보 장치를 감시하고 있었는데 Y2K로 혼란에 빠진 컴퓨터가 대륙간 탄도 미사일 발사 신호를 잘 못 보내 실제 반응을 유발시켜 새 천년을 너무나 짧은 천년이 되지 않도록 하기 위함이었다. 러시아의 공군 중령 Viktor는 그의 데스크탑 컴퓨터와 모스크바 시간을 알려주는 벽시계를 초조하게 계속해서 보고 있었다. "자정 3분전," "2분전…" 이라고 누군가 큰 소리로 외쳤다. 그 후 방안에 적막이 흐르면서 장교들은 가는 천년의 마지막 몇 초 동안 붉은 광장의 상공에서 전호를 그리며 치솟는 첫번째 불꽃을 보여주고 있는 TV화면을 보고 있었다.

09 아침 마다 그들은 함께 이동을 했습니다. 그리고 Mark는 택시를 타고 다시 그의 사무실로 돌아갔습니다. 비록 지금의 이런 일과가 예전의 일과 보다 돈이 훨씬 더 많이 들고 피곤하긴 하지만 Mark는 어느 정도의 시간만 지나면 Susan이 혼자 힘으로 버스를 타고 다닐 수 있으리라는 것을 알고 있었습니다. 시력을 잃기 전에 알고 있었던 Susan, 다시 말해서 어떤 도전도 두려워하지 않으며 결코 포기하지도 않으려 했던 Susan 을 그는 믿고 있었습니다.

10 Nelson Mandela 대통령이 모잠비크의 전 영부인이었던 Graca Machel 여사와 결혼을 하면서 그 동안 남아프리카에서 가장 서투르게 지켜져오던 비밀을 드러내고 말았다. Mandela 대통령과 Machel (52) 여사는 Mandela 대통령의 80세 생일날 부촌인 휴톤 요하네스버그 교외에 있는 대통령 관저에서 개인적으로 여러 종파의 의식에 따라 백년해로를 약속했다.

11 Theseus가 그 이유를 묻자, "우리가 전쟁에서 패했기 때문에 우리는 크레타의 왕에게 끔찍한 대가를 치루어야 한단다"라고 아버지는 말씀하셨다. 매년 우리는 가장 뛰어난 젊은이들 중에서 7명과 그리고 가장 아름다운 소녀들 중에서 7명을 크레타 섬에 보내서 Minotaur라고 불리는 괴물이 먹을 수 있도록 해야 한단다. 가련한 그 아이들을 검은 돛을 단 배에 태워 데리고 갈 사자가 오늘 아침에 도착했단다. 그래서 너희들은 우리 모든 사람들이 아주 슬퍼하는 것을 보게 된 것이란다.

12 아시아의 소비자들은 일본의 가치관과 생활방식에도 편안함을 느낀다. 홍콩의 TV 시청자들은 "한 지붕아래"라는 일본 드라마를 좋아하는데 그 이유는 어느 면에서 볼 때에 그들과 관련이 있는 주제, 즉 가족간 유대 관계와 어른에 대한 공경에 역점을 두고 있기 때문이다. 그 드라마는 3세대가 함께 모여 사는 것을 특징으로 그리고 있는데, 이런 것은 서구의 멜로 드라마에서는 흔치 않은 시나리오인 것이다. 문화가 신비주의에 젖어있는 인도네시아인들은 미국 만화의 왁자지껄한 이야기 보다는 일본 만화의 영웅주의와 마법이 더 친근하다고 말한다. 가장 인기를 끄는 아동 채널에서는 아동 프로그램의 95%가 일본에서 들어온 것이다. "일본 쇼 프로그램은 훨씬 더 색다르고 기묘한 등장 인물들이 출연하고 있다."라고 아홉 살의 Aditya Daniswara는 말하고 있다. 그는 그가 좋아하는 프로그램들 중 하나로 청색 우주복 차림의 로봇 고양이인 도라이몽을 좋아하고 있다. 그 고양이는 잘 못된 일을 바로

잡기 위해 마법을 이용한다. 아시아인들의 기호는 역시 정서적인 작품쪽으로 향한다. 할리우드가 특수효과가 뛰어나다면, 일본 제작물들은 인간관계를 세밀하게 파고들며 감정과 감상이 풍부한데, 바로 이런 면들을 아시아인들은 좋아하고 있다.

13 그들은 평생동안 고생을 하고있으며 가지고 있는 모든 것을 위해 일해야만 한다. 그들은 엄격한 도덕률(道德律) 발전시켜 서로 의지하며 살아야 했다. 그들에게는 마음을 달래줄 만한 환상이 거의 없다. 그들은 모든 사람들과 어울리며 할 수 있는 능력만 있다면 개혁을 위해 일을 할 것이다. 샨지에 발전이 있기를 바란다면 그들의 지도부와 귀족들의 지도부가 하나가 되어야 한다. "그들은 황제란 말을 생각하기도 싫어한다"라고 Kati가 말했다. 그들은 그를 대신하는 사람은 싫어하지 않을 것이다. Mengmoshu의 눈은 그녀의 눈에 고정되어 있었고 그들은 오랫동안 말없이 앉아있었다. Kati는 그녀의 뾰족한 손 뒤로 그를 보며 한숨을 쉬었다. 당신은 내가 샨지의 황후가 되길 원하지요. 네 그렇습니다. Mandughai도 그렇게 말했다. 그것은 Kati가 내린 결정이다. 그리고 Moshuguang이 그것을 지지하고 있다.

14 나는 그가 입원한 병원 침대 가까이 앉아 다시는 보지 못하게 되지나 않을까 정말 두려웠던 그의 얼굴에 시선을 고정시키고 있는데 남편 Dan이 그가 겪었던 이야기를 내게 해주었다. 그가 협곡 아래로 미끄러진 직후 자신의 상황이 심각하다는 것을 깨달았을 때에 그는 나를 생각하고 그리고 만약에 그가 되돌아오지 못한다면 나를 정말 보고 싶었을 거라는 말을 했다. 그는 울퉁불퉁한 벼랑아래에 누워서 여기저기 더듬거려 적합한 돌 하나를 찾았다. 아주 뾰족했던 그 돌을 이용해서 그가 누워있던 곳 근처의 큰 바위에 내게 남길 메시지를 용케 새겨놓았다. 혹시라도 최악의 상황이 발생한다면 내가 그 바위를 보고 그의 가슴에 안긴 채 늘 그와 함께 있었다는 것을 알아주길 그는 바랬던 것이다. 나는 다시 눈물이 나왔다. 나는 새삼 남편을 정말 사랑하고 있다는 것을 알았다. 그러나 나는 나에 대한 남편의 깊은 사랑을 받을 준비가 되어있지 않았었다.

Unit 2 외 치 (Extraposition)

01 그대 자신을 우유부단한 사람, 다시 말해 반 정도는 이성에 의해서 그리고 반 정도는 유치한 어리석음에 흔들리는 사람이 되도록 내버려 두지 말라. 그대의 어린 시절을 통제해 온 사람들의 기억에 불손함을 갖어다 줄까 두려워하지 말라. 그들이 당시에 그대에게 강하고 현명하게 보였던 것은 그대가 약하고 어리석었기 때문이었다. 그러나 그대는 약하지도 어리석지도 않으므로, 이제는 그들이 겉으로 강해 보이고 현명해 보이는 이유를 검토해 보고, 그리고 아직도 그대가 그들에게 습관 때문에 표하고 있는 그런 존경을 받을 만한 자격을 갖고 있는지를 고려해보는 것이 그대가 할 일이다.

02 여러 해 동안 농민들은 그저 농지에 비료와 농약 그리고 관개용수를 더 많이 쏟아 붓기만 하면 수확을 쉽게 늘릴 수 있었다. 그러나 그들은 지금 수익(수확) 체감의 법칙에 부딪치고 있다. 벌레들은 갈수록 살충제에 대한 저항성을 키워가고 있다. 거름과 퇴비 등 유기비료 보다는 오히려 화학비료에 의존을 하게 되면서 토양은 더 단단해지고, 그리고 그렇게 됨으로써 보다 쉽게 건조해지고 마침내 토양의 질이 떨어지게 된다. 잘못된 관개기술은 농지에서 수분을 너무 많이 증발시킬 수 있으며, 토양에 쌓여있는 염분을 그대로 남겨두고, 궁극적으로 토지를 척박하게 만드는 결과를 가져올 수 있다. 그래서 파키스탄의 광활한 지역이 소금 밭으로 변해 버린 것이다.

03 그러한 개혁은 IMF의 조항이 없었다면 생각할 수도 없었을 것이다. 재벌들의 저항 때문에 그런 개혁을 이루어 낸다는 것은 아주 어려웠을 것이다. 그래서 나는 우리가 21세기에 재도약을 준비할 수 있도록 우리의 경제 체제를 바꾸라는IMF의 개혁 조항을 이용하기로 결심했다. 이것은 우리에게 전화위복인 것이다.

04 변화가 사회에서 가속화되면서 여기에 나란히 우리 내부의 변화도 가속화 되어야 한다. 새로운 정보를 우리가 받아들이게 되면 우리는 계속해서 점점 더 빠른 속도로 우리의 이미지 목록을 수정해야 한다. 과거의 사실에 바탕을 두고 있는 낡은 이미지는 대체되어야 한다. 왜냐하면 우리가 그것들을 최신 정보로 바꾸지 않는다면

우리의 행동은 현실에서 유리되고 우리는 점차 현실에 대한 적응력이 떨어지기 때문이다. 우리는 현실에 대처할 수 없게 된다는 것을 알게 된다.

05 미국인들이 종종 식사를 하면서 그릇을 식탁 위에 내려놓으면서 몇 가지 관습들이 발달하게 되었다. 스푼을 수프 그릇이나 커피잔, 또는 다른 그릇에 놓는 것은 좋은 예절로 여겨지지 않는다. 스푼은 식탁보 위가 아닌 평평한 곳에 놓는다. 이렇게 하면 그릇을 쳐서 바닥에 떨어뜨리거나 음식을 엎지르지는 일이 줄어들게 된다. 관습에서 또 한 가지 다른 점은 미국인들은 스푼의 끝을 사용하지 않고 옆을 사용한다는 점이다.

06 Kamiya는 그의 집안 내력을 숨기기 보다는 오히려 교실과 일본 여기 저기에서 이야기를 했다. 처음에 그는 그의 아버지를 조금 아는 사람이라고 완곡하게 말했다. 그러나 1995년 한 젊은 일본 의회의원이 그녀의 세대는 전쟁시 저지른 만행에 대해 전혀 책임이 없다는 선언을 했다. 그것은 Kamiya를 경악케 했다. 그래서 그는 공개적으로 연설을 하기 시작했다. "그것은 단순히 진실을 이야기하는 문제만은 아니다. 나의 아버지와 같이 마음씨 따뜻한 분들이 어떻게 해서 그리고 왜 "No"라고 말할 수 없는 상황에 연루되게 되었는지가 더 중요한 것이다"라고 그는 말을 했다. Kamiya는 일본 아이들이 그의 아버지 세대의 과오를 반복하지 않도록 하기 위해서 보다 더 자율적으로 생각하고 행동하도록 가르치는 것을 그의 사명으로 삼고있다. 그러나 Minoru와 같은 사람들에 동기를 부여해주었던 것과 같은 부류의 민족주의적인 사고가 부활하고 있다는 여러 가지 우려되는 징후들을 보고 있다. Kamiya는 731부대의 망령이 아직도 살아있다는 말을 하고 있다.

07 Albert Einstein의 뇌가 여러분이나 나의 뇌와 달랐다는 것을 인정하는데 Einstein 같은 사람이 필요한 것은 아니다. 그 덥수룩한 머리 속에 들어있는 회색 물질이 그의 놀라운 생애 동안 바로 자연 현실의 기초가 되는, 시간과 공간과 운동에 대한 우리의 관념을 단 한번이 아닌 여러 차례에 걸쳐서 대변혁을 치르도록 했다. 그러나 Einstein의 두뇌에는 분명히 무언가 놀랄만한 점이 있었어야 했지만 이 위대한 물리학자가 죽고 난후 그의 두개골에서 뇌를 옮겨낸 병리학자는 그 뇌는 어느 모로 보더라도 완전히 정상적인 범주의 것이었다고, 다시 말해 다른 누구의 것보다 더 크거나 더 무겁지 않았던 것으로 보고했다.

08 저는 저의 형님을 방문하고 방금 돌아왔습니다. 우리가 여러 해 만에 만난 것은 처음이었습니다. 고맙게도 형님은 우리가 지난 번에 만났을 때에 나에게 정말 많은 마음의 상처를 주었다는 것을 깨닫고 친절하게도 나에게 전화를 해주었습니다. 한 아주머니가 내가 그녀에게 괴로움을 하소연한 후에 내 기분이 어떠했는가를 형님에게 말해 주었던 것이었습니다. 형님은 전화를 해서 정말 미안하다는 말을 내게 하며, 그리고 전화를 받아주어서 고맙다는 얘기를 했습니다. 우리가 만났을 때에 내가 까맣게 잊어버렸던 어떤 일로 인해 형님 역시 화가 나있었다는 것을 알았습니다. 나는 형님이 무슨 말을 해서 혹은 어떤 행동을 해서 내가 화가 났었는지 기억도 나지 않았습니다. 내가 알고 있었던 것은 내가 단지 화가 나 있었다는 것 뿐이었습니다. 우리가 많은 세월을 허비하게 되었던 것은 우리가 서로 대화를 갖지않았기 때문이었습니다. Abby 선생님, 독자들에게 전화기를 들어 그들이 화가 나있는 사람에게 전화를 걸어 대화를 나누도록 하세요. "미안해, 네가 보고 싶어"라는 말로 시작하도록 하세요. 누가 누구에게 무슨 말을 했느냐 혹은 무슨 짓을 했느냐 하는 것은 중요하지 않습니다. 만약 여러분이 화가 나있는 있는 사람을 사랑한다면 전화를 걸어 문제를 해결하세요.

09 프란체스카 존슨은 브랜디 잔을 널찍한 참나무 창틀 위에 내려놓고 그녀가 찍힌 8X10 사이즈의 흑백 사진을 들여다보았다. 그녀가 그 당시 22년 전에 어떤 모습이었는지 기억하기 어려울 때가 가끔 있었다. 색이 바랜 꼭 끼는 청바지, 샌들, 하얀 티셔츠 차림으로 울타리 기둥에 기대선 그녀는 아침 바람에 머리가 흩날리고 있었다.

10 어느날 Great Gable산을 오르다 그는 한 소녀가 위험해보이는 암벽에서 흥분해 손을 흔들고 있는 것을 보았다. 그는 그녀가 곤경에 처해있다고 생각하고 그녀에게로 서둘러 갔다. 그러나 서둘러 가다가 미끄러져 그는 발목을 삐었다. 그러나 그녀는 전혀 곤경에 처하지 않았었던 것으로 밝혀졌다.

11 수년에 걸쳐 반복적으로 상어를 관찰함으로써 Klimley는 귀상어들이 왜 무리를 지어 모여있는지에 대한 오랜 신비를 풀 수 있었다. 그것은 분명히 방어를 위한 것은 아니다. 왜냐하면 Klimley가 바다의 터프가이라고 부르는 상어를 잡아먹을 수 있는 것은 아무것도 없기 때문이다. 적어도 어느 정도는 그들이 정교한 짝짓기 의식을 위

해 모여 다니는 것이며, 그 의식을 거행하면서 크고 힘 있는 암컷들이 싸워 그 수컷 무리의 중앙으로 들어가는 것으로 밝혀지고 있다. 여기의 수컷들은 그 무리들 속에서의 위치를 보고 어떤 암컷이 가장 이상적인지를 구별하게 된다.

12 전문가들이 서로 그렇게 분명하게 의견이 대립되게 되면 이 분야는 연구의 대상이 된다. 나는 1890년대에 쓰여진 글은 틀림없이 이치에 맞지 않는다고 인식할 정도로 충분히 현대적이기를 바란다. 그러나 나는 1950년대에 쓰여진 글이면 반드시 이치에 맞는다는 견해를 가질 만큼 진보적인 사람도 아니다. 사실 이런 연구는 역사의 속성보다 훨씬 광범위한 주제로 빠져 들 수 있다는 생각을 여러분들이 벌써 했을 지도 모르겠다.

13 1950년대 중반부터 점차 분명해지고 있는 것은 이러한 산업들이 산업 국가에서 퇴보하고 있을 뿐만 아니라 쇠퇴하고 있다는 점이다. 예를 들어 미국에서는 노동력이 1965년과 1974년 사이에 21퍼센트 정도 증가했는데도 섬유 산업의 고용인구는 불과 6퍼센트정도 밖에 증가하지 않았으며 철강 산업의 고용인구는 실제로 10퍼센트 감소했다. 이와 유사한 양상이 스웨덴, 체코슬로바키아, 일본, 그리고 그 외의 다른 제 2의 물결 국가들에서도 분명하게 나타나고 있었다.

14 외국어를 유창하게 읽는 데에 주요 난점들은 어휘와 문장 구조에 있다. 여러분들이 이러한 장애를 극복하는 데에 도움이 될 수 있도록 이 책의 내용들은 분류되어 있다. 여러분이 이미 기본적인 영어 단어 약 3000개 정도를 알고 있고 영어의 구조에 대해 약간씩은 알고 있다는 것을 가정하고 있다. 비교적 흔하게 사용되지 않는 단어들은 점차적으로 소개되고 반복되어진다. 문장 구조도 독해 지문 여기 저기에서 점차적으로 복잡해져 간다.

15 진실만을 쓴다는 것은 글을 잘 쓰는 것만큼이나 뉴스 기사에 중요하다는 점도 기억해야 할 것이다. 사실이 잘못되었다면 아무리 잘 쓴 내용이라도 가치가 없는 것이다. 신문이 진실이 아닌 것들을 보도하게 되면 법적인 분쟁을 야기시킬 수도 있는 것이다.

16 출산 후 여성들의 한 특정 단체가 Jeane과 나의 호기심을 자극했다. 그들의 처음 불평은 그들 아이에 대한 걱정과 지나친 염려와 관련이 있었지만 우리를 당황케한 것은 이들 여성들이 전화로 말했던 두려움이 일단 그들이 우리 사무실에 들어온 다음 우리가 관찰한 정서상태와는 일치하지 않는다는 점이다. 전화를 했을 때에 그들은 고민으로 지칠 대로 지쳐있는 것 같았다. "긴급한 일이에요. 저는 들어가 봐야만 해요,"라고 그들은 우리에게 말하곤 했다. 그리고 나서 그들은 "저는 제 아이하고만 있는 것이 두려워요. 저는 아이를 떨어뜨리거나 함께 떨어질까 두려워요," 와 같은 이상한 말을 했다.

17 일반적으로 대화가 잘 될수록 당신이 영향력을 더 잘 행사할 수 있다. 만약 신변 안전 문제가 해결될 수 있다면 테러단들이 인질을 잡고 있건 어떤 폭력행위로 위협하고 있건 간에 그들과 대화를 시작하는 것이 이치에 맞는 일이다. 만약 당신이 상황을 순조롭게 만들어 놓는다면 그들이 당신에게 영향력을 행사하는 것보다 당신이 그들에게 영향력을 행사하기가 더 쉬워지게 된다..

18 우리가 흔히 불가피하다고 생각하기 쉬운 것은 Marner와 같은 입장에 있는 사람이라면 제비 뽑기를 해서 신의 판단에 호소하는 것이 타당한 것인지 의심을 품었을 것이라는 점이다. 하지만 그에게 있어서 이것은 그가 전엔 결코 알지 못했던 독자적인 생각을 하려는 노력이었을 것이다. 그리고 그는 그의 모든 에너지가 기대에 어긋난 믿음의 고뇌로 바뀌었던 순간에 그런 노력을 했음이 분명했다. 만약 인간의 죄 뿐만 아니라 슬픔을 기록하는 천사가 있다면 그는 어떤 사람도 비난 받지 않을 잘못된 생각으로부터 나오는 슬픔이 얼마나 많고 깊은지 알고 있는 것이다.

19 1985년 4월 25일 텍사스 달라스에 있는 TI사무실에 전화벨이 울렸다. 외국인 억양의 목소리가 회사의 보안 담당 이사와 만남을 요청하고 있었다. 미국에서의 정치적 망명을 요청했던 시리아의 전기 기사인 Sam Kuzbary는 위험 인물로 해고 되기 전 한때 TI에서 근무를 했다. 소문에 의하면 미 CIA가 그가 시리아에서 도망쳐 나올 수 있도록 도와 주었다는 것이다. 그곳에서 그는 한때 시리아 군에 근무한 적이 있었다. Kuzbary는 차에 총이 있었다. 그 때 그는 그가 TI의 마음에 들도록 행동을 해서 그의 일을 되찾고 싶다는 말을 했다. 그리고 그는 TI에서 훔친 중요한 비밀과 관련된 정보를 가지고 있다는 말을 했다.

20 손님들은 그녀가 바닥에 넘어지는 것을 보고 조롱하듯이 웃음을 터트렸다. 그녀는 너무나 창피스러워 땅속으로 기꺼이 빠져들고 싶을 정도였다. 그녀는 문으로 뛰어가 도망치려 했지만 계단에서 한 남자가 그녀를 제지해서 다시 데리고 왔다.

21 그들은 이제 우리의 앞에서도 꽤 편안해보였다. 그래서 그 다음 이틀동안 Elsa가 100야드 정도 떨어진 탁 트인 암염지(巖鹽地)에 그들을 남겨두었다는 사실에 우리는 놀랐는데 Elsa가 그들이 잘 보이는 곳에서 식사를 하는 동안에도 어떻게 훈련을 시켰는지 그들이 꼼짝 않고 있는 것을 보고 역시 놀랐다.

22 나는 많은 시간을 혼자 있는 것이 유익하다고 생각한다. 비록 가장 훌륭한 사람들이라도 함께 있게 되면 곧 지루해지고 시간 낭비를 하게된다. 나는 혼자 있는 것을 좋아한다. 나는 고독만큼 서글서글한 친구를 찾지 못했다. 우리는 대부분 밖에 있을 때보다 외출해서 사람들 사이를 돌아다닐 때에 더 외롭다. 사색에 잠겨있는 사람이나 일하고 있는 사람은 그가 어디에 있다 하더라도 항상 혼자 있는 것이다. 고독이란 한 사람과 그의 동료들 사이에 가로놓여 있는 공간의 거리로써 측정되는 것은 아니다.

23 그리고 나서 판사는 Springsteen에게 법정에 출두하라는 명령을 내렸다. Springsteen은 법정에 나왔고, 서버지니아에서 Springsteen의 치료를 담당했던 정신과 의사인 Jeffrey Harlow의 증언은 배심원들 앞에서 다시 읽혀져 확인되었다. 그 증언 가운데에는 Springsteen이 충동적인 화를 억제하기위해 도움을 청하는 부분이 들어있었다. Springsteen은 오늘 아침 법정에서 비교적 자신감이 있어보였다. 그는 앞 줄에 앉아있던 그의 아내에게 윙크를 해주었다. 만약에 배심원들이 금요일 밤까지 판결을 내리지 못 한다면 다시 정회를 하게 될 것이라고 린치 판사는 말했다. 하지만 그들이 월요일에 되돌아올지 혹은 주말까지 일을 할지는 분명하지 않다.

24 두 번째 실험을 하면서 Lowe는 센서가 장착된 상어를 넓은 바다에 풀어놓고 그 상어가 여기 저기 돌아다닐 때 뒤따라 다닌다. 이틀동안 계속해서 추적한 후 그와 기진맥진한 조원들은 그 새끼 상어가 어디로 가는지, 그리고 그것이 꼬리 흔드는 횟수를 세어 얼마나 많은 에너지를 사용하는지 정확한 기록을 얻게 된다. 우리는 아

직도 많은 자료를 모아야 하지만, 일단 우리가 실제로 귀상어 새끼들이 여기서 어떤 역할을 하는지 알게 되면 우리는 그것을 이용해서 어른 고래들이 넓은 바다의 생태계에 어떻게 적응하는 지 이해하게 될 것이다. 호놀룰루 뒤쪽, 오아후 맞은 편에서 타이거 상어에 꼬리표를 부착하는 것은 상어 행동의 다른 면을 이해하려는 또 다른 첨단 기술의 노력이다. 1992년 두 사람이 하와이 해역에서 타이거 상어한테 죽었는데 그런 죽음은 그곳에서 30년 만에 처음이었다. 초기에 사람들이 많이 죽게 됨으로써 타이거 상어 섬멸 총력 프로그램을 갖게 되었는데 그렇게 죽이는 것이 실제로 효과가 있었는지는 결코 분명하지 않았다.

25 1950년 TIME은 Winston Churchill이 자유를 구출한 구명 보트를 띄웠다고 말하며 그를 반세기의 인물로 선정했다. 사람들은 그의 눈부신 생애를 높이 평가했다. 50년 동안 국제적으로 탁월한 활동을 했으며, 세계 양대전 동안 고위 직책을 맡았던 유일한 사람이었으며, 글이 읽혀지는 한 살아남을 언어로 자신의 경험담을 글로 쓴 유일한 사람이었다. 공개적으로 소련의 위협을 가장 먼저 선언했던 사람으로서 Churchill은 그 위협을 제압한 금세기 승리의 건축가가 되었다. 양대전에서의 두 번의 승리는 금세기의 주요한 업적이 되고 있다. 아직도 진행중인 위대한 운동, 즉 시민권, 민주화, 시장 자본주의 등은 파시스트 사회나 마르크스주의 사회라면 불가능하거나 적어도 지체될 것이다. 만약 Churchill이 늘 그랬던 것처럼 살면서, 행동하고, 글로 쓰고, 그리고 말로 하지않았다면 오늘날 삶이 어떨지 상상할 수 가 없다.

26 시체들은 대부분이 자동차 내부와 주변에서 발견되어 금요일 저녁에도 여전히 터널 안에 있었는데 수사 요원들이 수사를 할 수 있도록 옮기지 않고 내버려둔 것이었다. 그 시체들이 언제 옮겨질지는 알려지지 않았다. 이번 화재로 터널 내부에 비상장치와 관련한 여러 가지 문제들을 제기되었다. 왜냐하면 그 터널은 통풍장치와 17개의 대피소가 설치되어 있으며 각각의 대피소가 수십 명을 수용할 수 있기 때문이다. 그 대피소는 2시간동안 열과 유독성 냄새에 견딜 수 있도록 설계되어있다. 단지 소수의 희생자들만이 그곳 대피소로 갈 수 있었다. 많은 사람들은 안전 조치가 충분하지 못했던 것으로 생각하고 있다.

27 오슬로에서 가진 저녁 기자회견에서 Steinar Killi는 이유는 분명치 않지만 충돌 바로 직전 운송관리 요원들과 기관사들간의 교신이 없었다고 말했다. 그는 역시 오늘 선로상에서는 어떤 기술적인 문제도 없었기 때문에 열차 중 한대가 정지신호를

보지 못한 것이 분명하다는 말을 했다. “그런 일은 일어나지 않았어야 했습니다. 이번 사고가 기술적 결함이었는지 아니면 사람의 실수였는지를 우리는 규명해내야 합니다”라고 말을 덧붙였다.

28 돈 없이 물건을 살 수 있다는 것은 어떤 꿈이 실현되는 것처럼 보일지도 모르겠다. 하지만 신용카드를 사용해 빚을 지게 되면 재정적으로 안정된 미래를 이룰 수 없다. 신용카드를 만들기는 아주 쉽다. 하지만 여러분들은 카드를 현명하게 사용하는데 익숙해져야 하며, 그리고 현명하게 사용해야 할 책임이 있다. 미국 소비자신용상담소의 상담원인 Paul Lavoie는 "신용카드는 신용을 쌓는데 좋은 수단이며, 여러분들이 지출을 조절할 수 있을 만큼 충분한 책임감이 있는지를 보여준다. 하지만 젊은이들이 신용카드를 책임감 있게 사용하는 방법을 배우지 않으면 좋지 않은 일이 생기게 된다"라고 이야기를 하고 있다.

29 자기가 살고 있는 세계에 공명하지 못한다면 작가가 된다는 것은 아무 소용이 없는 일이다. 문필은 서로 다른 목적을 위해 사용될 수 있다. 예컨대 그 시대의 지배적 추세를 지지하거나 반대하는 목적으로 사용할 수 있는 것이다. 그러나 작가 자신이 살고 있는 시대에 있어서 그 어느 목적을 위해서나 효과적인 것이 되려면 쓰여진 말이 그 작가와 동시대인들의 마음에 닿아 심금을 울리지 않으면 안된다. 만일 작가가 그렇게 할 수 없다면 그는 언젠가는 자기의 말이 그들에게 생생하게 살아날 것이라는 희망을 가지고 자기의 원고를 금고 속에 넣어두는 것이 좋을 것이다.

Unit 3 탈명사구 외치 (Extraposition from Noun Phrase)

01 중국 정부는 여러 차례 위엔화의 평가를 절하시키지 않겠다는 약속을 하며 상당한 정치적 자원을 투자하고 그리고 세계 여기 저기로부터 박수 갈채를 받고 있지만, 위엔화의 평가를 절하하라는 강한 압력을 받고 있다. 중국 정부는 이런 위험성들을 알고 있다. 즉 중국 정부는 대만, 한국, 인도네시아, 그리고 아주 최근에는 이웃하고 있는 러시아의 평가절하로 인해 이들 나라의 경제가 어려워지는 것을 주시하고 있다. 그러나 중국 정부가 고통의 문지방에 이르렀다는 여러 징후가 커지고 있으며, 지도부 가까이에 소식통을 두고 있는 한 민간 경제 전문가에 의하면 중국 정부는 수출이 추가적으로 잠식당하는 것을 막기 위해 내년 초 위엔화의 평가 절하를 고려하고 있다는 것이다. 이런 평가 절하는 외부요인에 따라, 특히 일본 엔화의 가치에 따라 30퍼센트씩이나 될 수 있다.

02 강물은 차가웠고 홍수로 범람하고 있었다. 그리고 강물이 불어나면서 강 뚝 멀리 떠다니던 많은 물건들이 흘러 지나갔다. 나는 운 좋게도 매달릴 수 있는 육중한 통나무 하나를 붙잡을 수 있었다. 그래서 나는 그 통나무 위에 턱을 받친 채 얼음처럼 차가운 물 속에 누워서. 두 손으로 최대한 힘 안 드는 자세로 버티고 있었다. 나는 경련이 일지나 않을까 염려하면서 우리가 물가로 나아가길 바랬었다. 나는 긴 곡선을 그리면서 강을 떠내려갔다. 날이 충분히 밝아 오기 시작하였다. 그래서 나는 물가 주변의 잡목 숲을 볼 수 있었다.

03 엄마가 마을로 돌아오던 날, 마을 사람들은 대부분 들에 나와 있었다. 엄마는 마을 외곽에 비워있던 곳으로 알고있던 오두막으로 가서 그 집을 청소하기 시작했다. 마을에서 상당히 떨어져 있고 비좁아서 아무도 살려고 하지 않는 집이었다. 엄마는 앞으로 일이 어떻게 될지 신경 쓰지 않았다. 그저 쉬고 싶었다. 마을 사람들이 하루 일을 마치고 집으로 돌아올 무렵에는 마을의 골칫거리가 다시 돌아왔다는 소문이 빠르게 퍼져 있었다. 하지만 처음에는 엄마에게 반감을 표시하는 사람도 없었지만 환영하는 사람도 없었다. 마을 사람들은 엄마의 존재를 묵인해 주기는 해도 받아들이지는 못했다. 가족 중 어느 누구도 엄마를 찾아오지 않았다. 친구가 있었을 지라도 위험을 무릅쓰면서까지 엄마와 함께 있다가 발각되는 망신을 각오하는 친구는 없었다. 그때부터 엄마는 마을에서 소외당한 채 살아 갔다. 엄마가 조용히 들판

에 있는 낡은 오두막으로 돌아올 때면 모두가 입을 다물었다. 그리고 아무도 엄마에게 말을 걸지도 않았다. 나를 낳을 때가 다가왔을 때에 엄마가 어떻게 생활을 꾸려나갔는지 모르겠다. 아마도 마을의 산파는 돈을 받는 대가로 엄마의 망신스러운 처지를 눈감아 주기로 했던 것 같다. 아마도 엄마가 혼자서 낳았을지도 모른다. 어쨌든 나는 건강하게 태어났고 그때부터 엄마에게는 딸이자 동지가 생겨났다. 자신의 처지나 과거의 잘못 따위에는 신경 쓰지 않는 사람이었다. 자신을 필요로 하고 사랑하며 매 순간 자기와 함께 있기를 원하는 그 누군가가 생겨난 것이다.

04 전 대통령이 양 김을 어떻게 할 것인지 분명치 않다. 서울 여기 저기에서는 전대통령이 4월 미국 방문에 앞서 정치 규제의 마지막 흔적들을 없앨 계획을 갖고 있다는 소문이 나돌고 있다. 그러나 한국의 분석가들은 전대통령이 김대중씨를 가까운 시일 내에 정치에 복귀하도록 할 가능성은 없는 것으로 보고 있다. 그렇다 하더라도 그의 정적(김대중)이 귀국하는 것은 분명히 전대통령을 곤혹스럽게 하고 있었다. 만약에 전대통령이 김대중씨를 마음대로 활동할 수 있도록 내버려둔다면, 야권에 불을 붙이는 꼴이 되어 그의 권위가 크게 실추되는 위험을 감수해야 하는 것이다. 그러나 전대통령이 김대중씨의 입에 계속 재갈을 물리는 한, 그가 남한을 민주화하는데 진정으로 관심이 있다는 것을 많은 한국인들과 많은 국제 사회에 납득시키기는 아마도 어려울 것이다.

05 사실상 죄의식이 훌륭한 생활의 원인이 되기는 커녕 그와 정반대가 된다. 그것은 인간을 불행하게 만들며 인간에게 열등감을 느끼게 한다. 불행하다는 이유로 그는 남에게 무리한, 그리고 그가 사람들과의 관계에서 행복을 누리는 것을 방해하는 요구를 하기 쉽다. 열등감을 느낀다면 그는 자기보다 나아 보이는 사람들에게 원한을 품게 될 것이다. 그는 다른 사람을 칭찬하는 것이 힘들고 질투하기는 쉽다는 것을 알게 될 것이다. 그는 대체적으로 사귀기 어려운 사람이 되고 점점 더 고독해질 것이다.

06 에이즈 전염의 정도를 올바로 보기 위해 인류 역사상 다른 어떤 질병보다 지난 20년 동안 에이즈로 죽은 사람이 더 많다는 것과, 또 2500만명 이상의 아프리카인들이 에이즈에 감염되어 있다는 것을 생각해보라. 이런 사실은 잔인하게도 에이즈 바이러스로 인해 아프리카 대륙이 빈곤에서 벗어날 수 있는 전망이 어두워지고 있다는 것을 의미한다. 그리고 이런 빈곤은 다시 아프리카 대륙의 에이즈 전염 억제 능

력에 제약을 가함으로써 사실상 에이즈 확산의 촉매로 작용하고 있다. 그러나 어떤 조치를 취해야 할 것인가 하는 의문은 여전히 남아 있다. 일부 정부들은 자국의 에이즈 위기를 인정하고 효과적으로 대처하는 용기 있고 찬양할 일들을 하고있다. 예를 들어 우간다는 주로 대중계몽운동을 펼쳐서 감염률을 1989년 14%에서 97년에 8%로 낮추는 데 성공했다.

07 위대한 역사는 사학자의 과거에 대한 안목이 현재의 문제에 대한 통찰력으로 조명될 때에 정확하게 쓰여지는 것이다. Mommsen이 공화국 붕괴 이후의 역사를 계속해서 쓰지 못한 것에 대한 놀라움이 종종 표명되고 있다. 그에게 시간이나, 기회, 또는 지식이 모자랐던 것이 아니라 Mommsen이 역사를 쓰고 있었을 때 독재가가 독일에는 아직 나타나지 않았었다. 그가 활발히 활동하는 동안에 독재자가 국정을 주관했더라면 어떠했을까 하는 문제는 여전히 현실적이지 못하다. 어떤 것도 Mommsen으로 하여금 이 문제를 로마의 무대에다 투영하도록 유도하지 못했던 것이다. 그래서 제국의 역사는 여전히 쓰여지지 않았다.

08 그는 기다리면서 그녀가 그것을 그녀에게로 가지고 들어오라고 자기에게 소리칠 것으로 기대했었다. 그러나 그녀는 그러지 않았다. 그 여자가 문으로 오더니 문틈으로 손을 내밀어 그 갈대를 받았다. 그녀는 아무 말도 하지 않았다. 그러나 그는 먼 길을 달려온 짐승이 헐떡거리는 것처럼 그녀가 숨을 거칠게 내쉬는 소리를 들었다.

09 그 다음 몇 주동안에 Nachum은 서서히, 그리고 고통스럽게 마비상태에서 벗어났다. 그의 손과 다리는 완전히 움직일 수 있게 되었다. 그러나 그 모든 날들이 한결같이 좋은 것은 아니었다. 좌절을 겪기도 했다. 음식물을 삼키도록 조절하는 근육이 자주 제대로 움직이지 않았고, 폐에 감염 징후가 나타났다. 우리는 한층 기도를 더 열심히 했고 약물 치료의 도움으로 그런 위기를 넘겼다.

10 그 지하철은 내 맞은편에 앉은 여자 승객 두 명을 제외하고는 텅 비어 있었다. 우리는 덜컹거리며 계속 달려가다 몇 차례 멈췄다. 그 다음 34번 가에 도착해 출입문이 열렸다 닫힐 즈음에 나는 더 이상 다음 단계의 일에 대해서는 관심이 없다는 생각이 들었다.

11 사회제도와 마찬가지로 생태계에 있어서 원인과 결과는 시간적으로 또한 공간적으로 현격하게 구별되는 경우가 많다. 따라서 우리의 개입이 예기치 않은 결과를 낳는 경우가 빈번한 것이다. 우리는 수년동안 해충을 죽이기 위하여 잘 분해되지 않는 살충제를 뿌리고 나서 우리는 국가적 상징인 흰머리 독수리를 거의 말살해 버릴 지경에 이르렀다는 끔찍한 사실을 알게 된 것이다. 즉, 먹이사슬을 통하여 농축되어 있던 살충제가 독수리와 일부 다른 새들의 조직에 번식을 해칠 정도까지 축적된 것이다.

12 한편 연안 앞바다에서 유전채굴 러시로 해저에서 "기름 재배"의 가능성은 희박해졌다. 바텐 메모리얼 인스티튜트의 Lawrence Raymond박사는 석유성분의 함유율이 높은 해초를 재배할 수 있는 가능성을 증명하고 그런 과정을 경제적인 면에서 효율적으로 바꾸기 위한 노력을 하고 있는 중이다.

13 1972년 9월 5일 뮌헨 올림픽경기는 무시무시한 비극의 현장으로 돌변했다. 이스라엘 선수 11명이 팔레스타인 해방기구(PLO) 산하의 비밀조직으로 자칭 '검은 9월단'이라는 팔레스타인 테러단체에 의해 살해당했다. 그러한 만행이 재발할 가능성이 있는 것일까? 그렇다. 이번에는 이런 차이는 있겠지만 2004년 올림픽에서 그런 사태가 발생할 가능성은 높다. 즉 이번 목표는 미국 선수들이 될 것이다. 믿어지지 않는 이야기인가? 2004년 올림픽 개최지인 그리스에서는 지난 25년 동안 과거 미국 외교관 한 명과 장교 3명이 암살됐고 30명의 정부 관리들을 살해하려다 부상을 입혔다. 더욱 믿기 어려운 것은 이 같은 테러가 극성을 부리는 동안 범인이나 용의자가 체포된 적이 없다는 것과, 유죄판결이나 경찰의 진지한 수사가 이루어지지 않은 점이다. 더군다나 그리스 정부는 아무 일도 하지 않았다. 다시 말해서 범죄자들의 신원 파악은 고사하고 범인 체포를 위한 아무런 조치도 취하지 않았다. 그리스에서 미국인 암살은 다반사로 굳어졌다. 가장 최근에는 테러단들이 아테네 중심부에 있는 미국 대사관에 폭탄공격을 했으며 영국 대사관 소속 무관 한 명을 암살했다. 그보다 앞서 네덜란드와 독일 대사에 대한 암살기도가 있었다. 범인이나 용의자 체포는 없었고 유죄 판결이나 진지한 수사는 이루어지지 않았다.

14 고화질 텔레비전과 오늘날의 가정용 비디오 화면과의 관계는 콤팩트 디스크와 고조할머니의 축음기에서 돌아가는 잡음 나는 음반에 비길 수 있다. 고해상도는 최상의 대형스크린 영화의 화질에 필적하는 화상을 텔레비전 화면에 나타낼 수 있다. 이것의 덕택으로 화상이 가장 섬세하게 인쇄된 출력물만큼 밝고 선명하게 보이는 컴퓨터 모니터를 압도할 수 있게 된다.

15 매주 금요일에는 다섯 상자의 오렌지와 레몬이 뉴욕에 있는 과일상으로부터 도착했다. 그리고 매주 월요일이면 바로 이 오렌지와 레몬들은 그의 집 뒷문에 과육이 제거된 반쪽으로 버려져 피라미드처럼 쌓였다. 식당에는 조그마한 버튼을 집사의 엄지 손가락으로 200번 누르면 30분만에 200개의 오렌지가 주스가 되어 나오게 할 수 있는 기계가 있었다.

16 여러분들은 미국 독립선언서에 서명한 56명에게 어떤 일이 일어났었는지 궁금해 해본 적이 있습니까? 서명한 다섯 명은 반역자로 체포되어 죽기 전에 고문을 당했습니다. 12명의 집은 샅샅이 수색을 당하고 불에 태워졌습니다. 열 두 명 은 미국 독립 전쟁 때에 군복무를 했던 아들들을 잃었습니다. 또 한 사람은 두 아들이 체포되었습니다. 오십육 명중 아홉 사람은 미국 독립 전쟁 때에 싸우다 부상을 당하거나 고초로 죽었습니다. 그들은 그들의 목숨, 재산 그리고 신성한 명예를 걸었습니다. 그들은 어떤 사람들이었는가? 스물 네 명은 변호사와 법학자들 이었습니다. 열한 명은 무역상이었습니다. 아홉 명은 농부와 농장주인 이었습니다. 모두가 재력가 이었고 교육을 잘 받은 사람들 이었습니다. 하지만 그들은 체포되면 벌이 사형이라는 것을 알면서도 독립 선언서에 서명을 했습니다.

17 "모든 회사는 자사 제품을 혁신시키고 개선할 능력을 갖추어야 한다," Gates는 워싱턴주 레드몬드에 있는 본사에서 이렇게 말했다. 하지만 세계 제일의 부자인 이 사람은 "법적 절차를 겪는 누구에게나 힘든 일일 수 있다"고 인정했다. 해결 대화에 대해 Gates는 "그것은 절대적으로 노력을 할 가치가 있다"고 말했다. 소송을 제기한 법무부와 주 법무장관들은 또한 마이크로소프트사가 불법 독점 행위를 했다는 결론에서 승리를 한 것이다. 그러나 정부와 여러 주들은 여전히 대법원에 상소하거나 타협안 마련을 위해 협상을 하려하거나 또는 하급 법원으로 되돌아가 새로운 처벌을 찾을 수도 있다. 부시 행정부에 해결안을 모색하라는 정치적 압력이 거세어졌다.

18 미 대통령 부인Laura Bush는 텔레비전 코미디 프로가 자기 남편을 비난하는 것에 대해 신경 쓰지 않으며, 그녀의 딸들에 대한 신문의 가십 기사도 곧잘 무시해 버린다. 대신 그녀가 가장 많이 기여할 수 있다고 생각하는 일, 즉 교육 홍보에 힘을 집중하고 있다. "가르치던 일이 그립다. 가르치는 일이 좋다. 그런데 늘 이 학교 저 학교를 방문하고 있기 때문에 아직도 아이들과 함께 책을 읽고 아이들과 함께 공부할 수 있는 기회는 있다." 라고 영부인 부시는 CNN '래리킹 라이브'에 출연해 인터뷰를 하면서 그와 같이 말을 했다. 그녀는 백악관에 입주하면서 얻게 된 자신의 영향력에 대해 놀라면서도 동시에 스릴이 느껴진다고 말했다. 그녀는 그런 부가적인 영향력을 더 많은 사람들이 가르치는 일을 전문직으로 생각하도록 장려하는데 쓸 계획이다. 그녀는 두 가지의 프로그램을 특별히 좋아하고 있다. 그 중 하나인 "장병에서 선생님으로"의 프로그램은 퇴역한 군인들이 교원 자격증이나 교육학 석사 학위를 취득할 수 있도록 학비를 보조해 주는 것이다. 또 하나인 "미국을 위한 교육" 프로그램은 시골이나 도심 지역에서 적어도 2년간 가르치는데 전념하는 최근 대학 졸업자들에게 혜택을 주는 것이다.

19 St. Bartholomew 병원과 Royal London 병원의 의료 종양학 교수인 팀 올리버 박사는 남자들이 15년 전보다는 더 많이 도움을 구하긴 하지만 증세를 발견하는 사람의 3분의 1정도는 최소 3개월을 기다린 후에야 의사를 찾는다는 것을 알았다. 암의 상처를 경험하면서 나도 내 환자들과 특별한 유대감을 갖게 되었다. 나는 부인과 의사로 일하면서 최소한 격주에 한번은 여자에게 난소암, 자궁암, 또는 자궁경부 암에 걸렸다는 소식을 알려야만 한다.

20 코펜하겐에는 이름이 아주 이상한 거리가 있었습니다. 그 거리는 'Hysken가(街)" 라 불립니다. 그런 이름이 어디서 유래했는지 그리고 그것이 무슨 의미인지는 확실하지 않습니다. 그것은 독일어라는 이야기 있습니다. 그러나 독일 사람들은 그것이 옳지 않다는 것입니다. 왜냐하면 당시에 그 말은 'Hysken'이 아니라 'Hauschen'이라 불렸기 때문입니다. 'Hauschen'은 조그마한 집을 의미하는 말입니다. 그리고 오랫동안 그곳은 조그마한 집 몇 채가 있었을 뿐이었으며, 그 집들은 장이 서는 날에 시장 터에서 보게 되는 판자 집보다 더 크지도 않았습니다. 아마도 그 집들은 약간 높았으며 창문이 있었던 같습니다. 그러나 창틀은 뿔이나 방광의 표피로 만들어져 있었습니다. 왜냐하면 당시에는 유리가 너무 비싸서 모든 집의 창문에 유리를 끼울 수는 없었기 때문입니다. 이 일은 오래 전 일입니다. 정말로 너무나 오래된 일이

기 때문에 우리의 할아버지들과 심지어 증조 할아버지들까지도 그 시절을 옛날이라고 말씀을 하시곤 합니다. 사실 그 이후로 수 세기가 흘렀습니다.

Unit 4 복합 명사구 이동 (Complex Noun Phrase Shift)

01 네덜란드 상원은 이번 주 안락사에 관한 법률을 찬반투표에 붙여 지난 가을 하원을 통과한 (안락사)법안에 대해 법적 효력을 갖게 했습니다. 이번 결의를 통해 네덜란드는 세계에서 가장 먼저 자발적 안락사를 합법화한 나라가 되었습니다. 비록 이번 법이 안락사의 요청이 허락되기까지는 따라야 할 엄격한 기준을 정하고 있기는 하지만 많은 비판론자들은 사람이 사람을 죽이는 것을 허용한다는 것과, 의사의 역할, 그리고 정책이 남용될 수 있다는 점에 대해 우려를 표명하고 있습니다. 이번 법안의 통과로 인해 네덜란드에서 수년동안 음성적으로 행해져 왔던 안락사의 관행이 지금까지 정부에 의해 공식적으로 승인된 적은 없었지만 공공의 장으로 들어오게 되었습니다. 이번 법안 통과는 사람들이 자신들의 생명과 죽음을 어느 정도까지 통제할 수 있는지 그리고 만약 누군가가 도울 수 있게 된다면 누구인지에 관한 토론에 불을 지펴놓은 것입니다. 네덜란드 사람들은 그들이 역사적으로 최초로 결정한 안락사를 자랑스러워 해야 할까요 아니면 부끄러워 해야 할까요? 그리고 이번 일이 나머지 유럽과 세계에는 어떤 의미를 갖게 될까요?

02 열 여섯 살이 되어 면도 한 번 해본 적이 없다는 것은 끔찍한 일이다. 내 생일날 나는 시판되는 최신형 면도기를 선물로 받았다. "머지않아 이게 필요하게 될 꺼야"라고 아버지는 확신에 찬 윙크를 하며 말씀 하셨다. 매일 아침 나는 거울을 유심히 보았지만 내 얼굴에는 수염이 돋아날 기미조차 없이 새해가 시작되었다.

03 그러나 평균여명에 대한 짐작은 말 그대로 짐작일 뿐이다. 애틀란타에서 활동하는 노인병전문가인 Jeff Lesesne박사는 어떤 병에 걸린 환자가 진단 후에 얼마동안 생존할 수 있는지를 예측하려고 할 때에는 신중함이 필요하다고 충고했다. 그는 일련의 일들이 환자에 따라 다양하게 진행될 수 있어서 어떤 일을 겪게 될 지는 정확히 예측하기는 어렵다고 말했다. 알츠하이머병은 뇌의 신경세포를 공격해 사람의

기억, 조율 기능과 감정 조절기능을 손상시킨다. 그리고 마지막 단계에서 그 병은 환자의 모든 정신기능을 빼앗아버린다.

04 우리가 제 1물결, 즉 농업에 의한 부 창출제도의 전반적인 속도와 제 2물결, 즉 산업제도의 속도와 비교해본다면 그것은 공장굴뚝 경제의 속도가 전통적 농업경제의 속도보다 훨씬 빠르다는 것을 분명히 해주고 있다. 산업혁명이 지나간 곳은 어디나 그것이 경제적 과정을 보다 더 높은 기어에서 돌아가도록 바꾸어 놓았다.

05 인간 지놈 프로젝트(HGP)는 미 국립 보건원(NIH)과 런던에 본부를 두고 있는 자선 단체인 웰컴 트러스트가 대부분 지원하고 있는 국제적인 컨소시엄이다. 그리고 셀레라 지노믹스는 매릴랜드 록빌에 있는 민간 기업이다. 이런 높은 수준의 국제적 협력이 대부분의 이번 프로젝트를 아주 빨리 마무리하는데 도움이 되었다고 월요일 미 국립 보건원의 Collins씨는 말을 했다. 물론 이들 공공 단체와 민간 단체가 인간 지놈 프로젝트를 하면서 다른 방법을 이용하고 있기는 하지만, 그들 양쪽 모두 인체를 구성하고 있는 대략 8만개의 화학 물질을 밝혀내는데 목표를 두고있다.

06 사람은 이삼십년 동안 매일 아침 면도를 하게 되면 반드시 무언가를 배우게 된다. 설사 그가 너무 게을러서 직접 면도를 하지 않고 이발사에게 면도를 맡긴다 하더라도 그가 중년쯤 되면 인간성에 대하여 무언가를 배울 수 밖에 없다는 것이다. 왜냐하면 이발사들도 부류에 따라 모든 다양한 인간성을 지닌 이발사들이 있기 때문이다.

07 책과 인간의 관계는 기억력과 개인의 관계와 같다. 책은 우리의 인류의 역사와, 우리 인간이 이룩한 발견과, 오랜 세월에 걸쳐 축적된 지식과 경험을 담고 있다. 또한 책은 우리에게 자연의 경이로움과 아름다움을 보여주며, 우리가 곤경에 처해있을 때 도와 주고, 슬픔과 고통에 빠져있을 때에 위로해주며, 따분한 시간을 즐거운 순간으로 바꾸어주며, 우리의 마음에 여러 가지 생각을 축적해주며, 그것들을 좋은 생각과 행복한 생각으로 채워주며 그리고 우리를 현재의 자신으로부터 끌어 올려보다 향상되도록 해준다.

08 청소년의 임신과 출산은 시민들과 정책 입안자들에게 있어서 현재 큰 관심사가 되고있다. 그들은 청소년 시절에 성적으로 문란한 생활을 하게 되면 10대 소녀들이 임신할 위험성이 훨씬 높다는 것을 분명히 밝히고 있다. 1993년 미주리 주에서는 10대 소녀들 평균 29명이 매일 출산을 했다. 높은 임신과 출산율로 인해서 부모로서 갖추어야 할 여러 가지 요건들을 잘 충족시키지 못하고 있는 젊은이들이 생겨나고 있다.

09 아마도 바로 어린 시절이 아니면 책이 우리의 삶에 깊은 영향을 주지 못 할 것이다. 이 보다 나중에 나이가 들어서도 (책을 읽으면) 감탄하고, 재미 있어 하고, 그리고 우리가 이미 가지고 있는 일부 생각들을 바꾸기도 하겠지만 우리는 책 속에서 단지 이미 우리의 마음속에 있는 것들에 대한 확증만을 찾는 경향이 오히려 두드러지게 된다.

10 나는 내 가방에서 전쟁의 여파를 찍은 사진들을 꺼냈다. 나의 왼쪽에 있던 간부가 소름이 끼치는 듯한 표정으로 그것들을 훑어보았다. 그리고 나서 그는 "나는 이런 것들은 원치 않아요," 라고 말했다. 그는 그 사진들을 그 대령에게 슬그머니 건네주었고, 그 대령은 그것들을 보고는 정중하게 나에게 돌려주었다.

11 사실, 미국과 서방 첩보 소식통은 수백 명의 러시아인 기사들과 기술자들이 테헤란 외곽의 미사일 시설을 정기적으로 방문해서 이란인들이 미사일 생산에 관한 상세한 계획을 세우는 것을 도와주고 있다는 것을 확인해왔다. 러시아는 이 사업을 완수하기 위해 미국회사가 만든 수퍼 컴퓨터를 이란 측에 전해주었을 수 도 있다. 그리고 이란인들은 기술적인 문제에 부딪치게 되면, 비행기 편으로 러시아의 극비 군사 연구소로 가서 러시아인들이 어떻게 비슷한 문제들을 해결했는지를 알아 보고 있었다.

12 아홉시 였다. 거의 바로 직후 나는 나의 시계를 보고 열시가 되었다는 것을 알았다. McKee씨는 마치 활동가의 사진처럼 두 주먹을 불끈 쥐어 무릎에 올려 놓고 의자에서 자고 있었다. 나는 손수건을 꺼내어 오후 내내 마음을 아프게 했던 그의 뺨에 있는 나머지 땀 자국들을 닦아주었다.

13 Dorian은 요하네스버그와 런던에서 10년 동안 컴퓨터 프로그래머로 일을 했다. 그는 남는 시간에는 바다에 관한 책을 읽으며 그가 다시 바다로 돌아갈 수 있을지 궁금해 했다. 그는 서른 두 살 때 결혼 생활의 실패로 일을 그만두고 새로운 출발을 찾아 아시아로 향했다. 그는 그렇게 하는 것이 바람직하다고 생각했다. 콜롬보에서 싱가포르로 비행기를 타고 가면서 그는 창문 밖 아래 멀리서 거품이 이는 물결을 응시하면서 바다가 그의 마음을 끌어 당기고 있는 것을 느꼈다.

14 이런 식으로 슬프지만 중요한 희망을 난민들과 불행한 고아들, 그리고 남편을 잃은 지친 여인들에게 주게 될 것이다. 희망은 특히 희망을 빼앗긴 사람들에게 중요한 것이다. 바로 우리 지도자들에게 이러한 사람들이 학살되거나 추방되지 않게 막아달라고 설득하는 일은 우리의 책임이다. 우리는 크고 또렷한 목소리로 희생자들에게 그들이 고통을 당할 때 그들과 함께 하고 있다는 사실을 말해야 한다. 만일 그들이 버림받았다는 느낌을 갖는다면, 우리의 위신은 땅에 떨어진 것이다. 만일 그들이 굴욕감을 갖는다면, 부끄러워해야 할 사람은 우리들이다.

15 비평가들에 의하면 궁극적으로 홍콩은 스스로 그런 근본적인 변화가 필요하다는 것을 시인해야 한다는 것이다. "홍콩에서는 열심히 일하지 않더라도 돈을 벌 수 있다고 생각하게 하는 잘못된 자만심이 있다."라고 홍콩 중국 대학의 정치학 교수 Peter N. S, Lee는 말한다. "우리가 해야 할 일은 주식시장에 투자하고 경영학 학위를 획득하는 것이라고 생각한다."라고 그는 덧붙인다. 이미 홍콩은 공학과 컴퓨터 과학을 공부하는 학생들이 부족하며, 홍콩이 배출하고 있는 전문가들은 본토에 있는 그들의 경쟁자들과 힘든 경쟁에 직면하고 있다. "WTO는 홍콩이 세계적 수준에 있음을 증명하도록 할 것이며, 홍콩은 단지 또 하나의 다른 중국의 도시로서는 생존할 수 없다." 라고 Mok은 이야기를 하고 있다. 홍콩이 신속히 재창조되지 않는다면, 홍콩은 자만보다 나쁜 결점, 즉 엉뚱함에 굴복하게 될 것이다.

16 HIV에 감염된 3400만중의 70퍼센트가 사하라 사막 이남 지역의 아프리카에 살고 있다. 그곳에서는 지난해 200만 명 이상이 에이즈로 죽었다. 사하라 사막 이남 지역의 아프리카에 살고 있는 사람 4명중의 1명은 이 지역의 주요 사망 원인이 되고 있는 에이즈로 죽게 될 것으로 추정하고 있다. 1999년에만 해도 이 지역에서 200만 명 이상이 죽었다. 전문가들에 의하면 에이즈가 의사, 교사, 그리고 엔지니어들

을 포함해서 국가 노동인구의 주요 부분이 되고 있는 전세대를 파괴하고 있다는 것이다. 부모가 죽음으로 인해 학교에 갈 수 없는 혹은 누군가가 그들에게 교육을 시켜주리라는 것을 알지 못하고 있는 고아들만 남게 된다. "처음으로 3-40대 보다는 6-70대 사람들이 더 많아지게 될 것이다,"라고 유엔 에이즈 프로그램인 UNAIDS의 소장인 Piot박사는 말했다.

17 그들이 초원에 도착했을 때, 공주는 잔디 위에 앉아서 머리를 풀어 내리고 있었다. 그것은 순금처럼 빛났으며, 꼬마 Conrad는 그 머리를 보고 너무 기뻐서 머리를 잡아 당기고 싶었다. 그러나 그는 그녀의 머리카락을 잡을 수 없었다. 그는 그녀의 머리를 잡지 못한 것을 바람 탓으로 돌렸다.

18 Suharto지도부가 벼랑 끝으로 몰린 가운데 모든 시선이 인도네시아의 강력한 군부에 쏠리고 있었다. 왜냐하면 그들은 자신들의 부대로 하여금 거리를 점령하도록 명령을 내릴 수 있었기 때문이었다. 탱크가 거리 곳곳을 누비고 다녔고, 짙은 연기 기둥이 자카르타 상공을 가로질러 뿜어대고 있었다. 폭도들이 자동차, 타이어, 상점, 그리고 집에 불을 질러 놓았던 것이다. 돌멩이를 던지는 십대들과 아이들은 수백여장의 유리창을 깨뜨리고 외국인들과 소수 민족들을 달아나게 할 정도로 광란의 파괴를 자행하고 있었다. "자카르타는 불에 타고 있어요. 우리는 아무 곳이라도 갈 거에요."라고 가족들에게 밖으로 나갈 비행기 표를 사주려고 하고 있던 27세의 한 중국계 여성인 Wen이 말을 했다.

19 교육부 장관 Segolene Royal씨는 일요일 1월부터는 국립 중등학교에서 근무하고 있는 의사와 간호원들이 피임약을 학생들의 요청이 있을 시에는 나누어 주도록 허용하겠다고 밝혔다. 이러한 결정은 10대들의 임신이 늘어나는 것을 막기 위해 시작되고 있는 전국적인 성교육 운동의 일환이다. 프랑스 십대 소녀 만 명 이상이 매년 임신을 하고 그 중 6천 7백 명이 낙태를 선택한다.

20 서울에 있는 대한민국 재향군인회는 공식적으로는 전투 재연을 포함해 연례 기념 열병식 행사를 취소하고 사진 전시회와 퇴역 군인들을 위한 만찬회로 대체하겠다는 한국 국방부의 결정을 지지했다. 그러나 화해에 대한 감정이 모두 다 같은 것은 아니었다. 일부 퇴역 군인들은 북한에 너무 많은 것을 양보하고 있다고 생각하는

것들에 대해서 분노를 하고 있다. "정부는 북한으로부터 전쟁을 시작한 점에 대해 사과도 받지 않고 국민들에게 6. 25전쟁을 잊으라고 말하는 것 같다"라며 훈장을 받은 전쟁 참전 용사들 한 단체의 회장이 미 연합 통신에 말했다. 이런 말은 남북이 정상회담으로 밝혀진 화해의 정신을 계속 유지하려는 가운데 아마도 앞에 놓여있는 여러 가지 어려움이 있다는 것을 시사하고 있다.

21 내가 오려둔 자료 중에는 결코 일어나지 않았던 것으로 알고 있는 이야기 하나가 있는데, 그것은 한 가지 사실을 명확히 설명하고 있다. 그래서 나는 그것을 다시 이야기하고자 한다. 이 어이없는 이야기에 따르면 한 농장 여자가 힘든 하루의 일과를 끝내고 수북한 건초 한 무더기를 농장 남자들 앞에 갖다 놓았다. 남자들이 화를 내며 그녀에게 정신이 나갔냐고 묻자 그녀는 "왜, 댁들이 눈치챌 줄 내가 어찌 알겠어? 난 지난 20년 동안 당신 남자들을 위해서 요리를 해 왔지만, 한 번도 당신들이 건초를 먹지 않는다는 것을 알려주는 말을 들어 본 적이 없어요" 라고 대답했다.

22 일리노이주에 있는 오크 브루크 체인은 손님들이 음식값을 지불하기 위해 현금 대신 조그만 회색 플라스틱 막대기를 사용하게 하는 마케팅 방법을 면밀히 검토하고 있다. 이러 생각은 신기하긴 하지만 전혀 새로운 것은 아니다. 하지만 맥도날드는 보이스에 있는 26개 점에서 시험 중에 있는데 이것이 좋은 아이디어가 될 수도 있다고 생각하고 있다. 2천명 이상이 이 프로그램에 가입했는데, 이 프로그램은 기본적으로 그들에게 음식값을 지불하기 위해서 전자 센서 앞에서 막대기를 흔들게 함으로써 편리함을 주고 있다. 잔돈을 찾거나 소액 지폐를 찾지 않아도 된다. "패스트푸드가 더 이상 빠르지 않다," 라고 미시건주 파밍턴힐스에 있는 요식업 컨설팅 그룹인 맥베티 앤 어소시에이츠 사장 Jerry McVety는 말한다. 이런 생각이 친숙하게 들린다면 그것은 이미 새로운 것이 아니다. 이와 똑 같은 기술이 통근자들이 톨게이트를 신속하게 빠져 나갈 수 있도록 점차 많이 이용되고 있다. E-Zpass라고 불리는 다른 형태의 지불 방식은 뉴욕시와 그 주변 지역에서 6백만 명 이상의 사용자를 확보했다. 맥도널드사가 시험 중에 있는 것과 흡사한 이 장치는 사용자들에게 톨게이트를 시속 5마일의 속도로 지나갈 수 있게 해준다. E-Zpass 응답기는 선불 계좌에서 통행료를 빼가는 것으로 자동차의 백미러 뒤 앞 유리 부분에 부착되어있다.

23 아버지는 언제나 나에게 인생을 즐겁게 살아야 한다는 점을 상기시켜 주셨으며 말씀하신 바를 그대로 실천하셨다. 아버지는 아무리 고된 일을 하시더라도 항상 즐거운 시간을 누릴 수 있는 충분한 여유를 남겨 놓으셨다. 아버지는 맛있는 음식과 술, 그리고 특히 좋은 친구들뿐만 아니라 볼링과 포커를 좋아 하셨다. 아버지는 언제나 나의 직장 동료들과 친하게 지내셨다. 내가 포드사에 재직하는 동안 아버지는 나보다도 포드사에 있는 사람들을 더 많이 알고 계셨던 것 같다.

Chapter 3. 도 치 (Inversion)

Unit 1 주어 동사 도치 (Subject Verb Inversion)

01 수천 건의 미국 중앙정보국(CIA) 비밀 문서와 이전에 여타 비밀로 분류됐던 자료들이, 그들 중 많은 것들이 Kennedy 행정부시절의 내부 외교 정책에 대해 논의되었던 내용을 문서화하고 있는 것들인데, 처음으로 공개되었다. 이들 문서들 중에는 Kennedy 대통령과 국가안보위원회의 McGeorge Bundy 보좌관 사이에 오고 간 비망록과 베트남전쟁 초기에 라오스 주재 미국대사관에서 국무부에 보낸 전신문, 쿠바의 정치적 전복 노력들이 포함되어 있다. 수백여명의 사학자들이 John F. Kennedy 도서관 겸 박물관에서 수요일 공개된 이들 문서의 4,500페이지를 면밀히 검토할 것으로 기대가 된다. "Kennedy 행정부의 의문점이 거의 완벽하게 들어있지만 구멍들도 분명히 있다"고 그 도서관의 책임자 모라 포터 여사는 말했다.

02 거리의 양지 바른 쪽의 창문은 닫혀 있었다. 택시가 보도 앞에 서있었다. 이층에 '호텔 몬타나'라고 쓴 간판이 보였다. 택시 기사가 가방을 가지고 들어와 엘리베이터 옆에 놓았다. 나는 엘리베이터를 작동시킬 줄 몰랐기 때문에 걸어 올라갔다. 이층에 '호텔 몬타나' 라고 쓰여진 깎아 다듬은 놋쇠 간판이 있었다. 내가 벨을 눌렀는데 아무도 문으로 나오지 않았다. 다시 벨을 누르자 시무룩한 얼굴의 하녀가 문을 열어 주었다.

03 이것은 음악이나, 의학, 건축, 그리고 사랑에 여전히 적용된다. 그리고 아마도 우리 문화에 살고 있는 사람들이 분명히 실패를 하고 있음에도 불구하고 왜 이 기술을 좀처럼 배우려 하지 않는가 하는 질문에 대한 해답이 여기에 있는지도 모른다. 사랑에 대한 뿌리 깊은 열망이 있음에도 불구하고 사랑 이외의 거의 모든 것들을 사랑보다 더 중요한 것으로 생각하고 있다. 즉 출세, 명성, 재력, 그리고 권력, 우리들은 우리의 거의 모든 에너지를 바로 이런 목표를 성취하기 위한 방법을 배우기 위해 쓰고 있지만, 사랑의 기술을 배우는 데는 어떤 에너지도 쓰고 있지 않다.

04 우리가 출발하는 샌프란시스코 바로 남부에는 오래된 거대한 삼나무 숲이 있는데 이곳은 넓기로 유명합니다. 샌프란시스코 남부에는 태평양 연안을 따라 지명이 초창기에 스페인 사람들이 이곳에 정착해 살았음을 반영해주는 산호세, 산타바바라, 산디에고와 같은 일련의 도시들이 있습니다. 오래된 저택들과 그 외의 빨간 타일 지붕의 하얀 치장 벽토로 된 건물들은 이곳이 스페인의 영향을 받았음을 보여주고 있습니다. 여러분들이 샌프란시스코를 떠나 동부쪽으로 이동해가면서 캘리포니아 중부지역을 지나게 됩니다. 그곳은 많은 감귤류와 채소를 미국 전역에 생산 공급하고 있습니다. 온화한 기후와 좋은 관개 시설로 이 지역은 연중 내내 생산성이 높습니다.

05 종교적인 관점에서 볼 때 합법적이고 정당한 방법을 이용해서 우리들의 현재의 세상살이를 개선하려고 애를 쓰는 것은 허용될 수 있지만 불만을 표시하는 것은 전혀 온당치 못한 것이다. 예수 그리스도는 포도원 일꾼들의 비유로 우리들은 우리들의 것이 아닌 물건에 대한 정당한 권리를 가질 수 없다는 것을 보여줌으로써 우리들에게 정의의 숭고한 교훈을 가르쳐주고 있다. 이런 분명한 진리에 미래에 대한 불확실함이 더해질 수 있고 아울러 살면서 우리가 필요로 하는 것과 관련해 무엇이 선이고 무엇이 악인지 모르는 그런 무지함이 역시 더해질 수 있다.

06 그의 생의 마지막 해에는 그의 친구들이 그에게 덴버 우체국의 사무원으로서의 일자리를 주었는데 사실 그 우체국은 그의 돈으로 지어진 것이었다. 그가 1899년에 죽으면서 베이비 Baby Doe에게 “매칠리스 광산을 끝까지 지켜라. 그것을 가지고 있으면 큰 돈을 벌게 될 것이다.”라고 유언을 남겼다. Baby Doe는 Tabor가 그녀에게 했던 말을 행동에 옮겼다. 그래서 그녀는 광산 입구에 있는 조그마한 오두막으로 이사를 갔다. 그 오두막집은 아직도 거기에 있는데 그녀가 그곳에 살았던 때와 아주 똑 같다. 간이 침대 하나 식탁 하나 그리고 한 두 개의 의자가 있다. 조그마한 석탄 난로가 한 쪽 구석에 놓여 있다. 벽에는 몇 개의 단지와 냄비가 있다. 카톨릭 재단이 한 쪽 벽에 기대어 있고 몇 개의 양초와 십자가 하나가 그 위에 놓여있다. Baby Doe의 편지는 방 한쪽에 있는 상자 안에 보관되어 있는데 그것들은 그녀가 죽기 전 몇 년 동안 누군가 광산에 들어오지나 않을까 염려가 되어 좀처럼 그 오두막을 떠나지 않았음을 보여주고 있다. 친구들이 그녀에게 식량과 석탄을 가져다 주었다. 시간가는 것을 놓치지 않기 위해 그녀는 그녀의 달력에 날짜를 표시해두었으며, 그 달력은 아직도 벽에 걸려 있다. 1935년 3월 중순에 날짜 표시가 멈춰있다. 그

73세 여성의 싸늘하게 언 시체가 몇 칠 후에 발견되었는데, 그녀는 아직도 그 매칠리스 광산을 지키고 있다(그 곳에 묻혀있다).

07 간호사가 화장실 문을 연다. 그리고 그 문은 해수욕장의 탈의실만한 방이지만 그녀의 목소리는 몸을 굽히고 좌석 밑에 있는 무언가에 말을 하고 있는 것처럼 들린다. "자 Beale, 나와 함께 가요."라고 그 간호사는 말한다. 그러자 Beale이 바지가 흘러 내린 채로, 그리고 바지 멜빵을 마루 위에 질질 끌며 커다란 실내복에 파묻혀 밖으로 나온다.

08 Francesca는 현관에서 내려와 서두르지 않고 잔디밭을 거쳐 문을 향해 걸어갔다. 그러자 픽업 트럭에서 Robert Kincaid가 나왔는데, 그는 '삽화로 본 무당사' 라고 불리는, 글이 쓰여져 있지않는 책에서나 나오는 모습처럼 보였다.

09 전쟁이 끝날 무렵 영국의 팔레스타인 점령이 최종적으로 국제 연맹의 인가를 받아 영국의 위임 통치로 바뀌면서 투쟁은 격해졌다. 이 위임 통치령에 1917년 후반에 영국 외상 Arthur Balfour가 내놓은 발포어 선언이 반영되게 되었다. 발포어는 유대인이 팔레스타인에 국가를 세우겠다는 생각을 지지했다. (하지만 팔레스타인에 거주하는 아랍인의 희생이 있어서는 안 된다는 것을 그 선언문에 규정하고 있다.) 영국인들은 아랍 지도자들이 오스만 제국에 대항해 그들을 지지해준 대가로 아랍 독립국가 건설을 돕겠다는 약속도 했었다. 하지만 오랫동안 얽히게 되는 한 가지 오해가 생기게 되었다. 즉 아랍인들은 팔레스타인이 새 아랍 독립국가의 일부가 되는 것으로 생각했던 것이다. 영국은 그런 의도가 없었다고 했지만 팔레스타인 전체를 유대 국가로 만들 의향도 없었다. 오히려 유대국가가 팔레스타인 내에 있게 될 것으로 말했다.

10 아이들을 상대로 하는 이런 섹스 산업에 불을 지핀 것은 미국, 캐나다, 영국, 독일, 스웨덴, 일본, 호주 그리고 뉴질랜드에서 온 수 만 명의 섹스 관광객들이다. 아이들을 성의 대상으로 하고 있는 은밀한 조직망의 도움을 받아 어린아이에 대한 섹스를 찾아 남부 아시아로 여행을 한다. 왜냐하면 그들은 잡힐 위험성이 적다는 것과 잡혀도 처벌이 가볍다는 것을 알고 있기 때문이다. 관광객들의 돈에 매료되어서 이 나라들의 정부와 법을 집행하는 공무원들이 눈감아 주고 있는 실정이다.

11 현대 문화의 독특한 또 하나의 특징은 이런 요인과 밀접한 관계를 갖고 있습니다. 우리의 모든 문화는 구매욕과 그리고 서로에게 이익이 되도록 교환한다는 개념에 기초를 두고 있습니다. 현대인의 행복은 진열장을 바라보는 설레임과 그리고 현금으로나 할부로 자기가 살 수 있는 모든 물건을 사는데 있습니다. 남자이건 여자이건 사람들을 비슷한 방법으로 보고 있습니다. 남자에게는 매혹적인 여자가, 여자에게는 매혹적인 남자가 바로 그들이 구하는 상품이 된다.

12 전시 수준의 경호를 받으며 부시 대통령이 금요일 오후 한 때에 번쩍이던 세계 무역 센터였던 참혹한 현장을 시찰하기 위해 도착했다. "이번 싸움은 상대방이 시기를 정하고 그들의 뜻 대로 시작되었습니다. 하지만 그것은 우리가 선택한 방법과 시간에 끝나게 될 것입니다." 라고 우울하고 비가 와 축축했던 이날 일찍 부시 대통령은 말을 했다. 부시 대통령의 헬기가 그 파괴된 현장을 선회하는 동안 전투기들이 상공에서 날고 있었다. 지상에서는 수색요원과 구조대원들이 그를 기다리고 있었다. 일부 사람들은 조그마한 미국 깃발을 흙 운반 장비에 부착했다. 그리고 어떤 사람은 자신의 무거운 작업모 뒤에 성조기를 매달고 있었다.

13 돌아가신 저의 아버지가 1951년 어머니 날을 기리기 위해 써놓으신 시 한 수가 동봉되어있습니다. 제 생각에 아마 당신은 이 시를 싣길 원하실 겁니다. 물론 그렇고 말고요. 당신 아버님의 시는 어머니와 떨어져 지내는 자식들에게 강한 메시지를 담고 있습니다. 만약 그 메시지를 가슴 깊이 새긴다면 어머니 날을 밝게 해주어 많은 어머니들을 기쁘게 할 것 입니다.

14 150페이지 분량의 탄원서에서 미 공익과학 센터는 연방식품 의약품국으로부터 안전한 것으로 널리 인정을 받지도 못하고 그리고 식품 첨가제로도 승인되지도 않은 약초 성분 첨가제가 들어있는 오두왈러 주스, 스내플과 아리조나 티, 프레쉬 사만떠 그리고 골든 템플 시리얼과 같은 유명 상품을 지적했다. 그리고 제품 성분 난에 불법적인 주장을 함으로써 연방 식품 의약 및 화장품 법령에 따르면 불순물을 첨가하고 허위 광고를 한 것으로 생각되는 제품들도 거명되었다고 이 소비자 단체는 말했다. 미 공익과학 센터는 연방식품 의약품국으로 하여금 이런 제품이 더 이상 판매되지 않도록 적법한 시행 조치를 취하도록 요구했다.

15 대략 9000년 된 케니윅맨은 지금까지 북아메리카에서 발견된 가장 오래된 유골 중 하나다. 1996년 여름 오리건주의 콜럼비아강 얕은 곳에서 보트경주를 관람하고 있던 사람들이 우연히 발견한 이 유골에서 과학자들은 매우 섬뜩한 사실을 발견했다. 전쟁의 상처가 있는 이 사람의 유골은 보존상태가 양호하며 연령이 40대로 추정되었으며 대략 90세기 전 엉덩이에 화살을 맞아 전사한 것으로 보이는 이 유골은 키가 약 5피트 10인치(175㎝) 정도 된 것 같았다. 이 보다 더욱 흥미로운 사실은 놀라울 정도로 긴 얼굴과 크고 높이 솟은 코였다. 이것은 현재까지 알려진 아메리카 인디언의 어떤 부족과도 닮지 않은 얼굴 생김새이기 때문이다.

16 경제 재제의 반대자인 Charles Rangel 미 하원의원이 요청한 보고서에 의하면 "미국의 대 쿠바 밀 수출은 연간 3200만 달러에서 5200만 달러 사이가 될 것이며 이는 최근 미국의 전체 밀 수출량의 대략 1%에 해당된다."고 한다. 이 보다 더욱 교훈적인 것은 다른 국가들의 경험이다. 월 스트리트 저널에 의하면 "멕시코와의 거래에서 쿠바는 약 4억 달러의 상업차관 상환을 연체하고 있다. 프랑스는 Castro가 과거 선적분에 대한 대금을 지불하지 않기 때문에 밀 선적을 보류했고 신용차관으로 1억6000만 달러를 제공하려 했던 것을 철회했다." 칠레는 지난해 쿠바에 수출한 2000만 달러 상당의 생선 대금 '지불계획'을 마련하기 위해 노력하고 있다. 요하네스버그 선데이 타임스에 의하면 남아프리카공화국은 쿠바가 1300만 달러의 부채를 청산해주지 않는 것에 실망했으며 이 부채가 청산될 때까지 신규차관 보증을 승인하지 않을 것이라고 한다.

17 알코올 중독과 마약의 탐닉은 이런 주신제 같은 의식이 없는 문화에서 개개인이 선택하는 형식들이다. 사회적으로 유형화된 해결책에 참여하는 사람들과는 대조적으로 그런 개개인들은 죄의식과 자책감으로 고통 받는다. 그들은 알코올이나 마약에 빠짐으로써 고립의식으로부터 탈피하려 하지만 알코올이나 마약 경험을 하고 난 후 더욱 심하게 고립감을 느끼게 되고, 그리하여 더욱 더 자주 그리고 더 심하게 그런 것에 의지하게 된다. 절제되지 않은 성적인 해결책에 의존하는 것은 이것과는 약간 다르다. 이것은 어느 정도 고립의식을 극복하는 자연스럽고 정상적인 방법이며, 고립 문제에 대한 부분적인 해답이 되기도 한다.

18 1996년에는 50만 명 이상의 십대들이 출산을 했다. 이들 10대들 대부분은 미혼이었으며 그 중 많은 수가 부모로서의 책임과 요구에 응할 준비가 되어있지 않았다. 상당수의 이들 신출내기 엄마들은 너무 일찍 출산을 함으로써 학교 교육을 충분히 받지 못하게 되고, 자신들의 발전을 제한하게 되며, 그리고 가난하게 살고 미숙한 성인으로 남에게 의존하게 될 가능성이 많게 된다. 마찬가지로 너무 이른 출산의 고통이 다음 세대에게로 돌아가게 될 것이라는 점도 예견할 수 있다. 10대가 출산한 아이들은 다른 아이들 보다 태어날 때에 평균 체중 이하가 되고, 적절할 학습 기회를 잃게 되고, 그리고 가난하게 살 가능성이 훨씬 더 크다. 그리고 이들 아이들은 성장하면서 공부를 도중에 그만 두고, 말썽을 일으키며 그리고 결국에는 그들 역시 10대 부모가 될 가능성이 더 크다.

19 자동차 1만 대당 교통사고 사망으로 평가해본다면 한국은 보츠와나 공화국과 모로코에 이어 세계에서 교통사고가 가장 많은 나라이다. 일치 단결된 캠페인으로 한국은 3년 만에 많이 개선되어 9위로 떨어졌다. 하지만 여전히 조심해야 한다. 하루에 30명이 도로에서 죽고, 17명이 평생 불구가 되고 그리고 950명 이상이 부상으로 치료를 받는다. 불안한 보행자들 역시 불안하게 운전하는 자동차 운전자들과 비슷하다. 5분 동안은 그들을 관찰해야 된다. 현대국가로서 한국은 우리와 마찬가지로 교통신호등과 횡단보도가 있다. 그러나 많은 뒷길은 횡단 보도와 인도가 없다. 특히 할머니들은 차에 치이지 않길 바라면서 주변을 살피지도 않고 도로를 건너는 것처럼 보인다.

20 탈북자 일곱 명이 6월 26일 아침에 유엔 난민 고등판무관 사무실에 와서는 그곳에서 나가기를 거부했다고 그 가족을 따라 건물 안으로 들어온 한 목격자는 전했다. 탈북자 일곱 명 중에는 17세의 화가를 포함하여 여자가 셋인데, 그녀가 북한 정부 하에서의 어려운 생활을 그린 그림들로 인해 그녀는 처벌을 받을 수도 있다고 Redmond는 말했다. "우리는 이 사람들에게 망명 자격이 있다고 생각하며 모든 관련 당국들과 함께 그들에게 해결책을 찾아주기 위해 도움을 구하고 있다"고 그는 덧붙였다. 유엔 난민 고등판무관 관계자들은 중국 당국과 그 가족을 받아들일 의향이 있을 것 같은 정부들과 접촉을 하고 있었다. "이들이 우리 사무실에 있으면 안전할 것으로 생각된다"고 Redmond는 말했다. 망명을 요청한 북한 사람들이 베이징 주재 유엔 난민 고등판무관 사무실의 도움을 요청한 것은 이번이 처음이다. 그러나 훨씬 더 많은 북한 사람들이 자신들의 공산통치 국가에서의 탄압과 기근 그

리고 비참한 생활 여건을 피해 중국으로 들어왔다고 Redmond는 말했다. "이번 일은 빙산의 일각에 불과하다. 다수의 북한 주민들이 중국에 입국했다는 여러 보고가 있었지만 그들은 국경 지역에 있기 때문에 우리가 그들과 접촉하는 데는 제한을 두고 있다"고 Redmond는 말했다. UNHCR은 수만 명의 북한 사람들이 자신들의 나라에서 중국으로 도망한 것으로 추산하고 있다.

21 옛날에 상냥하고 귀여운 소녀가 살았습니다. 그녀는 모든 사람의 사랑을 받았습니다. 하지만 아무도 그녀의 할머니만큼 그녀를 사랑하는 사람은 없었습니다. 어느 날 그녀의 할머니는 그 귀여운 소녀에게 빨간 우단 모자를 주었습니다. 그 모자는 그녀에게 너무 잘 어울려서 그녀는 항상 쓰고 다녔습니다. 그래서 사람들은 그녀를 "귀여운 빨간 모자"라고 불렀습니다.

22 미국이나 유럽과 같은 통합 시장에서는 식품 공급의 안전성을 보장해주는 일관성 있는 높은 기준이 적용되도록 책임질 단일 기관이 있어야 한다. 수준 높고 공식적으로 믿을 수 있는 식품의 안전성에 대해 결정을 내릴 수 있는 능력과 독립성을 갖춘 범 유럽 식품 안전기구가 있어야 한다. 벨기에에서 시작되어 대부분의 유럽으로 확산되고 있는 현재의 다이옥신 위기는 국경을 초월한 식품 안전성 문제를 다룰 효율적인 제도가 필요하다는 것을 보여주고 있다.

23 내 이름은 나의 엄마가 아주 사랑하는 외숙모 Madge의 이름을 따서 Margaret으로 지어졌다. 나는 사촌이 있는데 그녀는 나 보다 한 살 더 많고 그녀의 이름 역시 Margaret으로 지어졌다. 하지만 항상 Madge로 불리고 있다. (그녀의 아버지가 나의 엄마의 남동생이었다.) 나의 엄마와 외삼촌은 상처를 한 알코올 중독된 아버지로부터 충분한 보살핌을 받지 못했다. 바로 Madge 숙모는 엄마가 대학에 진학하고 그리고 후에 결혼을 하기위해 친정 집을 떠난 후에 나의 외삼촌에게 사랑이 가득한 가정을 만들어주었던 분이다. 이런 이유로 외숙모는 나의 엄마에게는 각별한 분이었던 것이다. 나에게 똑같은 이름을 지어준 것에 대해 나의 엄마에게 약간의 섭섭함이 있을 수 도 있다. 하지만 그렇다손 치더라도 나는 그런 섭섭함에 대해 들어본 적은 없었다. 우리는 같은 이름의 애칭으로 불렸는데 나쁜 감정은 없다.

24 중동에서 가장 위험한 화약고는 레바논 남부 크파르 슈바 마을 너머의 한 철책 가장자리에 있다. 빛깔이 엷은 풀로 덮여있고 사이프러스 나무가 듬성듬성 심어진 바위투성이 언덕에 찬 바람이 휘몰아친다. '위험, 죽음, 지뢰밭'이라고 하얀 표지판이 주의를 주고 있다. 철책 바로 너머의 언덕 꼭대기 감시초소에서 이스라엘군 병사들이 국경쪽으로 다가오는 차량의 움직임을 예의주시하고 있다. "지난 주에는 어떤 사람이 여기서 오랫동안 차를 끌고 왔다 갔다 하자 이스라엘군이 총격을 가했다"고 크파르 슈바에 살고 있는 농민 Khaled Khadry(25)는 말했다. Khadry는 지난해 11월 헤즈볼라 게릴라들이 대담한 작전으로 이스라엘 병사 3명을 납치해 갈 때까지 헤즈볼라 게릴라들의 기지였던 담장 옆에 방치된 한 판잣집을 가리켰다.

25 그는 경찰을 부를까 생각했었지만 이웃간의 분쟁을 일으키는 일은 현명하지 못하다는 결론을 내렸다. 그는 그가 이사 갈 때까지 말없이 고통을 감내했다. 불행히도 그러한 일이 드문 것만은 아니다. 대부분 우리들은 이웃과 크고 작은 갈등을 가지고 있다. 이웃간의 분쟁을 다루고 있는 많은 지방 단체들은 무너진 울타리, 시끄러운 음악소리, 파티, 버릇 없는 아이들과 관련된 그런 분쟁들이 증가 추세에 있다는 이야기를 하고 있다. 샌프란시스코 대학의 법학부 학장인 Jay Folberg교수는 때때로 그런 분쟁은 법원에까지 간다고 말한다. 일부는 심각하지만 또 다른 것들은 웃음을 자아내게 한다.

Unit 2 주어 조동사 도치 (Subject Auxiliary Inversion)

01 나의 아버지는 Su Jinsan이라는 시인이셨는데 1957년 헤난성에서 가장 악명 높은 우파 중의 한 분으로 비난을 받았다. 나의 어머니는 아버지와 이혼을 하려하지 않는다는 이유로 극우파라는 꼬리표가 붙어 다녔다. 그분 둘 다 문화혁명기간 동안에 또 다시 공격을 받았다. 1989년 나는 나의 아이들 특히 큰 아들이 염려가 되었다. 그래서 나는 오월에 나의 아버지가 편찮으시다는 핑계로 그를 고향으로 보냈다. 나는 막내 아들 Zhao Long이 죽으리라고는 결코 상상도 하지 않았다. 6월 4일 새벽 4시가 되었는데도 Zhao Long은 아직 집에 돌아오지 않았다. 그래서 나는 그를 찾기 시작했다. 나는 (천안문) 광장을 향해 갔는데 광장은 이미 군인들이 꽉 메우고 있었다. 나는 그의 사진을 들고 인근 병원으로 갔다. 나는 어렵게 환자실을 거쳐 시체 공시장으로 갔다. 시체들이 장롱 속에 들어있었다. 우리는 그를 찾느라 시체를 한 구씩 한 구씩 끌어냈다. 마침내 남편과 나는 6월 6일 3번 병동에서 Zhao Long을 찾아냈다.

02 "저게 마지막 잎이야" Johnsy가 말했다. "난 분명 그것이 밤새 떨어졌을 거라 생각했어. 바람소리를 들었거든. 오늘은 떨어질 거야. 그리고 난 죽게 되겠지." "무슨 소리야! 너 자신을 생각하지 않겠다면 나를 생각해줘. 내가 어떻게 하면 될까?" 라고 Sue는 그녀의 지친 얼굴을 베개에 기대며 말했다.

03 다음날 아침 비행기가 우리를 태우러 오기 전 나는 엄마한테 나와 함께 돌아가 영국이나 미국에서 함께 살고 싶은지를 물었다. "그러나 그렇게 한다면 나는 무얼 해야 될까?" "물론 그게 문제가 되네요. 하지만 나는 엄마가 아무 일도 안 했으면 좋겠어요. 엄마는 일은 충분히 했어요. 이제는 쉴 때가 되었어요." "아니다. 너의 아버지는 나이가 들어가고 있고 나를 필요로 하고 계신다. 게다가, 나는 앉아있을 수만은 없다. 만약에 네가 무슨 일을 하고 싶다면 소말리아에다 내가 지칠 때에 갈 수 있는 집을 하나 사주렴. 이곳은 내 고향이다. 이 곳은 내가 알고 있는 전부이다. 나는 엄마를 껴안았다. 엄마, 사랑해요. 돌아올 거에요. 그 말 잊지 말아요."

04 우리는 이러한 새로운 가능성들로 눈을 돌리기에 앞서 우선 현재 사장되어가는 제도를 분석해 볼 필요가 있다. 또한 우리는 시대에 뒤떨어진 우리의 정치제도를 투시해 보고 이 제도가 제2물결 문명의 틀에 어떻게 맞았는지, 그리고 그것이 산업사회의 질서와 그 엘리트들에게 어떻게 기여했는가를 살펴볼 필요가 있다. 그때서야 비로소 우리는 왜 그 제도가 더 이상 적절하지 않고 혹은 더 이상 존속될 수 없는 지를 이해할 수 있게 된다.

05 Arafat는 혁명을 위한 테러분자이다. 그리고 Arafat가 팔레스타인 자치정부를 다스리는 한 중동에 평화는 실현되지 않을 것이다. 캠프 데이비드 회담에서 Ehud Barak 이스라엘 총리와 Clinton 대통령은 가장 관대한 조건을 제시했다. Arafat는 그 제안을 단호하게 거부했다. 그가 제안을 받아들였다면 이스라엘의 팔레스타인 점령은 끝났을 것이며, 오늘날 팔레스타인 국가가 수립되어있을 것이다. 더 이상의 폭력사태가 벌어질 필요도 없었을 것이다. Yasser Arafat가 테러 단체의 수반으로 앉아있는 한 팔레스타인 국가 수립이 불가능하다는 점은 국제사회와 팔레스타인 주민 및 이스라엘 국민에게 분명히 밝혀져야 한다. Arafat는 평화의 동반자가 아니다. 그래서 그는 물러나야 한다. 분명히 팔레스타인 자치정부에 혁명적인 변화를 가져오는 것은 팔레스타인 주민들에게 달려있다.

06 나는 성공했다는 생각이 인생을 더 쉽게 즐길 수 있도록 해준다는 것을 부인하지는 않는다. 가령 젊은 시절 내내 무명으로 지내던 화가가 그의 재능을 인정 받게 된다면 더 행복해질 수 있을 것이다. 그리고 나는 돈으로 어느 정도까지는 행복을 키울 수 있다는 것도 부인하지 않는다. 그러나 그 정도를 넘게 되면 돈으로 그렇게 할 수 없다고 생각한다. 내가 주장하고 있는 것은 성공은 단지 행복의 한 요소에 지나지 않으며 그 외의 모든 다른 요소들을 희생해가며 성공을 얻는다면 너무 비싼 대가를 치르게 된다는 점이다.

07 국제적인 위기를 대처하는데 있어서 일관성 있는 외교정책은 필요 불가결한 것이다. 정치적압력과 경제적 압력도 마찬가지이다. 그러나 그것들이 군사력에 의해 결코 지원을 받지 못한다는 것이 확실해 보이면 좀처럼 그것들만으로는 충분하지 못하다. 그리고 군사력은 항상 공군력에 한정될 수 있는 것으로 가정해서도 안 된다. 만약 폭격만으로 분쟁이 해결되지 않는다면 어떻게 되겠는가? 그러면 미국은

그냥 철수만 하면 되는 것인가? 미국이 무시되지 않기를 바란다면 지상군의 이용을 결코 배제시킬 수 없는 것이다. 아주 다양한 의견을 갖고 있는 미국 정치인들은 미국이 지도력을 발휘하는데 있어서 그것의 필요성에 대해서 계속 해서 얘기를 하고 있다. 그러나 지도력은 금전적인 측면과 때때로 인명적인 측면에서 볼 때 그 대가는 비싼 것이다. 우리가 진정으로 어느 정도 세상다운 세상을 이끌고 이룩하려고 한다면, 우리는 더 이상 그 일을 값싸게 그리고 리모콘만으로 할 수 있는 척해서는 안 된다. 많은 상황을 고려해보건대, 평화가 유지되기를 원한다면 우리는 평화유지만 하려고 해서는 안될 것이다.

08 Hitler는 선동가로서 오랫동안 일을 하면서 '군중 독약'의 영향에 대해 연구해서 그 자신의 목적을 위해 그런 영향을 이용하는 방법을 알게 되었다. 그는 연설가가 인간의 행동에 동기를 부여하는 그런 숨겨진 힘에 작가 보다 훨씬 더 효과적으로 호소할 수 있다고 믿었다. 작가는 오직 평상시의 맨 정신으로 책 앞에 앉아 있는 개인에게만 이야기할 뿐이다.

09 Bannet양의 놀라움이 곧 누그러지게 된 것은 Elizabeth에 대한 어떤 칭찬도 아주 당연한 것으로 보이게 해주는 언니로서의 강한 편견 때문이었다. 모든 놀라움은 다른 감정들 때문에 곧 사라지게 되었다. 그녀는 Darcy씨가 그들의 호감을 사기에 그리 적절치 못한 태도로 그의 감정을 전했다는 것을 유감스럽게 생각하고 있었지만, 그녀는 그녀의 동생이 거절함으로 인해서 그가 받아야만 하는 불행 때문에 훨씬 더 슬펐다.

10 한 여인이 신발가게에 들어가서 열 두 켤레의 신발을 신어보았으나 잘 맞는 것을 찾을 수가 없었다. 마침내 지친 점원은 그 여인에게 "부인, 부인의 한 쪽 발이 다른 발보다 커서 당신께 맞는 신발을 골라 드릴 수가 없군요."라고 말했다. 그 여인은 아무것도 사지 않고 그 상점을 나왔다. 그 옆 가게에서도 발에 맞는 신발을 고르다는 것은 마찬가지로 어려웠다. 마침내 미소를 머금은 점원은 "부인, 부인의 한 쪽 발이 다른 발 보다 더 작다는 것을 알고 계시지요?"라고 말했다. 그 여인은 두 켤레의 새 구두를 겨드랑이에 끼고 그 가게를 나왔다.

11 부모님들은 나중에 그들 자녀들의 입에서 나오는 말을 듣고 놀랄 수 있는 말은 우연히 라도 하지 않도록 각별히 조심할 필요가 있습니다. 자기 남편에게 '입 닥쳐'라고 하는 아내와 이웃 사람을 바보라고 부르는 아버지는 그들 자녀들이 그들에게 똑같이 말하는 것을 들을 수 있습니다. "만약 우리가 올바른 예절을 생활화하지 않는다면 어떻게 우리가 우리 자녀들에게 그런 것을 기대할 수 있겠습니까?"라고 예의범절의 저술가이자 "Ms. Demeanor"의 기고가인 Mary씨는 지적합니다. 격려하고 칭찬을 해주십시오. "너 정말 지저분한 녀석이구나. 너는 방 청소하는 것을 볼 수가 없구나." "그런 사례 편지를 써야지 그렇지않으면 너 TV 못 본다." "감히 나한테 언성을 높이다니." 대부분의 부모님들은 이런 말들을 그들 자녀들에게 하고 있습니다. 그들의 행동을 바로 잡기위한 것입니다. 그런데 왜 그들은 철저하게 그렇게 하지 않는 건가요? 왜냐하면 아이들의 버릇없는 행동은 자주 의도적인 반항이기 보다는 오히려 부주의함의 결과이기 때문입니다. 비난, 욕설, 그리고 명령은 아이들을 단지 화나게 하고 수동적이게 할 뿐입니다. 그런 것들은 아이들이 강압 없이는 올바른 행동을 할 수 없다는 생각을 강화시켜줍니다.

12 그는 자기 엄마를 잘 알고 있으며 그녀가 모든 사람을 정말로 화나게 한다는 것도 잘 알고 있습니다. 하지만 지금까지 우리는 좋은 해결책을 내놓을 수가 없었습니다. 저는 그의 어머니를 존경하고 있습니다. 결코 저는 그분에게 말대꾸를 해본 적도 없고, 그분이 아무리 옳지 않다고 생각되더라도 그분과 논쟁을 해본 적도 없습니다. 그런 이유의 일부 역시 만약 그분이 여러분에게 훈계를 하고 계시는데 여러분이 그분에게 무언가를 말하려고 한다면, 그분은 여러분의 귀가 파열되어 체념할 때까지 목소리가 점점 더 커지는 경향이 있기 때문이다. 여러분은 정말 참을 수 없지만 함께 지내야만 하는 사람을 다루는 방법에 대해 저에게 조언을 해주실 수 있는지요? 저는 우리의 미래에 대해 이런 점이 매우 걱정됩니다.

13 산책을 하라. 스위스에서 행해진 한 연구에 의하면 햇빛이 밝게 빛나지 않더라도 낮에 밖에서 한시간만 있으면 기분을 상당히 끌어올릴 만큼의 햇빛을 받는다는 것이다. 재미있게 시간을 보내라. 여름에 가족들은 저녁 식탁 접시를 치우고도 뒤뜰에서 캐치볼 놀이나 프리스비 놀이를 할 충분한 시간을 가질 수 있다. 겨울이 오면 우리는 실내에 있게 된다. 겨울 날씨에도 우리가 필요로 하는 신체적인 활동을 즐겁게 할 수 있는 여러 가지 방법이 있다.

14 내가 집에 돌아왔을 때는 대략 새벽 두시였음에 틀림없다. 나는 초인종을 울려 아내를 깨우려 했지만 아내는 잠이 깊이 들어 있어서 정원에 있는 헛간에서 사다리를 가져와 벽에 걸쳐놓고 침실 창으로 오르기 시작했다. 내가 거의 다 올라갔을 때 아래서 빈정거리는 목소리로 "이런 밤 시간에 창문을 청소할 필요가 없다고 생각하는 데요."라고 누군가 말했다. 나는 아래를 내려다보았다. 그리고 나는 경찰을 보고 하마터면 사다리에서 떨어질 뻔했다. 나는 즉시 그렇게 대답한 것을 후회했지만 "나는 밤에 창문 닦는 것을 좋아해요."라고 말했다. "나도 그렇소"라고 그 경찰은 같은 톤으로 대답했다. "실례하겠소. 나는 일하느라 바쁜 사람을 방해하는 것을 싫어하오. 하지만 당신은 나와 함께 경찰서로 가주셔야 겠소." "글쎄요, 나는 여기 있고 싶은데요. 당신이 보다시피 내가 열쇠를 두고 나왔오."라고 나는 말했다. "당신의 뭐라고요?" 라고 그는 외쳤다. "제 열쇠요."라고 나는 외쳤다. 다행히도 그렇게 외치는 소리에 내 아내는 깨어나서, 그 경찰이 나를 향해 올라오기 시작한 바로 그때 창문을 열어주었다.

15 그 해 가을 바네사는 임신한 사실을 알고 기뻐했다. 그러나 그녀와 남편 Robert이 함께 임신을 축하하며 출산계획을 세우자마자 그녀는 유산을 하고 말았다. 여러 달 동안 그녀와 Robert은 그 유산을 슬퍼했다. 그 해 겨울은 몹시 추운 것 같았다. 그러나 봄이 되자 이들 부부는 다시 아이 가질 생각을 하기 시작했다.

16 미 연방 항소법원은 6월 28일 만장일치로 법원의 마이크로소프트사 분할 판결을 기각했지만 소프트웨어계의 이 거대기업이 독점금지법을 위반했다는 판결을 내렸다. 이례적으로 비난을 하면서 항소 판사들은 예심판사가 Bill Gates와 그의 제국 마이크로 소프트사에 대한 모욕적인 발언으로 이번 사건을 심각하게 손상시켰다고 말을 했다. 7 대 0 판결에서 콜럼비아순회 재판구 항소법원은 회사 분할 명령을 기각하고 독점금지 사건을 좁혔으며 신임 판사에게 보내어 소프트 업계의 이 거대기업의 분할이나 다른 처벌이 정당한지를 결정토록 했다. 비록 Thomas Penfield Jackson 지방법원 판사가 심각한 실책을 저지르긴 했지만 "우리는 마이크로소프트사가 경쟁 원칙에 위배되게 행동했으며 이 같은 행위들이 회사의 독점력 유지에 도움을 준다고 하는 지방법원의 판결에 동의한다"고 항소 판사들은 말했다. 아직 법적인 문제들이 해결되지 않았지만 마이크로소프트사 중역들의 사기와 마찬가지로 주가도 치솟았다. 회사 중역들은 해결을 위해 대화를 계속하겠다는 약속과 함께 새로운 윈도우 XP 운용체제와 인터넷 서비스 계획을 추진했다.

17 요즈음은 육체 노동을 하는 사람들이 종종 사무실 직원들보다 훨씬 더 많은 봉급을 받는다. 사무실에서 일하는 사람들은 그들이 칼라가 하얀 와이셔츠를 입고 넥타이를 메고 일터로 간다는 단순한 이유로 자주 '화이트 칼라 직장인'이라고 불린다. 인간의 본성이 대단히 강한 것이어서 아주 많은 사람들이 종종 화이트 칼라 직장인이 되는 특권을 위해 더 많은 봉급을 기꺼이 포기하고 있다.

18 "당신 영국인이세요?"라고 내가 아마도 좀 재치 없이 물었는지 모르겠다. 물론이죠. 제가 미국인처럼 보인다고 생각하시는 것은 아니겠죠? 토박이 영국인입니다. 그리고 그게 바로 현재의 저입니다. 그는 영국인이라는 것을 증명하기 위해서 그의 호주머니에서 여권을 끄집어 내어 내 코앞에서 가볍게 흔들었습니다. 영국에는 이상한 사람이 많다. 그는 유창하게 말은 했지만 영어다운 점은 하나도 없었다. 내가 그의 여권을 좀더 면밀히 검토해 보았더라면 Kelada씨는 일반적으로 영국에서 볼 수 있는 것보다 더 푸른 하늘에서 태어났다는 사실을 드러냈을 거라는 확신이 들었다.

19 인간은 이성을 타고 난다. 인간은 생명 그 자체를 의식하는 생명체이다. 인간은 그 자신과 자신의 동료와 자신의 과거 그리고 자신의 미래의 가능성을 의식한다. 이렇게 자신을 독립된 실체로서 의식하는 것, 자신의 수명이 짧다는 것을 의식하는 것, 자신의 의지와는 관계없이 태어나 자신의 의지와 관계없이 죽는다는 것을 의식하는 것, 그가 사랑하는 사람들보다 자기가 먼저 죽거나 사랑하는 사람들이 자기보다 먼저 죽으리라는 것을 의식하는 것, 자신은 고독하고 분리되어 있다는 것을 의식하는 것, 자연의 힘과 사회의 힘 앞에서는 무력하다는 의식, 이런 모든 의식이 홀로 떨어져 고립되어있는 그의 존재를 견디기 어려운 감옥으로 만든다. 만약 그가 이런 감옥에서 해방되어 밖으로 손을 뻗쳐, 어떤 형태로든 사람들과 그리고 외부 세계와 결합하지 못한다면 그는 미쳐버릴 것이다.

20 그러나 휴대폰 소지자들에 대해 일고있는 무례하다는 비난은 때로는 공평하지 않은 경우도 있다. "그들이 단지 과시를 하고있다"는 것이 다른 모든 사람들이 정당하게 하고 있는 일들, 즉 버스를 타고 가면서 이야기를 하는 것, 인도에서 전화를 거는 것, 그리고 차를 몰고 가며 수다를 떠는 것 등을 하기 위하여 휴대폰을 사용하고 있는 사람들에게 쏟아지는 비난이다. 비싼 전화가 지위의 상징으로 생각될 수 있다. 그러나 분명히 별로 쓸모도 없으면서 대중의 분노를 불러 일으키지 않는 많

은 다른 것들도 그렇게 생각되고 있다. 휴대폰은 단지 하나의 도구에 지나지 않는다는 것을 인정해야 한다. 무례함을 결정하는 것은 휴대폰을 어떻게 사용하느냐이다. 자신들의 휴대폰에 대고 소리를 질러야 하는 사람들은 보다 더 좋은 전화를 필요로 하고 있는 것이다. 하지만 소리를 지르는 그 자체는 이미 에티켓을 어기고 있는 것이다.

21 미국은 자유 국가인가? 전통적인 기준으로 볼 때 아니다. 서양문명사에서 자유는 경제적 의미와 법률적 의미를 지닌다. 미국은 이 두 가지 자유의 기준에 미달한다. 이번 주에 닥쳐 온 4월 15일 세금의 날은 미국에 경제적 자유가 없다는 것을 상징하게 되었다. 미국인들은 중세의 농노나 마찬가지로 자기 수입에 대해 권리를 주장할 수 없다. 가장 성공한 미국인들이라 할지라도 노예에 비교될 만하다. 자유를 위한 오랜 투쟁은 자신의 신체와 노동가치를 소유하기 위한 투쟁이었다. 유럽의 농노는 자신의 노동을 소유하지 못했다. 그 결과 농노에게는 자신의 노동을 시장에서 임금을 받고 팔 수 있는 자유가 없었다.

22 소크라테스는 사람들이 잘못된 사회적 통념과 감언이설의 속박으로부터 벗어나 창의적인 분석과 객관적인 평가의 자유스런 영역으로 가기 위해서는 마음속에 어느 정도 긴장을 불러일으킬 필요가 있다고 생각했습니다. 마찬가지로 우리는 비폭력적인 주장을 하는 사람들이 사회에서 긴장을 불러일으킬 필요가 있다는 것을 알아야 합니다. 왜냐하면 그런 긴장이 사람들로 하여금 편견과 인종차별주의의 깊은 나락에서 벗어나 이해와 형제애의 웅대한 정상으로 가는 것을 도와줄 수 있기 때문입니다. 우리의 직접적인 행동계획의 의도는 위기감이 팽배한 상황을 만들어서 어쩔 수 없이 협상의 문을 열도록 하는데 있는 것입니다. 그러므로 나는 여러분들이 협상을 요구하는 것에 동의합니다. 너무나도 오랫동안 사랑하는 우리의 남부는 대화 보다는 오히려 혼자만의 중얼거림 속에서 살려는 처절한 노력을 기울이며 꼼짝 않고 있습니다.

23 영국에서는 잉여 자금을 가진 지주와 사업가들이 그 돈을 안전하게 금은 세공 업자들에게 맡기기 시작했다. 그러면 금은 세공 업자들은 그 돈을 높은 이자로 빌려주곤 했었다. 점차 금은 세공 업자들의 대출부서는 너무나 많은 이익을 보게 되었다. 그래서 그들은 예탁자들에게 그들의 재산을 보호해주는 대가를 요구하던 것을 중단했을 뿐 만 아니라 실제로는 그들에게 그렇게 해준 것에 대해 오히려 대가를 지

불했다. 그는 물론 대출자에게 물리는 이자보다는 낮은 율의 이자를 예탁자들에게 지불했다. 금은 세공 업자들이 예탁자들에게 지불하는 이자와 대출자에게 청구하는 이자간의 차액이 이윤이 되었던 것이다. 근대의 은행은 금은 세공업을 그만두고 돈을 예탁받고 대출해주는 것을 전문으로 해오고 있는 것이다.

24 민주주의는 정치적 책임과 성숙뿐만 아니라 행복과 번영을 가져다 준다고 합니다. 민주주의가 한때 공산주의 치하에서 고생을 했던 사람들에게 기쁨을 가져다 주고 있는 것을 보십시오. 아프리카 독재 국가들의 희생자들을 불쌍히 여기십시오. 왜냐하면 아프리카의 독재사회가 민주주의 혜택을 누릴 수 있다면 그들 사회도 우리의 사회와 비슷할 것이기 때문입니다. 유고슬라비아와 이라크에 민주주의가 없는 것을 슬퍼하십시오. 만약 이들 국가들이 그런 독재의 굴레를 떨쳐버릴 수 있다면 나토의 회원국들 만큼 공정하고, 좋고 그리고 정의로우며 합리적인 국가가 될 것입니다.

25 그는 계속 연락하지 않았다. 그녀 또한 마찬가지였다. 1년 후 이혼 서류가 오자 그는 서명하고, 다음 날 비행기를 타고 오스트레일리아로 날아갔다. 그녀는(메리언은) 자유 외에는 아무 것도 요구하지 않았다.

26 Matt은 친구인 일학년 Engen과 사학년 Grandt 두 친구와 함께 영화 보러 가도 좋다는 허락을 받았다. 그러나 그 소년들은 영화는 보러 가지 않고 18살의 Amy Pestor의 아파트로 향했다. Amy의 12살 먹은 여동생인 Karin이 그 곳에 있었다. 마찬가지로 Matt의 같은 반 친구인 Milbrandt와 Raymond 두 사람도 거기에 있었다. 그 일곱 명의 아이들은 이야기하며 텔레비전을 보았다. 아무도 냉장고안의 맥주는 건드리지 않았다.

27 집 밖의 미국 생활에서 여성들의 새로운 역할로 인해서 사회 구조와 미국 가정의 생활 양식이 변하게 되었다. 더 이상 가족의 재산이 남자들의 손에만 있게 되지 않았으며, 여자가 사업을 하고자 한다 해도 더 이상 남편의 동의가 필요하지 않게 되었다. 점차 여성들은 그들 남편과 재산의 공동 소유주가 되어가고 있으며 혹은 독립 소유주가 되어가고 있다. 점차적으로 그들은 그들 혼자서 사업을 하고 있다. 여성들이 가족의 재산에서 일정 몫을 갖게 됨에 따라 여성들은 가족 수입이 어떻게

지출되어야 하는지를 결정하는데 있어서 예전보다 더 많은 발언권을 가지게 되었다. 재정, 종교, 정치, 아이들 양육 정책, 건강, 그리고 여가 활동 문제에 대한 가족의 결정은 일반적으로 부부간의 토의 결과에 따르고 있다.

28 1872년에 그는 Marian Hooper와 결혼했는데 그녀는 상당한 재산을 상속 받은 사람으로서 멋진 성격의 소유자였다. 그러나 그녀는 1885년 자살했다. Adams는 그의 인생에서 누이와 아내 단지 두 명의 여자만을 사랑했는데, 둘은 모두 비극적으로 인생을 마감했다. 그의 자서전 어디에서도 그의 결혼에 대한 언급은 그리 많이 찾아볼 수 없다. 그 상처는 규명하기에는 너무 깊은 것이었다.

29 그들은 서로 20야드도 떨어져 있지 않았다. 그리고 너무 뜻밖에 그가 나타났기 때문에 그의 시선을 피할 수는 없었다. 그들의 시선이 곧 바로 마주쳤다. 그러자 두 사람의 뺨은 새빨간 홍조로 뒤덮였다. 그는 바로 움직이기 시작했다. 그런데 잠시 놀랐던지 몸을 움직일 수 없는 것처럼 보였다. 그러나 곧 제정신으로 돌아와 일행 쪽으로 가서, 완전히 침착하다고는 할 수 없어도 적어도 아주 정중하게 Elizabeth에게 말을 걸었다.

30 인생을 살아가면서 사랑을 키워나가는 데 너무 늦는 법이란 없습니다. 그저 여러분은 새로운 방법을 배우면 되는 것입니다. 여러분이 치료를 받고 있건 그렇지 않건 간에 만일 이성과의 보다 만족스러운 관계를 원한다면 이 책을 권합니다. “화성에서 온 남자 금성에서 온 여자”를 여러분들과 함께 나누는 것은 기쁜 일입니다. 여러분들의 지혜와 사랑이 커지길 바랍니다. 이혼은 줄고 행복한 결혼이 많아지기를 바랍니다. 우리의 자녀들은 보다 나은 세상에서 살아야 합니다.

31 이런 국가의 기도와 추모의 날에 즈음하여 우리는 전능하신 신께 우리나라를 지켜주고 앞으로 일어날 일에 있어서 우리에게 인내와 결연한 의지를 허락해주실 것을 요청하는 바입니다. 우리는 신께서 슬픔 속에서 걷고 있는 사람들을 위로와 격려를 해주실 것을 기도합니다. 우리는 신께 지금 어쩔 수 없이 슬퍼하고 있는 개개의 삶과 앞으로의 삶에 대한 약속에 감사 드립니다. 우리가 확신하고 있는 바와 같이 죽음도, 삶도, 천사들도, 권세자들도, 권력도, 현재의 일도, 앞으로의 일도, 높음도, 깊음도 우리를 신의 사랑으로부터 떼어놓을 수 없습니다. 신께서 죽은 자들의 영

혼에 축복을 내려주시길 빕니다. 신께서 우리를 위로해주시길 빕니다. 그리고 신께서 우리의 나라를 인도해주시길 빕니다.

32 나는 수면 장애에 대한 보고서를 우연히 읽고 나서야 비로서 뭔가가 잘못되어 있음을 알게 되었다. 그 보고서는 수면에 관한 퀴즈를 담고 있었는데 나는 비참할 정도로 그 질문에 낙제점을 받았다. 그 결과는 심각한 수면 장애를 시사하고 있었다. 바로 그때서야 나는 단잠에 대한 몇 가지 기본적인 조언을 따르기 시작하면서 회복의 길로 들어섰다.

33 약 5년 전에 저는 생모로부터 한 통의 편지를 받았습니다. 그리고 우리는 몇 번 만났습니다. 저의 생모와 가족들은 좋은 사람들이고, 우리가 계속 만나기를 원하지만 저는 원치 않습니다. 그래서 그들에게 제 마음을 넌지시 비추었지만 이해하지 못하는 것 같습니다. 저는 그분들에게 솔직하게 말하고 싶지만 아내는 제가 그렇게 하면 그 분들에게 상처를 주게 될 것이라고 말합니다. 그리고 제 마음이 변할 수도 있으니 마음을 열어 놓고 지내라는 것입니다. 저는 제 마음을 확신하며 아내의 말에 동의하지 않습니다. 저는 제 생모께서 저를 임신한 상태에서 쓰라린 이혼을 하시게 되었다는 것을 알게 되었습니다. 돈이 거의 없어서 그녀는 셋째인 저를 키울 여유가 없었던 것입니다. 저의 생모는 생부가 그러하셨던 것처럼 나중에 재혼을 하셨습니다. 저는 생부를 한번 만난 적이 있습니다, 그러나 아버지는 제 마음을 더 헤아려 주십니다. 아버지는 저의 사생활을 존중해 주십니다.

34 "우리는 과학과 약초학을 병합시킬 수 있습니다. 이것은 우리가 제조 약에만 의존했을 때보다 더 나은 약을 제공해줄 것입니다. 우리는 약초를 테스트해보기 위해, 다시 말해 무슨 약초가 가장 효능이 좋은지를 알아보기 위해서 과학을 이용할 수도 있습니다. 문제는 과학 대 자연이 아니라, 오히려 문제는 최고의 약을 얻어내기 위해 그 약이 천연 약이건 혹은 합성 약이든 간에 과학을 어떻게 이용하느냐 입니다,"라고 Duke는 말을 했습니다.

Chapter 4. 기 타

Unit 1 분열 구문 (Cleft Construction)

01 바로 게으른 사람들은 자기가 원한다고 생각하는 일을 할 시간이 없다고 불평하는 것이 일반적이다. 사실 사람들은 일반적으로 그들이 하고 싶은 일을 할 시간을 낼 수 있다. 사실 부족한 것은 시간이 아니라 바로 의지이다.

02 6년째 되던 해 후반에 그 죄수는 언어, 철학, 그리고 사학을 열심히 공부하기 시작했습니다. 그는 이들 학문에 열심히 몰두했습니다. 너무나 열심히 몰두한 나머지 그 은행업자는 그가 주문한 책을 구해주기가 힘들었습니다. 4년 동안 그의 요청에 따라 약 6백 여권의 책이 조달 되었습니다. 바로 이 기간동안에 그 은행업자는 죄수로부터 다음과 같은 편지를 받았습니다.

03 얼마 전 나는 한 외과 의사가 미묘한 뇌 수술을 하는 것을 볼 기회가 있었다. 그 의사의 손이 약간만 미끄러졌어도 그 환자는 죽었거나 마비가 되었을 것이다. 내가 그 의사에게 깊은 인상을 받았던 것은 그의 능숙함이 아니라 그의 놀라운 침착성이었다.

04 Sheets가 모든 일을 직접 했던 것은 그 당시에는 그가 그 일들을 하지 않으면 안되었기 때문이었다. "요즘 다 큰 그의 자녀들이 집을 찾아와서 그들이 가장 즐겁게 회상하는 것은 바로 그가 보여준 사랑의 노동이다. 그 시절을 그처럼 특별한 것으로 만들어 준 것은 그 집도 아니고, 호수도 아니었다. 우리가 한 가족이 되어 그 속에 쏟아 부은 즐거움이었다,"라고 Sheets는 말한다. 행복한 가정은 개인적인 노력을 수반하는 기쁨을 소중히 하는 것처럼, 할머니의 결혼 반지와 같은 개인적인 의미가 있는 물건도 소중히 한다. 그러나 불행한 가정은 소유물을 개인적인 의미가 있어서라기보다는 금전적인 가치가 있고 쓸 데가 있어서 더 소중히 여기는 경향이 있다.

05 그녀를 놀라게 한 것은 그들의 관계가 정말로 빠르게 변화되었다는 것이다. Jim이 그녀에게 훨씬 더 상냥해졌고 더 많은 관심을 갖게 되었다. 2주만에 Jim이 자기의 예전의 모습으로 되돌아오기 시작했다. 그는 항상 그녀에게 즐거운 일을 해주고 싶어했고 데이트 계획을 시작했다. 그가 의욕을 되찾게 된 것이다.

06 나는 성공했다는 느낌을 가지면 인생을 즐기기가 한결 쉬워진다는 것을 부인하지는 않는다. 가령 젊은 시절 내내 세상에 이름이 알려지지 않았던 화가가 그의 재능이 인정을 받게 된다면 더 행복해질 수 있을 것이다. 그리고 나는 어느 정도까지의 돈은 행복을 증진시킬 수 있다는 것도 부인하지도 않는다. 그러나 그 정도를 넘어서면 돈이 행복을 증진시킬 수 있다고 생각하지는 않는다. 내가 주장하고 있는 것은 성공은 단지 행복에 있어서 하나의 요소가 될 수 있을 뿐이며, 성공을 얻기 위해 그 외의 다른 요소들이 희생된다면 너무나 비싼 대가를 치르고 얻어진다는 점이다.

07 나는 Addison 부부의 거실 창에서 당신을 처음 보았을 때부터 수년동안 사랑해왔어요. 그래요 그분들이 당신에게 만나도록 하고 싶었던 사람은 바로 저였어요. 그러나 당신은 어떤 사람에게도 우리를 다른 사람에게 소개할 수 있도록 해주지 않았어요. 당신은 Addison부부에게도 우리를 서로에게 소개 시킬 기회를 주지 않았어요. 당신은 우리가 서로 좋아하게 될 거라는 Karen의 말을 받아들이지 않으려 했던 거예요. 저는 당신을 만나지 않으려고 생각을 했었어요.

08 교육의 문제들은 교육이 사회제도 안에서 그리고 사회제도를 위해서 행해지고 있음에도 불구하고 사회제도와 전혀 관계가 없는 것처럼 자주 논의된다. 이것이 바로 교육문제에 대한 해답이 불만족스러운 가장 흔한 이유들 중의 하나가 되고 있다. 바로 특정 사회제도 안에서만 어떤 교육제도가 의미를 갖는 것이다. 만약 오늘날 교육이 타락한 것처럼 보인다면 그리고 점점 더 혼란스럽고 무의미한 것처럼 보인다면 그것은 일차적으로 우리가 확고하고 만족스러운 사회제도가 없기 때문이며 우리가 원하는 부류의 사회에 대하여 모호하고 다양한 의견을 갖고 있기 때문이다. 교육이란 허공 속에서 토론될 수 있는 주제가 아니다. 우리의 문제들이 다른 사회적, 경제적, 재정적, 그리고 정치적인 문제를 불러일으키기 때문이다. 그래서 교육은 이것들 보다 더 궁극적인 문제와 관련이 있다. 우리가 교육으로부터 무엇을 원하는지 알기 위해서는 우리가 일반적으로 무엇을 원하고 있는지 알아야 하

고 우리의 교육이론을 생활철학으로부터 끌어와야 한다. 그 문제는 종교적인 문제라는 것이 드러나게 된다.

09 저는 지금 슬픔에 잠겨있습니다. 어제 남편과 저는 초콜렛 색의 세살 짜리 Labrado를 영원히 잠재워야 하는 끔찍한 경험을 했습니다. 2-3일 동안 그는 먹으려고도 마시려고 하지 않았습니다. 그리고 무기력하고 구토를 했습니다. 그래서 우리는 그를 동물 병원 응급실로 데리고 갔습니다. 수의사들이 그를 진찰해보고는 복부 속에 무언가 들어있다는 것을 알았습니다. 그래서 그것을 끄집어 내기 위해서 수술을 해야 했습니다. 그들이 그의 장안에서 발견한 것은 바로 주방용 타월 조각이었습니다. 불행히도 그 타월 주변 조직은 이미 감염되어 장으로 혈액 공급이 안되어 죽어 있었습니다. 그 상처는 예상했던 것보다 더 심각한 것이었습니다. 그래서 장에서 피가 흐르기 시작했습니다. 그는 너무 쇠약해져서 회복할 수 없었습니다. 그래서 우리는 그를 영원히 잠재워야 했습니다. 우리가 비탄에 잠겨 있다고 말하는 것은 전혀 지나치지 않습니다.

10 오늘날의 사회운동 단체들의 활동이 늘어나기 전에도 Eliot은 이미 그런 사람들과 그들의 우선순위가 무엇인지를 알고 있었다. 그는 1950년에 쓴 글에서 이렇게 말했다. "이 세상에서 일어나는 해악의 절반은 자신을 대단하다고 생각하고 싶어하는 사람들 때문에 생긴다. 그들은 남에게 해를 끼칠 생각은 없으나 그런 해악에 대해 아무런 관심도 없다. 아니면 그들은 자신들을 좋게 생각하기 위한 끝없는 노력에 몰두하기 때문에 그런 해악을 보지 못하거나 그것을 정당화한다."그런 사람들을 변화시킬 가망은 거의 없다. 그러나 우리 나머지 사람들이 할 수 있는 일은 어리석게도 그들의 자아도취적인 행동을 다른 사람들을 위한 이상적인 노력으로 받아들이는 떨쳐버리는 것이다.

11 Abby 선생님께서는 "Used in North Carolina"라는 사람에게 몇 가지 좋은 점을 말씀해 주셨습니다. 그는 임신한 여자 친구와 결혼을 하고 9년 후에 자기 아들이 "자기 자신의 아들이 아니다"라는 것을 알게 되었더군요. 그리고 이 아버지는 그가 "자기 자신의 아이가 아닌" 아이를 돌보아야 한다는 것에 정말 화가 났더군요. 그러나 선생님께서는 한 가지 중요한 점을 빠뜨리셨습니다. 선생님의 칼럼은 아주 널리 읽혀지고 있기 때문에 아이를 자기 자신의 아이로 만드는 것이 정말 무엇인지에 대해서 주의를 환기시켜주는 것이 중요합니다. 저는 소아과 의사입니다. 저는 매일

모든 부류 집안의 아이들과 접촉을 합니다. 아이들의 관점에서 볼 때에 아이가 진정 부모의 아이가 되도록 하기 위해서는 부모와 아이간의 정서 심리적인 유대관계가 있어야 합니다. 아이가 정서적으로 건강하게 자라기 위해서는 바로 그런 사회적 유대관계가 안정되어야 합니다. 이런 정서적 유대관계는 생물학적 혈연관계와 상관없이 아이들에게 필수적인 것입니다. 저는 우리의 아이들을 위해서 이런 말을 하지 않을 수 없습니다.

12 시간이 지나면서 그 반 학생들은 인문과학 분야의 천재가 그들 가운데 있다는 행운을 예전 보다 더 많이 의식하게 되었다. 나는 세미나가 있을 때에 아주 많은 단체에 이런 질문을 한적이 있다. 그러면 대답은 항상 같았다--여러분은 누군가가 우는 것을 보면 그들에게 다가가서 보통 무슨 말을 합니다. 여러분은 뭐라고 말하나요? 모두 이렇게 대답한다. 무슨 일 있니? 그러나 Jimmy는 결코 그런 말을 하지 안았다. 그의 질문은 항상 이렇다. 무얼 도와 줄까?

13 맨 처음 그들 뒤에서 일어난 폭발을 기억하고 무엇 때문에 그 폭발이 일어났는지 알아 보려고 돌아서 간 사람은 벨이었다. 그가 본 것은 바로 Keck 중사가 이상할 정도로 기이한 자세로 두 눈을 감고, 그리고 여전히 그의 오른쪽 손에 수류탄의 고리와 안전핀을 잡고 드러누워있는 모습이었다. Bell이 소리를 치자 그를 향해 달려온 그들은 그 중사를 조심스럽게 돌려 보고 그를 위해 해줄 수 있는 것은 아무것도 없다는 것을 알았다. 그의 오른쪽 엉덩이 전체와 등의 일부분이 날아가 버렸던 것이다. 그의 장기 일부가 보였는데 아무일 없는 듯 각기 제 활동을 하고 있었으며, 맥박은 바쁘게 뛰다가 순식간에 사라져갔다. 끊임없이 피가 상처 난 부위에서 흘러나왔다. 그들은 조심스럽게 그를 다시 눕혔다.

14 이상을 가지고 사는 삶은 성공적인 삶이다. 사람을 강하게 만들어 주는 것은 사람이 무엇을 하느냐가 아니라 무엇을 하려고 노력 하느냐인 것이다. 끊임없는 노력을 해야 성공할 수 있다. 우리가 온 힘을 다해 일을 하지 않을지라도 다른 사람들은 온 힘을 다해 일을 할 것이다. 그리고 그들은 인생이라는 경주에서 우리를 물리치고 우리의 손아귀로부터 상을 빼앗아갈 것이다. 성공이 행운과 우연에 의존하는 일이 점점 줄어들고 있다. 자기 불신이 우리 대부분의 실패의 원인이 되고 있다. 성공에 크고도 필요불가결한 도움이 되는 것은 인격이다. 인격은 결정화된 습관이며 훈련과 신념의 결과이다. 세상에서 가장 어리석은 바보는 보거나, 느끼거나 혹은 맛볼

수 없는 것은 어떤 것도 인정하려고 하지 않는 사람이며, 다시 말해 상상력이나 통찰력 또는 믿음의 여지가 없는 사람이다. 사람은 다양한 종류의 교육을 받을 수 있다. 사람은 육체적, 사회적, 종교적, 지적 그리고 도덕적인 능력을 소유하고 있다. 이런 모든 능력의 교육은 사람을 완전하게 해주지만 단지 일부분만의 교육은 결함을 갖게 한다. 교육을 받은 사람은 뭔가를 할 수 있는 사람이며 그가 하는 일의 질은 그의 교육의 정도를 나타내준다. 젊은이들이 하는 최고의 투자는 좋은 책에 있다. 왜냐하면 그 책들을 공부하게 되면 마음이 넓어지기 때문이다.

15 그녀는 아마 그의 이러한 반응을 반기지는 않겠지만 존중할 것이다. 물론 그녀는 그가 언제나 사랑이 넘치는 사람이기를 바란다. 하지만 혼자 있을 필요가 있다면 그것은 그의 타당한 욕구인 것이다. 그는 그가 갖고 있지 않은 것을 줄 수는 없다. 그가 할 수 있는 것은 사태의 악화를 피하는 일이다. 해결의 열쇠는 그녀의 욕구뿐만 아니라 그의 욕구를 모두 존중해주는데 있다. 그는 필요한 시간을 가져야만 하고 그런 다음 돌아가서 그녀가 필요로 하는 것을 주어야 한다. 남편들이 아내에게 많은 관심을 표하기 어려운 상황이어서 아내의 상한 기분을 귀 기울여 들어줄 수 없다면, 남편들을 이렇게 말할 수 있을 것이다. "나는 당신이 기분이 상한 건 이해해요. 거기에 대해 생각할 시간이 좀 필요한데 우리 잠시 생각할 시간을 가집시다." 남편들이 이런 식으로 자신의 입장을 설명하고 아내의 이야기에 귀를 기울이지 않는다 하더라도 이것이 그녀의 상한 감정을 적당히 둘러대고 무시해버리려는 것 보다는 훨씬 낫다.

16 공산 중국의 현실을 동화 같은 이야기로 모호하게 만들어서는 안 된다. 중국은 세계 최대의 상비군을 보유하고 있음에도 불구하고 매년 8%씩 국방예산을 증액하면서 유례를 볼 수 없는 비율로 군비를 증강하고 있다. 그리고 사실 이 지역에는 다른 국가나 혹은 국가연합에 의한 전쟁 도발 위험이 현재나 먼 장래에 전혀 없다는 점이다. 대만과 중국은 협상을 반복하겠지만 양안간 협상은 중국정부의 좌절감이나 더 심한 것만을 가져올 것이다. 대만의 Lee Teng-hui (李登輝) 전 총통은 이렇게 말한 바와 같이 "대만이 통일을 원하지 않는 것은 아니다. 대만 국민들이 공산주의 체제 아래서 살기를 원하지 않을 뿐이다."

17 그래서 그녀는 부드럽게 생쥐를 부르며 뒤따라갔다. "귀여운 생쥐야, 다시 돌아오렴. 네가 고양이와 개를 싫어한다면 우리 역시 그것들에 대해서는 이야기를 하지

않을 거야. 생쥐는 이 말을 듣고 방향을 돌리더니 천천히 그녀에게로 다시 헤엄쳐 왔다. 생쥐의 얼굴은 아주 창백해져 있었다. 그리고 생쥐는 나지막이 떨리는 목소리로 말했다. "물가로 가자. 그런 다음 너에게 나의 예전의 이야기를 해줄게. 그러면 너는 내가 왜 고양이나 개를 미워하는지 알게 될 거야."

18 "Grieving Grandmother"과 Ann Coakley의 편지는 우리나라의 총기문제에 대해 깨우쳐주는 비극적인 내용이었습니다. 불행히도, 그런 일들은 지방 뉴스 방송이나 지방신문의 뒷면에서나 취급되는 것 외에는 대중매체에서 별 주목을 받지 못하고 있습니다. 그런 일은 이제 "뉴스"도 아닙니다. 너무 자주 일어나는 일인 것입니다. 학교에서 대량 살상이나 생겨야 전국적인 주목 거리가 됩니다. 뉴욕의 타임즈 광장의 상황 변화에 따라 바뀌는 "게시판"을 만들어서 매년 초부터 전국에서 발생한 총기 사망자의 수치를 계속 적어놓는 겁니다. 그 수치는 우발적인 사고나 살인으로 인한 사망과는 구별해도 되겠지요. 수시로 변화하는 메시지는 죽은 날짜, 장소, 희생자의 나이와 관련하여 최근 총기 사망의 세부 사항을 제공해줄 수 있을 것입니다.

19 나는 그런 구절을 말하고 어떤 반응이 나오는지를 지켜보기로 했다. 나는 결과에 늘 실망했다. 그 남자는 대개 멍한 표정으로 나를 바라보며 화제를 바꾸던가 아니면 "그게 무슨 소리야?"라고 물었다. 내가 대답해 주면 그는 "흠, 그런데 왜 그런 걸 외고 있지?"라고 묻곤 했다. 그런 질문은 결코 내가 기대했던 것이 아니었다. 나는 그런 글귀를 듣고 나와 똑같이 느끼는 사람이 있기를 바랐다.

20 마음에 상처를 주는 것은 우리가 무슨 말을 하느냐가 아니라 그 말을 어떻게 하느냐 이다. 남자들은 도전 받고 있다고 느끼면 그들의 신경은 옳다는 데에 집중한 나머지 사랑하는 마음 따위는 역시 잊어버리는 것이 보통이다. 자연히 그는 상대를 배려해주고, 정중하고, 그리고 편안하게 해주는 목소리로 의사를 전달하는 능력이 떨어지게 된다. 그는 자신의 이런 말투가 얼마나 무정하게 들리는지 그리고 이런 것이 여자에게 얼마나 큰 상처가 되는지 알지 못한다. 그럴 때에는 사소한 의견 차이도 여자들에게는 공격으로 받아들여질 수 있게 되어 부탁이 명령으로 들리게 된다. 여자들은 다른 때 같으면 남자들이 하는 말을 충분히 받아들일 수 있는 내용이라도 이런 식의 애정 없는 접근 방식에는 저항감을 느끼게 된다.
남자들은 자기도 모르게 무정한 말투로 말을 해 자신의 아내들에게 상처를 주고 한 술 더 떠서 그녀가 왜 기분 나빠해서는 안 되는지 조목조목 설명한다. 남자들은 사실 그들의 애정 없는 말투에 여자들이 당황해 하면 여자들이 그들의 의견을 무시하는 것으로 잘못 생각한다. 남자들은 여자들의 반응을 이해하지 못하기 때문에 그들이 하는 말투는 고치려고 하지 않고 그들이 하는 말이 옳다는 것만을 설명하는데 기를 쓴다. 남자들은 자기가 한 말을 여자들이 못마땅하게 여기고 있다고 생각하겠지만, 사실 여자들이 언짢아 하는 것은 남자들의 애정 없는 말투이다. 여자들의 반응을 이해하지 못하는 남자들은 말투를 고칠 생각은 전혀 안 하고 자기 말이 왜 옳은지 기를 쓰고 설명하려 한다.

21 저는 14살의 소녀입니다. 저에게는 한 가지 큰 문제가 있습니다. 오늘 아빠와 제가 슈퍼마켓에 갔는데 재미있어 보이는 책이 한 권 눈에 들어왔습니다. 그 책의 제목은 "사랑에서 승리하는 방법"이었습니다. 제 사랑에 문제가 있어서가 아니라 사랑에 대한 호기심이 있어서 그 책을 집어 들었습니다. 그리고 몇 페이지를 읽고 나서 사기로 했습니다. 아빠가 그 책 제목을 보시고는 제게 화를 내셨습니다. 그때 저의 한 언니는 제가 마치 이상한 사람이나 되는 것처럼 저를 보기 시작했습니다. 이제 저는 저의 아빠와 언니가 엄마에게 일러 바칠까 두렵습니다. 그러고 나면 엄마 역시 화를 내게 될 것입니다. 저의 엄마는 제게 학교를 마칠 때까지는 남자친구를 사귀지 말라고 말씀하셨습니다. 제가 단지 호기심에 그런다는 것을 어떻게 말을 해야 될까요? 제가 알기로는 저의 부모님은 두분 모두 제가 남자친구를 사귀기에는 너무 어리다고 생각하고 계십니다. 그러나 그건 그렇지 않습니다. 그 책은 남자들과 결혼에 관한 책이 아닙니다. 그것은 자신을 바꾸고 자기 자신의 삶을 책임지는 것에 관한 책입니다. 제가 사랑에 호기심을 갖는다는 것은 저의 잘못이 아닙니다. 그것은 저의 부모님이 저와 사랑에 대해 대화를 나누려 하지 않기 때문입니다. 제가 사랑에 대하여 무얼 물으면 항상 그분들은 "네가 왜 알고 싶어하는데? 너 남자친구 있어?라고 말씀하십니다. 저는 그게 싫습니다. 만약 제가 부모님과 사랑에 대해서 이야기 조차 나눌 수 없다면 그분들과 어떤 이야기를 나눌 수 있겠습니까? 그럴 수 없다는 것이 가장 마음이 아픕니다.

22 그녀가 회복되어가면서 그 두 사람은 Karen의 집중력을 돕기 위해 카드놀이를 하기 시작했다. 약간의 회복을 위해서라도 오랜 시간동안, 때로는 하루에 여덟 시간까지 놀아주어야 했다. Karen이 회복이 되어가고 있었지만 속도는 더뎠다. 스트레스가 그 두 사람에게 감당하기 힘들 정도가 되어가고 있었다. 아빠가 무엇을 해줄 수 있을까? 어느 날 아침 샤워를 하던 중 그런 생각이 떠올랐다. 사실 그는 의사가

아니었다. 전문 치료사도 아니었다. 하지만 그는 컴퓨터 과학자였다. 그런데 아마도 그 점이 Karen을 가장 많이 도울 수 있었다.

23 그 세미나에서 Sandra는 이렇게 말했다. "저는 20년이라는 세월을 Larry에게 말을 시켜 보려고 애를 쓰면서 보냈어요. 그가 좀 허심탄회하게 마음을 털어놓고 허점도 있는 사람이기를 바랐죠. 제가 그리워한 것은 저로 하여금 속마음을 털어놓고 허점이 있어도 저를 격려해줄 사람이라는 것을 미처 깨닫지 못했던 겁니다. 그걸 제가 정말로 필요로 했던 거예요. 이번 주말에 저는 저의 남편과 지난 20년을 합친 것보다 따뜻한 감정을 더 많이 나누었습니다. 저는 정말 사랑을 받고 있다는 느낌이 들어요. 이것을 제가 그리워해왔던 것입니다. 저는 남편이 달라져야 한다고 생각했었어요. 이제 저는 저의 남편이나 저에게 아무 잘못이 없다는 것을 알게 되었어요. 단지 우리가 서로를 격려하는 방법을 몰랐던 것뿐이었어요."

24 일본에서 35년 이상 살고 있는 작가 겸 교사인 Kerr씨는 오늘날 일본의 거의 모든 측면을 비판하고 있다. 교육제도는 경직되어있고 창의력을 고무시키지 못하고 있으며 권위에 순종하도록 가르치는 것이 교육의 최고 목표가 되고있다. 학생들은 불안감에 시달리며 점차적으로 학교에서 서로를 따돌리고 헐뜯는 경향이 있다. 언론은 당국과 결탁하여 불미스러운 진실들을 은폐하고 있다. 외국인과 외국 사상들은 대체로 불신 받고 폄하 되고있다. Kerr씨는 "입으로는 아무리 국제화를 떠들지언정 일본의 기본 정책은 쇄국"이라고 기술하고 있다. 모두가 타당한 주장이지만 이 책은 약간 지나치게 수선을 피우는 느낌이다. 책의 말미에 가서야 Kerr는 오랫동안 이어져온 일본의 여러 가지 저력을 인정하면서도 거의 항상 마지못해 그렇게 하고 있다.

25 (고아원을) 떠나던 날, 나는 빨강과 하얀 색의 체크 무늬로 가장자리를 장식한 무명 원피스와 발목까지 오는 양말을 받았다. 그런 옷들은 내가 입고 있던 밤색 바지와 셔츠와 마찬가지로 미국 교회가 우리에게 보내 준 헌 옷이었는데 불편하고 낯설었다. 그 원피스는 내게 너무 컸다. 나는 조그맣고 빨간 꽃무늬가 찍힌 초록색 고무신을 신고 내 양부모가 될 사람들의 사진을 받았다. 그리고 나는 '맘(mom)'과 '대드(dad)'를 포함해 몇 가지 간단한 말들도 배웠다. 내가 알고 있었던 것은 그 단어들이 이 사진 속에 있는 낯선 사람들과 관련 있다는 것 뿐이었다.

26 그러나 그 일요일이 지난 후 Gretchen은 다시는 그렇게 외롭다는 것을 느껴 본적이 없었다. 아무리 귀엽다 하더라도 보통 아이는 그렇게 신비롭고 즐겁게 그녀의 기분을 고양시킬 수는 없을 것이라는 사실이 그녀에게 떠올랐던 것 같다. 대신에 그 아이를 그녀의 고통을 이해하고서 그녀의 아픔을 위로하고 낫게 하기 위하여 손을 내민 누군가가 보내었던 것이다. 아마도 그 사람은 Fred였을 것이다.

27 24년 전 Jim Ketler는 전형적인 그리고 적극적인 고등학생 이었다. 그는 고교 축구와 씨름 팀의 주장이었으며, 야구를 했고 트램폴린에 타고난 재능이 있었다. 그는 공중에서 몸을 한 바퀴 반 비틀며 세 바퀴를 회전할 수 있었다. 16살 때에 그의 삶이 영원히 바뀌게 되었다. Jim은 어느 여름 워싱턴의 몬테사노의 소도시에 있는 그의 아버지 목재소에서 일을 하고있었다. Jim은 금요일에는 대개 일하러 가지 않았다. 그러나 그의 아버지가 새벽 4시30분에 그를 깨워서 아버지와 함께 일을 하러 갈 수 있는지를 물었다. Jim은 아버지가 적하기를 운전하고, 전기 톱을 사용하고 그리고 벌목 트럭을 운전하는 것을 돕고 나서 낮잠을 자기 위해 통나무를 집어 올리는 갈고랑 쇠 안으로 기어들어갔다. 그는 그의 발을 한 쪽에 두고 그의 머리는 반대쪽에 두고 해먹처럼 그 안에서 자고 있었다.

28 우정은 이유를 초월한다. 왜냐하면 여러분이 친구에게서 좋은 점들을 발견한다 하더라도 그것들을 발견하기에 앞서 그는 여러분의 친구이기 때문이다. 우정은 우리가 당연히 주어야 하기 때문에 주는 선물인 것이다. 좋은 점에 대한 보답으로 우정을 주는 것은 우정에 값을 매기는 일이 될 것이고, 그리고 그렇게 하는 사람들은 줄 우정도 없는 사람들이다. 만약에 여러분이 덕이 있고 그래서 덕이 있는 사람들과 함께 있는 것을 원하기 때문에 친구를 선택한다면 여러분이 상업적인 이유로 친구를 선택한 것 만큼이나 진정한 우정과는 가까이 있지 않는 사람이다.

29 우리 아버지는 선생님들을 가르쳤다. 그래서 선생님들의 선생님이 되었다. 내 부자 아버지는 늘 젊은 사람들에게 자신의 사업 방식을 가르쳤다. 돌이켜보면 그분들은 아는 것을 너그럽게 주었기 때문에 더 똑똑해졌다. 이 세상에는 우리 보다 훨씬 더 똑똑한 사람들이 많다. 우리가 그곳에 스스로 갈 수도 있지만 그런 사람들의 도움을 받으면 더 쉽다. 여러분에게 필요한 것은 자신에게 있는 것을 너그럽게 주는 것 뿐이다. 그러면 그런 똑똑한 사람들도 우리에게 너그러워질 것이다.

30 과학자들이 그런 질문에 정확한 답을 제시해줄 수 없다는 것이 국민들을 불안하게 하고있다. 모든 자료가 이용가능 하다면 규제결정을 내리는 일은 어렵지 않다. 다만 어려운 것은 그런 불확실한 경우에 정확한 판단을 내릴 수 있느냐 하는 것이다. 공공보건에 역점을 두고 국민의 신뢰를 받는 식품안전규정의 강력한 제도만이 이런 예측할 수 없는 일들을 성공적으로 처리할 수 있다.

31 뒤늦게 서야 "Nightline"의 Ted Koppel은 실제 Mitch Snyder와 마주 앉아서 통계수치의 근거를 물었다. 그때 Snyder는 그것은 언론 매체가 실시하고 있는 조사를 원하는 대로 충족시켜주기 위해 날조한 것이라고 시인했다. 더구나 노숙자 옹호자들은 Snyder가 한 행동을 지지하면서 그런 행동을 "정의를 위한 거짓말"이라고 불렀다. 사람들은 수세기 동안 거짓말을 해오고 있다. 통계수치의 거짓말이 오늘날 이토록 위험한 까닭은 언론 매체에 종사하는 아주 많은 사람들이 운동 단체들이 자신들의 매체의 진보-좌익 성향을 공감하는 경우에 불순한 의도를 가지고 그런 운동단체들이 제시하는 통계수치를 기꺼이 받아들여 방송을 내보내고 있기 때문이다. 잘못된 통계수치는 문제의 일부에 지나지 않는다. 심지어는 정확한 통계수치조차도 사실을 분명하게 부각시키지 않고 오도하는 경우가 있다.

Unit 2 "THOUGH" 이동 ("THOUGH" Movement)

01 호주가 호주의 국가수반을 갖는다는 것은 당연하고 기본적으로 정당하다. 영국 여왕이 정말 훌륭한 분이긴 하지만 계속해서 우리의 국가 수반이 된다는 것은 불합리하고 옳지도 않다. 나는 압도적인 다수의 호주인들이 이런 제안을 받아들이고 있다고 믿고 있다. 그리고 사실 거의 모든 호주인들은 이런 문제와 관련된 모든 사실에 접근할 기회가 주어진다면 그런 제안을 받아들일 것으로 믿고 있다.

02 이와 같은 조사 결과는 평등주의와 관련이 있는지는 모르겠지만 당초 여권주의의 명분 아래 설계된 화려한 신세계에는 좋은 징조가 못 된다. 이 결과는 수많은 미국 여성들의 소위 '해방된' 생활이 엄청난 그리고 어쩌면 너무나 과중한 대가를 치르고 있다는 것을 시사하고 있다. 이런 해방된 여성들은 절망감으로부터 욕망에 이르는 여러 가지 이유로 인해 물경 75%에 이르는 이 나라의 아이들을 어떤 형태의 탁아 시설에 맡기는 것을 적합한 것으로 생각하고 완전 고용된 직장생활을 확대하거나 유지하고 있다. 과학적으로 측정된 행동불량 성향이 가장 높은 어린이들은 실제로 어린 시절을 탁아 시설에서 일주일에 30시간 이상 지낸 아이들이라는 점을 비추어 볼 때 이번 연구는 바로 이런 엄마들에게 아주 간곡하게 호소하고 있다.

03 한 부자 상인의 집에서 어린애들의 파티가 있었는데 부잣집과 신분이 높은 사람들의 자식들이 그곳에 있었다. 그 상인은 아버지가 그를 대학에 보내주고 시험에 합격을 해서 제법 학식이 있는 사람이었다. 그의 아버지는 처음에는 소장수였다. 그러나 항상 정직하고 근면했다. 그래서 그는 돈을 벌게 되었다. 그리고 상인으로서 그의 아들이 그의 가게를 용케 잘 키웠다. 그는 약삭빠르기도 했지만 인정이 있었다. 하지만 사람들은 그의 인정보다는 그의 돈에 대한 이야기를 많이 했습니다. 지적인 사람뿐만 아니라 집안이 좋은 모든 부류의 사람들이 그 상인의 집에서 머물렀다. 이런 내세울만한 것들 중 아무 것도 없는 사람들 일부도 그곳에서 머물렀다.

04 Presely는 즉시 테이블에서 일어나 모자를 쓰고 서둘러 거리로 나갔다. 그곳에는 이미 가로등이 불을 밝히고 있었다. 그러나 Presely는 찾고자 했지만 다시는 그 젊은 여인을 만날 수가 없었다. 그는 그 여자인 불행한 독일인의 딸을 보았던 생각을 했

다. 마침내 그는 찾는 것을 포기하고 이 시간에는 거의 아무도 없는 클럽으로 돌아오며 담배 몇 대를 피웠다. 그리고 도서관에 있는 많은 에세이들 중에서 일부를 골라 읽으려고 했지만 그렇게 되지않았다. 결국은 초조함과, 산만함으로 기진맥진해 잠자리에 들었다.

05 이번에는 우리 아이가 수술에서 깨어나지 못했습니다. 수술이 끝나고 얼마 후 그는 죽었습니다. 이 아이를 떠나 보낸다는 것이 정말 괴로운 일이었지만 남편과 나의 관계는 여전히 원만합니다. 우리 아이 Derian이 우리에게 서로를 보다 더 깊이 사랑할 수 있는 선물을 준 것 같았습니다. 그런 고통에도 불구하고 우리는 여전히 기도, 기적, 위대한 신, 그리고 무엇보다도 우리가 지금 Derian이라는 꼬마천사로부터 받고 있는 영적 지도를 믿고 있습니다.

06 며칠 후에 그는 제네바 참사회장으로 임명되었다. 그는 결코 줄어들지 않는 열정으로 종무(宗務)를 처리했다. 그는 불쌍한 사람들을 애정으로 보살피고 고해실에서는 가장 낮은 자들의 요구에 특별한 관심을 가지고 헌신했다. 그의 설교의 말투는 아주 간결해서 듣는 사람들을 매료시켰다. 그는 학자이었지만 설교를 일반적으로 라틴어와 그리스어 인용을 자제하고 그리고 신학적으로 미묘한 점들의 언급을 자제했다.

07 내 아내 Bonnie는 '기분이 우울해지는' 이런 경험은 마치 캄캄한 우물 속으로 들어가는 듯한 느낌이라고 말한다. 여자들이 자신의 우물 속으로 들어갈 때 의식적으로 무의식의 세계와 어두움 그리고 혼란스러운 감정 속으로 빠져들어가고 있는 것이다. 여자들은 갑자기 많은 설명할 수 없는 감정과 분명치 않은 느낌을 경험할지도 모른다. 그리고 어쩌면 아무도 없는 곳에 혼자 외로이 있다거나 혹은 아무런 지지도 받지 못하고 있다고 생각하며 절망감을 느낄 지도 모른다. 그러나 곧 절망의 맨 밑바닥에 닿은 후 자신이 사랑을 받고 있고 지지를 받고 있다는 느낌이 들면 자신도 모르게 기분이 더 좋아지기 시작할 것이다. 갑자기 여자의 기분이 와르르 무너졌다 하더라도 여자들은 자신도 모르게 기분이 좋아져서 자신과 맺은 관계 속에서 다시 사랑을 발산할 수 있게 될 것이다.

08 미국의 Thompson 보건-인간 봉사부 장관이 직접 장기기증운동을 시작했던 4월17일 현재 7만5863명의 미국인이 장기의 기증을 기다리고 있었다. 지난해 5500명 이상의 미국인이 장기이식을 기다리다 사망했다. 현재 더 많은 장기 기증자가 시급하게 필요하다. 그리고 장기를 기증하는 방법만 알아도 금년에 수천명의 목숨을 구할 수 있을 것이다. Thompson 장관이 주도하는 이번 일은 학교와 기업체와 같은 곳에 장기기증에 관한 지식을 확산시키는데 목적이 있다. 그는 또 이식 전문 의사들과 협력하여 장기를 필요로 하는 사람들을 돕기 위해 연구를 확대할 계획이다. 그러나 Thompson장관이 주도하는 이번 일은 그 명분이 훌륭함에도 불구하고 이번 운동 계획이 수반하는 여러 가지 일들이 잘못 알려져 논란에 휘말리고 있다.

09 그가 떠난 뒤에 나는 방으로 갔다. 얼마 후 나는 아무 소리도 듣지 못하고 밖으로 나와 남쪽을 향해 바라볼 수 있는 돌계단으로 올라갔다. 협소한 안마당의 어두움과 비교해볼 때에 내가 접근할 수 는 없었지만 광활하게 확 트여 있어서 다소 자유스런 느낌이 들었다. 이런 광경을 보면서 나는 사실 감옥에 갇혀있다는 느낌이 들었고 밤이었지만 신선한 공기를 마시고 싶다는 생각이 들었다. 나는 이런 야행성의 생활이 나에게 영향을 주고 있다는 것을 느끼기 시작하고있다. 그것은 나의 신경을 파괴하고 있는 것이다. 나는 내 그림자를 보고 놀라서 온갖 무시무시한 상상으로 가득 차 있다.

10 Rostov는 이전에 전투를 시작하면 두려운 느낌이 들었으나 이제는 두려운 감정 같은 것은 전혀 없었다. 그가 두려움을 느끼지 않는 것은 포화에 익숙해 있기 때문이 아니라--위험에 익숙해진다는 것은 있을 수 없기 때문에--위험에 직면했을 때 자기의 사고를 조절할 수 있는 방법을 터득했기 때문이다. 그는 전투를 하면서 그의 주의를 가장 끌 것 같은 일은 제외하고 즉 당면한 위험만은 제외하고 그 밖의 온갖 것을 생각하는 습관을 들였던 것이다. 그가 처음 군복무를 할 때에 아무리 노력해도 그리고 아무리 자신의 소심함을 질책해도 이것을 터득할 수 없었으나 해가 감에 따라 지금은 저절로 그러한 기분이 될 수 있었다.

11 그 동안 그 꽃은 창가에서 시들어가며 잊혀졌다. 그리고 마침내 그 꽃은 살던 사람들이 이사 가던 날 거리의 쓰레기 더미로 내버려졌다. 이 가엾은 꽃은 비록 시들었지만 우리의 꽃다발과 합쳐지게 되었다. 왜냐하면 그 꽃은 여왕의 정원에 있는 가장 아름다운 꽃 보다 더 큰 진정한 기쁨을 주었기 때문이다.

12 이런 주장의 일부는 사실과 유리되어 있고 아직 입증된 것도 없지만 유럽의 다른 지역에 살고 있는 소비자들은 동물 사료 속에 들어가는 내용물과 관련해서 이보다 훨씬 더 무시무시한 이야기를 듣고 있다. 지난 주 네덜란드에서는 식당이나 병원에서 나오는 식용 폐기물인 구정물이 1986년 이래 사용하지 못하도록 금지되어 있음에도 불구하고 아직도 돼지 사료로 사용되고 있다는 보도가 있었다. 지난 주 스페인의 한 텔레비전 방송국은 Andalucia에서는 동물 사육원에서 나온 죽은 애완 동물들이 사료로 재활용 되고 있다는 주장을 보도했다.

13 마찬가지로 그녀의 부모는 그녀가 돌아와 그들과 함께 살 것으로 생각했기 때문에 당혹스러워 했다. 그들은 딸을 대단히 사랑했었지만 한 집에서 함께 산다는 것은 잘못 된 일이 될 거라는 생각이 들었다. 그러나 Margaret는 독립해서 살기로 하고 노팅힐게이트의 다소 허름한 하숙집에다 방을 구하기 전에 일주일 동안만 부모님과 함께 살았다. 그러나 임대료는 비쌌지만 이렇게 하는 것이 중요한 일이라는 것을 알고 있었다. 그리고 나서 그녀는 친구 Julia가 해준 충고에 따라 지하철 역 근처에 있는 고용기관에 등록했다.

14 상대방이 보는 것처럼 상황을 볼 수 있는 능력은 어려운 일일 수도 있겠지만 협상자가 가질 수 있는 가장 중요한 기량 중의 하나이다. 상황을 서로 다르게 보고 있다는 것을 아는 것만으로는 충분치 못하다. 당신이 상대방을 움직이려 한다면, 상대방의 견해를 잘 이해하는 동시에 상대방이 그 견해를 믿고있는 감정의 세기도 느낄 수 있어야 한다. 그것은 현미경으로 딱정벌레를 들여다보듯이 상대방을 들여다보는 것만으로는 충분하지 못하다. 오히려 딱정벌레가 된다는 것이 어떤 느낌인지도 알아야 한다. 이 일을 하려면 상대방의 견해를 시험해보며 잠시 판단을 유보할 준비가 되어 있어야 한다. 당신이 당신의 견해가 옳다고 믿고 있는 것 만큼이나 상대방도 자신의 견해가 옳다는 믿는 것은 당연한 일이다. 당신은 식탁 위에 냉수가 반이나 담긴 컵을 보고 있는데, 당신의 아내는 마호가니 식탁에 원형의 물자국을 남길 지저분하고 절반이 비어있는 컵을 보고 있을 수도 있다.

15 최근에 나는 게잇웨이 컴퓨터 한 대를 구입했는데 그 컴퓨터는 운영체제 윈도우 ME를 사용하고 있다. 문제는 바로 이것이다. 때때로 철자 A키와 Caps Lock키가 연결되어있어서 A를 한 번 치면 Caps Lock이 켜지고 다시 A를 치면 Caps Lock이 꺼

진다. 연속해서 A를 치면 이와 같다. AaAaAaAa. 이상하게 시작되는 것처럼 이상하게 멈추어버렸다. 이런 일이 자주 일어났다. 우리는 키보드 새것을 사용해 보기고 하고 윈도우 운영체제를 다시 설치하기도 했다. 무엇 때문이냐?

16 그러나 Theseus는 위대한 영웅이었음에도 불구하고 그의 아버지의 뒤를 이어 왕이 되었을 때에 소란을 피우는 아테네 사람들을 통제할 수 없었다. 그는 나이가 들어 그 도시에서 쫓겨나 유배의 몸으로 죽었다. 나중에 그의 동포들이 그가 했던 모든 공로를 잊지 않고 기억했다가 도의적인 면에서 그의 시신을 다시 가져와 신의 대열에 넣었다.

17 그러나 그녀는 위험으로부터 구출되었지만 마치 또 다른 위험에 빠져든 것 같았다. 술탄은 그녀에게 말을 한 마리 주도록 명령했다. 그리고 그녀를 그의 궁궐로 데리고 가서 그곳에 있는 아름다운 방으로 그녀를 안내해주었다. 술탄은 여자 하인들을 뽑아 그녀의 시중을 들도록 했고 환관들을 뽑아 그녀를 보호하도록 했다. 그리고 나서 술탄은 그가 한 행동에 대해서 그녀에게 감사의 말을 할 시간도 주지 않고 그녀가 했던 모험이야기를 다음날 해달라며 쉬도록 했다.

18 나는 내가 결점이 많다는 것을 정확히 알고 있었다. 한국에서는 짐승만도 못한 존재였다. 그리고 나는 이교도였다. 나는 어느 누구에게도 좋은 사람이 아니었고 나는 완전히 절망감에 빠져있었다. 나는 어떤 사람의 기준에도 부합되지 못했다. 부모님은 내가 하느님의 형상대로 재창조되기 위해 한국에서 구원된 것이라고 하셨지만 나는 충분히 잘 빚어질 만한 점토는 아니었다. 이런 모든 이야기가 되풀이 되는 것 같지만 그 집에서 보낸 내 삶이 얼마나 단조로운 것이었는가는 도저히 말로 표현할 수 없었다. 나는 똑 같은 리듬으로 끝없이 돌아가는 수레바퀴에 갇힌 기분이었다.

19 지난해 저의 부모님은 회갑연을 갖았습니다. 적당한 선물을 찾는다는 것은 정말 힘든 일이었습니다. 저의 여동생이 추억으로 가득한 스크랩북을 해드리자고 제안했습니다. 저의 형제들은 8남매인데 각각 자기들이 선택한 추억들로 3페이지씩 채우도록 할당 받았습니다. 저는 아무리 노력을 해도 제가 맡은 페이지에 채워넣을 추억거리를 생각해낼 수가 없었습니다. 결국 저는 저의 부모님께 이런 편지를 썼는

데, 사랑하고 소중히 하는 부모님이 있는 모든 분들을 위해 당신이 그 편지를 실어 줄길 희망합니다.

20 이것은 우리들이 밤에 연안에서 상륙하는 것이 불가능하다는 것을 확인케 해주었다. 그런데 낮엔 어떻게 해서 상륙하느냐, 이것 또한 큰 문제가 아닐 수 없었다. 왜냐하면 야만인의 손에 잡히는 것은 사자나 표범한테 당하는 것과 다를 바 없는 일이었기 때문이다. 적어도 우리들은 야만인에게 잡히는 위험이나 야수에게 당하는 위험은 똑같이 염려하고 있었다. 어쨌든 물을 구하기 위하여 어디든 상륙하지 않으면 안 되었다. 배에는 1바인트(약 반 리터)의 물도 남아 있지 않았기 때문이었다. 그런데 언제 어디서 물을 구하느냐가 문제였다.

21 그러나 Marx는 사회주의는 피할 수 없다는 확고한 믿음을 가진 과학자 이면서 동시에 철학자이었지만 단순한 연구가가 아니었다. 그는 1848년 독일혁명에 참여했고 그 해의 혁명을 준비하는데 적극적이었으며 그의 시대를 위해 가능한 경우에는 언제든지 자본주에 대한 노동자들의 투쟁에 참여했다. 그는 항상 그런 투쟁을 사회주의 혁명의 준비로 알고 있었다. 파리의 노동자들이 파리 코뮌을 수립했던 1871년에 Marx는 그것을 인류역사상 가장 위대한 사건중의 하나라고 일컬었다.

22 아마도 여러분들은 내가 왜 영화 'Clash of the Titan'으로부터 강력한 제우스신을 인용해서 페르세우스에 대해서 이야기를 하고 있는지 궁금해 할지도 모르겠다. 왜냐하면 이것은 분명히 헤라클레스 아들의 영화이기 때문이다. 그리고 페르세우스는 그리스의 위대한 영웅임에도 불구하고 헤라클레스의 아들은 아니었다. 틀림없이 어떤 관련이 있다. 아무튼 헤라클레스는 죽을 운명의 한 여인과 호색가인 제우스사이에서 태어났다. 페르세우스도 마찬가지였다. 헤라클레스는 아버지의 부정 때문에 화가 난 제우스의 아내인 헤라로부터 화를 샀다.

Unit 3 "WITH" 주술관계 ("WITH" Nexus)

01 뒤 이은 합의에 의하면 팔레스타인인들은 유대국가 제거를 요구하는 문구를 국가 설립 강령에서 삭제하는데 동의했으며 이스라엘인들은 추가로 서안 지구의 13%에 해당하는 영토를 양보하는데 동의했다. 동시에 최종적인 평화 협정을 체결하기 위하여 2000년 9월 13일까지의 최종기한을 정해두었다. 2000년 중반 평화협정의 그 최종기한은 다가오고 협상타결의 기미가 보이지 않자 Clinton은 메릴랜드 대통령 휴양지인 캠프 데이비드에서 열릴 3자 정상회담에 Barak와 Arafat를 초청했다. 이 회담은 7월 11일에 시작해서 양측이 주로 예루살렘의 주권 및 관할권 문제를 놓고 교착상태에 빠진 가운데 아무 협정도 가시화 되지 못하고 15일 후 끝났다.

02 8개월 후 1994년 11월 26일 71세의 Margaret Garrish는 Kevorkian이 보는 가운데 일산화탄소 중독으로 죽었다. Garrish는 스물 한번째로 Kevorkian으로부터 도움을 받은 사람이었다. Kevorkian의 말에 의하면 그때부터 그는 이들 외에도 백 명 이상을 일산화탄소를 흡입케 하거나 정맥에 독극물을 투입해서 죽는 것을 도와 주었다는 것이다. 그의 이런 일은 1998년 9월 17일 Thomas Youk이 죽으면서 절정에 이른다. 왜냐하면 Kevorkian자신이 그 쉰 두 살 먹은 사람에게 치사량의 화학물질을 주입하는 장면을 녹화해서 나중에 CBS의 "60 Minutes"이라는 프로에서 Mike Wallace에게 틀어주었기 때문이다.

03 저는 이웃에 사는 사람들과 그들의 아이 때문에 괴롭습니다. 남편과 저는 활동적이고 외향적이어서 뜰 일이나 정원 일 같은 일을 좋아합니다. 그런데 이 이웃 사람들은 우리와 완전히 반대입니다. 그들은 주말을 대부분 소파에 파묻혀 지내면서 자기들이 얼마나 게으른지 과시하고 있지요. 우리가 밖에서 아이들하고 놀고 있으면, 그들은 우리가 오라고 하지도 않고 오는 걸 원하지도 않는데 자기들의 아이를 보냅니다. 저는 평생 아이들을 싫어한 적이 없지만, 그 애는 버릇이 없고, 무례하며 예의가 없어서, 솔직히 말해 우리 아이들과 함께 놀지 않았으면 하는 그런 아이입니다. 그 애는 부모의 보살핌을 제대로 받지 못했다는 것을 저는 알고 있습니다. 그래서 그에게 동정을 느끼지 않을 수 없습니다. 그래도 그 애가 우리 집에 오지 않았으면 좋겠어요. 저는 "네 이웃을 미워하라"는 관계를 시작하고 싶지 않기 때문에 그 애의 부모님께 무슨 말을 해야 할지 모르겠어요. 남편은 조용히 살기 위

해 그런 것을 참을 수 있지만, 이제 여름도 다가오면서 그것이 더 심해지리라는 것을 저는 알고 있습니다.

04 이 모든 집단들이 미국인을 구성하고 있음에도 불구하고 미국 사회가 아주 동질적이라는 점이 놀랍게 보일 지도 모른다. 미국 문화는 전형적인 특징이 있는데, 아마도 가장 주요한 특징 중 하나는 모든 다양한 특성들을 혼합해서 미국의 관습과 이상을 만들어 내고 있다는 점이다.

05 Rudy는 강물이 턱 있는 데까지 넘실대는 가운데 다리의 가장자리를 움켜잡고, 단단한 다리 표면 위로 몸을 끌어올리려고 안간힘을 썼다. 그러나 그는 몸을 움직일 수 없었다. 그는 자기의 왼쪽 다리가 견지낚시용 모터를 고정시키기 위해 사용했던 굵은 노란색 견인용 밧줄에 얽혀있다는 사실을 깨닫지 못하고 있었다. 모터 보트가 누르는 무게는 닻과 같았으며 그의 하체를 다리 밑으로 끌어당기고 있었다. 한 편으로 그는 머리가 수면 아래 잠기지 않도록 하기 위해 버둥거리고 있었다. 설상가상으로 고무보트의 나머지 절반이 Rudy의 등 뒤로 접히고 보트와 그녀의 몸 사이에 커다란 낚시 도구 상자가 쐐기처럼 박혀서 그의 머리와 양 어깨를 두드려대고 있었다.

06 그 물체는 소리없이 출발했다. 그리고 Delgado는 그의 순찰차로 돌아왔는데, 그의 말에 의하면 그의 도움 없이 그 차 안의 점화장치와 여러 개의 등과 그리고 경찰 무선 통신기가 저절로 다시 켜졌다는 것이다. Delgado가 도와 달라고 무선 연락을 한 지 4분 후인 새벽 3시 56분에 세 대의 순찰차가 요란한 소리를 내며 왔다. Bartley 경사는 Delgado가 그의 순찰차에 앉아서 문을 열어 놓고 부들부들 떨고 있는 것을 발견했다. 그날 아침 늦게 Delgado는 신체검사와 정신 진단을 받았는데 그 중 어떤 것에서도 부상이나 정신이상의 증거는 발견되지 않았다. Bartley경사는 지금은 경찰에서 퇴직했지만 Delgado의 말을 믿을 수 있다고 단언하고 있다. 그래서 그는 Delgado가 그날 새벽에 이상한 물체를 그 곳에서 보았다는 것을 의심치 않는다고 이야기를 하고있다.

07 몹쓸 장난을 좋아하는 한 양치기 소년이 있었다. 그 소년은 마을에서 상당히 떨어져 있는 곳으로 양 떼를 몰고 가서, 늑대가 양 떼를 습격했다고 말하면서 마을 사람들에게 도와달라고 외치곤 했다. 두 세 번이나 마을 사람들은 놀라서 부랴부랴 달

려왔다가 되돌아 가고 양치기 소년은 그들을 보고 재미있어 했다. 그러나 결국은 몇 마리의 늑대가 실제로 나타나게 되었다. 늑대들이 양치기 소년과 양 떼들 사이로 뛰어들자 소년은 그를 도와 달라고 이웃 사람들을 불렀다. 그러나 사람들은 의례 장난을 치는 것으로 생각하고 아무도 그 소년을 염려하지 않았다. 그래서 소년은 그의 양을 잃게 되었다.

08 그가 죽은 다음날, 모든 여자들은 우리의 관습대로 그 집을 방문해서 조의를 표하고 도와줄 준비를 했다. Emily양은 문 앞에서 그들을 맞이했는데 평상시와 똑같은 옷차림으로 얼굴엔 슬픈 흔적조차 찾아볼 수 없었다. 그녀는 사람들에게 아버지는 돌아가지 않으셨다고 말했다. 그녀는 사흘동안이나 그렇게 했다. 그래서 목사들이 그녀를 찾아갔고 의사들은 그녀에게 자신들이 시신을 처리하도록 해달라며 설득하기 위해 애를 쓰고 있었다. 그들이 법과 완력에 호소하려 하자 그녀가 포기를 했고 그래서 그들은 곧 그녀의 아버지의 시신을 땅에 묻어 주게 되었다.

09 Tom은 이야기가 진행되는 동안 서서 마치 꿈을 꾸고있는 사람처럼 그의 두 손을 들어 올리고 눈을 크게 뜨고 있었다. 서서히 그리고 점차 그 이야기의 의미가 그에게 와 닿게 되면서 그는 그의 낡은 의자에 앉기보다는 오히려 의자 위에 쓰러지고 말았다. 그리고 그의 무릎 위에 머리를 떨구었다.

10 물은 차가웠고 홍수로 범람하였다. 그리고 강물이 불어나면서 강 뚝 멀리 떠다니던 많은 물건들이 흘러 지나갔다. 나는 운 좋게도 매달릴 수 있는 육중한 통나무 하나를 붙잡을 수 있었다. 그래서 나는 그 통나무 위에 턱을 받친 채 얼음처럼 차가운 물 속에 누워서. 두 손으로 최대한 힘 안 드는 자세로 통나무를 움켜지고 있었다. 나는 경련이 일지나 않을까 염려하면서 물가로 나아가길 바랬었다. 나는 긴 곡선을 그리면서 강을 떠내려갔다. 날이 충분히 밝아 오기 시작하였다. 그래서 나는 물가 주변의 잡목 숲을 볼 수 있었다.

11 Anne Sterling 부인은 두 남자를 쫓아 숲 속으로 뛰어 들어가면서 자신이 처하게 될 위험을 생각하지 않았다. 그들은 그녀가 핸드백을 가지고 숲 가장자리에서 소풍을 즐기던 중 그녀에게 달려들었다. 실랑이를 벌이던 중에 가방 끈이 끊어졌고 가방이 그들 손아귀에 들어오자 두 남자는 나무사이로 도망치기 시작했다. Anne Sterling

부인은 너무나 화가 나서 그들을 뒤쫓았다. 그녀는 숨이 차 왔으나, 계속해서 달렸다. 그녀가 그들을 따라잡았을 때, 그들은 앉아서 가방의 내용물을 꺼내보고 있었다. 그래서 그녀는 그들을 향해 똑바로 달려갔다. 그 두 남자는 너무 놀라서 가방을 떨어뜨리고 도망갔다. '가방 끈을 수선해야 겠지만 아무것도 훔쳐가진 않았어요.' 라고 부인은 말했다.

12 "외국어를 읽는 방법"에 관한 도입부에서 저자들은 여러분들이 문법 형식을 선별해서 단어 하나씩 읽는 것보다는 오히려 단어군 별로 읽을 수 있는 능력을 개발해야 된다는 것을 언급했습니다. 이러한 방법으로 하게 되면 여러분들은 보다 더 빠르게 그리고 이해를 더 잘하며 읽게 될 것입니다. 이러한 능력개발에 도움이 되려면 여러분의 선생님이 큰소리로 다음 문장들을 읽는 동안 여러분들은 책을 덮고 들으십시오.

13 은 공황이었던 1893년도까지는 모든 일이 잘 되어갔다. 그러나 미국은 은을 더 이상 화폐의 본위로 사용하지 않았다. 은의 가격이 내려가면서 Tabor는 Matchless 탄광을 운영할 수 없게 되었다. 그는 사치스러운 생활을 하는데 그의 모든 돈을 써버렸기 때문에 덴버에서 일당 노동자로 일을 하는 수 밖에 없었다. 소문에 의하면 한 번은 그와 Baby Doe가 집에 먹을 것이 없었을 때 (위자료) 120만 달러로 편안하게 살고 있던 그의 조강지처가 그들이 온 겨울을 지낼 수 있도록 마차 1대분의 식량을 보냈다고 한다.

14 커다란 차 한 대가 헤드라이트를 켜고, 경적을 울리며 상점가를 따라 오면서 갑자기 침묵이 깨졌다. 그 차는 보석상점 앞(밖)에서 멈추었다. 한 명은 운전석에 그대로 머물러 있었고, 다른 두 명은 얼굴에 검은 스타킹을 뒤집어 쓴 채 차 밖으로 뛰어내려 쇠파이프로 상점 유리를 깼다. 이 일들이 벌어지는 동안, Taylor씨는 위층에 있었다. 그와 그의 직원은 창문 밖으로 가구들을 던지기 시작했다. 의자와 탁자들이 상점 안으로 날아들어 갔다. 도둑들 중 한 명이 무거운 조각상에 맞았지만, 그는 다이아몬드를 훔치느라 정신이 없어서 아무런 아픔도 느끼지 못했다. 이 약탈은 도둑들이 차로 돌아가 놀라운 속도로 사라짐으로써 3분만에 끝났다. 차가 막 떠나려고 할 때에 Taylor씨는 서둘러 재떨이와 꽃병을 던지며 그들을 쫓았지만, 도둑들을 멈춰 세우는 것은 불가능했다. 그들은 수천만 파운드에 달하는 다이아몬드를 가지고 도망쳤다.

15 소방 대원들의 말에 의하면 한 아이로 인해서 수요일 밤 남 오스틴에서 주택 화재가 발생했다는 것이다. 대원들이 화재를 신속히 진압했지만 화재로 인해서 7만 달러 상당의 피해가 있었다. 서른 여섯의 한 남자는 손에 2도 화상을 입었지만 상태가 괜찮다. 그의 여섯 살 된 딸은 상태가 좋지만 연기를 많이 마셔 치료를 받고 있는 중이다. 다른 세 명의 아이들은 사고 현장에서 바로 치료를 받아야만 했었다.

16 그들은 출발했다. 이번에는 그가 앞장을 섰다. 그리고 그들이 그 작은 거실에 다시 도착했을 때 그녀는 그녀가 잘 알고 있는 배낭에 그가 속옷과 슬리퍼를 챙겨넣는 것을 보았다. 필사적이었지만 예의 바르게 그녀는 그가 얼굴이 상기된 채 하는 모든 행동들을 지켜보았다. 그는 그녀를 안심시키기 위해 그녀의 목에 손을 얹었다.

17 목격자들 말에 의하면 200여명 이상의 약탈자들이 다른 폭도들이 불을 질러 놓은 백화점에 갇혀 죽었다고 한다. 친척들이 그들 주변에서 오열하고 있는 가운데 주민들이 시신을 거두기 위해 모여들었다. 그러나 시신들은 검게 타서 알아볼 수가 없었다. 그리고 경찰관들과 구조대원 들은 동부 자카르타의 Kelender구역의 빈민가 근처에 위치하고 있는 그 백화점 어디에서도 볼 수 없었다. 지난 주 수하르토 대통령이 수 십년 만의 인도네시아 최악의 경제위기를 극복하기 위해 국제 통화 기금이 부여한 430억 달러의 구조개혁안의 새로운 긴축 정책을 도입한 후에 불안이 심화되었다.

18 그것은 조그마한 창문이었습니다. 그런데 강풍이 급습해올 때 창문이 깨지는 것을 막기 위하여 조그마한 종이 조각들이 창문을 가로질러 붙여져 있었습니다. 중앙에 종이조각이 붙여지지 않고 남아 있던 작은 공간에다 안경을 낀 작은 남자가 조심스럽게 시계를 진열하고 있었습니다. 그러나 그는 또 하루를 서둘러 시작하는 많은 런던 사람들에게 전혀 주의를 기울이지 않고 있었습니다.

19 주교들은 Milingo가 서약을 배반했다고 말했다 왜냐하면 그는 여전히 성직자로서의 의무를 지켜야 하는 신분이었기 때문이었다. 잠비아 로마 가톨릭교의 대변인인 Denis Dejong 주교는 Milingo가 결혼을 함으로써 교회에 등을 돌린 것이라고 말했다. "이렇게 하여 Milingo는 스스로 가톨릭교를 떠났다. 우리는 전 대주교인

Milingo를 신뢰했지만 지금은 배신당하고 버림받았다고 생각하는 많은 사람들과 공감한다"고 Dejong 주교는 말했다. Milingo는 오랫동안 로마 가톨릭 교회의 제도와 사이가 좋지 않았다. 그는 루사카의 대주교로 있는 동안 신앙 치료와 주술을 펼쳐 교황청과 마찰을 일으켜왔다. 그는 1983년 압력에 못 이겨 사임했는데 이런 일은 정년이 안된 나이와 건강 상태가 좋은 대주교로서는 매우 드문 경우였다. 그런 다음 그는 이주자와 떠돌아 다니는 사람들을 치료하는 주교 위원회의 일원으로 로마에 오게 되었다. 그러면서도 그는 치료와 주술 모임을 계속했다. 지난 해 Milingo는 조용히 그 자리에서 물러났다.

20 남부는 여러 가지로 대조를 이루고 있는 땅이다. 이곳에서는 아직도 지난 세기의 유적인 몇 개의 농장저택을 볼 수 있을 것이다. 이런 건물들의 특징은 하얀 기둥들이 현관을 받치고 있다. 그런 집은 종종 봄에 만발한 많은 관목들이 있는 아름다운 정원으로 둘러싸여있다. 남부에는 역시 백인이나 흑인 소작인들의 페인트칠이 안된 오두막집들이 있고, 그런 집들 옆에는 조그마한 담배 밭이나 목화 밭이 있다.

21 나의 성장한 아이들은 자신들의 문제들은 스스로 풀려고 한다. 그리고 좀처럼 내게 도움을 청하러 오지 않는다. 내 아내의 아이들은 그들 결혼 생활에 문제가 생기면 우리 집에서 머무른다. 한 아이는 지금 몇 달째 우리와 함께 지내고 있다. 또 다른 아이는 우리가 일주일에 두세 번은 애들을 보살펴주어야 하는 것으로 생각하고 있다. 내가 아내에게 무슨 말을 하면 그녀는 기분 상해한다. 나는 이제 은퇴를 했다. 그래서 나는 나의 가정이 나의 아내와 내가 우리의 은퇴를 즐길 수 있도록 돌아가길 바란다. 나는 은퇴를 즐기기 위해 40여년을 일했다. 지금 나는 은퇴생활의 하루 하루가 싫다. 나는 그녀와 헤어질 것을 고려하고 있다. 하지만 현재의 법대로라면 그녀가 나의 퇴직금의 절반은 받게 될 것이다. 그런데 그녀는 나의 퇴직금을 위해 한 일은 아무것도 없었다. 하루가 지나갈 때마다 나는 재혼을 하지 않았더라면 좋았을 텐데 라고 생각한다. 나는 혼자 살았더라면 지금 보다 더 행복했을 것이다.

22 금세기가 저물어 가면서 다음 세기의 여러 가지 도전들이 이미 나타나고 있다. 1989년 소련 연방이 몰락하면서 이전의 공산주의 국가들이 아주 오랫동안 억압 받아왔던 주체성과 민족성에 대한 의식을 열망하게 되었다. 그 이후 이 십여 개국 이상이 독립을 하게 되었고 새로운 민족주의 도래를 알리게 되었다. 이런 민족주의는 칭찬할 만한 것이면서도 그 자체가 지난 십년 동안 불안정과 국지적 갈등의 주

요한 원인이 되어왔고, 그리고 앞으로도 수 십년 동안 불안의 요인이 될 것임을 보여주고 있다.

23 우리들 대부분은 예를 들어 우리들이 집을 나설 때는 모자를 쓰는 습관을 갖게 된다. 그리고 우리가 계속해서 그렇게 하는 것은 우리의 머리를 날씨로부터 보호하기 위해서 라기 보다는 오히려 우리가 어린 시절부터 항상 그렇게 해왔기 때문이다. 요즈음 모자를 쓰지 않고 돌아다니는 사람들이 많이 있지만 여전히 그들에 대해 거부감을 갖는 편견이 팽배해 있다.

24 나는 내가 옳다고 믿고 너는 네가 옳다고 믿는다면 우리는 이런 믿음의 차이를 이용할 수 있다. 우리 양측이 각각 승리를 자신한다면, 공정한 중재자로 하여금 그 문제를 해결하도록 하는데 동의할 수 있을 것이다. 만약 노조 지도부의 두 파가 어떤 임금 제안을 놓고 의견 일치를 볼 수 없다면 그들은 그 문제를 회원들의 투표에 일임하는데 합의할 수 있다.

25 벽장 정리가 마무리되고 양복장이 텅 비면서 그 방에서 외로움이 스며 나왔다. 아빠는 이제 떠나고 안 계신다. 그리고 그분이 쓰시던 물건들이 하나씩 없어지고 있고 내 인생의 새로운 시대가 시작되고 있었다. 여러분은 정말로 사랑하는 사람이 더 이상 없다면 다시 말해 여러분이 그를 가장 필요로 할 때에 그 사람이 그곳에 없다면 어떻게 하나요? "아빠, 사랑해요."라고 말하기 위해 전화를 하면 이제는 누가 그 전화를 받아줄까요?

26 나는 수술을 받고 작은 오두막집으로 돌아와 오랜 회복기를 가졌다. 그 동안 나는 등을 대고 누워 있거나 똑바로 서있을 수 밖에 없었다. Leigh가 요리와 빨래를 맡아 했고 그 애만의 독특한 방식으로 거의 24시간 꼬박 나를 간호해 주었다. 딸애는 내게 셰익스피어를 읽어주었다. 딸애는 우리가 함께 마실 차를 끓이고 불과 몇 년 전 내가 책을 읽어 줄 때 그랬던 것처럼 손에 책을 든 채 잔뜩 쌓아 둔 베개 위에 웅크리고 누웠다.

27 때는 1991년이었으며, 피닉스의 부동산 시장은 엉망이었다. 사람들은 모두 집을 헐값에 팔고 있었다. 나는 나의 동창생에게 뮤추얼펀드에 있는 돈의 일부로 집을 하나 사도록 권유했다. 그 친구는 그런 아이디어에 흥미를 느꼈고 우리는 그 가능성을 의논하기 시작했다. 그 친구의 가장 큰 걱정은 새로 집을 사는데 필요한 은행융자를 받을 수 없다는 것이었다. 이미 다른 융자를 받아서 신용이 제한되어있기 때문이었다. 나는 그 친구에게 은행 말고 다른 방법으로 부동산을 사는 방법이 있다고 얘기했다.

28 일을 시작한 후 나는 사실 그가 얼마나 인정이 많고 나를 잘 이해해주었는지를 알게 되었다. 집값이 워싱턴에서 현재의 가격으로는 내가 감당해 낼 수 있는 집을 찾기가 힘들었다. 그래서 나는 조그마한 방을 임대했다. 그것은 주말에 가족을 방문하기 위해서는 8시간 동안 집으로 차를 몰고 가야 한다는 것을 의미한다.

참고 문헌

Akmajian, Adrian. 1970. On Deriving Cleft Sentences from Pseudo-cleft Sentences. *Linguistic Inquiry* 1: 149-168.

Abraham, Werner. 1995. Discourse-Functional Focus: The Assignment of Rheme. *The Prague Bulletin of Mathematical Linguistics* 63:5-19.

Acuna Farina, Juan Carlos. 1995. Left-Dislocation Revisited. *Revista Alicantina de Estudios Ingleses* 8:7-23.

Allerton, D. J. 1978. The Notion of 'Givenness' and its Relation to Presupposition and Theme." *Lingua* 44: 133-168.

Baker, C. L. 1995. English Syntax. Cambridge, MA: MIT Press.

Ball, Catherine N. 1994a. The Origins of the Informative-Presupposition It-Cleft. *Journal of Pragmatics* 22:603-628.

Ball, Catherine N. 1994b. Relative Pronouns in it-Clefts: The Last Seven Centuries. *Language Variation and Change* 6:179-200.

Berman, Arlene, 1973. A Constraint on Tough Movement. In Claudia Corum, T. Cedric Smith-Stark, and AnnWeiser (editors), *Papers from the Ninth Regional Meeting of the Chicago Linguistic Society*. 34-43. University of Chicago: Chicago Linguistic Society.

Birner, Betty, and Mahootian, Shahrzad. 1996a. Functional Constraints on Inversion in English and Farsi. *Language Sciences* 18:1-2.

Birner, Betty J. 1996b. *From Discourse Process to Grammatical Construction: On Left-Dislocation in English.*

Birner, Betty J., and Ward, Gregory. 1996c. A Crosslinguistic Study of Postposing in Discourse. *Language and Speech* 39:2-3.

Birner, Betty J. 1997. The Linguistic Realization of Inferrable Information. *Language and Communication* 17:133-147.

Birner, Betty J., and Ward, Gregory. 1998. *Information Status and Noncanonical Word Order in English.*

Bolinger, Dwight. 1992. The Role of Accent in Extraposition and Focus. *Studies in Language* 16:265-324.

Chafe, Wallace. 1976. Givenness, Contrastiveness, Definiteness, Subjects, topics, Point of Views. In Li (ed.) 1976. 25-26.

Cinque, Guglielmo. 1977. The Movement Nature of Left Dislocation. *Linguistic Inquiry* 8:397-412.

Collins, Peter. 1991a. *Cleft and pseudo-cleft constructions in English*. London ; New York: Routledge.

Collins, Peter. 1991b. Pseudocleft and Cleft Constructions: A Thematic and Informational Interpretation. *Linguistics* 3:481-519.

Collins, Peter. 1992. Cleft Existentials in English. *Language Sciences* 14:419-433.

Collins, Peter. 1994. Extraposition in English. *Functions of Language* 1:7-24.

Collins, Peter. 1995. *From Discourse Process to Grammatical Construction: On Left-Dislocation in English.*

Culicover, Peter. 1982. Though-Attraction. *IULC.*

Culicover, Peter W., and Rochemont, Michael S. 1990. Extraposition and the Complement Principle. *Linguistic Inquiry* 21:23-47.

Declerck, R. 1984. "Some Restrictions on Clefts that Highlight Predicate Nominals." *Journal of Linguistics* 20. 131-154.

Delin, J. L. 1991. Cleft Constructions in Discourse.

Delin, Judy. 1992. Properties of It-Cleft Presupposition. *Journal of Semantics* 9:289-306.

Delin, Judy. 1995. Presupposition and Shared Knowledge in It-Clefts. *Language and Cognitive Processes* 10:97-120.

Delin, Judy, and Oberlander, Jon. 1995. Syntactic Constraints on Discourse Structure: The Case of It-Clefts. *Linguistics* 3:465-500.

E Kiss, Katalin. 1998. Identificational Focus versus Information Focus. Language 74:245-273.

Emonds, Joseph E. 1976. *A Transformational Approach to English Syntax*. New York: Academic Press.

Enkvist, N. E. 1980. Motives for Topicalization. Occasional Papers in *Linguistics and Language Learning* 7:1-15.

Fichtner, Edward G. 1993. Cleft Sentences in English: A Comprehensive View. *Word* 44:1-30.

Foley, William A., and Van Valin, Robert D., Jr. 1984. *Functional Syntax and Universal Grammar.*

Frascarelli, Mara. 2000. Cleft Constructions and Small Clauses: *An Analysis of English. Lingua e Stile* 35:417-446.

Geluykens, Ronald. 1988a. Five Types of Clefting in English Discourse. *Linguistics* 5:823-841.

Geluykens, Ronald. 1989b. Information Structure in English Conversation: The Given-New Distinction Revisited. *Occasional Papers in Systemic Linguistics* 3:129-147.

Geluykens, Ronald. 1991a. Discourse Functions of It-Clefts in English Conversation. *Communication and Cognition* 24:3-4.

Geluykens, Ronald. 1991b. Topic Management in Conversational Discourse: The Collaborative Dimension. *Papers from the Regional Meetings, Chicago Linguistic Society* 27:182-195.

Geluykens, Ronald. 1992. *From Discourse Process to Grammatical Construction: On Left-Dislocation in English.*

Grosz, Barbara J., and Ziv, Yael. 1998. *Centering, Global Focus, and Right-Dislocation.*

Gueron, Jacqueline. 1980. On the Syntax and Semantics of PP Extraposition. *Linguistic Inquiry* 11:637-678.

Gundel, Jeanette K. 1975. Left Dislocation and the Role of Topic-Comment Structure in Linguistic Theory. *Ohio State University Working Papers in Linguistics* 18:72-131.

Gundel, Jeanette K. 1985. Shared Knowledge and Topicality. *Journal of Pragmatics* 9:83-107.

Haider, Hubert. 1997. Extraposition. In *Rightward Movement* ed. by Beerman, Dorothee, LeBlanc, David, & Van Riemsdijk, Henk C. Amsterdam: John Benjamins. 115-151.

Halliday, Michael A. K. & R. Hasan. 1976. *Cohesion in English*. London: Longman.

Halliday, M. A. K. 1985. It's a Fixed Word Order Language Is English. *ITL, Review of Applied Linguistics*:91-116.

Huck, Geoffrey J., and Na, Younghee. 1990. Extraposition and Focus. *Language* 66:51-77.

Huck, Geoffrey J., and Na, Younghee. 1992. Information and Contrast. *Studies in Language* 16:325-334.

Iannucci, David E. 1979. Verb Triggers of Tough Movement. *Journal of Linguistics* 15:325-329.

Jackendoff, R. 1972. *Semantic Interpretation in Generative Grammar*. Cambridge, Mass.: MIT Press.

Jespersen, O. 1933. *Essentials of English Grammar*. London: Allen and Union.

Jeong, In-Sik. 2003. The Inversion of Comparative Constructions and Information Structure in English. *The Linguistic Association of Korea Journal* 11:23-43.

Jones, Larry B., and Jones, Linda K. 1985. Discourse Functions of Five English Sentence Types. *Word* 36:1-21.

Jucker, Andreas H. 1996. Cleft and Pseudo-Cleft Constructions in English.

Kim, Kyu-hyun. 1995. WH-Clefts and Left-Dislocation in English Conversation: Cases of Topicalization. In *Word Order Discourse* ed. by Downing, Pamela, & Noonan, Michael. Amsterdam, The Netherlands: John Benjamins Publishing Co. 247-296.

Kuno, Susumu. 1972. "Functional Sentence Perspective." *Linguistic Inquiry* 3: 269-320.

Kuno, Susumu. 1987. *Functional Syntax*. Chicago: University of Chicago Press.

Kuno, Susumu, and Takami, Ken-ichi. 1997. Structural or Functional Accounts?. In *Directions in Functional Linguistics* ed. by Kamio, Akio. Amsterdam: John Benjamins. 221-249.

Lee, Chungmin. 1996. Generic Sentences Are Topic Constructions. In *Reference and Referential Accessibility*, ed. Thorstein Fretheim and Jeanette K. Gundel. Amsterdam: John Benjamins Publishing Company.

Lee, Chungmin. 1999. Contrasive Topic: A Locus of the Interface-Evidence from Korean and English. In *The Semantics/Pragmatics Interface from Different Points of View (CRiSPI 1)*, ed. K. Turner: Elsevier Science.

Lee, Chungmin. 2002. Contrastive Topic and Proposition Structure. In *Asymmetry in Grammar*, ed. Ann-Morie Di Sciullo. Amsterdam: John Benjamins Publishing Company.

Li, Charles N. 1976. *Subject and Topic*. Academic Press.

Lambrecht, K. 1994. *Information Structure and Sentence Form*. Cambridge: Cambridge University Press.

Michaelis, Laura A., and Lambrecht, Knud. 1996a. Toward a Construction-Based Theory of Language Function: The Case of Nominal Extraposition. *Language* 72:215-247.

Michaelis, Laura A., and Lambrecht, Knud. 1996b. The Exclamative Sentence Type in English.

Nakajima, Heizo. 1999. Irregular Though Though-Attraction Seems To Be. In *Linguistics: In Search of the Human Mind* ed. by Masatake Muraki and Enoch Iwamoto. 520-539.

Oberlander, Jon, and Delin, Judy. 1996. The Function and Interpretation of Reverse Wh-Clefts in Spoken Discourse. *Language and Speech* 39:2-3.

Pereira, Fernando. 1981. Extraposition Grammars. *American Journal of Computational Linguistics* 7:243-256.

Prince, Ellen F. 1978. A Comparison of WH-Clefts and it-Clefts in Discourse. *Language* 54:883-906.

Prince, E. F. 1981. "Topicalization, Focus Movement and Yiddish Movement: a

Pragmatic Differentiation." *BLS* 17. 249-264.

Prince, Ellen F. 1985. Fancy Syntax and 'Shared Knowledge'. *Journal of Pragmatics* 9:65-81.

Prince, Ellen F. 1988. Yiddish Wh-Clauses, Subject-Postposing, and Topicalization. *Proceedings Eastern States Conference on Linguistics* 5:403-415.

Prince, Ellen F. 1997. On the Functions of Left-Dislocation in English Discourse. In *Directions In Functional Linguistics* ed. by Kamio, Akio. Amsterdam: John Benjamins. 117-143.

Quirk, R., S. Greenbaum, G. Leech and J. Svartvik 1985. *A Comprehensive Grammar of the English Language*. London: Longman.

Rodman, Robert. 1974. On Left Dislocation. *Papers in Linguistics* 7: 3-4.

Walker, Marilyn A., Joshi, Aravind K., and Prince, Ellen F. 1998. *Centering Theory in Discourse.*

Walton, Charles. 1997. The Uses of Pseudo-Cleft Sentences in Sama Narrative Discourse. *Journal of Translation and Textlinguistics* 9:15-34.

Ward, Gregory, and Birner, Betty. 1996. On the Discourse Function of Rightward Movement in English. In Conceptual Structure, Discourse And Language ed. by Goldberg, Adele E. Stanford, CA: Center Study Language & Information: 463-479.

Ward, Gregory L. 1990. The Discourse Functions of VP Preposing. *Language* 66:742-763.

Ward, Gregory L., and Prince, Ellen F. 1991. On the Topicalization of Indefinite NPs. *Journal of Pragmatics* 16:167-177.

Weinert, Regina, and Miller, Jim. 1996. Cleft Constructions in Spoken Language. *Journal of Pragmatics* 25:173-206.

Wiedenhof, Jeroen. 1996. Nexus and the Birth of Syntax. *Acta Linguistica Hafniensia* 28:139-150.

Wirth, Jessica R. 1978. The Derivation of Cleft Sentences in English. *Glossa* 12:58-82.

Yang, In-Seok. 1993. Remarks on English VP-Preposing. *Linguistic Explorations: Syntax, Semantics, Pragmatics*, 1-24. Seoul: Hanshin Publishing Company.

Yang, In-Seok. 2000. *Grammatical Rules of English*. Hankuk University of Foreign Studies Press.

Yu, Ella Ozier. 1988. Agreement in Left Dislocation of Coordinate Structures. *Papers from the Regional Meetings, Chicago Linguistic Society* 24:322-336.

Ziv, Yael. 1994. Left and Right Dislocations: Discourse Functions and Anaphora. *Journal of Pragmatics* 22:629-645.

저자 정 인 식

■ 학력
- 한국 외국어 대학교 대학원 영어과 문학박사
- 한국 외국어 대학교 대학원 영어과 문학석사
- 한국 외국어 대학교 영어과 문학사

■ 약력
- 서울디지털대학교 영어학부 교수
- University of Texas at Austin – Visiting Scholar
- 서울대학교 인문학연구소 선임연구원
- 한국 외국어 대학교 외국어 교육연구소 연구원
- 한국 외국어 대학교 영어과 강사

영어독해를 위한

영어특수구문

영·특·구

2001년 9월 30일 초 판 발행
2002년 12월 20일 개정판 발행
2012년 5월 1일 제 3 판 발행

저자와의 협의에 의하여 인지첨부를 생략합니다.

지은이 : 정 인 식
발행인 : 이 재 철
등 록 : 1994.7.26. 제15-199호

발행처 : 새암 法學社
주 소 : 서울시 관악구 신림2동 116-2 201호
전 화 : (02) 876-9977
팩 스 : (02) 876-9960
ISBN 978-89-6289-346-5 13740

정 가:23,000원